FINANCIAL ACCOUNTING

By John Arnold and Tony Hope
ACCOUNTING FOR MANAGEMENT DECISIONS
(Prentice-Hall International)

FINANCIAL ACCOUNTING

John Arnold, Tony Hope and Alan Southworth

Department of Accounting and Finance, University of Manchester

Englewood Cliffs, NJ · London · Mexico · New Delhi · Rio de Janeiro
Singapore · Sydney · Tokyo · Toronto · Wellington

British Library Cataloguing in Publication Data
Arnold, John, 1944–
    Financial accounting.

    1. Accounting
    I. Title   II. Hope, Tony   III. Southworth, A.J.

    657′.48   HF5635
    ISBN 0-13-316746-1

© **1985 by Prentice-Hall International (UK) Ltd**

ISBN 0-13-316746-1

Prentice-Hall Inc., *Englewood Cliffs*, *New Jersey*
Prentice-Hall International (UK) Ltd, *London*
Prentice-Hall of Australia Pty, Ltd, *Sydney*
Prentice-Hall Canada, Inc., *Toronto*
Prentice-Hall Hispanoamericana, SA, *Mexico*
Prentice-Hall of India Private, Ltd, *New Delhi*
Prentice-Hall of Japan, Inc., *Tokyo*
Prentice-Hall of Southeast Asia Pte Ltd, *Singapore*
Editora Prentice-Hall do Brasil Ltda, *Rio de Janeiro*
Whitehall Books Ltd, *Wellington*, *New Zealand*

10 9 8 7 6 5 4 3 2 1

Typeset by HBM Typesetting Ltd, Chorley, Lancs.
Printed by A. Wheaton & Co. Ltd, Exeter

To all those accounting students who prefer labour to labor, centre to center, and inside-forwards to quarter-backs.

Contents

Chapter 11   Financing   200

PART 5   INTERPRETATION AND EVALUATION   333

Preface

In an increasingly complex world, characterised by private sector and public sector organisations of all shapes and sizes, the importance of efficient systems of communication between organisations and those who participate in them is of vital importance. Financial accounting is one means by which an organisation provides information to its participants (e.g. shareholders and other providers of funds, employees, customers, suppliers and government). Our aim in this book is to provide a foundation for understanding the principles upon which financial accounting systems are based, by explaining underlying concepts, existing practices, and possible alternatives to existing practices. We believe that the importance of such an understanding is not restricted to accountants; almost all of us come into regular contact with numerous organisations, whether as customers, employees, shareholders or in some other capacity. Our ability to get the most from such contacts will be enhanced by an ability to understand financial accounting systems.

This book should be of interest to those with little previous knowledge of financial accounting. Its contents should be of value to first and second year university and polytechnic students and others who wish to understand the bases upon which organisations prepare their accounts and who wish to appreciate the strengths and limitations of those accounts. It should also be of value to those who are familiar with accounting practice but who lack knowledge of its conceptual underpinnings. The book is divided into five parts. The first provides a basic framework for financial accounting and introduces the main concepts to be used subsequently. The second describes the fundamentals of the accounting model of the organisation and introduces its two basic statements, the income statement and the position statement or balance sheet. The third part deals with some particular problems of asset valuation and long-term financing. Parts 2 and 3 are concerned essentially with existing practice. In the fourth part we describe and discuss alternative methods which might be used to measure an organisation's performance and position. The fifth part explains how accounting statements might be interpreted and evaluates the alternative accounting methods discussed in Parts 2, 3 and 4. The structure of the book is explained more fully in the Introduction.

At the end of each chapter are discussion topics, suggestions for further reading and, where appropriate, numerical exercises. We hope that these will be of interest and use to the reader who wishes to increase his understanding of financial accounting. For teaching purposes the book should fit neatly into a typical undergraduate course of twenty lectures. A teacher should be able to select class problems from amongst the discussion topics and exercises provided at the end of each chapter.

We owe a great debt to the people who have contributed to the preparation of the book. Giles Wright and Ruth Freestone of Prentice-Hall International have managed to maintain sufficient pressure on us to ensure that the book was finished, while at the same time managing not to pressure us to finish it so quickly that we were forced to cut corners. We are also indebted to those who have read and commented critically and helpfully on earlier drafts of the book: G.R. Booth, Angela Filmer, Tom Lee, Michael Mepham, Bob Parker, Peter Sénèque, Michael Sherer and John Whitman. Michael Sherer was also generous enough to provide us with several exercises for use in and at the end of chapters. Of course, any errors or omissions which remain are ours alone. Susan Gore, Julie Gorton, Kay Sanders and Maureen Scapens patiently, and often under great pressure, typed successive drafts of the book in their usual efficient manner. We are grateful to Methuen London for permission to reproduce the extract from *Monty Python's Big Red Book* on page 9. We are grateful also to Boddingtons plc, John Lewis Partnership plc and Marks and Spencer plc for permission to reproduce the Statements of Sources and Uses of Funds shown on pages 402, 405 and 407 respectively. We also wish to thank Mozart, Puccini, Verdi and Wagner for providing titles for the end-of-chapter exercises (and much more!). During the past ten years or so, all three of us have been heavily involved in the teaching of financial accounting to first and second year undergraduate students at the University of Manchester. The frequent reluctance of those students to accept our 'instruction' without justification and explanation has forced us to clarify our own thinking and to question many accepted practices; such merit as the book has, owes much to them. Finally, and most importantly, we thank Lynne, Pamela, Gill and the kids for reminding us always that there are more important things in life than accounting!

John Arnold
Tony Hope
Alan Southworth

FINANCIAL ACCOUNTING

Introduction

The subject matter of this book, *financial accounting,* is concerned with the ways in which organisations communicate information about their performance to the 'outside world'. The book is aimed at readers who may have little previous experience or knowledge of accounting. For that reason, our primary intention is to provide a *conceptual* foundation and framework for financial accounting, i.e. we will attempt to provide the reader with a thorough understanding of the ideas which underlie the preparation of financial accounts, and the concepts which might be used to choose between alternative methods of financial accounting. Clearly such an understanding is incomplete without some knowledge of how accounting is practised. This we also attempt to provide. It is, however, a difficult task to write an introductory accounting book which balances well the (often conflicting) theories and practices of accounting. The balance must in the end be determined by what the authors believe to be the purposes of an introductory accounting text.

We believe that a detailed study of the practice of accounting, without a prior understanding of underlying concepts, is likely to be of relatively short-term benefit. The detailed conventions and rules of accounting can and do change quickly—largely as a result of changes in the environment in which organisations operate and as a result of developments in accounting theory and thought. Thus we have chosen to direct attention primarily to the conceptual foundations of financial accounting and to its broad practical basis. We do not intend to offer a detailed and extensive examination of current accounting practice, as embodied in company law and in the recommendations of the professional accountancy bodies.

Our emphasis means that, if the sum total of the reader's knowledge of financial accounting is limited to the contents of this book, he would almost certainly *not* be able to prepare the financial accounts of ICI, Marks and Spencer, Unilever, Fords, Sainsburys, or even his local newsagent or solicitor, in accordance with the current rules specified by company law and by the professional accountancy bodies! On the other hand, he should be able to understand the concepts upon which those organisations' financial accounts have been prepared and, perhaps more important, he should be equipped to evaluate both current accounting practices and the changes which will inevitably be made to those practices in the future. To summarise, our purpose is to provide the reader with a foundation in financial accounting which will be useful for decades, rather than with practical knowledge which may be out of date within a few years or even months.

The book contains five main parts and we now discuss each one in turn, both to explain its importance and to explore its interdependencies with the other parts.

Part 1—Basic Framework. Part 1 provides an overview of the role and purposes of financial accounting. The financial accounts or reports of an organisation are one source of information available to those who wish to evaluate its performance and prospects. It is important to recognise that the information in these reports comprises only one of a number of sources of information available about an organisation. Thus, in order to assess the impact and usefulness of financial reports it is necessary to evaluate the additional or incremental information they contain, over and above that which is available from other sources. In order to identify the incremental effects of a particular piece of accounting information, the following questions must be asked (and answered). Who are the existing and potential users of the information? For what purposes will they use the information? How will the information influence the beliefs and, in consequence, the decisions and actions of users? How will the actions of users affect other members of the community? How much will it cost to produce the information? The answers to these questions are necessary in order to estimate the benefits and costs of providing the information.

In Chapters 1, 2 and 3 we examine the role of accounting and organisations in society, and discuss the information requirements of different users of accounting reports. Of particular importance are the distinctions between different kinds of organisations (e.g. private and public sector organisations, large and small organisations, organisations which are guided largely by the profit motive and organisations, such as charities, which have other predominant objectives) and between different groups of users of accounting information (e.g. owners, employees, customers, government, suppliers). The existence of different types of organisations and of users with different information requirements means that there is no one system of financial accounting which is best for all organisations and users. Nevertheless there is, as we shall see, substantial common ground—for example, all interested users are concerned in one way or another with the survival of the organisation. In Chapter 4 we attempt to use this common ground to develop a set of criteria which might be used to assess the desirability of alternative accounting methods. We use these criteria in subsequent chapters to evaluate alternative accounting treatments of an organisation's transactions.

Part 2—The Accounting Model of the Organisation. For many years, the financial accounts prepared by most organisations have consisted primarily of an *income statement* or *profit and loss account,* describing the results of the organisation's performance during a past period, and a *position statement* or *balance sheet,* showing its position at the end of the period covered by the income statement. The approach which accountants have adopted (i.e. the basis for the figures appearing in each statement) emphasises measurement of the transactions of the organisation. The revenues arising from the transactions are matched with the costs incurred in earning the revenues. This matching of revenues and costs determines the organisation's *net income* or *net profit*. Expenditures which have not been matched with revenues are shown in the balance sheet as assets. This *transactions-based* approach to the measurement of net income and financial position remains by far the most widely used approach in the Western world. Furthermore, the costs which are matched with revenues generally represent the original or *historical costs* of the resources utilised.

In Part 2 we describe the fundamental concepts underlying the preparation of historical cost transactions-based accounts. We begin in Chapter 5 by explaining how an organisation's accounts reflect a real, *physical* process of transforming inputs (e.g. raw materials and labour time) into outputs (e.g. products for sale). In Chapters 6 and 7 we explain the basic principles by which the results of the physical transformation process are expressed in *financial* terms in the form of a balance sheet and income statement and introduce the accountant's recording technique—that of double-entry book-keeping. In Chapter 8 we explain an important aspect of financial accounting—the meaning and treatment of 'accruals'. These arise when expenditures or revenues have been incurred or earned but not paid for, or where costs have been paid in advance. We conclude Chapter 8 with an example of double-entry book-keeping which illustrates the principles explained in Part 2.

Part 3—Asset Valuation and Long-term Financing. In Part 3 we extend the framework introduced in Part 2 to consider the accounting treatment of transactions which affect the organisation for more than one accounting period. Expenditures which involve the acquisition of resources to be used by, and to provide benefits to, an organisation over a number of periods are termed *assets*. Broadly speaking, assets are *fixed* if they represent part of the productive capacity of the organisation and are expected to be owned by the organisation for some years, or *current* if they are held for resale or for conversion to a form suitable for resale. Chapter 9 discusses the accounting treatment of fixed assets and the methods of charging to the income statement the periodic cost associated with their use. Such charges are known as *depreciation*. In Chapter 10 we discuss the accounting treatment of stock, the major current asset of most organisations, and explain the variety of methods available for charging the cost of stock used to the income statement. In Chapter 11 we turn to the organisation's long-term obligations, both to its owners and to others who have provided long-term finance or *capital*. We describe the characteristics and accounting treatments of the sources of long-term capital available to the three main types of private sector, profit-orientated organisations—individuals, partnerships and limited liability companies. Although we concentrate primarily on such private sector, profit-orientated organisations to explain the basic framework of accounting in Parts 2 and 3, most (but not all) of the principles discussed are applicable also to both public sector and not-for-profit organisations. The usefulness of such principles can, of course, be evaluated only in the context of the type of organisation to which they are applied.

We conclude Part 3 with an appendix which provides a detailed example of double-entry book-keeping and which illustrates the historical cost transactions-based approach described in Parts 2 and 3. After reading the first eleven chapters (i.e. up to the end of Part 3) the reader should have a sound understanding of the principles underlying the accounting model of the organisation. In the remaining chapters of the book we make use of the basic framework introduced in Part 1 to evaluate and interpret the principles and procedures described in Parts 2 and 3 and to assess the likely usefulness of alternative measurement methods.

Part 4—Alternative Measurement Methods. The historical cost transactions-based approach to financial accounting (more commonly termed *historical cost accounting*) is not the only one available, although it is the approach most widely adopted in current practice. Alternatives to both its transactions-based emphasis and its use of historical costs have been advocated and warrant attention. In Part 4 we consider the nature and merits of some of these alternatives. Chapter 12 discusses the major weakness of historical cost accounting—its inadequacy as a means of measuring income and valuing assets when prices are increasing (or decreasing) at significant rates. It is important to recognise that even price changes of, say, 4% or 5% per annum may be 'significant' for this purpose. For example, an organisation which purchased a piece of land for £100,000 fifteen years ago will, under historical cost accounting, continue to show it in its current balance sheet at its original cost of £100,000. And yet if land prices have risen by only 5% per annum since purchase, the current value of the land will be over £200,000.

In Chapter 13 we discuss an alternative to transactions-based approaches—the *forecast-based* approach. Under this approach, the value of the organisation and its periodic income are based on forecasts of future performance rather than on the results of past transactions. This approach derives its source from the writings of economics and, in consequence, the performance and position measures which it produces are often referred to as measures of economic income and economic value. In Chapters 14 and 15 we consider various transactions-based approaches which use measures other than unadjusted historical costs. The two main alternatives which we describe are *current purchasing power accounting* (Chapter 14) and *replacement cost accounting* (Chapter 15). Both alternatives attempt to deal, in very different ways, with the problems within the transactions-based framework created by the use of historical costs when prices are changing. Under current purchasing power accounting, the historical cost numbers are adjusted by a *general* price index (such as the Retail Price Index), whereas under replacement cost accounting, the historical costs of resources are increased to their current replacement costs, often by the use of price indices which are *specific* to the resources concerned. The differences between the figures produced by the two methods tend to be small when relative price changes are low (i.e. when all prices tend to change at very similar rates) but may be very large when substantial relative price changes occur.

Part 5—Interpretation and Evaluation. In Part 5 we attempt to draw together many of the threads running through the first fifteen chapters. The threads are drawn in three stages. The first stage (Chapter 16) describes how users of financial reports might interpret the information contained in the income statement and balance sheet by calculating a variety of ratios designed to measure both the liquidity and the profitability of an organisation. Our primary emphasis is on the use of ratios calculated from historical cost accounts, but we also discuss the extent to which the use of ratios based on current replacement costs might be helpful. This chapter provides an important link between the basic framework introduced in Part 1, the various accounting methods described in Parts 2, 3 and 4, and the evaluation of those methods which follows in Chapter 17. Chapter 17 thus represents the second of the three stages.

A recurrent theme in the book is the relationship between an organisation's net income and its net cash flow. The amounts of the two seldom correspond. In Chapter 4 we explain the reasons why accountants adjust an organisation's cash flows in order to measure its income and position. Such an explanation is, however, insufficient to convey the importance of the role of cash in any detailed assessment of an organisation's performance and prospects. Such an assessment requires an evaluation of the organisation's ability to generate sufficient liquid funds (i.e. cash and near-cash assets) to meet its periodic obligations to pay employees, suppliers, lenders and so on. Thus in Chapter 18 we discuss the third stage of evaluation via the flow of funds statement which is concerned directly with this particular aspect of an organisation's activities. The final chapter—Chapter 19—is a brief summary of the main themes of the book and of the conclusions we have reached.

We may thus summarise the main objectives we hope to achieve in the book. They are:

1. To provide a framework for the evaluation of alternative methods of financial accounting, based on the assumption that the primary purpose of financial accounting is to provide information which is useful for decisions.
2. To explain the fundamental concepts and principles underlying historical cost accounting, so that the reader of financial reports may understand more clearly the basis upon which such reports are prepared, and appreciate both their strengths and their limitations.

3. To describe and evaluate alternative approaches to the measurement of an organisation's performance and position.
4. Perhaps most important, to instil in the reader a critical and analytical attitude to financial accounting, which will enable him to understand and evaluate the changes to financial accounting practices that will inevitably be made in the future and maybe even to make some contribution to those changes!

Part 1

Basic Framework

Chapter 1

The Role and Context of Accounting

1.1 An Introduction to Accounting and Accountants

This may be the first book on accounting that you have ever read. As
authors, therefore, we have a great opportunity to influence your percep-
tions of accounting for many years to come. We have also a great responsibility to stimulate and maintain your interest in the subject. You may already
have some preconceptions about accounting and accountants. These may be
similar to those expressed by the chairman of the accounting department at
the University of California[1] who commented, "Suddenly students see
accounting as a glamorous, sexy profession, thanks to the expanding role
accountants play in business and government, and to the increasingly attractive salaries." Or they may be closer to those expressed in the following
extract from *Monty Python's Big Red Book*.[2]

> **Why Accountancy Is Not Boring by Mr A. Putey**
>
> First let me say how very pleased I was to be asked on the 14th inst. to
> write an article on why accountancy is not boring. I feel very strongly that
> there are many people who may think that accountancy *is* boring, but they
> would be wrong, for it is not at all boring, as I hope to show you in this
> article, which is, as I intimated earlier, a pleasure to write.
> I think I can do little worse than begin this article by describing why
> accountancy is *not* boring as far as *I* am concerned, and then, perhaps, go on
> to a more general discussion of why accountancy as a whole is not boring.
> As soon as I awake in the morning it is not boring. I get up at 7:16, and my
> wife Irene, an ex-schoolteacher, gets up shortly afterwards at 7:22. Break-
> fast is far from boring, and soon I am ready to leave the house. Irene, a keen
> Rotarian, hands me my briefcase and rolled umbrella at 7:53, and I leave
> the house seconds later. It is a short walk to Sutton station, but by no means
> a boring one. There is so much to see, including Mr Edgeworth, who also
> works at Robinson Partners. Mr Edgeworth is an extremely interesting
> man, and was in Uxbridge during the war. Then there is a train journey of
> 22 minutes to London Bridge, one of British Rail's main London termini,
> where we accountants mingle for a moment with stockbrokers and other

---

[1]See Lohr, S., 'Goodbye to the ink-stained wretch', *The Atlantic,* August 1980.
[2]*Monty Python's Big Red Book,* Methuen, 1971 (p.16).

accountants from all walks of life. I think that many of the people to whom accountancy appears boring think that all accountants are the same. Nothing could be further from the truth. Some accountants are chartered, but very many others are certified. I am a certified accountant, as indeed is Mr Edgeworth, whom I told you about earlier. However, in the next office to mine is a Mr Manners, who is a chartered accountant, and, incidentally, a keen Rotarian. However, Mr Edgeworth and I get on extremely well with Mr Manners, despite the slight prestige superiority of his position. Mr Edgeworth, in fact, gets on with Mr Manners extremely well, and if there are two spaces at lunch it is more than likely he will sit with Mr Manners. So far, as you can see, accountancy is not boring. During the morning there are a hundred and one things to do. A secretary may pop in with details of an urgent audit. This happened in 1967 and again last year. On the other hand, the phone may ring, or there may be details of a new superannuation scheme to mull over. The time flies by in this not at all boring way, and it is soon 10:00, when there is only 1 hour to go before Mrs Jackson brings round the tea urn. Mrs Jackson is just one of the many people involved in accountancy who give the lie to those who say it is a boring profession. Even a solicitor or a surveyor would find Mrs Jackson a most interesting person. At 11:05, having drunk an interesting cup of tea, I put my cup on the tray and then...

(18 pages deleted here—Ed.) . . . and once the light is turned out by Irene, a very keen Rotarian, I am left to think about how extremely un-boring my day has been being an accountant. Finally may I say how extremely grateful I am to your book for so generously allowing me so much space (Sorry, Putey!—Ed.)

Accountants and prospective accountants probably view themselves as 'glamorous and sexy' although they may view other accountants as 'Mr Putey' stereotypes. What is your view? It will depend to some extent upon your understanding of what an accountant does. You may have heard that an accountant records financial events—and certainly his role includes that task. You may even be aware of certain financial statements which are the product of the accounting process—for example, the *profit and loss account* or *income statement* and the *balance sheet,* and an illustration of these two statements is provided in Table 1.1. The income statement reports the results of an organisation's activities (its revenues less expenses) *over a period* of time, and the balance sheet reports the financial position of an organisation *at a point* in time, i.e. what the organisation owns (assets) and how those assets have been financed. We should point out here that the title of the organisation, Seaview Ltd, refers to a limited company (hence Ltd). We discuss this type of organisation in Chapter 2. At first glance these two financial statements may appear simply to be aggregations of various trans-actions recorded during the year. But if this is accounting, you may wonder why it merits being studied as an academic subject and why it is now taught in most British universities and polytechnics. There has to be something else. Fortunately there is.

Table 1.1   Seaview Ltd – Financial statements

Income Statement for the year ended 31 December 19X0

		£
Sales		300,000
less: Expenses		
Cost of goods sold	120,000	
Depreciation	30,000	
Wages and salaries	70,000	
Administrative expenses	20,000	
		240,000
Income before tax		60,000
Taxation		25,000
Net income		£35,000

Balance Sheet at 31 December 19X0

Assets employed:		£
Property, plant and equipment		
(net of depreciation)		80,000
Stock		20,000
Debtors (amounts receivable)		50,000
Cash		15,000
Total assets		165,000
less: Creditors (amounts payable)		(40,000)
Net assets		£125,000
Financed by:		
Shareholders' funds		100,000
Long-term bank loan		25,000
		£125,000

Accounting should not be confused with book-keeping. Whereas book-keeping is the mechanical task of maintaining accounting records according to some pre-established rules and procedures, accounting is a much more complex process. It is concerned, among other things, with story-telling, bargaining and accountability. *Above all accounting is concerned with decision-making.* Every individual or group in society makes economic decisions about the future, and each requires economic information in order to make a rational decision. For example, the management of the Ford Motor Company needs to know which models have been successful before deciding which lines should be phased out and/or which should be promoted more vigorously; potential employees and investors wish to satisfy themselves as to Ford's financial viability before accepting a job or investing money in the company; and the managers of a non-profit-making organisation, such as a local authority or a charity, require economic information before planning their social programmes (and social information before planning their economic programmes). Accounting has something to contribute to each of these decisions. Specifically, accounting is concerned with *identifying* which information will help the various decision-makers, how it should be *measured* and how it should be *communicated* to them. This involves accountants in designing and implementing systems within which financial information can be processed, and in establishing the rules and procedures to be used in processing the information. One important reason, then, for studying accounting is to acquire the knowledge and the skill to search through available economic and financial information for clues that will serve as guides for future action.

In the remainder of this chapter and in Chapter 2 we try to explain the role of accounting systems in present day organisations. We discover that there is no unique role, and that the use made of the accounting information depends upon not only the type of organisation whose transactions are being reported, but also the people involved in the organisation, and the society within which the organisation operates.

1.2   Organisations and Participants

We have now reached an important stage in our discussion. In order to progress further we must identify the objectives (or goals) of the reporting organisation, whatever its nature, for example whether it is a snack bar, a multinational company, or a charity. However, an organisation as such cannot have goals. Only the individuals who comprise the organisation can have goals.[3] So where do we go from here? At this stage you might feel like abandoning accounting as all we have given you are unanswered questions. Still, at least you should no longer believe that accounting is simply a matter of recording and aggregating, and that the accountant is simply a book-keeper. Instead, you may be thinking in terms of 'decision-makers', 'objectives', and 'information'. What we must do now is construct a framework, using these ideas, in order to facilitate our further study of the subject. In an attempt to identify the objectives of an organisation, we shall begin by examining the relationship that exists between the individuals within an organisation and the organisation itself.

We stated above that organisations, as such, cannot have goals, and yet one aim of accounting is to report on how an organisation is achieving its objectives. We must, therefore, identify which people are involved in a particular organisation and ascertain whether their individual goals can be

[3]See, for example, Cohen, K.J. and Cyert, R.M., *Theory of the Firm: Resource Allocation in a Market Economy,* Prentice-Hall, 1965, p.331.

transformed into the objectives of the organisation. This material is fundamental to an understanding of the remainder of the book and thus warrants
particularly careful reading.

The correlation between the goals of the people involved or *participants*
in an organisation and those of the organisation itself will differ from
organisation to organisation. In some organisations there will be a wide area
of agreement on, and commitment to, organisational goals. Professional
bodies and charities fall into this group. One objective of the Institute of
Chartered Accountants in England and Wales (of which all three authors are
members) is "to do all such things as may advance the profession of accountancy in relation to public practice, industry, commerce and the public
service".[4] This objective should correlate very closely with the objectives of
its seventy thousand members. In other organisations the objectives of the
participant groups may be in direct conflict. Consider, for example, two of
the main objectives of the staff of a prison (and presumably those of society)
which are to ensure that no prisoner escapes, and to restrict the availability
of certain civil liberties. Presumably neither objective is shared by the
prisoners. In such a case the goals of the organisation are often taken to be
the goals of the dominant group, i.e. the group which has the power, through
force or influence, to impose its own goals.

Most business organisations lie between the two extremes of a professional body and a prison. Different groups of participants may have conflicting goals, but no one group has sufficient power to impose its goals upon the
others. This raises the question of organisational survival. The survival of a
charity or professional body is ensured as long as there is a sufficient number
of people willing to work towards a common objective. A prison will continue to operate as long as the dominant group retains sufficient power to
pursue its own goals to the exclusion of others. But how does a business
organisation survive if various groups have different, and maybe conflicting,
objectives and no one group has the power to impose its own goals?

To answer this difficult question we must develop the concept of an
organisation as a collection of individuals or groups. For a business organisation or *entity* these individuals may be classified into several groups: employees, management, owners (shareholders), creditors, customers, suppliers,
etc. (Figure 1.1)[5] These groups come together to set up and perpetuate the
particular organisation, but each group has a variety of alternative opportunities—the employee may hand in his notice at Ford's and, if he is prepared to move house, seek employment at Vauxhall Motors; shareholders

---

[4]*Supplemental Royal Charter of 1948*, Institute of Chartered Accountants in England and
Wales, 1973.

[5]The diagram in Figure 1.1 is based upon diagrams included in McDonald, D. and Puxty,
A.G., 'An inducement – contribution approach to financial reporting,' *Accounting, Organisations and Society*, Vol. 4, No. 1/2, 1979, pp.53–65.

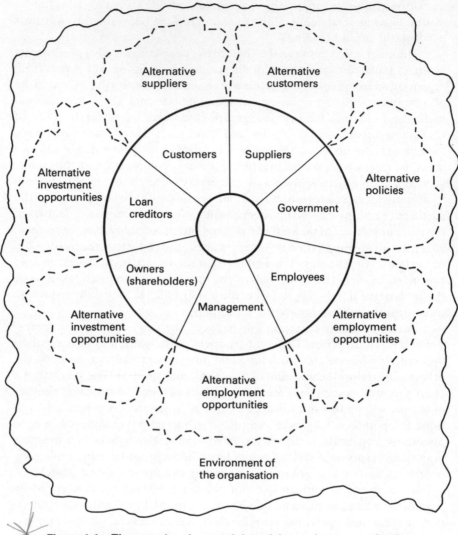

Figure 1.1   The actual and potential participants in an organisation.

may sell their shares and invest in other organisations; creditors may with-draw their funds and loan them elsewhere; customers may buy from a competitor, and suppliers may give preference to other customers. To sur-vive, the organisation must somehow ensure the continuing participation of these groups.

In order to persuade participants to contribute to, and remain with, an organisation, the organisation must, in turn, offer some *inducements.* Thus an employee might be induced to join a company because of monetary rewards in the form of high wages, and non-monetary rewards such as the friendship of colleagues, the status attached to his position and the proximity of the company to his home. His *contributions* will include not only his work output, but also his ability to motivate those working with him. A customer's inducements may be competitive prices, good service and a convenient location. His contributions include regular purchases and prompt payments. Each individual participant will stay with the organisation as long as the inducements offered by the organisation exceed the contributions made by the individual. However, the value of the inducements offered to participants will be influenced by the objectives of those participants—and these objectives may be in direct conflict with one another. For example, the desire by shareholders for higher returns from the organisation (termed *dividends*) might conflict with an employee's objective of higher wages, and a customer's goal of lower prices.

The survival of an organisation thus appears to depend upon its ability to satisfy a set of disparate and often conflicting objectives. That many organisations do survive can be attributed to the role of one participating group—the managers. Like other employees, the managers are induced to participate by the promise of monetary and non-monetary rewards in the form of salary, fringe benefits, status and job satisfaction, in return for which they contribute effort. One of the functions of the managers is to coordinate the activities of other participants. In particular, managers have the power to increase inducements to ensure the participation of other individuals. Because the role of managers is necessary for the survival of an organisation, the other participants will agree to accept the managers' powers as long as organisational survival suits their own purposes. Only by ensuring that the inducements offered to each participant exceed his contribution can the managers guarantee the continued existence of the organisation. Therefore, we can view management's role as that of attempting to satisfy the objectives of all participants, including themselves.

The situation is made more difficult because participants' objectives are not static. The environment in which an organisation exists is dynamic. For example, changes in the alternative opportunities available to the various groups will affect the inducements they require from the company. Hence, the managers must ensure that an organisation adapts to changes in its environment and pursues courses of action that will enable it to continue satisfying participants' needs. It is not surprising, therefore, that the lives of business organisations are characterised by periods of conflict between participants, during which compromises are reached over the distribution of inducements, followed by periods of apparent consensus during which the agreements are implemented. Numerous examples are provided by the economic recession in the UK during the late 1970s and early 1980s. In those years, new wage, productivity and staffing level agreements were negotiated in industrial and commercial organisations throughout the private and public sectors as one means of helping such organisations to survive in the increasingly competitive environment created by the recession. For a variety of reasons many organisations failed to reach the compromises necessary to survive in the changed environment and, in consequence, ceased to exist. This period provides a rather dramatic illustration of the problems experienced by organisations in a dynamic environment.

This is the context within which accounting exists. From our view of an organisation, accounting must have at least two functions. First, accounting represents one source of information which enables the managers to steer the organisation towards the satisfaction of participants' objectives. It provides information for both planning and control purposes. *Planning* is the process of formulating a course of action. It involves the setting of goals, the identification of alternative ways of achieving those goals, and the choice of one of those alternatives. The task of accounting is to provide clear statements of the financial consequences of each of the alternatives. *Control* is the process of monitoring the outcome of the chosen alternative, of checking whether the plans are in fact being carried out. The task of accounting is to provide information on actual costs and revenues in a form which facilitates comparison with the planned costs and revenues. This branch of accounting is known as *management accounting*.

Secondly, accounting provides information for planning and control purposes to groups other than management. Here the role of accounting is to help those groups to evaluate management's performance in achieving organisational goals and to assess their own positions in relation to other groups and the organisation as a whole. It should also give some indication of any likely changes in organisational performance and the impact of those changes on the position of each group (other than management) relative to other groups. This branch of accounting is known as *financial accounting,* and is the subject matter of this book.[6] It is clear that both branches of accounting are concerned with providing accounting information to decision makers.

1.3   Financial Accounting and the Readers of Financial Statements

Consider an individual who wishes to make an economic decision which concerns himself and Seaview Ltd, whose financial statements were presented in Table 1.1. The financial statements might comprise the only information the individual possesses about Seaview Ltd, as most readers of financial statements do not have access to the detailed information concerning an organisation's transactions. Financial statements, therefore, provide

---

[6]Management accounting is explored in detail in Arnold, J. and Hope, T., *Accounting for Management Decisions,* Prentice-Hall International, 1983.

readers with *summarised information* about an organisation's transactions, and financial statements similar to those illustrated in Table 1.1 are prepared by organisations of various sizes operating in both the private sector (from a university campus snack bar run by the owner and his family, to very large organisations such as Imperial Chemical Industries (ICI)) and the public sector (e.g. British Gas Corporation). Even charities such as Oxfam, and other non-profit-making organisations (e.g. The University of Manchester) produce financial statements. The intention of each is to provide information to their readers; but who are 'their readers'?

Readers of financial statements differ from organisation to organisation. The readers of the financial statements, sometimes loosely termed the 'accounts' of ICI and British Gas may have similar characteristics, but they are not identical. Readers usually consist of individuals and institutions who are interested in the activities of the organisation and who need information for some purpose of their own, for example in order to make a decision. The accounts of Jack's Snack Bar, for example, should be of interest to the owner, to the manager of the local bank, if the bank has lent money to the business, and to the Inland Revenue (the tax authority). The readers of ICI's accounts might include the owners (called shareholders), the managers, various financial institutions and individuals who have loaned money to the company, the Inland Revenue, the workforce, competitors, customers, suppliers, and the government. Oxfam's accounts will presumably be read by the administrators of the organisation, together perhaps with those who have loaned or donated money to (or received money from) the organisation, its employees, and the Charity Commissioners. Thus the terms 'readers' and 'participants' may often by used synonymously although, of course, certain participants may not read the financial statements and certain interested readers (e.g. potential shareholders and creditors) may not (yet) be participants.

Some of the readers we have identified (e.g., a bank) are common to all three organisations, and some (e.g., the Charity Commissioners) are exclusive to only one type. But does it matter that different readers (often referred to as *user groups*) exist for different organisations? If all user groups require similar information, then a standard set of accounts should suffice for all types of organisation. For example, irrespective of the size difference between a snack bar and ICI, one might suppose that the readers of the accounts would be interested in the *profits* earned by those two organisations.[7] That may be true, but it is unlikely that the readers of Oxfam's accounts are interested in its profitability. A charity does not view the generation of profit as its primary objective, so a reader might instead require information on how effectively Oxfam has pursued its own particular

---

[7]We do not, at this stage, expect you to understand exactly what the accountant means by the word profit. Its calculation is a complex matter and we look at it in detail in Chapter 7.

objectives. In fact, as we have suggested earlier, it is unlikely that the snack bar and ICI are concerned solely with making profit, and readers of their accounts might also require information on how effectively they have been achieving their other objectives.

Discussion Topics

1 Discuss the relationship between accounting information and economic decisions. How can accounting help to resolve problems?

2 List the main types of private and public sector organisations with which you are familiar. What characterises the differences between them?

3 Why cannot organisations themselves have goals?

4 List the main participant groups interested in organisational survival. Do you believe that any of these groups dominate the others? What characteristics do the dominant groups (if any) possess?

5 Which are the two most important financial statements prepared by the accountant? What purposes do they seek to serve?

Further Reading

Cooper, D., 'A social and organizational view of management accounting' in Bromwich, M. and Hopwood, A. (eds), *Essays in British Accounting Research*, Pitman, 1981.

McDonald, D. and Puxty, A.G., 'An inducement—contribution approach to financial reporting', *Accounting, Organisations and Society*, Vol. 4, No. 1/2, 1979.

Poole, M. and Groves, R., 'The modern accountant: anatomy of a species', *Accountancy*, August 1982.

Chapter 2

Accounting, Organisations and Society

2.1 Accounting and Society

In Chapter 1 we described the general context within which accounting functions and distinguished between management accounting and financial accounting. We now turn to a more detailed consideration of the role of financial accounting. In *general,* the role of financial accounting is to provide information to groups other than managers so that they might assess how far their goals have been achieved, and to what extent and in what respects they are likely to be able to influence the behaviour of the organisation in the future. In other words, financial accounting information should be of crucial importance to participants in deciding what action to take in respect of their involvement with the organisation including, in the extreme, the decision as to whether to continue or terminate their involvement. However, the *specific* role of financial accounting is determined largely by the society within which it operates. Different societies produce different types of organisation and different participating groups, and these, in turn, produce different inducements, contributions and objectives.

For example, in the first written work on double-entry book-keeping published in 1494 Luca Pacioli[1] emphasised the importance of accounting records as follows: "...it would be impossible to conduct business without due order of recording for without rest, merchants would always be in great mental trouble". This may seem to us, 500 years later, to be quite a restricted viewpoint, and yet, given the structure of society in fifteenth century Italy it would have seemed strange indeed had Pacioli recommended the disclosure of information about the merchant's business to, say, the employees. (Much of the merchant's trade required the hiring of ships and men to bring goods back from the Middle East. The men were hired for one 'venture' at a time—they had no continuing part to play in the merchant's business.) The function of accounting was to aid the merchant (owner *and* manager) himself.

---

[1]Pacioli, L., *Summa de Arithmetica, Geometrica, Proportioni et Proportionalita,* 1494.

Let us take another, more recent, example to illustrate the argument. A different society from that of Pacioli existed in Germany in the 1930s. A rapid rearmament programme and productivity drive was accompanied by the creation of new organisations designed for the complete control of specific industries. Companies and even industries were regrouped in order to attain self-sufficiency. The role of accounting was to provide statistics to serve as 'barometers' for the use of the public, or semi-public, organs of control. For this purpose uniformity was essential, and in 1937 some 200 uniform charts of accounts were made compulsory for the different branches of German industry and commerce. These compulsory charts were enforced in each occupied country during the Second World War and although they ceased to be compulsory in Germany in 1945, they were retained in France and are still used by the state in the planning and controlling of economic growth.

Accounting in the UK and the USA has concentrated more upon the micro-level rather than the macro-level, as suggested by the German and French examples. The emphasis in the UK and USA has been on disclosing to interested groups the details of the financial performance and position of individual business organisations. The number of such groups has increased as society, generally, has become more open and, as a consequence, demanded more accountability from business. In 1966, the American Accounting Association (AAA) defined accounting as:[2]

> the process of identifying, measuring and communicating economic infor-
> mation to permit informed judgements and decisions by the users of the
> information.

In 1975 a discussion document published for comment by the Account-ing Standards Committee (ASC), representing the UK professional accoun-tancy bodies, declared that:[3]

> the fundamental objective of corporate reports is to communicate
> economic measurements of and information about the resources and per-
> formance of the reporting entity useful to those having reasonable rights to
> such information.

Although we shall develop our own view of accounting based upon these last two definitions, it should be clear that there is no single definition of the objective and subject matter of accounting or of its role. Accounting does not exist independently of society. By providing information about the activities of an organisation to interested parties, accounting must respond to the changing needs of society. Its role depends on, amongst other things, the type of reporting entity and the participants who need information.

---

[2]American Accounting Association, *A Statement of Basic Accounting Theory,* American Accounting Association, 1966, p.1.

[3]Accounting Standards Committee, *The Corporate Report,* ASC, 1975, p.28.

Hence, the individual merchant was the focus for fifteenth century Italian accounts; the state was the major influence upon accounting in Germany in the 1930s and remains so in several countries today; and, in the UK and the USA, the accounting process seeks to aid the decision processes of a variety of individual and institutional user groups.

Taken at their face value these recent definitions of the accounting process presented by the AAA and the ASC (given above) imply that accounting in the USA and the UK has adapted well to changes in society. But does current practice reflect the thinking of these academic (AAA) and professional (ASC) bodies? In the nineteenth century, accounting was criticised by Marx as a *tool* of the capitalist. Marx saw it as serving an ideological role, because it distorted the true nature of the social relationships which generate wealth through productive effort. He pointed out that financial statements emphasised the efforts of the labourer as "bare material labour-power, a commodity",[4] and in so doing they confirmed the capitalist's view that wages are merely one more expense incurred in generating a profit for the owners. We have noted that, in the late twentieth century, accounting in both the UK and the USA is defined in terms of helping a variety of users of accounts, rather than simply the owners, and we have emphasised the joint efforts of participants in ensuring an organisation's survival. However, some indication of how far current accounting practice lags behind changes in society and developments in accounting thought can be obtained from an examination of the income statement presented in the previous chapter in Table 1.1. In its present format this statement would have attracted Marx's criticism because wages and salaries are classified as a *cost* or *expense* of generating profit for the owners along with the cost of goods sold, depreciation, and administrative expenses.[5] The focal point of this statement (the 'bottom line') is *net income,* which figure represents the amount available to the *owners* of the business after accounting for all costs.

2.2   Business Organisations and Accountants in the UK

In the previous section we considered how business organisations and the role of accounting have been influenced by the societies in which they operate. Later in this section we shall describe the role of accountants as it has developed in the UK. But first we introduce three types of business structure which dominate the UK private sector in the 1980s and which will

---

[4]Marx, K., *Capital,* Vol. III, Part 1, Progressive Publishers, 1966, p.45.

[5]Note however that the form of Value-Added Statement advocated by *The Corporate Report,* Accounting Standards Committee, 1975, goes some way to counter this criticism. The wages paid to employees are shown as applications of value-added rather than as costs.

be referred to frequently throughout this book. The three business structures are those of *individuals, partnerships* and *companies*.

The first type of business stucture refers to a business owned by one person. Usually the owner is also the manager and such organisations tend to be rather small. Examples of individual businesses are found amongst farmers, shopkeepers, accountants, solicitors and doctors.

A partnership structure is similar to that of an individual in many respects except that it has more than one owner. Once again this form of business structure is common amongst accountants, solicitors and doctors. Some accounting partnerships may have only two partners whereas the international accounting firm of Peat Marwick Mitchell and Co. has over 70 partners in London alone, and over 1,000 partners worldwide.

The financial statements of both individuals and partnerships report upon the financial position and performance of the business entity, i.e. for reporting purposes, the business activities of the owners are separated from their personal activities.

Individual businesses and partnerships have existed in the UK for several hundred years. However, the limitations of these business structures were exposed during the rapid industrialisation of the UK in the mid-nineteenth century. The Industrial Revolution led to the creation of large, highly mechanised, manufacturing organisations. These organisations required funds to finance their large-scale operations and long production cycles, and few individuals were sufficiently wealthy to supply them. The problem was how to encourage a large number of individuals and institutions to invest funds in an organisation without giving them a voice in the day-to-day management of the business. A new business structure, the limited company, emerged, which not only encouraged investment in private enterprise but also protected investors from unscrupulous and/or incompetent managers.

A company is a business organisation created by law. Individuals who wish to *incorporate* their businesses must register their company with the Registrar of Companies. Upon incorporation the company becomes a *legal entity* separate from its owners, and accounts are prepared annually to report the financial position and performance of the company. The accounts are also filed with the Registrar of Companies and are open to public inspection by interested parties. A company must have at least two owners (called shareholders) and ownership is evidenced by the possession of share certificates. In contrast to the owners of individual businesses and partnerships, the shareholders of a company generally have *limited liability*. This means that if a limited company is experiencing financial difficulties, the creditors (e.g. banks which have lent money, and companies which have supplied goods) can look only to the company's assets for repayment of their outstanding claims. The creditors cannot ask the shareholders to pay any more cash into the company should the company's assets be insufficient to meet their claims. The shareholders' liability is limited to the amount they have paid or agreed to pay for their shares. Thus when Laker Airways went into liquidation in 1982, Sir Freddie Laker, as a major shareholder, lost all the money he had invested in the company. However, the creditors, including those customers who had paid for flights and holidays in advance, did not have any claims upon Sir Freddie's personal wealth. In contrast, if the assets of an individual business or a partnership are insufficient to meet the claims of creditors, the creditors can look to the owners' personal assets for repayment. The liability of these owners is unlimited.

Limited companies may, since 1980, include either 'plc' (public limited company) or 'limited' (private limited company) in their title. The difference lies in the restriction placed on the issue or transfer of their shares. Public limited companies offer their shares for public subscription, whereas private limited companies restrict their ownership. Most public limited companies issue shares which are traded on the London Stock Exchange, and are thus known as *quoted* or *listed* companies. Most of the companies which are household names in the UK, e.g. ICI plc, National Westminster Bank plc and Boots plc, are quoted companies. However, the vast majority of companies in the UK are private limited companies, which are often owned and managed by the same people.

Large quoted companies have so many shareholders that they cannot all be involved in the management of the company. For example, in 1983, ICI plc had issued 612 million shares which were owned by 365,000 different individual and institutional shareholders. In such companies the shareholders appoint *directors* (i.e. managers) to exercise day-to-day control of the company's activities, and it is the directors who are responsible (and accountable) for ensuring that the annual accounts are prepared and published. Thus, in large companies, ownership is divorced from operational control and both owners and creditors rely upon financial information supplied by the directors. In order to protect shareholders and creditors there is a statutory obligation for the accounts of limited companies to be audited.

An *audit* involves an independent accountant, appointed by the shareholders, in examining the accounting system of the business, in collecting information about business activities, and in verifying the information to be included in the published accounts. The results of this audit enable the auditor to express an independent opinion on the fairness and reliability of the company's financial statements and thus on the directors' stewardship of the owners' funds. We can thus say that the need for regular financial statements exists because of the separation of ownership and control, and an audit is needed to check the accuracy of such statements. In particular, the auditor's report expresses an opinion as to whether the financial statements comply with statutory requirements (embodied in various Companies Acts) and accounting standards (statements of accounting practice issued by the

Accounting Standards Committee)[6] and give a 'true and fair view' of the company's position and performance.

Table 2.1   Auditors' Report

To the Members of Imperial Chemical Industries plc

We have audited the financial statements on pages 26 to 47 in accordance with approved auditing standards.

In our opinion the financial statements on pages 26 to 43, 46 and 47, which have been prepared under the historical cost convention, give under that convention a true and fair view of the state of affairs of the Company and the Group at 31 December 1983 and of the results and sources and applications of funds of the Group for the year then ended and comply with the Companies Acts 1948 to 1981.

In our opinion the supplementary current cost accounts for the year ended 31 December 1983 on pages 44 and 45 have been properly prepared, in accordance with the policies and methods described in the notes, to give the information required by Statement of Standard Accounting Practice No. 16.

	Thomson McLintock & Co.
London	Price Waterhouse
1 March 1984	Chartered Accountants

Table 2.1 reproduces the Auditors' Report to the shareholders (here termed 'members') of ICI plc. Independent audits are carried out not only on private sector companies, but also on nationalised industries, local authorities, and charitable organisations, in which cases the auditors report to the appropriate minister, the members of the council and the trustees respectively.

Accountants are involved in both the preparation and the auditing of financial statements, and can, perhaps, be categorised into three broad groups: those who work for companies in the private sector (industrial accountants); those who work for organisations in the public sector (public sector accountants); and those who work for accounting firms (accountants in professional practice).

Industrial accountants are employed by a company, e.g. in manufacturing by (say) Ford, in retailing by Sainsburys, in construction by Wimpey, etc. Typically they will help to determine the cost of products, prepare budgets, prepare tax returns and provide information for decision making by business management—for example, the opening up or closing down of factories and shops—as well as preparing the published accounts for external users. They may also design and develop new accounting systems or revise the existing systems of a business.

---

[6]We examine the role and usefulness of accounting standards in Chapter 4.

Public sector accountants work for all types of public sector organisations, including local authorities, health authorities and government agencies. Many of their duties coincide with those of an industrial accountant, e.g. involvement in budgeting, and the provision of information for management decisions. However, because the profit objective has a lower priority in the public sector, the information provided has a somewhat different emphasis.

Accountants in professional practice offer a variety of accounting services to companies, individuals, governments, etc. As we have noted they may carry out an audit of the records of a business organisation. In addition they may provide a variety of tax services for their clients including tax planning and tax return preparation, and more general advice to management about the running of the business, i.e. management consultancy work. Accounting firms range from individuals offering a book-keeping service and tax and general advice to individuals and small businesses, to international partnerships offering the whole range of professional services. The accounting profession is dominated by the eight largest partnerships, known collectively as the Big Eight, each of which has offices throughout the Western world and sometimes beyond. The largest of these firms has over 1,000 partners worldwide, and revenues in excess of $1,200 million per year (Table 2.2). Most of the largest business organisations in the UK and the USA are clients of (i.e. are audited by) one of the Big Eight (Table 2.3).

Table 2.2   Worldwide revenues of the Big Eight accounting firms

	Worldwide fee income 1982 ($million)
Peat Marwick Mitchell	1,219
Arthur Andersen	1,168
Coopers and Lybrand	1,098
Price Waterhouse	1,003
Arthur Young	977
Deloitte Haskins and Sells	920
Ernst and Whinney	914
Touche Ross	832

Source: *Accountancy Age*

2.3   Accounting as a Social Science

Our argument so far has been to try to convince you that accounting is not simply a technique. It is something more than that. Thus the AAA's defini-

Table 2.3   The ten largest UK business organisations and their auditors

Business organisation	Net assets (1982–83) £million	Auditors
Electricity Council	32,605	Deloitte Haskins and Sells
British Petroleum	17,306	Ernst and Whinney
Shell Transport and Trading	11,962	Ernst and Whinney
British Gas	10,996	Price Waterhouse
British Telecom	8,437	Ernst and Whinney
Imperial Chemical Industries	5,421	Thomson McLintock/Price Waterhouse*
Rio Tinto Zinc	5,162	Coopers and Lybrand/Spicer and Pegler*
BAT Industries	4,607	Deloitte Haskins and Sells
Shell UK	3,704	Price Waterhouse
Esso Petroleum	2,890	Price Waterhouse

*Joint auditors
Source: Annual reports

tion that accounting is[7] "the process of identifying, measuring and communicating economic information to permit informed judgements and decisions by the users of the information" links accounting to several other allied disciplines. For example, it is closely related to economics because it reports upon economic activities, and to political science because the resolution of participants' conflicting goals may be a political process. Perhaps we might, with some justification, describe accounting as a social science. The social sciences examine man's relationship with society and we have noted that the existence and the role of accounting are dependent upon the society in which it operates. The standing of accounting as a social science was reinforced in a later pronouncement of the AAA[8] which emphasised the importance of accounting in enhancing 'social welfare' rather than the welfare of individual decision-makers. We might also add that most university departments of accounting are located in faculties of social studies or social sciences.

[7]American Accounting Association, *A Statement of Basic Accounting Theory*, American Accounting Association, 1966, p.1.

[8]American Accounting Association, 'Report of the Committee on Concepts and Standards for external financial reports', *Accounting Review Supplement*, 1975.

2.4   The Communication Process

Much of this book examines that part of the accounting process concerned with "identifying and measuring... economic information", i.e. which items should be selected for inclusion in the financial statements, and how should they be measured. However, appropriate identification and measurement of information are of little use unless the information is adequately communicated. We therefore close this chapter by examining the communication aspect of the process.

If the accounting process comprises the identifying, measuring and communicating of economic information, then the financial statements (hereafter also referred to as the 'published accounts', or 'annual reports') are the vehicles of communication, i.e. they constitute the medium by which information is conveyed to the various interested groups.

But what do we mean by 'communication'? Let us explore the notion by asking a question. If you are an accounting student, did your lecturer 'communicate' with you in your last accounting lecture? He no doubt talked to you, but communication is much more than the transmission of a message—it implies an attempt by one person to *influence the behaviour* of another.

Figure 2.1 describes the communication process involved in the delivery of an accounting lecture in October 1984. The process began in the previous January when the lecturer agreed to teach an introductory accounting course. His objectives were to stimulate the students' interest in accounting and, ultimately, to make them proficient in accounting. At some time between January and October he expressed his thoughts in note form, and on 17 October 1984 he delivered the lecture. Each student who was present heard the lecture and took appropriate notes in his or her own language.

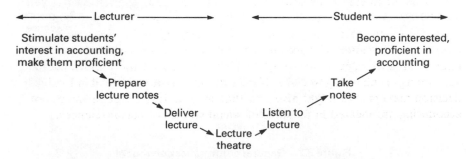

Figure 2.1   Communication model of an accounting lecture.

Intuitively we might suggest the following effects (or non-effects) of the lecture:

(a)   no student would have taken down every word spoken;
(b)   it is most unlikely that any two students would have had identical notes at the end of the lecture; and
(c)   no student's notes would have been the same as those used by the lecturer to deliver the lecture.

If our suggestions are correct, communication by lecture is clearly not a straightforward process; each student may have had a different summary of the lecture, and each may have taken away different impressions of the purposes and messages in the lecture.

The involvement of the students in the communication process has so far been short-term. They have listened, observed and taken notes. However, the aim of the communication was to influence their *future* behaviour. The lecturer, an optimist, was hoping that the lecture would cause the students to behave in a particular way, e.g. by making them feel sufficiently stimulated to spend time in the library, attend tutorials and ultimately obtain a good degree. It is possible that the message contained in the lecture influenced the behaviour of some students for several weeks or longer. The process of communication is thus more complex and extends over a longer time period than the mere transmission of a message.

2.5   Financial Statements and Communication

The example of the accounting lecture in the previous section is one illustration of a process which has been formalised elsewhere as a general communication model. Figure 2.2 illustrates this general model.[9] The originator determines the objective of the communication—an objective which

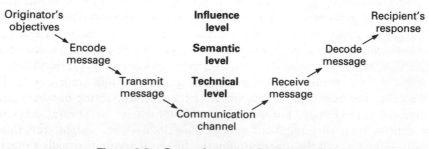

Figure 2.2   General communication model.

[9]The model in Figure 2.2 is an adaptation of the communication model first suggested by C. E. Shannon and W. Weaver in *The Mathematical Theory of Communication,* University of Illinois Press, 1964.

attempts to influence the recipient's behaviour. Hence there is a relationship between the originator's objective and the recipient's actions and we refer to this level of the communication process as the *influence level*. In the case of an annual report, the originators are accountants working within the organisation and other members of the management team. As the managers have access to all the transactions and economic events which involve the organisation during the year, one might expect them to select the best abstract of those events to communicate to the readers. But what is meant by the 'best' abstract? If we were considering only the interests of the users of the accounts, 'best' could mean that abstract which helped users to make the most informed judgements and decisions. However, we have already seen that management, as a participating group itself and as the group which must manage the demands of all other participants, might not wish to select such an abstract. Indeed, managers may be tempted to deliberately select an abstract of events which is sub-optimal from the users' point of view, in order to produce in the users a response which serves the needs of management rather than those of the users. An example of such behaviour is provided by a US corporation, Peabody International Inc. In 1979, the managers of Peabody reported a profit figure for the final three months of its accounting year of 71 cents per share. They did not disclose that this figure included 30 cents per share from "hoped-for court awards". A leading US analyst[10] claimed: "In my 10 years of analyzing income statements, I've never seen anything quite like this. Here was a high-flying company that, when faced with a disappointing profit performance, decided to move heaven and earth to keep its growth record from falling apart." Hence managers may seek to provide users with an abstract of events which is 'best' from the users' standpoint or one which is 'best' from the managers' own standpoint. In both instances, however, the managers must be aware of the requirements of users and of how their behaviour can be influenced by the content of the financial statements. They must also, of course, be aware of the constraints imposed upon them by statute and by accounting standards which may limit their ability to manipulate the information contained in financial statements.

Having selected the appropriate abstract, the originator encodes the message in a form suitable for transmission. In some communications this might involve the use of a different language, for example, morse code. In the case of annual reports, it involves the use of accounting numbers and financial terminology. For example, although there are several ways in which an item of equipment can be described—size, weight, function, value—the basis of the description in the financial accounts usually reflects the *cost* of the particular item, and only items which have an identifiable cost are reported. In addition, a language has developed in which everyday

---

[10]*The Wall Street Journal*, 'Paper profits', 20 June, 1980.

phrases may take on very specific meanings, e.g. 'depreciation', 'provision', 'reserve', 'current liability', etc. In the 1983 annual report of ICI, the various plants, factories and offices owned by that company are described as follows:

Land and buildings at the end of 1983
Cost	£1106 million
Depreciation	412 million
Net book value	£ 694 million

Just as it is essential that the recipient of a message sent in morse is using the same code book as is the originator, so it is essential that the recipient of financial statements understands the method by which the financial message has been encoded. This level of the communication process is called the *semantic level.*

Finally, effective transmission of the message requires that the message is received clearly. This final stage of the process is called the *technical level.* In some fields—radio, telecommunications, etc.—this is an extremely sensitive area. It may seem less important in accounting as it appears to involve only the typing, printing and distribution of the reports. We should note, however, that at present only shareholders receive the annual report as of right and, although there may be few problems of typing and distribution, many decision makers may never in fact receive the information included in the accounts.

All three stages together comprise the communication model. The success, or effectiveness, of a 'neutral' communication in accounting might be judged on whether the recipient of the information makes the same response that he would have made had he been given access to all the original information. A 'biased' communication might be deemed effective when the recipient responds in a manner intended by the originator. Whichever way we view the accounting model, an effective communication requires that the communication process is operating efficiently at all three levels. If there is interference or *noise* at any one level, it may be sufficient to distort the whole communication process. This analysis gives us an insight into the problems presently being encountered in financial accounting. *Noise exists at all three levels.*

Noise exists at the influence level if the management of a company is unaware of, or deliberately ignores, the information needs of a participant group. For example, the managers of the National Coal Board, when considering closing down one of its mines, might ignore the employees' need for disaggregated financial information for each mine. We shall examine the informational needs of several groups of participants in Chapter 3. Semantic noise occurs when the preparer and the reader of the financial statements place different interpretations upon key terms or figures. A common misinterpretation concerns the figure attached to a company's assets. In Table 1.1 (p.11) the stock of Seaview Ltd is disclosed in the balance sheet at £20,000. What meaning should be attached to this message? Does it mean that similar stock would now cost £20,000 (its replacement cost), or that the company would recieve £20,000 if it sold the stock now (its resale value), or that the original cost of the stock was £20,000 (its historical cost)? Each of these alternatives can be used, in certain circumstances, in accounting reports.

It may be argued that if organisations stated clearly, in 'plain English', what they meant, there would be no semantic noise. However, as can be seen from the following newspaper headlines, even 'plain English' is open to misinterpretation:

'Star's broken leg hits box office'.
'Man who received trousers loses appeal'.
'Antique dealer thought girl was older'.

In Chapter 4 we shall examine various ways of reducing the risk of such misinterpretation.

One aspect of technical noise which may be significant in accounting relates to the physical capacity of the receiver to process all the information being transmitted. Too much information may lead to 'information overload', with the result that the most important aspects of the message are lost, buried in a mass of other information, and in consequence the ultimate behaviour of the receiver is different from that intended by the sender.

This chapter has described in broad terms the role of financial accounting within business organisations. Accounting is not concerned solely with the mechanical recording of business transactions, but with the much more complex process of economic decision-making. All groups involved in an organisation make decisions about the future and all require information to aid them in their decision-making. Accounting is concerned with identifying and measuring financial and other economic data which are then communicated to the various participant groups. The information communicated will be influenced by the society in which the organisations exist, because that society will influence both the objectives of the participants receiving the information and the type of reporting organisation. The extent to which the information communicated is of use to the recipients depends upon the efficiency of the communication process at the influence, semantic and technical levels.

We now turn our attention in Chapter 3 to an examination of the problems which exist at the influence level of communication and consider whether the information currently provided is of much help to decision-makers.

Discussion Topics

1 Explain the reasons why the type of society dictates the type of accounting information which organisations provide.

2 Contrast the purposes of producing accounting information in a modern industrial society such as the UK with a modern industrial society such as East Germany, where all large-scale production is under state ownership.

3 Discuss and explain each of the aspects of the AAA's 1966 definition of accounting, as outlined on page 20.

4 Explain the essential differences between the main types of private-sector business structure which exist in the UK.

5 Why do you suppose that so few large accounting firms dominate the auditing profession in so many different countries? What historical reasons exist for such dominance?

6 What are the attributes of a social science? Do you believe that accounting can justifiably be classified as one?

7 Do you believe that the financial accounting communication process can hope to influence all possible users of financial statements?

Further Reading

Bird, P.A., *Accountability: Standards in Financial Reporting*, Accountancy Age Books, 1973.

Freear, J., 'Historical background to accounting', in Carsberg, B. and Hope, A. (eds), *Current Issues in Accounting*, 2nd ed, Philip Allan, 1984.

Haggie, D., 'The annual report as an aid to communication', *Accountancy*, August 1984.

Lee, T.A., 'The modern audit function' in Carsberg, B. and Hope, A. (eds) *Current Issues in Accounting*, 2nd ed, Philip Allan, 1984.

Parker, R. H., 'History of accounting for decisions', in Arnold, J., Carsberg, B. and Scapens, R. (eds), *Topics in Management Accounting*, Philip Allan, 1980.

Renshall, M., 'A short survey of the accounting profession', in Carsberg, B. and Hope, A. (eds), *Current Issues in Accounting*, 2nd ed, Philip Allan, 1984.

Smith, M. and Taffler, R., 'Improving the communication function of published accounting statements', *Accounting and Business Research*, Spring 1984.

Chapter 3

Accounting and Decision-making

We suggested in the previous chapter that if the managers of an organisation wished to act in the best interests of the other participant groups, they should select that summary of the organisation's economic activities which best meets the participants' needs for information. If, however, management is unaware of the needs of other participants, or deliberately ignores them, there will be noise in the communication system at the influence level. In this chapter, we consider how the needs of particular participants (users) might be identified, and examine the implications of those needs for the development of a financial reporting system.

3.1 The Users of Financial Statements

One approach to the identification of users' needs might be to ask them which information they would like to receive. However, this approach has many difficulties—in particular, users may be prejudiced by the type of information they receive currently and may be unaware of information which is at present unavailable to them. An alternative approach would be to first identify the types of decisions users might make, and then *deduce* the information they would need to make those decisions in as *rational* a manner as is possible. This is known as a *normative* approach. It is concerned with what people *ought* to do. This approach to the identification of the information requirements of user groups has played an important part in the development of accounting in recent years and we adopt it below. We identify some of the decisions taken by each of five participant groups (employees and trades unions, government, creditors and lenders, customers, and shareholders and investment analysts), and consider the sort of information which organisations might provide in order that these groups might make informed judgments and decisions. We do not consider here or elsewhere the decisions of managers.

Employees and trades unions
A discussion of the information requirements of employees is hampered by a lack of clearly defined models which describe employee and trades union

decision processes. There are at least two reasons for this. First, many negotiations between employee and employer are conducted by trades union officials acting on behalf of the employees. (For example, the wage rates and conditions of employment for coal-face workers are usually determined after negotiations between officials of the National Union of Mineworkers and members of the National Coal Board management team.) For some decisions we need to identify the decision models of union officials, and for other decisions, the decision models of individual employees. Secondly, as we noted in Chapter 1, participants join an organisation for a variety of reasons, not all of which are for monetary gain. Most of the research into loan creditors' and shareholders' needs has concentrated upon the monetary needs of these groups. However, a more complex relationship exists between the organisation and the employee. For example, the employee requires not only a monetary reward for his contribution to the organisation, but also respect from his peers, recognition from his superiors, a safe, clean workplace and stimulating tasks to perform.

Because this book concentrates upon the information contained in financial statements, we shall restrict ourselves to a brief review of some of the decisions which employees (or their representatives) must take, and which are likely to be based, at least in part, upon financial information.

If job opportunities are available, one decision facing all employees is whether to remain with their existing employers or to seek alternative employment. The factors influencing this decision will obviously vary from employee to employee. However, in almost all cases, financial reward will be an important consideration, although it will not always be the only one. Other factors such as (non-financial) job satisfaction, conditions of work, health and safety provisions and job security may affect decisions. In deciding whether to change jobs, an employee would presumably like estimates of future salary prospects, future job satisfaction, future working conditions and future job security, both from his existing employment and from other possible job opportunities.

Employees also make decisions concerning bargaining procedures with their existing employers; for example, regarding claims for wage increases and other conditions of employment. Employees, or their representatives, must decide what demands to make initially in the bargaining process and what financial and non-financial conditions to accept eventually. It is outside our scope to discuss such matters in detail. Indeed, as we noted earlier, the decision processes of trades unions and employees are not well understood at the present time. Nevertheless, it seems likely that, when bargaining, employees will need information about the likely amount of future cash available to their current employers both to pay wages and to create other conditions of employment that benefit employees. This will depend, in part, on the future operating profitability of the employer's business and on the ways in which resources generated from operations are to be divided between such various participants as shareholders and employees. The employee's bargaining position will also be influenced by the existence of, and opportunities offered by, alternative employment possibilities. In other words, decisions about bargaining procedures and decisions about changing jobs are not independent. In some cases, market forces will operate to ensure that similar rewards are offered for similar work by different employers.

Government

A government's need for information from *public sector* entities such as nationalised industries, is self-evident. A government generally bears the ultimate responsibility for the running of nationalised industries and its position may be thought of as similar to that of shareholders in private sector companies. A government's decision models may differ from those of shareholders, however, because its objectives differ from those of private individuals and organisations. For example, a government is likely to attach importance to such social factors as the level of unemployment, protection of the environment, distribution of wealth, and so on. These factors will not generally concern shareholders. Also, because the government spends tax-payers' money in providing funds to public sector entities, it will wish to scrutinise expenditure plans and to monitor the use made of cash invested. One might thus expect that the government would require, from each nationalised industry, the following types of information:

(a)   forecasts of future cash flows;

(b)   the amount of cash to be provided from government sources;

(c)   the particular industry's expectations of the impact of its policies on the level of employment in that industry and on the environment; and

(d)   reports of actual cash receipts and expenditure, and of the effect of past and current policies on employment and the environment.

Governments must also make various decisions which are directly affected by the behaviour and performance of *private sector* entities. A major decision facing any government concerns the determination of its future taxation policy. In making this decision, the government will consider factors such as the effects of different taxation policies on national economic performance, on national wealth distribution, on total taxation revenues likely to be raised from different policies, and on the ability to pay of those who are to be taxed. The information required from private sector entities will depend on the bases of taxation being considered. Thus, the effects of a tax on profits will depend on estimates of the future 'profitability' of private sector firms, the effect of a tax based on sales revenue or employee remuneration on estimates of firms' expected sales revenues and wages costs, and so on. The effects of taxation policies will also depend on the ability of firms to pay the tax due under each policy, i.e. on the future cash they are likely to have available for this purpose.

Governments may also make decisions about other aspects of economic policy, for example relating to the control of prices, the granting of investment subsidies, and the regulation of wages and profits. Each of these decisions requires information from private sector entities, including estimates of their future performance in the areas to be covered by the relevant policies.

Government must also decide how much tax should be raised from each taxpayer, in the light of its taxation policy. In order to do this, each entity's taxable profit, taxable sales revenue, taxable employee remuneration, and so on, must be calculated according to the rules prescribed in the relevant legislation. As taxation assessments are rarely based on estimates of future performance, the calculations involved generally relate to some aspect of an entity's past performance. For the year ended 31 December 1983, ICI's tax bill amounted to £201 million, based on a reported pre-tax profit figure of £619 million.

Creditors and lenders

Creditors and lenders are individuals or organisations to whom an entity owes money. As the name suggests, lenders are those who have loaned money to the entity on the understanding that it will be repaid at some future time. The reward to the lenders is usually termed 'interest', and this is normally payable by the borrower for the period from incurrence to repayment of the loan. An entity's liability to its creditors normally arises because the creditors have supplied goods or services to the entity for which it has not yet paid. On 31 December 1983, ICI owed £1,800 million to those who had loaned money, and £650 million to those who had supplied goods and services, to the company.

The two main decisions facing creditors and lenders, as far as their relationship with a particular entity is concerned, are first, whether to advance further credit (or make further loans) and second, whether to require accelerated or even immediate repayment of amounts due to them. Crucial questions in the minds of creditors and lenders when making such decisions presumably concern the security for their loans and also whether the entity will have sufficient cash available in the future to pay its debts, i.e. interest payments and loan repayments to lenders and payment of amounts owing to creditors. Such an estimate will depend *inter alia* on the cash the entity is expected to generate from its future operations, the other sources of funds available to it, the extent of its likely future expenditure on plant, machinery, property, fixtures, fittings and other assets and the claims of other parties to whom it owes money.

Customers

Strictly speaking, all individuals need information from all the organisations of which they may become customers—both for goods or services for immediate consumption (e.g. food, drink, travel, entertainment) and for capital investment goods such as property, cars, washing machines, refrigerators and so on. Such information is concerned with the performance, quality and price of the goods and services to be acquired at the time they would likely be acquired, i.e. at some time in the future. The customer may also need information about the credit arrangements offered by the supplier, if the goods are not to be paid for at the time of purchase, and, in the case of items which are not to be consumed immediately on purchase, the supplier's 'after-sales service'. An evaluation of after-sales service will include an assessment of its cost, quality and availability. The last of these will depend, in part, on the overall future prospects of the supplier. If the supplier is unable to generate sufficient resources to stay in business, it may be difficult for the customer to obtain satisfactory after-sales service!

It is unlikely that many individuals would go so far as to scrutinise a supplier's financial statements before buying a washing machine, or a microcomputer, but consider, for example the case of BL, which buys many of its electrical components from one particular supplier, Lucas Industries. BL's forecasts of its own future performance depend in part upon the continued survival of Lucas, and the price and quality of Lucas products as well as on the availability of alternative suppliers. Thus, in common with many other users of accounting reports, major customers will be interested in an entity's future prospects and profitability. (The interest in survival may be mutual. If a significant proportion of Lucas' output is sold to BL, then Lucas, as a *supplier,* has a vested interest in the continued existence of BL.)

In addition, the interest of customers in the price and quality of goods and services implies that they will require information which allows them to monitor price movements and changes in the quality of both goods and services. This monitoring role is often carried out by consumer organisations, for example the Consumers' Association, and their findings may be used to influence future policies of the organisation. In 1981, the Post Office Users' National Council persuaded British Telecom to reduce a proposed price increase by citing the (large) accounting profit of £180 million made by British Telecom in 1980/81.

Shareholders and investment analysts

This last group of participants has been the subject of more research in accounting than that devoted to all the other groups together. This may be because the basic decision model assumed to be used by shareholders is relatively straightforward (i.e. often only one, quantifiable objective is assumed—to maximise shareholders' financial wealth) and because of the historical importance of owners' information needs (which were discussed in Chapter 2). This basic model has been the subject of several quantitative refinements, and most of the research has focused upon shareholders of the larger listed companies, the shares of which are quoted on a Stock Exchange.

   Under the heading 'Shareholders and investment analysts', we include those who already own shares in a company (shareholders), potential shareholders, and those who advise shareholders and potential shareholders (investment analysts). A frequent decision facing these users is whether to buy, hold or sell shares in a particular company. To make such a decision, the shareholder (or his adviser) must estimate the value to himself of owning shares in the company and compare that value with the current market buying and selling price of the shares. As with many other goods, the buying price for the shareholder (customer) will normally be above the price at which he can sell, to allow for the costs and profit of the share 'dealer' (a person who trades in shares). A shareholder cannot buy shares directly from a company. He must use the services of an intermediary dealer, usually called a stockbroker. If the value of the shares to the investor exceeds the buying price, he should buy shares. If the value is less than the selling price, he should sell shares, or refrain from buying if he does not own shares. If the value is between the buying and selling prices, he should simply maintain his existing holding. Thus the crucial part of this particular process is to estimate the value of a particular company's shares to an investor. Many ways of estimating share values are discussed in the accounting and finance literature. One of the most widely advocated share valuation models is known as the 'dividend valuation' model. This involves the discounting of expected receipts from a shareholding (dividends and capital distributions) to their present (i.e. today's) value using a rate of interest which is appropriate for the risk attached to the expected receipts. The model may be formally stated as follows:[1]

$$V_0 = \frac{d_1}{(1+i)} + \frac{d_2}{(1+i)^2} + \cdots + \frac{d_n}{(1+i)^n}$$

$$V_0 = \sum_{j=1}^{n} \frac{d_j}{(1+i)^j}$$

where V_0 is the current value of a shareholding to an investor, d_j is the receipt he expects from the shareholding at time j, (i.e., the dividend or capital distribution), n is the last time at which a receipt is expected from the shareholding, and i is the appropriate discount rate.

   In order to use the model for buy, hold or sell decisions, the investor needs information to enable him to estimate V_0, i.e. he requires estimates of future receipts from the shareholding and information about the risk associated with the expected receipts in order to select an appropriate discount rate. For this purpose, the notions of *portfolio analysis* which show how and why risk can be diversified, are of particular importance.[2]

---

[1] Readers not familiar with the notions of discounted cash flows and the time value of money may find it helpful at this point to refer to the appendix at the end of this chapter.

[2] For an introduction to portfolio analysis, see for example, Arnold, J. and Hope, T. *Accounting for Management Decisions,* Prentice-Hall International, 1983, pp.68–78.

A different decision facing existing shareholders is whether to intervene in the running of the company. In general, the running of a company is in the hands of its directors and managers. Shareholders generally intervene only if things go badly wrong. Nevertheless, the right of intervention is always available to shareholders—after all they *own* the company. The case of Lonrho plc provides an illustration. In 1973 a boardroom dispute erupted over the chief executive's style of management and eight Lonrho directors signed a resolution calling for the dismissal of Mr Tiny Rowland as chief executive. The shareholders subsequently held an extraordinary meeting to determine whether to remove Mr Rowland as chief executive and managing director and/or to remove the eight directors from the board. The shareholders voted by 29.5m to 4.5m in favour of retaining Mr Rowland and by 26m to 8m in favour of dismissing the eight directors. (Mr Rowland was still chief executive in 1984.)

The impact of one shareholder's intervention depends very much on the size of his shareholding. The owner of 51% of the shares in a small company may intervene with great effect. The owner of 0.001% shares in ICI may find it extremely difficult to exert any influence, even though a 0.001% holding in ICI represents approximately 6,000 shares and an investment at 1984 prices of approximately £40,000.

In order to decide whether to intervene in the running of a company, a shareholder needs information that will enable him to assess the impact of his intervention on the value he attaches to the company's shares and on their market value. Such information will include the probability of intervention by other shareholders, the probable consequences of intervention, including the likelihood of its being effective, and the effect of each possible consequence on the future dividends expected from the company and on their associated risk.

3.2   Organisational Size and Financial Statements

In Chapter 1 we pointed out that not all participant groups are common to all types of organisation, and in Section 3.1 above we identified the information requirements of certain participant groups, e.g. trades unions, customers, shareholders and the government, which relate to the financial performance of organisations. In this section, we consider the means by which financial information is communicated to participants and, in particular, we consider why participants in large organisations are more interested in the *published financial statements* of the organisations than are participants in small organisations.

Consider again the snack bar which is owned and managed by an individual. As the owner is involved in the daily management of the bar, he should be well aware of its financial position, and the annual accounts, which measure past performance and current position, will tell him little that is new. The employees of the bar work alongside the owner and, by observing the general level of custom, will normally be aware of the financial position. Negotiations over pay and conditions of employment will be held directly with the owner. The bank manager may have known the owner for a considerable period of time, and the business's overdraft may be secured by the deposit of deeds of the owner's house with the bank. In such circumstances, the bank manager is normally supplied with information upon request, e.g. monthly takings, breakdown of expenses, future plans, etc. Suppliers are paid either in cash or within the stated credit period, and customers pay cash. For such an organisation, the annual financial statements might be viewed as providing confirmatory evidence of the financial performance and position of the business for the owner and the bank, and a basis upon which a tax charge will be levied. The importance of the annual accounts is diminished because more direct lines of communication exist between the various participants.

For larger organisations, these direct lines of communication do not exist and the importance of the published financial statements increases. The shareholders and potential investors in ICI are divorced from the daily activity of the company and the directors will rarely venture onto the 'shop floor'. The shareholders rely upon company reports, press comments and market data for information about ICI: the employees (approximately 118,000 in 1983) are not involved in company decision-making and, as they are unable to assess the company's performance by simple observation, they require more information concerning their employment. In addition, the immense size of ICI implies that it will be the major customer for many of its suppliers (materials and services used totalled £5,700 million in 1983), and in turn will itself be the major supplier for many of its own customers (sales were £8,200 million in 1983). The survival of these suppliers and customers may depend upon ICI maintaining a specific output level.

As organisations become larger and more complex, not only do they involve more groups of participants, but they may also have a greater influence over the behaviour of those groups. At the same time, many informal channels of communication disappear and more emphasis is placed upon formal channels of communication. The published financial statements represent one such formal channel of communication.

3.3   Implications of Users' Information Requirements

In the preceding sections we have considered briefly the sort of information which participants might require from financial statements. We have not attempted to develop detailed decision models in order to determine information requirements. Nevertheless, our *ad hoc* review provides a flavour of the sort of information users might be looking for if they are to make rational decisions.

Our analysis reveals an interesting phenomenon. In all but one of the decisions discussed in Section 3.1 (the assessment of entities' taxation liabilities by the government), the information required by users relates in part to some aspect or aspects of an entity's *future* performance. This revelation is hardly surprising. We have emphasised the role of accounting information in the decision processes of users. Decisions are concerned with choices between alternative future courses of action and thus information useful for decisions generally relates to the future. As part of the process of estimating aspects of future performance, users will require 'control' information. By control information we mean information about past performance which may be compared with the (past) estimates available to users. Such information should ideally include explanations of differences between previously estimated performance and the performance actually achieved. This helps users to evaluate the estimating procedures used, and make appropriate adjustments to existing forecasts. This sort of control information, involving the regular comparison of budgeted and actual performance, is a familiar part of management planning procedures. It should be an equally important part of the decision processes of other participant groups.

Our reasoning suggests that in general all users of accounting reports have two main, interdependent information requirements:

(a) forecasts of some aspects of the future performance of the reporting entity, and

(b) regular reports explaining both differences between forecast and actual performance, and changes in forecasts if expectations have changed.

The aspects of an entity's performance for which forecasts are required may, of course, differ from user to user. However, we noted in Chapter 1 that the survival of an organisation depends upon its participants receiving regular inducements from the organisation, and that many of these inducements are of a monetary nature. The review of user decisions and informational requirements in Section 3.1 suggested that many users are interested in the cash flows of the entity. These users include investors, creditors, employees, customers and the government.

It is significant that these user groups are concerned more with *cash flows* than with other measures of performance such as *accounting profit*, which we discuss at length in later chapters. There are two reasons for this. First, as we noted when describing the dividend valuation model, financial and economic theory suggests that all financial transactions be specified as cash flows to incorporate the impact of the time value of money, e.g. shareholders value their holdings on the basis of discounted *cash flows* rather than discounted *profits*. Interest is paid and received upon the amount of cash borrowed or loaned. Second, cash flows in and out of an organisation are fundamental to business events. Business activity is normally on a 'cash to cash' basis in that most transactions involve some cash movement either in the short or the long term. "Without cash the company could not survive in the economic world today, no matter how skilled its managers and workers. Cash at the end of the day determines its fate; indeed cash may be linked to the lifeblood of the company".[3]

If such a variety of users of financial statements desires information about forecasted and actual cash flows, and if cash is fundamental to the survival of the business, it would seem logical for entities to provide two types of financial statement:

(a)   a statement of forecasts of the entity's expected future cash flows, and
(b)   a statement of the entity's actual cash flows together with an explanation of the differences between the forecast and the actual cash flows.

However, such statements are not, at present, provided. Published financial statements for participants other than management generally do not include forecasts of future cash flows. Typically these statements report on the *past* performance (the Income Statement) and *current* financial position (the Balance Sheet) of an organisation, and, in some cases, as we explain in Chapter 18, include a Funds Flow Statement which attempts to show the sources and application of funds for the period. Also, the traditional focus of published financial statements has been upon income, or profit, rather than upon actual cash flows. In the next section we consider why entities have generally been reluctant to provide users with estimates of *future cash flows*, and in Chapter 4 we examine the reasons why published financial statements focus upon an entity's income for a period rather than on its *actual cash flows*.

3.4   Forecasts of Future Cash Flows

Although we are here concerned specifically with forecasts of future cash flows, the arguments presented are applicable equally to forecasts of income or profit.

The provision of forecasted information would directly facilitate decision-making by external users of financial statements. Many decisions of external users are based upon estimates of future events (see Section 3.1). In changing economic conditions, financial information about the past and present, as published in the annual financial statements, may be an unreliable guide to an organisation's future activities and performance. Although

---

[3]Lee, T.A., 'A case for cash flow reporting', *Journal of Business Finance*, Summer 1972.

it would be impractical to allow external users unrestricted access to an organisation's internal records in order to obtain data on which to base their own forecasts, the provision of management-prepared forecasts offers an alternative solution. This may be a preferable alternative for two reasons. First, it would involve relatively few additional costs, as most responsible managements already prepare forecasts for internal planning. Second, management is in the best position to assess the demand for an entity's products, the corresponding input requirements for the production processes, and the various input and output prices in the industry in which it operates.

Such forecasts, however, would need to be treated with caution. Forecasts, by their very nature, are uncertain, and it is possible that shareholders, lenders, employees and others might not recognise management forecasts as merely the most probable outcome from a whole range of outcomes. Nor might they recognise that such forecasts may be based upon rather tenuous assumptions about future events. If users were to interpret the forecasts as precise estimates by management, they might, as a result, take poor decisions, and should the forecasts subsequently turn out to be inaccurate, they may lose confidence in both management and the financial reporting process. Given the central role of management in 'managing' the various participants in an organisation, and the delicate balance that exists between the participants' inducements and contributions, such a loss of confidence in management could threaten the survival of the organisation itself.

It is not easy to predict how users might react to the publication of management forecasts. 'Sophisticated' investors, such as financial institutions, stockbrokers and financial analysts will be aware of the uncertainty attached to forecasting and will recognise the limitations of management forecasts. Presumably, management's best estimate of the entity's prospects would be only one of many inputs to the sophisticated investor's forecasting model. On the other hand, a less sophisticated investor, or a trades union with insufficient resources to obtain proper financial advice, might not appreciate the limitations inherent in the forecasts.

Nevertheless, management-prepared forecasts should be more reliable as an aid to decision-making than many other information sources. As we noted above, managers already produce detailed budgets internally for the purpose of planning and controlling the future operations of the company. Some of these budgets may be in physical terms—quantity of material used, number of hours worked, etc.—but most are translated into monetary amounts, i.e. cash flows. A lack of sophistication in financial matters by some users is not a valid reason for not publishing forecasts. Users will continue to make decisions about an entity whether or not the management provides them with forecasts, and a lack of sophistication could be lessened by increasing the level of financial education amongst users.

The publication of management's cash forecasts would provide the other participant groups with a yardstick against which to compare and evaluate management's future performance. Although this is likely to be seen as useful additional information by most participants it is less likely to appeal to managers. We suggested in Chapter 1 that, as a participant group itself, management has its own goals which, at any one time, may conflict with the goals of other groups. For example, it may not be in management's best interests to provide a warning to suppliers, customers or shareholders of a possible decline in future cash flows. In order to prevent management from issuing overly optimistic, or deliberately misleading, forecasts, it is important that they be held accountable for their forecasts. For example, it may be desirable for auditors to audit the assumptions underlying the forecasts, or for users to be allowed to take legal action against the managers should the users suffer losses as a result of acting upon misleading forecasts. However, the more stringent are the *ex post* controls, the more managers may be motivated to provide conservative and easily achievable forecasts, and the less willing they will be to undertake potentially profitable but risky ventures. The degree of control which should be exercised over management forecasts is thus difficult to determine. Too little control might encourage the managers of some companies to publish deliberately misleading forecasts, whereas too much accountability might cause them to become unduly conservative in both their forecasts and actions.

Further, the disclosure of assumptions regarding management's likely future actions might involve the disclosure of confidential information (e.g. the introduction of new products, the closing down of a factory, etc.) to competitors. The detrimental effects of such disclosures would at least be tempered if all companies were forced to comply with the requirement. However, as compliance would presumably be restricted to UK companies and UK subsidiaries of foreign companies it might still be possible for foreign companies to gain a competitive advantage in international markets from such disclosures.

In 1975 two influential committees[4] considered and rejected the arguments in favour of disclosing cash forecasts as part of a company's published financial statements. Thus despite the considerable potential benefits which might accrue to users from the disclosure of cash forecasts, it is unlikely that they will be published in the foreseeable future.

3.5   Analysis and Interpretation of Financial Information

Managers, who may have most to lose by the disclosure of forecasted information, comprise a powerful lobby opposing such disclosures. The uncertainty of the impact of published forecasts upon management policies

---

[4]*The Sandilands Report,* Report of the Inflation Accounting Committee, HMSO Cmnd 6225, 1975, para 229; and *The Corporate Report,* Accounting Standards Committee, 1975, p.56.

and upon the behaviour of 'financially naive' user groups and 'financially sophisticated' competitor firms has added weight to this opposition. The implication for students of accounting is clear: we do not start with a clean slate. Estimates of future business performance might appear to be a natural candidate for disclosure in financial statements, but what appears beneficial to the interests of one group of participants may be detrimental to the interests of another.

As a result, some external users of financial statements are deprived of a basic input to their decision models, i.e. management-prepared forecasts of future cash flows. The information currently disclosed is concerned more with *past* performance and *present* position, which is, of course, determined by the results of *past* transactions. External users must analyse and interpret this historical information in order to estimate an entity's *future* business performance and financial position. This state of affairs raises the following fundamental question:

How should users of financial statements analyse and interpret the (historical) data provided in order to obtain the (predictive) information required?

This question has greatly influenced our approach in the writing of this book. It means that in the following chapters we will not always accept current accounting practices at face value, but, where necessary, will examine how easily they can be translated into information which might be useful for decision-makers; and whenever a choice exists between alternative accounting methods we will stress the need to consider the extent to which each method translates into information useful to decision-makers.

In Chapter 4 we begin this process by considering why accounting practice has for so long focused upon the income of an entity rather than upon its actual cash flows, and we introduce the criteria against which we might evaluate alternative methods of reporting business performance.

APPENDIX A
The Time Value of Money

The share valuation model introduced in Section 3.1 involves the discounting of expected receipts from a shareholding (dividends and capital distributions) to their present value using a rate of interest (or discount rate) which is appropriate for the risk attached to the expected receipts. The central feature of this model is that cash receipts expected at different times in the future are not simply added together to obtain a measure of the present values of those cash receipts. The model recognises that £1 now is worth more than £1 at some time in the future, and the rationale for this is explained below.

The time value of money is the result of the existence of investment, lending and borrowing opportunities, of the preference that many individuals have for immediate rather than future consumption, and of expected inflation. These factors mean that those who wish to have cash for spending sooner rather than later incur a cost (pay a price) in so doing, and that those who are willing to defer having cash available for spending enjoy a benefit (receive a price). The prices paid or received are normally expressed in terms of interest rates which represent the costs or benefits of transferring money from one period to another, in much the same way as costs or benefits arise when other resources are acquired or disposed of.

In practice, a spectrum of interest rates exists at any time in the capital market (i.e. the market in which funds are borrowed and loaned). Rates of interest vary depending upon the amounts and risks involved, the status of the individual or entity concerned, and so on. To simplify our discussion of the role of interest rates in the measurement of wealth we make two rather unrealistic assumptions at this stage.[5]

First, we assume that there are perfect markets for borrowing and lending funds, i.e. perfect capital markets. Three conditions must be satisfied if this assumption is to hold:

(a)   No lender or borrower is large enough for his transactions to affect the ruling market price for funds (the interest rate).
(b)   All traders in the market have equal and costless access to information about the ruling price and all other relevant information.
(c)   There are no transactions costs involved in using the market and no taxes that would alter economic decisions.

Second, we assume that the future is known with certainty. If these two assumptions hold, there will be a unique market rate of interest, which we shall call i, at which all users of the capital market are able to borrow or lend as much as they wish. Under the conditions assumed, competitive forces are likely to eliminate opportunities to lend or borrow at any interest rate other than i. The assumption of a unique market rate of interest leads to a useful simplification in the measurement of wealth; cash flows which arise at different points in time may be compared without any ambiguities which might arise if there existed a number of different possible interest rates.

Given the unique market rate of interest, i, an individual presently in possession of £C could lend it to yield £$C(1+i)$ after one year, i.e. return of capital, £C, plus interest £$C \times i$. (In these expressions and all relevant subsequent ones in this chapter, i should be interpreted as the rate of interest expressed as a decimal of 1. Thus, for example, an interest rate of 6% would be written as 0.06 and one of 20% as 0.20.) If capital and interest are loaned

---

[5]Some of the implications of relaxing these assumptions are discussed in Arnold, J. and Hope T., *Accounting for Management Decisions,* Prentice-Hall International, 1983, Chapter 12.

for a further year the total returns at the end of the second year will be $£C(1+i)(1+i)$, which equals $£C(1+i)^2$. In general, if an amount $£C$ is invested for n years at an annual compound rate of interest, i, the amount to which it will have accumulated after n years will be $£C(1+i)^n$. This process is known as *compounding*, and enables us to re-express present values in terms of equivalent future values. A rational individual should be indifferent between $£C(1+i)^n$ after n years and $£C$ immediately, because possession of the latter could be converted to the former by lending at the market rate of interest.

For purposes of measuring present wealth we are interested not so much in re-expressing present values in terms of equivalent future values as in the opposite process of re-expressing expected future cash flows in terms of equivalent present values. This process is known as *discounting,* and provides us with a common basis for measuring wealth, in terms of (discounted) present values.

Suppose an individual expects to receive $£C$ after one year. What is the present value (PV) of the expected receipt? Let us think of PV as the immediate amount the investor would have to lend in order to accumulate $£C$ after one year. Then:

$$PV(1+i)=£C, \text{ and}$$

$$PV=\frac{£C}{(1+i)} \quad \text{(sometimes written as } £C(1+i)^{-1})$$

By similar reasoning, it may be shown that the present value of $£C$ receivable or payable after two years is $£C/(1+i)^2$ and, in the general case, that the present value of $£C$ receivable or payable after n years is $£C/(1+i)^n$. A rational investor should be indifferent between any expected future amount and its present value. For example, in the general case an individual expecting to receive $£C$ after n years could convert it to $£C/(1+i)^n$ immediately by borrowing, and an individual with $£C/(1+i)^n$ could convert it to $£C$ after n years by lending.

The equivalence between an expected cash receipt or payment and its discounted present value enables us to measure the impact of a future cash flow on an individual's or firm's present wealth. It also provides us with a means of calculating the total wealth of an individual or firm, and the present value of the shares of a company, provided we can estimate the amount and timing of all relevant future cash flows, i.e., the process is to estimate the future cash flows, discount them to present values and sum the present values.[6]

---

[6]Although we have assumed the existence of a unique interest rate for discounting purposes, the procedure described is often valid in an environment where multiple interest rates exist. Of course, such environments create the additional problem of selecting a discount rate or rates which reflect the individual's or firm's particular borrowing and lending opportunities and the risk associated with expected cash flows.

Illustration. A company expects to receive, and distribute to its share-holders as dividends, net cash inflows (i.e. cash receipts from sales, etc., less operating costs) of £50,000 after one year, £65,000 after two years and £100,000 after three years, and nothing thereafter. The relevant interest rate, *i,* is 15% (0.15) p.a. compound. Mr Windsor owns 10% of the company's shares. What is the present value of Mr Windsor's shareholding? Calculating the discounted present value of the expected dividends (net cash inflows) to Mr Windsor, and summing gives:

$$PV = \frac{5,000}{(1+i)} + \frac{6,500}{(1+i)^2} + \frac{10,000}{(1+i)^3}$$

$$PV = \frac{5,000}{(1.15)} + \frac{6,500}{(1.15)^2} + \frac{10,000}{(1.15)^3} = £15,837.90$$

The present value of Mr Windsor's shareholding is £15,837.90.

We can now provide a symbolic representation of the model used above to calculate present value. The present value of a shareholding to an investor may be described by the expression:

$$V_0 = \frac{d_1}{(1+i)} + \frac{d_2}{(1+i)^2} + \frac{d_3}{(1+i)^3} + \cdots + \frac{d_n}{(1+i)^n}$$

where V_0 is the present value of a shareholding to an investor, d_1 is the dividend or other cash receipt expected at time 1 (i.e. after one year), d_2 is the dividend or other cash receipt expected at time 2 and so on, n is the last time at which a receipt is expected from the shareholding, and i is the appropriate interest rate.

This expression may be more conveniently written:

$$V_0 = \sum_{j=1}^{n} \frac{d_j}{(1+i)^j}$$

Discussion Topics

1 Discuss the information requirements of the following user groups:
   (a) employees
   (b) government
   (c) shareholders.

2 Which government departments might be particularly interested in the infor-mation contained in financial statements? For which purposes?

3 Are you aware of any instances in which trade unions have used published accounting information as a basis for wages demands? How were these negoti-ations resolved?

4 Why are managers so reluctant to publish forecasts? Can you think of any circumstances in which publication would be beneficial to managers?

5 Are there many decisions which are common to shareholders and lenders, and would thus require similar information?

6 Can you think of any circumstances in which participants other than managers might not like to see published forecasts? For what reasons?

7 Explain the relationship between organisational size and formal communication.

Further Reading

Arnold, J., 'The information requirements of shareholders', in Carsberg, B. and Hope, A. (eds), *Current Issues in Accounting,* 2nd ed, Philip Allan, 1984.

Carsberg, B., 'Directions into the future: the prospects for research', in Carsberg, B. and Hope, A. (eds), *Current Issues in Accounting,* 2nd ed, Philip Allan 1984.

Cooper, D., 'Information for labour', in Carsberg, B. and Hope, A. (eds), *Current Issues in Accounting,* 2nd ed, Philip Allan, 1984.

Cooper, D. and Essex, S., 'Accounting information and employee decision making', *Accounting, Organisations and Society,* Vol 3, 1977.

Gray, R. and Perks, R. 'How desirable is social accounting?', *Accountancy,* April 1982.

Maunders, K. and Foley, B. *Accounting Information, Disclosure and Collective Bargaining,* Macmillan, 1977.

Sherer, M. and Southworth, A. 'Accounting and accountability in the nationalised industries', in Carsberg, B. and Hope, A. (eds), *Current Issues in Accounting,* 2nd ed, Philip Allan, 1984.

Exercises

3.1 Mr Alfonso is the owner of a small business, the Jago Co., which manufactures and sells footballs. Mr Alfonso expects that the business will earn net cash receipts of £5,000 after one year, £6,000 after two years, and £8,000 after three years. At the end of three years he expects to sell the business to Despina Ltd for £40,000.

Assume that Mr Alfonso will withdraw all net cash receipts from the business for his personal use as they arise, that no cash flows are expected other than those described above, and that there is no uncertainty associated with the receipt of any cash flow. Mr Alfonso's discount rate is 20% per annum.

• Calculate the discounted present value of the Jago Co., now and at the end of *each* of the next three years, immediately after the annual net cash receipts have been distributed to Mr Alfonso.

3.2   Mr Nabucco owns a 20% stake in a small, but prosperous, company which is considering investing £50,000 in a new process which will offer the following positive cash flows at the end of the following years:

Year 1	£30,000
Year 2	£25,000
Year 3	£10,000

Mr Nabucco is unhappy about the proposed investment because he would have liked an immediate distribution of cash so that he could have indulged himself, his wife and his six children in a Carribean cruise at a cost of £10,000.

Mr Nabucco can borrow and lend at the same annual rate as the company which is 10%.

●   Explain to Mr Nabucco what he should do to maximise his satisfaction. What would happen if the best rate of interest available to Mr Nabucco for borrowing was 20% per annum?

3.3   Once upon a time, many years ago, there lived a feudal landlord in a small province of Central Europe. The landlord, known as the Red Bearded Baron, lived in a castle high on a hill, and this benevolent fellow was responsible for the well-being of many peasants who occupied the lands surrounding his castle. Each spring, as the snow began to melt and thoughts of other, less influential men turned to matters other than business, the Baron would decide how to provide for all his serf-dependents during the coming year.

One spring, the Baron was thinking about the wheat crop of the coming growing season. "I believe that 30 acres of my land, being worth five bushels of wheat per acre, will produce enough wheat for next winter", he mused, "but who should do the farming? I believe I'll give Idomeneo the Indefatigable and Idamante the Immutable the task of growing the wheat." Whereupon Idomeneo and Idamante, two serfs noted for their hard work and not overly active minds, were summoned for an audience with the Baron.

"Idomeneo, you will farm on the 20 acre plot of ground and Idamante will farm the 10 acre plot", the Baron began. "I will give Idomeneo 20 bushels of wheat for seed and 20 pounds of fertiliser. (Twenty pounds of fertiliser are worth two bushels of wheat.) Idamante will get 10 bushels of wheat for seed and 10 pounds of fertiliser. I will give each of you an ox to pull a plough but you will have to make arrangements with Arbace the Ploughmaker for a plough. The oxen, incidentally, are only three years old and have never been used for farming, so they should have a good ten years of farming ahead of them. Take good care of them, because an ox is worth 40 bushels of wheat. Come back next autumn and return the oxen and the ploughs along with your harvest."

Idomeneo and Idamante genuflected and withdrew from the Great Hall, taking with them the things provided by the Baron.

The summer came and went and after the harvest Idomeneo and Idamante returned to the Great Hall to account to their master for the things given them in the spring. Idomeneo, pouring 223 bushels of wheat onto the floor, said, "My Lord, I present you with a slightly used ox, a plough broken beyond repair, and 223 bushels of wheat. I, unfortunately, owe Arbace the Ploughmaker three bushels of wheat for the plough I got from him last spring. And, as you might expect, I used all the fertiliser and seed you gave me last spring. You will also remember, my Lord, that you took 20 bushels of my harvest for your own personal use."

Idamante, who had been given 10 acres of land, 10 bushels of wheat and 10 pounds of fertiliser, spoke next. "Here, my Lord, is a partially used-up ox, the plough for which I gave Arbace the Ploughmaker three bushels of wheat from my harvest, and 105 bushels of wheat. I, too, used all my seed and fertiliser last spring. Also, my Lord, you took 30 bushels of wheat several days ago for your own table. I believe the plough is good for two more seasons."

"Knaves, you did well," said the Red Bearded Baron. Blessed with this benediction and not wishing to press their luck further, the two serfs departed hastily.

After the servants had taken their leave, the Red Bearded Baron, watching the two hungry oxen slowly eating the wheat piled on the floor, began to contemplate what had happened. "Yes," he thought, "they did well, but I wonder which one did better?"

● Prepare for each farmer (Idomeneo and Idamante) a statement of 'net income' for the period and a statement of 'financial position' at the end of the period. Provide full explanations of your calculations and note any reservations you have.

Chapter 4

Understanding the Message: Cash Flows and Accounting Standards

In Chapter 3 we pointed out that the users of financial statements do not receive directly (i.e. in published reports) the future-orientated information they require to make rational economic decisions. To make such decisions they must, therefore, analyse and interpret the historical information provided. It is important that this historical information is clear and unambiguous: only then will it provide a sound basis for further analysis. In the terminology of the communication model it is important that no noise exists at the semantic level (see Figure 2.2, page 28). In Sections 4.2 and 4.3 we consider the reporting of actual (or historical) cash flows as a way of minimising noise in published financial statements. The evaluation of historical cash flows as a reporting method leads us to develop, in Section 4.4, a set of criteria against which we might evaluate all alternative reporting methods. Finally, in Section 4.5, we describe how the accounting profession in the UK has attempted to increase the usefulness and the understandability of published financial statements by 'standardising' accounting practice.

4.1 Understanding the Message

To achieve success in any form of communication, it is essential that the receiver understands the language used by the sender in constructing his message. Suppose an organisation was not obliged to disclose its method of arriving at the figures appearing in its financial statements. It would be virtually impossible for a reader of those statements to evaluate the organisation's business performance, or to compare its results with those of other organisations. And yet, such a situation existed in the UK until the 1930s. The directors of a company were not legally obliged to disclose separately the components of a company's balance sheet or profit and loss account. For example, the profit and loss account of Rylands and Sons Ltd for 1930 included an item: "Dividends and Interest received, and Transfers from

52

Contingency Accounts, and after charging Maintenance, Repairs, Depreciation, Income Tax, Salaries of Managing Directors, Bad Debts and other expenses, £106,752/16/9".[1] The reporting of a profit figure down to the last nine pennies implies that the underlying calculations were very precise, and yet no information is provided on the relative size of the components of that figure. It is difficult to imagine any decisions for which such aggregated information would be useful.

This type of extreme problem could be eliminated by requiring entities to explain how each figure in the accounts has been calculated. However, this might entail the publication of long and tedious 'explanatory notes' (leading to information overload), and the comparison of the accounts of two or more entities would be an equally long and tedious process. An alternative would be to require all entities to report each item in the balance sheet and income statement in accordance with a predetermined set of detailed procedural rules. However, the activities of companies in different industries may be sufficiently diverse as to be incapable of being described satisfactorily by a single set of *accounting policies*—as we noted in Chapter 1, it is most unlikely that the activities of a charity could be reported adequately using accounting policies designed for reporting on the activities of profit-seeking companies. Complete uniformity, therefore, does not appear to be the answer. A compromise solution would be to require all entities to adhere to a set of *basic guidelines* (to ensure a certain degree of comparability) and, where choice exists between alternative accounting policies, to disclose which policy has been adopted. This describes current practice, and in Section 4.5 we shall examine this in some detail.

However, it may seem that there is an obvious solution to the semantic problem in financial statements—all entities should report their activities in terms of actual cash flows paid and received. This proposal has several advantages. First, most of us understand the meaning of cash. It is not a nebulous concept like income or profit. Second, cash is a relatively objective measure. It is more difficult for an entity to manipulate a cash flow figure than to manipulate an income figure (for example, by changing an accounting policy). Hence published financial statements should be more comparable. Third, as we noted in Chapter 3, cash is fundamental to the survival of an entity and the reporting of past cash flows might provide some indication of the entity's future prospects. Yet, despite these advantages, the reporting of historical cash flows does not form the basis of conventional accounting practice. The reasons for this are examined in the next section.

---

[1]Edwards, J.R., 'The accounting profession and disclosure in published reports, 1925–35', *Accounting and Business Research,* Autumn 1976.

4.2   Historical Cash Flows and Accrual Accounting

Cash has long been used as a medium of exchange. It is well understood and is suitable for a wide variety of transactions. Students often judge the state of their well-being by reference to the balance in their bank accounts. At the beginning of each term cash is paid into the bank account when the grant is received, and over the course of the term cash is paid gradually, or rapidly, out of the account as expenditures are made. An assessment of a student's ability to manage his or her financial affairs might be carried out by examining the size of the cash balance (or overdraft) at the end of the year. In a sense, as we explain below, any surplus cash might be seen as profit. In addition, if prices were to remain stable and the student's spending pattern remained the same, the amount of surplus cash this year would give an indication of what might be saved next year also.

Cash balances fulfilled a similar role for Italian merchants in the fifteenth and sixteenth centuries. A 'trading venture' might have involved the exchanging of goods for silks and spices in the Eastern Mediterranean. Merchants would spend cash in purchasing the goods to be exchanged, in leasing or buying ships, in hiring crew and so on. Cash inflows arose only at the end of the voyage when the silks and spices were eventually sold in Italy. The success of the venture could be measured by counting the surplus cash after all expenses had been paid and the original investment recovered. This surplus cash represented profit from the venture, and *ceteris paribus* the size of the profit gave an indication of the likely profitability of similar ventures in the future.

A similar situation might exist today for a fruit and vegetable stallholder (see Table 4.1(a)). Suppose the stallholder begins the day with £100 which he uses to purchase fruit and vegetables at the wholesale market on Monday morning. He pushes his (rented) barrow to a suitable pitch and sells all his produce for £150 by the evening. He pays his barrow rental of £2 and returns home with £148. The surplus cash of £48 represents his profit for the day and if trading conditions (including prices) are not expected to change, then Monday's cash surplus is a good indicator of the likely profit to be earned on Tuesday and on each subsequent day.

On first reading it might appear that the disclosure of cash receipts and cash payments and of the balance of cash held at the beginning and end of the period would provide the reader with information useful for decision making. We noted in Chapter 3 that users would like, ideally, an estimate of the entity's future cash flows and a report of actual cash flows together with explanations of any differences between forecast and actual results. In the examples above actual cash flows have been disclosed and it is suggested that if conditions are stable, the amount of surplus cash at the end of the current period provides an indication of the likely cash surplus in future periods. In these cases, surplus cash reflects *maintainable profit*.

Table 4.1   Cash flow statements for stallholder

	(a) Monday		(b) Tuesday	
	£	£	£	£
Cash receipts from sales		150		120
Cash payment:				
Purchases	100		–	
Barrow rental	2		2	
	——	102	——	2
Cash surplus		48		118

However, the position is not so clear-cut in practice. Each of the above illustrations is characterised by reference to a complete *trading cycle* the student's 'profit' was calculated at the end of the academic year; the merchant's profit was calculated at the completion of the venture; and the stallholder's profit was calculated at the end of the day, at which time a full cycle of purchase and sale had been completed. In the real world such completeness is rare, at least over a fairly short period. The student's bank balance would have been less reliable as a measure of profit for the past year and an indicator of next year's surplus had he recently (i.e. near the end of the year) purchased food, books, etc. using a credit card, and had not yet settled his account. Similarly, the stallholder might not trade solely on a cash basis. Hence, his trading cycle might not be completed at the end of each day. Suppose that on the following day: (a) the market allows him to settle his account at the end of the week, and (b) although he sells all his produce for £150, he receives only £120 cash. A regular customer had forgotten his wallet and the stallholder allowed him twenty-four hours to pay. Does the day's cash surplus of £118 (see Table 4.1(b)) measure the stallholder's business performance on Tuesday and can it be used to estimate his likely performance for the rest of the week?

This illustration suggests that a statement of cash payments and receipts might not reflect business performance or economic activity when transactions do not involve the immediate transfer of cash, for example when buying and selling on credit. Even so, credit transactions would not create reporting problems if we could wait until the cash was paid or received before preparing the financial statements, i.e. until the trading cycle was completed. However, most businesses buy and sell goods and services continuously, so that at any one point in time there will always be bills outstanding in relation to sales and purchases. Consequently, conventional accounting practice records transactions at the time of sale and purchase rather than at the time of cash receipt and cash payment.

Table 4.2   Income statements for stallholder

	(a) Monday		(b) Tuesday	
	£	£	£	£
Sales		150		150
Expenses:				
Cost of goods sold	100		100	
Barrow rental	2		2	
	—	102	—	102
Profit		48		48

A conventional financial statement for the stallholder is illustrated in Table 4.2. On Tuesday, sales (as distinct from cash receipts) are £150, purchases (as distinct from cash payments) are £100, and as all the produce is sold, the *cost of goods sold* is £100 also. After deducting the barrow rental the profit for the day amounts to £48. This would seem to be a more realistic assessment of the stallholder's performance on the day (i.e. compare this with his performance on Monday when the same economic activities generated an identical profit of £48) and it gives some indication of his future performance too. If he continues to sell £150 worth of goods each day then he should continue indefinitely to earn a profit of £48 each day. The cash surplus of £118 could not be so maintained even if conditions (prices) were stable because, for example, it ignores the amount which must be paid to the market at the end of the week.

The convention which distinguishes between the receipt of cash and the right to receive cash, and the payment of cash and the obligation to pay cash is known as the accrual convention. Conventional accounting is often termed *accrual accounting* to distinguish it from cash flow accounting.

At the end of the week when the stallholder's trading cycle is complete, the cash surplus should be identical to the reported profit. Table 4.3 reconciles the two methods of reporting business performance. The results of the stallholder's operations on Monday and Tuesday are reproduced from Tables 4.1 and 4.2. On Wednesday the stallholder again purchases goods for £100, on credit, from the market. His account will be settled on Saturday. He sells all these goods for £150 cash and in addition collects £30 from the customer who had forgotten his wallet the previous day. On Thursday and Friday he again purchases £100 goods on credit and sells them for £150 cash. On Saturday he sells £150 worth of goods and settles his account at the market. This amounts to £500 representing purchases of £100 each day from Tuesday to Saturday. For each of the first five days he has generated a (fluctuating) cash surplus, but on Saturday the settlement of his outstanding

Table 4.3   Reconciliation of stallholder's cash flow and income statement

	Monday £	Tuesday £	Wednesday £	Thursday £	Friday £	Saturday £	Totals for week £
Cash flow statements							
Cash receipts from sales	150	120	180	150	150	150	900
Cash payments:							
Purchases	100	–	–	–	–	500	600
Barrow rental	2	2	2	2	2	2	12
	102	2	2	2	2	502	612
Cash surplus/(deficit)	48	118	178	148	148	(352)	288
Income statements							
Sales	150	150	150	150	150	150	900
Expenses:							
Cost of goods sold	100	100	100	100	100	100	600
Barrow rental	2	2	2	2	2	2	12
	102	102	102	102	102	102	612
	48	48	48	48	48	48	288

account produces a cash deficit, or net cash outflow, of £352. Totalling the daily figures we can produce a cash flow statement for the week. This is presented in the right-hand column of Table 4.3 and shows a cash surplus of £288.

The stallholder's income statement is identical for each day of operations, from Monday to Saturday. Irrespective of when the cash was actually paid and received, he has purchased goods costing £100 and sold them for £150 each day. For each of the six days he has generated a profit of £48, which amounts to £288 by the end of the week. Thus the cash surplus and the profit generated at the end of the week are identical. This is an important point. It does not matter how large is the organisation, nor how complex its transactions, all measures of profit will produce the same aggregate figure at the completion of the trading cycle and that profit figure will be identical to the cash surplus over the period.

This identity hides two major problems. First, as we shall see in the following section, many organisations do not complete their trading cycle until the business is wound up, which in most cases is many years after they have begun to trade. Secondly, although the aggregate profit figure over the life of the organisation will be identical to the aggregate cash surplus, the pattern of cash and income figures reported within that period can differ significantly. We can see from Table 4.3 that a reader of the stallholder's accounts might make a different assessment of the stallholder's past performance, and a different prediction of his future performance, depending upon whether he was provided, at the end of each day, with a cash flow statement or an income statement.

This is one dilemma facing all accountants. At the end of an organisation's life, all methods of cash flow and income measurement will produce identical aggregate figures measuring the surplus/profit generated since the organisation was created. Participants, however, require information on a more regular basis in order to make their decisions. The aggregate surplus/profit is therefore *allocated* over a series of reporting periods—usually of twelve months duration. The choice of accounting method will determine the pattern of the surplus/profit figures reported in these periods, and this pattern may have a significant influence on participants' decisions.

4.3   The Allocation of Expenditure

Some cash outflows are used not to pay immediate running expenses, but to purchase *assets,* items which will produce benefits for the entity over a period of time, e.g. the student might use any excess of his grant over his living expenses (!) to purchase stereo equipment, and the Italian merchant might purchase a ship which will be used on future ventures. If, after the first voyage, the merchant reports a cash deficit after taking into account the

entire cost of purchasing the ship, does this mean the venture was unprofitable and that future ventures should not be undertaken? In this instance the
trading cycle has not been completed because the ship has not been recon-
verted into cash.

Because users need regular information, most entities are currently
required to produce financial statements every twelve months. However, as
most organisations are *going concerns* (i.e. they are expected to continue to
operate for the foreseeable future) they do not reconvert their assets into
cash for the purpose of calculating a cash surplus. How, then, should an
entity account for cash spent on assets which are still in existence at the end
of the year?

Suppose our stallholder was successful. Having accumulated £20,000
he decides to open a shop. He purchases a truck for £10,000, signs a three
year lease on a shop at a cost of £6,000 and purchases shop fittings for
£3,000. His bank balance is reduced to £1,000. He has spent cash of £19,000
on items which he hopes will last beyond the first twelve months and will
contribute towards the generation of revenues and profits in future years. It
would therefore seem inappropriate to charge the whole £19,000 as an
expense in the first year of trading when the truck, the shop and the fittings
are all available for use in the second year. On the other hand, neither does it
seem appropriate to ignore these items altogether in calculating how the
business has performed in its first year. These items cost £19,000 and
eventually they will be 'consumed', i.e. will wear out or expire.

This example illustrates another difficulty in relying on actual cash flows
to measure past performance and provide an indication of future cash flows.
Organisations often purchase assets which will last, and provide benefits, for
several years. This may involve the payment of large amounts of cash in
some years, but little or none in others. For example, if the truck for which
the stallholder has paid £10,000 in year 1 lasts for five years, he will have no
comparable expenditure in each of the next four years.

To include the whole £10,000 as an expense in the first year would
distort an evaluation of that year's business performance and could mislead
users in estimating business performance in years 2, 3, 4 and 5. Major cash
expenditures tend to be 'lumpy' and can distort year-by-year evaluations.
Hence, conventional accrual accounting aims to smooth out the lumps by
allocating the cost of assets to the years in which they are consumed. If the
truck is expected to last for five years, the £10,000 would be allocated over
the five year period by means of an annual *depreciation* charge. The £6,000
lease would be allocated over three years, and the £3,000 spent on fittings
over their *estimated useful life*.

By recording transactions at the time of sale and purchase rather than at
the time of cash receipt and cash payment, and by allocating cash expenditure on long-lived assets over several periods, the accrual accounting method
produces an income or profit figure which, historically, has been deemed to

be more useful and more understandable to the users of financial statements than the more erratic cash flow figures. We might ask ourselves why this is. First, the income figure is thought to be a good measure of *business* performance insofar as it reports on the *economic* activity of buying and selling goods rather than the *financial* activity of paying out and receiving cash. Secondly, in spreading capital expenditures over the useful life of the assets purchased, it adopts a longer-term view of the business. By looking beyond the current year the system produces an income figure which, it is argued, is a better indicator of future business performance. In Chapter 3 we suggested that most participant groups would benefit from some estimate of an organisation's future business performance. We also suggested that, when evaluating accounting alternatives we should consider how easily the information provided could be translated into information useful for decision-makers. As direct forecasts are unavailable at present, it would seem helpful for users to receive an income figure representing maintainable profit, if such a figure could be used for estimating future performance, including that based on future cash flows.

But does an income figure calculated according to conventional accrual accounting provide a sound basis for further analysis? In practice, the calculation of accounting income poses several difficulties for managers and accountants. For example, in spreading the cost of an asset over its useful life, they must consider various factors which may contribute to the determination of that useful life. Thus an asset's useful life may be affected by the intensity of its use, by its location or by economic and technological trends. Managers must also consider how best to allocate the cost over that useful life, for example should an equal amount be allocated each year, or should some weighting factor be applied?

Managers and accountants can and do provide several alternative, equally justifiable answers to these questions[2] and yet if other participants are to understand and have confidence in the figures reported by management there must be some *consistency* in the manner in which business organisations prepare their financial statements. If published financial statements are not to contain reasonably objective, easily understood cash flows, then guidelines and *standards* must be provided to ensure a degree of comparability between the information included in the financial statements of different organisations. These will enable the reader of the statements to decode successfully the messages contained therein. In Section 4.5 we shall examine the role of such accounting standards in the UK, and their usefulness generally as a means of governing accounting practice.

In Chapter 3, we examined the arguments for and against the publication of cash forecasts. In Sections 4.2 and 4.3 we have considered the case for reporting historical cash flows to external readers, and have introduced the

(margin annotation: IMPORTANT)

---

[2]For a further discussion of the issues involved in allocating the costs of assets, see Chapter 9.

basic system of accrual accounting which underlies conventional practice. We have referred repeatedly to the decision models of the users of accounting reports. We believe that *relevance to user decision models* is of prime importance in the choice of reporting method. Nevertheless, other criteria have been suggested. Some of these are also relevant to user decision models and we have already mentioned the need of users for information which is objective, easily understood and which can be expressed in terms enabling the user to compare one entity's results with those of another. In the following section we describe some of the more important criteria which a financial reporting method should strive to satisfy, and which might provide useful guidelines for those responsible for developing accounting standards.

4.4   Criteria for Choice of Reporting Method

As a rather rough distinction, we may categorise all the main criteria as relating to either the *usefulness* or the *feasibility* of alternative reporting methods. Within the category of usefulness we may include relevance to user decisions (which we have already discussed at length), timeliness, comparability, objectivity and understandability. In the feasibility category may be included verifiability and measurability. However, classification of the criteria into particular categories is much less important than an understanding of their significance in helping to develop reporting guidelines.

Timeliness
The criterion of timeliness suggests that the usefulness of accounting information is reduced, the longer is the time period between an event occurring and its being reported. Hence, a dedicated imbiber of alcoholic drinks planning to spend his evening drinking either beer or whisky, may not be much assisted in a choice between the two if he receives the information that in 1962 a pint of beer cost 1s 3d and one sixth of a gill of whisky 1s 7d, even if the prices were converted to decimal currency! He is presumably interested in their current prices. One might also expect that the information contained in the financial statements of ICI plc for the year ended 31 December 1983, and published in March 1984 would have been less useful to readers had the statements not been published until March 1985.

Comparability
The criterion of comparability has two dimensions; comparability through time (often referred to as consistency) and comparability between entities. As we shall see in later chapters, accountants are permitted sufficient flexibility in choosing methods of recording and reporting transactions to produce any one of a large number of figures as a measure of the outcome of a particular series of transactions. If accounting information is being used, for

example, to monitor the profitability of a particular entity through time, it is important that the methods adopted to measure the components of profit are not varied from period to period. If the methods are varied, changes in reported profitability may result solely from changes in accounting methods. Similar considerations apply when aspects of the performances of two or more entities are being compared, i.e. similar underlying performances may result in very different reported measures if different accounting methods are used. For example, suppose two companies purchased identical items of computer equipment on the same day. The equipment has a cost of £15,000 and both companies expect the equipment to last for five years. Under the cash flow method of accounting, each company would disclose a payment of £15,000 in year one and no payment in the remaining four years. However, conventional accrual accounting would require each company to allocate the £15,000 over the asset's useful life. It is conceivable that one company would charge depreciation of £3,000 each year for five years and the other company would charge depreciation of £5,000 in year one, £4,000 in year two £3,000 in year three, £2,000 in year four and £1,000 in year five. Even if all other revenues and expenses of these two companies were identical, their choice of different methods of depreciation would result in different reported income figures.

Objectivity
The objectivity criterion is concerned primarily with the extent to which accounting information is free from bias. For example, an accounting system that involves the reporting only of bank account transactions during a period would probably be more free from bias than one that involves the reporting of forecasts of future performance (although it may be less relevant). Perhaps the most helpful measure of the objectivity of an accounting method is the extent to which the method reflects a *consensus* view. For example, suppose that 1,000 spectators watch an exciting and high-scoring basketball match but receive no indication, apart from their own observations, of the score. On leaving the stadium they are asked two questions: What was the score? Was the game entertaining? One might expect intuitively that the answers to the first question would be more 'objective' than the answers to the second. Yet there may well be a greater consensus about the game's entertainment value than about its score. In this sense, the latter 'measure' is more objective than the former.

Understandability
The usefulness of accounting information depends in part on the extent to which those who use it understand the basis on which it has been prepared, i.e. that there are few problems at the semantic level of communication. Non-accountants might, for example, be surprised to learn that the reported income of an entity for a period may bear little resemblance to the change in

its cash and bank balances during the period. Anyone who believes that reported income does indicate the change in an enterprise's cash resources (i.e. who does not understand the basis on which income is measured) may make incorrect decisions in consequence. Hence, understandability is an important attribute of accounting methods.

Verifiability

It is not generally possible for the users of most entities' accounting reports to verify the recording of each transaction undertaken by the entity. There are both too many users and too many transactions. In consequence, a limited checking of the transactions leading to items in the reports is generally carried out by an auditor. Thus verifiability has two dimensions—it is concerned both with checking for some documentary support for transactions (e.g. invoices, cash receipts) and also with their proper recording in the organisation's books. In order to facilitate the auditor's task, it is helpful if the accounting procedures adopted by the entity are such as to enable the auditor to satisfy himself as far as possible that transactions have been properly recorded. It is also helpful to the auditor's client if he can accomplish his task in as short a time, and hence as cheaply, as possible.

Measurability

Accounting is concerned primarily with the quantification of behaviour. It follows that, all things being equal, a particular accounting system is to be preferred if it enables more events to be measured than other accounting systems. In the extreme, a reporting system which permits nothing to be measured or quantified will be of little interest or use to accountants or users. The reporting methods which we have introduced so far have been based upon the reporting of some future (contemplated) or past (actual) transactions involving either the flow of cash or the establishment of a right to receive, or an obligation to pay, cash. We should stress here that these methods would neither report an increase in the *value* of an asset after it has been purchased, nor measure the benefit to the business of a skilled and loyal workforce.

The above descriptions of criteria that might be applied to the choice of alternative accounting methods are intentionally brief and somewhat imprecise. Our main aim at this stage is to highlight the range of criteria available. Ideally, we would favour the accounting method that best satisfied all the criteria we have mentioned. Unfortunately, conflicts exist which result in different methods scoring more highly under different criteria. For example, an accounting method based on the reporting of forecasts of future performance may go a long way to satisfying the criterion of relevance to user decisions but would be unlikely to do well under the criterion of verifiability.

Conflicts between criteria considerably complicate the problem of choosing best accounting methods. As a first step in resolving this difficulty we might attempt to rank the criteria, for example by gathering information from users about the criteria they think are most important to their decisions. However, such a ranking would not be a sufficient basis for establishing the most beneficial accounting method. Suppose that an agreed ranking of the four most important criteria was:

1. Relevance
2. Objectivity
3. Timeliness
4. Verifiability

How could this ranking be used to choose between method A (which is relevant and verifiable) and method B (which is objective and timely)? In order to make this choice, we would need to quantify the importance of each criterion (perhaps by developing some form of weighting scheme). Such a quantification is unavailable at present. Indeed, there is not even any agreement about the ranking of the available criteria. In these circumstances, the best we can do in evaluating alternative accounting methods is to assess the extent to which they satisfy each of the criteria, and then attempt to identify the methods that appear to satisfy substantially more criteria than do others. Or we could introduce our own value judgments as to which are the most important criteria, and how much more important they are than other criteria.

The criteria discussed above are concerned mainly with assessing those attributes of accounting methods which are helpful to the users of accounting reports. A final criterion which clearly must be considered is the *cost* of providing information. Ultimately, any accounting method must be evaluated according to the benefits it provides (i.e. the extent to which it satisfies some or all of the criteria we have discussed) and the cost involved in its implementation.

4.5   The Role of Accounting Standards

In the previous section we examined a number of criteria which a financial reporting method should strive to satisfy. We noted also that within the overall framework of conventional accrual accounting there is scope for individual entities to choose between alternative, equally acceptable accounting policies, e.g. methods of depreciation. During the last twenty years or so, the professional accountancy bodies in the UK (and elsewhere) have produced several statements of standard accounting practice intended to limit this choice. The use of accounting standards to narrow the choice of reporting methods is, however, only one aspect of accounting regulation in the UK. These standards complement legal regulation of accounting practice. Thus the range of accounting methods which is available to most reporting entities is limited both by legal requirements and by the recommendations of professional accountancy bodies. In the UK the main legislation governing the preparation and content of published accounts is embodied in the Companies Acts 1948, 1967, 1976 and 1981, which are concerned only with the accounts of limited liability companies. The Companies Acts deal mainly with minimum disclosure requirements, and are designed primarily for the protection of creditors and shareholders. In effect, the Companies Acts provide a framework for *general* disclosure and specify that certain financial statements (e.g. a balance sheet and profit and loss account) and certain items (e.g. depreciation, directors' salaries and audit fees) must be disclosed. Accounting standards, on the other hand, have traditionally been more flexible and have dealt rather with methods of valuing assets and liabilities. Although they are not legally binding, an accountant who ignores the recommendations of professional accountancy bodies may face disciplinary action by the professional body of which he is a member. Since 1971, recommendations from professional accountancy bodies in the UK have been in the form of Statements of Standard Accounting Practice (SSAPs). Each standard is prepared by the Accounting Standards Committee (ASC), whose membership is drawn largely from the major professional accountancy bodies in the UK.[3] The procedure preceding the issue of a standard is broadly as follows. The ASC identifies an area of accounting practice on which it believes a recommendation is necessary. It then establishes a working party to prepare a draft standard, containing recommendations as to measurement and disclosure of the relevant topics. When the draft has been approved by the ASC it is issued for comment as an Exposure Draft (ED) for a period typically of three or six months. At the end of this period the ASC reviews the ED in the light of submissions it has received and amends it as it thinks appropriate. The amended document is generally issued as an SSAP individually by each of the professional accountancy bodies represented on the ASC.

We refer to several SSAPs throughout this book, although it is not our intention to deal specifically with their recommendations. Accounting standards are not immutable and we do not wish to give the impression that they represent the only possible method of dealing with particular topics. Before we discuss their usefulness, it may be helpful to an understanding of the profession's perception of the role of accounting standards to quote selectively from the explanatory foreword to its SSAPs issued by one of the major professional bodies:[4]

---

[3]The Institute of Chartered Accountants in England and Wales, the Institute of Chartered Accountants of Scotland, the Institute of Chartered Accountants in Ireland, the Chartered Association of Certified Accountants, the Institute of Cost and Management Accountants, and the Chartered Institute of Public Finance and Accountancy.

[4]The Institute of Chartered Accountants in England and Wales, *Members' Handbook,* Part II, Section 2.100.

Statements of Standard Accounting Practice describe methods of accounting approved by the Council of the Institute of Chartered Accountants in
England and Wales ... for application to all financial accounts intended to
give a true and fair view of financial position and profit or loss.

Significant departures in financial accounts from applicable accounting
standards should be disclosed and explained.

The Council expects members of the Institute who assume responsibilities
in respect of financial accounts to observe accounting standards.

Accounting standards are not intended to be a comprehensive code of rigid
rules. It would be impracticable to establish a code sufficiently elaborate to
cater for all business situations and circumstances and every exceptional or
marginal case. Nor could any code of rules provide in advance for innova-
tions in business and financial practice.

Methods of financial accounting evolve and alter in response to changing
business and economic needs. From time to time new accounting standards
will be drawn at progressive levels, and established standards will be
reviewed with the object of improvement in the light of new needs and
developments.

In other words, accounting standards are regarded as generally applicable to accounting reports prepared for external users, although it is recognised that a particular standard may not be appropriate for all present and
future situations. Where the recommendations of a standard are not followed, the reasons for and effects of the departure from recommended
practice must be given.

In 1983 the ASC reviewed the standard setting process and concluded
that accounting standards will henceforth:[5]

deal only with matters of major and fundamental importance affecting the
generality of companies and will therefore be few in number.

As a result of this conclusion, a new category of pronouncement, the Statement of Recommended Practice (SORP) has been introduced. A SORP is
issued when a need is seen for a pronouncement on a specific topic but when
that topic is not deemed to be a matter of "major and fundamental importance affecting the generality of companies". Although companies are
encouraged to comply with SORPs, compliance will not be mandatory.

The basic philosophy of the ASC is contained in SSAP 2.[6] This standard
lists four *"fundamental accounting concepts"* (defined in the standard as
"broad basic assumptions which underlie the periodic financial accounts of
business enterprises"), which are regarded as having general acceptability.
Indeed since the 1981 Companies Act, all company accounts must now

---

[5] Accounting Standards Committee, 'Review of the standard setting process', *Accountancy,*
July 1983, p.115.

[6] Statement of Standard Accounting Practice Number 2, *Disclosure of Accounting Policies,*
The Institute of Chartered Accountants in England and Wales, November 1971.

incorporate these four concepts as a matter of law. Although it is acknow-
ledged in the standard that the four concepts are "practical rules" rather
than "theoretical ideals", they are recommended as "working assumptions"
to be adopted in the preparation of accounting reports. The four concepts
are as follows:

1. The *going concern* concept: It is assumed that the enterprise will con-
    tinue to operate for the foreseeable future, and that no cessation of
    business or significant curtailment of operations will occur.
2. The *accruals* (or *matching*) concept: Revenues and costs are recognised
    as they are earned or incurred, not necessarily when the cash flow
    relating to them is received or paid, and are *matched* with one another as
    far as possible. Hence the term 'matching concept' is often used instead
    of 'accruals concept'.
3. The *consistency* concept: The accounting treatment of like items should
    be consistent both within each accounting period and from one period to
    the next.
4. The *prudence* concept: Revenues and profits should not be anticipated;
    they should be included in income only when realised in cash or in the
    form of other assets whose ultimate cash realisation can be assessed with
    reasonable certainty. Provision should be made for all known liabilities,
    using the best estimate available of the size of the liabilities. In the event
    of conflict between this concept and any of the others, in particular the
    accruals concept, the prudence concept prevails.

The above concepts are of great practical importance in the development of accounting standards in the UK; they are used by the ASC, when
preparing a new standard, to aid its choice between alternative accounting
methods. And, as we have noted previously, they now have legal backing.
Yet they are a disparate collection. Consistency and prudence are criteria for
choosing between accounting methods. Going concern is an assumption
about the economic position and prospects of the reporting enterprise. The
accruals (or matching) concept defines a broad set of rules for measuring
income. It implies that income should be based on transactions which have
occurred and should represent the difference between revenues actually
earned and appropriately matched costs.

Our main concern here is to consider the usefulness of the sort of
accounting standards that have been and are likely to be developed from the
above 'fundamental concepts' and, more generally, to discuss the desirability of the setting of accounting standards by professional accountancy bodies
or by other groups. Although our discussion relates primarily to the UK, our
conclusions about the role and usefulness of accounting standards have some
applicability to other countries.

In order to evaluate the role and usefulness of accounting standards we
must attempt to answer a number of questions. What does standard account-

ing practice mean—uniform practice or best practice? What are the advantages and disadvantages of imposing standards on the preparers of accounting statements? Who should be responsible for developing accounting standards and controlling their implementation?

The meaning of standard accounting practice

We have explained previously that there exists a range of accounting treatments for measuring and reporting the results of many types of economic activity. The aim of standardisation is to ensure as far as possible that different entities apply similar accounting treatment to similar transactions. A crucial question is whether standardisation should be based on *best* accounting practice, which implies an evaluation of alternative treatments and the choice of one that best satisfies selected criteria, or on *uniform* accounting practice, which may imply little more than the random choice of one accounting treatment from the range available. This distinction reflects two of the (many) definitions given to the word 'standard' by the *Concise Oxford Dictionary*: "Degree of excellence, etc. required for particular purpose" and "...measure to which others conform...". There seems little doubt that, other things being equal, best accounting practice is preferable to uniform accounting practice. There seems even less doubt, in view of our previous discussion, that best accounting practice is at present an unattainable ideal, and will remain so until agreement is reached about the relative importance of alternative criteria for the choice of accounting methods. However, this is not a view that is accepted without reservation by the professional accountancy bodies in the UK. The terms of reference of the ASC include the following:[7]

> ... to advance accounting standards and to narrow the areas of difference and variety in accounting practice by publishing authoritative statements on *best accounting practice* which will wherever possible be definitive...
>
> (italics added)

Unfortunately, with the exception of the four 'fundamental accounting concepts' discussed above, the ASC has no criteria or framework against which it can evaluate alternative accounting methods. In consequence the standards it issues are *de facto* statements of uniform practice rather than statements of best practice.

Advantages and disadvantages of (uniform) accounting standards

Uniform standards of measurement are of great help in many spheres of life. For example, it is helpful for a decorator to know that if he buys ten (standard) metres of wallpaper, the quantity he receives (based on the

---

[7]Accounting Standards Committee Constitution, reprinted in *Accounting Standards 1983*, The Institute of Chartered Accountants in England and Wales, 1983, p.x.

supplier's understanding of the length of a metre) should correspond to the quantity he expects to receive (based on his understanding of the length of a metre). The application of uniform standards to the preparation of accounting statements also has advantages. Perhaps the main one is that accounting numbers, both between organisations and through time, are comparable. In the extreme, if all accounting methods were standardised, two organisations which had undertaken identical transactions during a period and which were identical at the start of the period would report identical income numbers for the period and would have identical position statements at the end of the period. A further advantage of the development of uniform standards is that their application should reduce the size, and hence the cost of preparation, of accounting statements. There would be no need to include explanations of the bases upon which particular figures had been calculated because only one (uniform) basis would be acceptable. (We should make two things clear at this point: first that the above advantages apply strictly to situations where all accounting methods are standardised, and secondly that such situations do not exist either in the UK or elsewhere.)

The application of uniform accounting standards may also have some undesirable consequences. We noted in Section 4.1 that such standards limit the extent to which the preparer of accounts is able to tailor them both to meet the needs of those who use the accounts and to reflect environmental factors particular to the reporting entity. This inflexibility is a disadvantage insofar as it may restrict the usefulness of accounting statements. It is also likely to restrict the extent to which new and modified accounting methods are developed—such that progress towards better methods is stifled. Finally, we should not underestimate the possible confusion of the meaning of the terms 'best' and 'uniform' in the minds of users. The consequences of such confusion are not illusory. Many UK users of accounts, on reading the terms of reference of the ASC quoted earlier, may be led to believe that UK accounting standards are concerned with best rather than uniform practice and as a result may make incorrect decisions. As we have explained, this interpretation would not be correct at the present time.

Responsibility for accounting standards

In the UK and elsewhere the responsibility for issuing accounting standards lies primarily with professionally qualified accountants. These accountants represent mostly the preparers and auditors of accounting statements rather than those who use them. For example, 18 of the 20 members of the ASC are members of one or other of the UK professional accountancy bodies and the great majority are either partners in firms of auditors or employees of large reporting enterprises.

It is no easy task to identify where the power to influence the content of accounting standards really lies. We know who are the members of the ASC and we may examine the public submissions of those organisations and individuals that comment on exposure drafts. It is much more difficult to identify other (informal) sources of power, such as the influence exerted on auditor members of the ASC by their clients, and the extent to which the ASC considers the likely responses of government to particular accounting standards. Formal power, however, is firmly in the hands of the members of the ASC and of the Councils of its six sponsoring bodies, who decide ultimately whether or not to adopt a particular standard. Our earlier discussion of the range of reporting entities and of the information needs of the variety of interested users suggests that if accounting standards are to be as useful as possible, the body responsible for issuing them and controlling their implementation should represent the interests of all groups who are affected by accounting standards.

Summary

For communication to be effective, the message must be understood by the recipient. In this chapter, we have examined various ways in which the understandability of the accounting message can be increased. The proposal to use cash flows as a method of reporting has merit. Cash is well understood and, in certain circumstances, the method produces relevant information for users' decision models. However, the business practice of buying and selling on credit and of purchasing long-lived assets leads to some ambiguities in the cash flow message, and conventional acounting practice has long been based upon the accruals (matching) principle. But the greater subjectivity of an income-based, rather than a cash-based, reporting method has produced its own problems of understandability. Similar economic events can be reported in different ways because entities can choose to report those events on the basis of one of several, equally acceptable, accounting policies.

The response of the accounting profession has been to limit the number of acceptable accounting policies which can be used in financial statements. This limiting of choice by the recommendation of standard accounting practices should increase the comparability between the financial statements of different entities. However, the usefulness of the information contained in those statements will depend upon whether the recommendations are statements of best practice or simply uniform practice. As no agreement exists as to which are the most important criteria by which accounting methods should be evaluated, it seems that best practice is at present an unattainable ideal. Some of the recommendations of the ASC suggest that they may have settled for more easily attainable goals, i.e. increased comparability and a better understanding of the accounting message are more easily achievable by the imposition of uniform accounting practices.

As a result, the ASC could claim to be eliminating noise at the semantic level, but noise is still very loud indeed at the influence level.

Discussion Topics

1 Explain why you think the reporting of past cash flows may be more understandable to users than the reporting of income figures.

2 Under what assumptions will the cash surplus from business activities reflect the business's maintainable profit. Is it likely that such assumptions are likely to be realistic representations of actual situations?

3 Distinguish between cash accounting and accrual accounting. Which expenses are likely to be measured in different ways if either of the two methods is chosen?

4 Discuss the main criteria applicable to the choice of reporting method. Can you think of any potential conflicts which would exist if such criteria were to be put into practice?

5 Which of the above criteria do you believe to be the most important? What are your justifications for your choice?

6 Do you believe the British system of regulating accounting practice via both the law and the accounting profession to be the best available? What alternative systems of regulation would be possible?

7 Distinguish between 'best' and 'uniform' accounting practice. Which characteristics do you associate with each of the two forms?

Further Reading

Accounting Standards Committee, *Disclosure of Accounting Policies SSAP 2*, Institute of Chartered Accountants in England and Wales, 1971.

Accounting Standards Committee, 'Review of standard setting', *Accountancy*, July 1983.

Bird, P.A., 'The development of standard accounting practice', in Carsberg, B. and Hope, A., *Current Issues in Accounting*, 2nd ed, Philip Allan, 1984.

Egginton, D.A., 'Distributable profit and the pursuit of prudence', *Accounting and Business Research*, Winter 1980.

Weetman, P., 'Updating the prudence concept', *Accountancy*, September 1983.

Part 2
The Accounting Model of the Organisation

Chapter 5

The Transformation Process

This chapter is the first of four which introduce and develop the traditional accounting model of an organisation. A model can be defined as a simplified approximation of real world conditions, constructed from a set of observed relationships. The real world conditions which the accounting model seeks to simplify are the results of the economic and financial activities undertaken by the organisation. There are two principal elements of the accounting model of the organisation, representing the two main statements of financial accounting: namely the balance sheet (or statement of financial position at a point in time) and the income statement (or statement of the results of operations over a period of time). A third statement, the funds flow statement (or statement of the sources and uses of funds employed by the organisation over a period of time) has become increasingly popular in recent years, and we shall look at this statement in Chapter 18.

As we saw in Chapters 1 and 2, whatever their size or compexity, most organisations—a local pub, a cricket club, Marks and Spencer plc, the Post Office—produce some form of balance sheet and income statement, the two primary accounting statements, although not all organisations are required to disclose the same type or same amount of information. The structure of the organisation in large measure determines the form and content of the two primary accounting statements—thus, for example, limited companies must meet the minimum disclosure requirements laid down by company law, whereas local pubs and clubs are not subject to such constraints.

5.1 Accounting Statements and the Organisation's Operations

We should perhaps begin this section with a statement of belief—a belief that has, in many ways, both provided the impetus for writing this book and also determined its content. *We believe that an understanding of the purpose of financial accounting, and its major financial statements, can best be achieved by placing the accounting function firmly within the context of the organisation's business. To see most clearly how, and why, the accountant prepares the balance sheet, income statement and funds flow statement, it is necessary to understand the nature of the operations conducted by the organisation.* To divorce the accounting figures from the operations to which they relate is to make the subject matter abstract and lifeless.

Because financial statements are prepared for a large variety of types of organisation—for example, for *public limited companies* such as ICI plc and Marks and Spencer plc; for *partnerships* such as Peat Marwick Mitchell & Co. (one of the 'Big Eight' firms of chartered accountants); for *individuals* or *sole traders,* such as the local butcher or greengrocer; and for *nationalised industries* such as British Rail and the Post Office, we can best begin to appreciate the role of each of the elements of the accounting model by first considering the reasons *why* such organisations exist at all. In most cases the reasons are clear. In Western societies most limited companies, partnerships, sole traders and nationalised industries operate to provide goods and services to the public at a price sufficient to make profits large enough to reward their participant groups over an indefinite time period, and thus ensure their future existence. This objective, as we have seen in earlier chapters, is the prime—though by no means the only—reason for business activity in capitalist and mixed economies.

Let us now examine the nature of the organisation's business—it is this which determines *how* profits are made. To determine how a large manufacturing company such as ICI makes profits we must examine the nature of its operations, i.e. we must examine the process undertaken to manufacture and sell its many different products. This process is known as the *transformation process,* because it reflects the method by which the factors of production are transformed into the finished products sold by the company.

In the case of ICI, the transformation process will differ as between the manufacture of fibres, chemicals, agricultural products, paints, plastics, fertilisers and all the other various activities undertaken by this large diversified company. As we have intimated in Chapter 4, and as we shall explain in detail in Chapter 7, the profit of the organisation is not usually recognised until the finished goods or services have been sold or provided to the customer, and thus the total costs of the transformation process comprise all the costs necessary to place the goods in a saleable state (i.e. to the production costs must be added the costs of selling and marketing, administration and finance). The total of all such costs must then be deducted from the revenue to be received from the sale of goods to determine the organisation's profit.

That the transformation process determines how profits are made is true of all organisations. For example, to determine how such financial institutions as banks or insurance companies make profits, we should examine and understand the *process* by which they provide financial services. Such organisations do not manufacture finished goods in the same way as ICI, but rather their process is to 'produce' and 'sell' such financial services as lending to customers, providing financial advice and paying benefits to claimants. The costs of providing these services must be covered by attendant revenues (in the form of interest charges, premiums, etc.)

before profits can be shown. Understanding the process by which an organisation operates is the key to understanding the role of the financial accountant and the statements he must prepare.

Most organisations of any size and complexity employ a financial accountant (often with a responsibility for other accounting personnel) who records, measures and reports the results of the organisation's transformation process, and its position at the reporting date. This role is, in many larger organisations, distinct and physically separate from that of the management accountant, whose primary concern as we saw in Chapter 1 is with the provision of information to managers, rather than to external parties. To illustrate the financial accountant's function we will, throughout this and subsequent chapters, devote most of our attention to the processes of manufacturing organisations. In the remainder of this chapter we will look at the *physical* process of the organisation, i.e. at the method by which physical inputs are converted into physical outputs. This will provide an initial perspective of the need for, and the function of, the accountant's basic financial statements, the income statement and the balance sheet. In the immediately following chapters we shall see how the accountant places monetary values on these physical flows, such that all facets of the organisation's operations which are recorded in the financial statements are expressed in financial terms. Thus Chapter 6 deals with the balance sheet, and Chapter 7 with the income statement.

5.2   The Transformation Process

We shall use the term *'transformation process'* to describe the process by which the organisation links the markets in which it purchases its production factors, with the markets in which it sells its goods. As we have explained, the costs of the transformation process include all costs necessary to place the goods in a saleable state, i.e. they include purchasing, production, selling, administration and financing costs. Let us begin our analysis of the transformation process with a single-product company, which operates to produce and sell components. In order to be sold, components must first be produced, and their production requires certain input factors. Some of these input factors might be easily guessed—for example, most manufacturing organisations require people, machines and raw materials to produce their goods. Others are somewhat less obvious, for example, light and heat and the supervision of men, machines and materials. The amounts of these input factors are not selected at random, but rather they are combined in certain predetermined proportions. Thus, to produce completed components each machine might be combined with men and raw materials in certain fixed proportions (say one machine, two men and four tons of raw material—a proportion of 1:2:4). Such a combination is termed a *production unit.* Other production expenses might comprise an amount which varies directly with the volume of production (for example, the power used in a factory) and an amount which is fixed for the year, irrespective of the actual volume of production (for example, the annual salary of a supervisory foreman). In order to undertake production in the first place, the organisation must buy, or lease, or rent, the buildings necessary to house the machines, men and raw materials. In most cases the organisation will own, rent or lease not only the buildings (factory, warehouse, offices, etc.), but also the land on which they stand.

We can now begin to see a little more clearly the nature of the transformation process which converts the various factors of production, purchased in the various resource markets (for example, the market for machines, the labour market and the market for raw materials) into the finished components sold on the selling market. The process begins when the organisation (or more correctly, the manager responsible) purchases the production factors—usually in sufficient quantities to ensure the continuity of the production process. The organisation obviously will wish to avoid any shortage of input factors, as this interrupts the flow of production. As production proceeds in the agreed proportions, and at the agreed rate, some of the resources are used up—for example, raw materials physically enter the production process and become part of the finished product, some machinery is 'used up' through wear and tear, and some labour hours are spent on the process. We shall see later that labour hours are not 'used up' in quite the same way as raw materials or machine hours, and this, at least in theory, poses a major recording problem for the financial accountant. Some light and heat is also expended in production—the bill from the electricity supplier will tell the organisation the cost of lighting and heating the premises during the hours of production.

At any point in time, there will be resources which have not yet been used up, and which await introduction to the production process. The organisation will usually have a *stock* of *raw materials* (for example, a brewery will have stocks of untreated hops). There will also, at the same point in time, be partly finished goods, on which further work is necessary before they can be sold. These partly finished goods are called *work in progress* (the brewery, for example, will have vats of beer in different stages of fermentation). Finally, as it is unlikely that all production is sold immediately, there will be *finished goods* in the form of completed units which await sale (just as the brewery will have barrels of beer ready for sale). Thus the organisation will, at any point in time, hold three qualitatively different types of stock: stocks of raw materials (awaiting use); work in progress (awaiting completion); and finished goods (awaiting sale). It is also likely that these different types of stocks will be housed in different factories, or at the very least in different parts of the same factory.

We can now show the organisation's transformation process (from the purchase of the individual factors of production to the sale of finished products) in the form of a diagram. Figure 5.1 depicts such a process for an organisation producing just one product. If, as may be more likely in practice, an organisation produces several products, there will be more than one production process—in fact, there will be a different process for each product, using its own machinery, labour force, materials, etc. However, it is also likely that a multi-product organisation will use common resources, especially labour and machinery, to produce its different products, and this situation presents difficult problems for the accountant. Basically, the accountant must decide how much of the common resource is used by each product in order to arrive at a suitable measure of the cost of production and thus of the product's profitability. In most cases, the accountant devises a method of *allocation* which apportions the use of common resources to individual products. We deal with these issues in more depth in Chapter 10. We now turn to a discussion of Figure 5.1.

Figure 5.1 reveals that the transformation process, the aim of which is to generate a profit for the organisation by ensuring that the revenue from the sale of its finished products is greater than the cost of their transformation, is in *five* stages. The process thus involves five distinct types of operations.

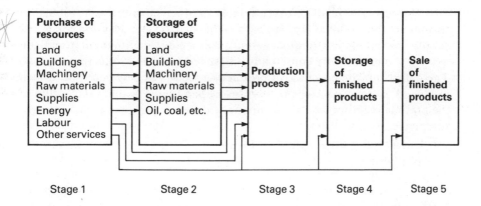

Figure 5.1   Transformation process of a manufacturing organisation.

Stage 1—Purchase of resources

In order for production to take place, input factors must first be acquired. We will assume that the resources in Figure 5.1 have all been purchased and are owned by the organisation. It is possible for assets such as machinery to be rented or leased. Labour, of course, cannot strictly be 'owned' in the way that other resources are. Rather the organisation purchases the services which labour will provide. Two types of resources may be distinguished. The first type we might term long-lived or 'fixed' resources, such as land, buildings and plant and machinery. These fixed resources—or as they are more commonly termed, *fixed assets*—constitute the organisation's productive capacity, i.e. the organisation can produce only up to the maximum capacity of its fixed plant and machinery (which is usually expressed in terms of machine hours) irrespective of the amount of raw material and labour it can acquire. These fixed assets are not expected to be consumed speedily and are intended to provide benefits or services over a long period of time. In fact, unless the organisation is, say, a mining company, land is unlikely to be used up at all, and buildings only over a very long period. In relation to these assets the term 'fixed' is probably appropriate; in relation to plant and machinery it is less appropriate, though still commonly used. The period of use of plant and machinery is rarely immutably fixed, and in practice depends upon a variety of factors such as the number of working hours, the degree of obsolescence, the amount of technological change, etc. Manufacturing plant and machinery may give services for any number of years in a range from, say, five to twenty. The estimate of the machinery's productive life is of great importance, as it directly determines the annual charge for the use of machinery, termed *depreciation*, in the income statement, and thus can significantly affect the organisation's annual income. We return to this topic in Chapter 9.

The second type of resource relates to other shorter-lived production factors such as raw materials, supplies, light and heat, etc. Raw materials and supplies are commonly termed *current assets* (to distinguish them from fixed assets), and are used up continually and speedily in the production process. The balance of the purchase of production factors as between those which are 'fixed' and those which are 'current' depends greatly upon the nature of the production process as well as upon the different prevailing market prices for the factors. For example, some processes are more capital intensive than others, and thus require a greater proportion of machine hours. Others are labour intensive and depend less on the use of machinery. The organisation will in the long term seek to produce a particular output at the minimum cost to ensure the maximum profit. We have, up until now, omitted any reference to the 'purchase' of labour from our categorisation of fixed and current resources. At first sight, it may appear odd that the workforce is not treated as a fixed asset, even though it is likely that at least some of the workers (and managers) will remain with the organisation for many years—in some cases they will provide services for much longer than certain items of plant and machinery. However, in practice accountants do not usually treat 'human' assets in the same way as plant and machinery, i.e. labour is not 'stored' awaiting entry to the production process, but rather it is treated as being 'used up' in production as and when weekly and monthly payments are made to the workforce.

Stage 2—Storage of resources

Once the production inputs have been purchased they must be physically 'stored' to await entry to the production process. Storage of production inputs is most easily imagined in the case of raw materials, which are usually kept in a warehouse and, depending on the nature and perishability of the materials, stored in bins, shelves, vats, cartons, etc. prior to use. Production factors such as energy and lighting are not stored in bins and cartons, but rather they are drawn upon when needed (although, of course, if power or energy is provided by oil or solid fuel, physical stores of such forms will exist). As we noted above, labour hours are not physically stored in the same way as raw materials or machine hours—workers go home at the end of the day! The amounts of production factors in storage at any time represent those which have not yet entered the production process. They represent both fixed and current assets.

Stage 3—The production process

As and when demanded by the production manager, the raw materials are physically removed from the warehouse to the place of production (the manufacturing department), where they are 'combined' with the machinery (machine hours), the workers (labour hours) and other resources in the predetermined proportions to produce the finished product. The length and form of the production cycle (the process of converting the raw input factors into finished goods) will depend upon the nature of the process. This is true both in terms of the number of units produced during the cycle (the production run), and also in terms of the time taken to operate the cycle. Some production cycles, particularly in heavy industry, may take weeks or months; others, for example the baking of bread and the brewing of beer, may take from a few minutes to a few days. This helps to explain why heavy engineering and contracting organisations have very large amounts of work in progress, whereas bakeries and breweries have very little. Whatever the method or speed of production, the mechanics of the process are essentially the same—at one end, input factors enter the process in agreed proportions and, at the other end, finished products emerge.

Stage 4—The storage of finished products

On completion of the production run the finished products are transferred to the appropriate warehouse prior to their ultimate sale and delivery to customers. One major aim of the organisation is to ensure that it strikes a balance between the number of finished units produced and the number which can be sold. Both under- and over-production can entail costs to the organisation, not all of which are immediately evident. Thus, too much production may tie up scarce warehouse space which might be used more profitably, and also incur additional (and unnecessary) financing costs to support the high level of stocks. Too little production may entail lost orders and a deterioration in the relationship between the organisation and its customers. The number of finished units in storage at any time represents the unsold amount of completed production. The units are treated as a current asset.

Stage 5—The sale of finished products

The final stage of the transformation process is the sale of the completed product to the customer. As we shall discuss in Chapter 7, a sale is usually deemed to take place when the finished goods are delivered to the customer. Thus the transformation process is complete on final delivery of the finished good, rather than on the date on which the cash is received from the customer.

5.3   The Transformation Process—An Illustration

We have argued strongly that an understanding of the mechanics of the transformation process is fundamental to an appreciation of the nature of both the balance sheet and the income statement. We now provide a numerical illustration of the process to aid this appreciation. Figure 5.2 shows data relating to the activities of Fratton Ltd, a component producer, for the calendar year 19X0. To simplify the illustration, we will assume that 19X0 is the first year of operation of Fratton Ltd, i.e. no resources are owned at 1 January 19X0.

During the year to 31 December 19X0 Fratton Ltd purchases all the resources shown in Stage 1 of Figure 5.2. Machinery, labour and materials are combined in a ratio of 1:2:4 (i.e. 1 machine hour: 2 labour hours: 4 lb of raw material) to produce the finished component. Stage 3 shows that 19,000 completed units are produced during the year, and 1,000 units require a further 250 labour hours before they are completed, i.e. 1,000 units of work in progress are in hand at 31 December. Thus in producing the 20,000 completed and partly-completed units, Fratton Ltd has used up 20,000 machine hours, 80,000 lb of raw materials, 39,750 labour hours, 15,000 litres of oil, and 10,000 kilowatts of electricity used to heat and light the factory. One fiftieth (i.e. one year) of the factory's useful life is deemed to have been 'used up' in production.

The information shown under Stage 2, the storage of resources, shows that, at the end of the year, there remain in storage the following physical means of production: 10 acres of land (no land having been used up in production); a factory with 49 years of useful life; 10 machines with a revised capacity of 80,000 hours (20,000 hours having been used in production); 20,000 lb of unused raw material; and 10,000 litres of unused oil.

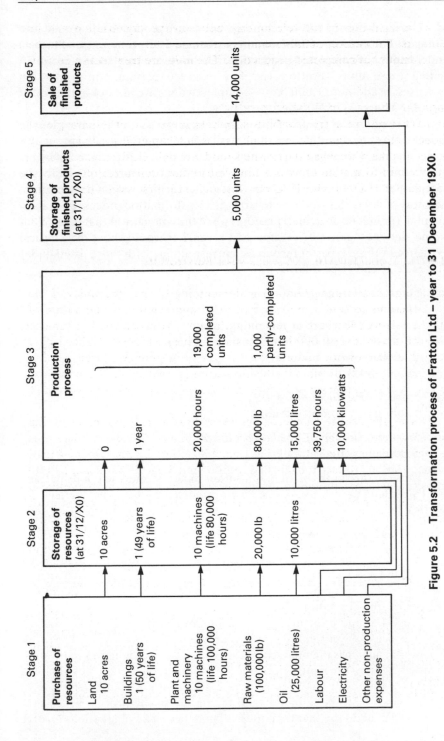

Figure 5.2   Transformation process of Fratton Ltd – year to 31 December 19X0.

During the year 19,000 completed units were produced and passed into storage. Of these units, 5,000 remain in stock on 31 December (see Stage 4) and 14,000 have been sold and delivered to customers (see Stage 5). In selling these units, Fratton Ltd has incurred certain non-production expenses. In addition, 1,000 partly-completed units are in stock at the end of the year (Stage 3).

What can we glean from this simple example as to the nature of the balance sheet and the income statement? Remember that we are, at this stage, dealing with physical quantities only. Suppose first that the managers of Fratton Ltd wish to know the levels of physical resources owned by the company at 31 December 19X0, the last day of the first year of its operation. One way of doing this would be to stop the transformation process and take a 'mental' (or indeed an actual) photograph of the company at that date. What would the photograph of Fratton Ltd reveal? It would show the physical existence of three types of resources, corresponding with those listed under Stages 2, 3, and 4, as follows:

(a)   *Stage 2—Storage of resources*
      10 acres of land
      1 factory (49 years of remaining life)
      10 machines (80,000 hours remaining life)
      20,000 lb of raw material
      10,000 litres of oil

(b)   *Stage 3—Production process*
      1,000 partly completed units

(c)   *Stage 4—Storage of finished products*
      5,000 completed units

These photographs of an organisation, taken at specific points in time, are equivalent to *balance sheets,* or *position statements.* They reflect the physical levels of resources owned by the organisation, although as we shall see in the next chapter, the organisation will likely possess financial as well as physical resources, and these financial resources will also appear in the balance sheet. Thus the (physical) balance sheet of Fratton Ltd would show a listing of the physical assets appearing under Stages 2, 3, and 4. We can now appreciate that an organisation's balance sheet includes assets in various degrees of transformation.

Second, suppose the managers wish to know the *result* of the transformation process of Fratton Ltd for the year. Result is a tricky word. The result of a football match is the final score; the result of an examination is the mark awarded. Neither the match score nor the examination mark tell us anything about how the result has been achieved. We need a working definition of 'result' which helps us to understand the nature of the process which produces it. We might say that both football matches and examinations involve (or in some cases fail to involve) *efforts* on the parts of the players and students in order to produce *accomplishments,* i.e. that the result of an activity is the difference between what has been accomplished and what has been expended in effort, or more simply, is the difference between *accomplishments* and *effort.* Thus to determine the result of Fratton Ltd's transformation process, the managers must identify the accomplishment and effort involved in the process. Without some basic principles from which to work, the managers might have some difficulty in doing this. Fortunately, as we saw in Chapter 4, there exist in the language of accounting certain basic principles which are widely used and understood. Accomplishment is measured by the *realisation principle*—which may be defined in physical terms as the quantity of finished goods *sold* to customers. Thus, in accounting terms, accomplishment equals sales. Fratton Ltd's accomplishment for the year has been to sell 14,000 components. From the extent of the accomplishment is deducted the extent of the effort involved—the effort is to be matched with the accomplishment, and thus the *matching principle* determines the amount of effort expended to produce the result. In accounting terms, effort equals the sacrifices linked to all the aspects of the transformation process. The total of Fratton Ltd's efforts for the year is represented by the sacrifices involved in producing and selling 14,000 units. The result is the difference between the accomplishment and the effort involved in producing and selling 14,000 units. The income statement of an organisation can, in general terms, be represented as follows:

Income statement for the period . . .

Sales (Level of accomplishment —determined by the realisation principle)		X
less:		
Production costs	(Level of	X
Selling and	effort—	
marketing costs	determined by	X
Administration costs	the matching	X
Financing costs	principle)	X
Net income (*accomplishment less effort*)		X

We have now reached a most important stage in our analysis. It has been our intention in this chapter to provide an intuitive 'feel' for the contents of the two main accounting statements, the balance sheet and the income statement, by understanding the processes undertaken by any particular organisation. A few simple essentials of accounting should now be apparent. For example, when a customer buys a pair of socks at Marks and Spencer, he is reducing the level of finished goods in Marks and Spencer's *balance sheet* (he is, of course, also increasing Marks and Spencer's cash resources by the amount of the purchase, and we will see in the next chapter how the accountant deals with this); and, provided that its costs of transformation are less than the price paid for the socks, Marks and Spencer will show a profit on this transaction, which will appear in its *income statement*. In other words, an organisation's financial statements are (financial) models of the results of the organisation's activities and operations during a particular period. An understanding of the underlying activities and operations of the organisation should greatly facilitate an appreciation of the nature and role of its financial statements.

Discussion Topics

1 Describe the transformation processes of the following types of organisation:
   (a) a brewery
   (b) a bank
   (c) a food retailing company.

2 Describe the five main stages of the transformation process of a manufacturing organisation. Discuss the relationship between the stages, and the relationship between the various stages and the contents of the financial statements.

3 Discuss the relationship between the various physical assets of an organisation. What determines their balance sheet classification?

4 Discuss the production cycles of manufacturing organisations with which you are familiar. What determines the length of such cycles?

5 Explain the terms 'accomplishment' and 'effort'. Do you believe these terms are applicable to accounting? What types of revenue or expense would you expect to see under each heading?

Further Reading

See end of Chapter 8 for reading for Part 2.

Chapter 6

The Balance Sheet

This chapter describes a major element of the accounting model of an organisation—its balance sheet. In many ways the balance sheet, which is sometimes referred to as 'the statement of financial position' is the most basic statement in all accounting. Some justification for this claim might be provided by the following observations:

(a)   The balance sheet is the basis for the derivation of such other important statements as the income statement and the flow of funds statement.

(b)   The balance sheet, as we shall see later in this chapter, is the formal expression of the *accounting equation*, the book-keeping equation which seeks to ensure that the assets of the organisation are exactly equal to the claims on them.

(c)   The balance sheet is the most 'intuitive' and easily understood document of accounting. Most of us, at some stage in our lives (for example, when negotiating a loan from a bank or a building society) will be required to compute a listing of our possessions. Such a listing of possessions is a major element in the construction of a balance sheet.

In the previous chapter we suggested that the purpose of a balance sheet was to present a photograph of an organisation at a particular point in its life. We should stress that a balance sheet can be drawn up at any date in an organisation's life. Thus the fact that ICI prepares its annual balance sheet on 31 December, and Sainsburys prepares its annual balance sheet on 31 March does not mean that these large organisations could not produce balance sheets at dates other than 31 December or 31 March. The notion of a photograph of an organisation holds at any time in its life—although of course, in practice, very frequent compilations of balance sheets would be costly and probably unnecessary.

6.1   The Physical Balance Sheet

We saw in the last chapter how, as a result of the physical activities undertaken by a manufacturing organisation, we might identify those resources (or assets) which comprise its 'physical' balance sheet. Such resources are represented by the organisation's stock of unused raw materials, its stock of partly-completed production and finished goods awaiting sale, as well as its unused productive capacity—its fixed assets.

The accountant does not, however, report the organisation's position in purely physical terms. For example the listing of resources as shown in Table 6.1 would never be prepared by the accountant. Perhaps the reasons are obvious. The physical resources are expressed in different terms, or units of measurement, which makes it difficult to appreciate their significance and, because such terms are not additive (e.g. 4 acres + 2 factories + 45 machines do not equal 51 units of anything!), it is not possible to form an overall view of the organisation's position by adding up the total of these resources. Thus, in order to give some meaning to these non-comparable figures, the accountant expresses resources in terms of a common measuring unit. The measuring unit chosen by the accountant is the monetary unit. As we shall see in later chapters, the use of money as a common measuring unit is not without its difficulties. This is particularly so if there is a lapse of time between the date at which the organisation acquires its resources and the date at which it uses them, and if in the intervening period inflation has affected the stability of the measuring unit.

**Table 6.1   Resources of an organisation as at
31 December 19X0**

Land	4 acres
Buildings	2 factories
Plant and machinery	45 machines
Stocks:	
Raw materials	2,500 lb of raw materials
Work in progress	520 partly finished units
Finished goods	600 completed units

6.2   Physical and Monetary Assets

By expressing the organisation's position in monetary terms we can build a much clearer picture of its different *types* of resources. Two types of resources are important—*physical resources* and *monetary resources*—and the difference between them is fundamental to an understanding of balance sheets. Most physical resources represent input factors to the production process (although certain physical resources such as office equipment and cars do not affect the production process directly), whereas monetary resources represent the means of providing physical resources. Thus for a manufacturing organisation to undertake its transformation process, it must have a sufficient stock of monetary resources, i.e. it needs sufficient cash to buy the requisite machinery and raw materials as well as to pay the labour force. The balance between physical and monetary resources for any organisation will depend upon the nature of its business. A comparison of the asset structure of a large manufacturing company (ICI plc) with that of a large bank (Barclays Bank plc) may help to clarify the point. The balance sheet of ICI as at 31 December 1983, extracts from which appear below, shows that physical (P) assets and monetary (M) assets total £7,621 million, *in terms of the amounts originally paid for the assets* (their historical costs).

ICI plc
Historical cost balance sheet as at 31 December 1983

	£m
Fixed assets	3,376 (P)
Trade investments	348 (M)
Stocks	1,462 (P)
Debtors (amounts owed by customers)	1,661 (M)
Liquid assets	774 (M)
	£7,621m

The composition is approximately 63% physical assets, 37% monetary assets. A very different picture is presented by the asset structure of Barclays Bank as at 31 December 1983, a summary of which is given below:

Barclays Bank plc
Historical cost balance sheet as at 31 December 1983

	£m
Fixed assets	1,363 (P)
Trade investments	381 (M)
Advances to customers	48,236 (M)
Cash and short-term investments	12,098 (M)
Equipment leased to customers	2,826 (P)
	£64,904m

Of the total assets of approximately £65 billion, monetary (M) assets contribute 94%, whereas physical (P) assets contribute only 6%. The preponderance of monetary assets in the balance sheet of a large bank is, of course, to be expected—the very nature of banking operations concerns the acquisition and disbursement of cash or near-cash assets. The importance of the difference between the two types of asset will assume more significance when, in Chapters 14 and 15, we discuss the impact of inflation upon the organisation's performance and financial position.

We can now return to the relationship between the two types of asset by means of a diagram. Figure 6.1 shows the relationship between the generation of cash (the financial side of the organisation's activities) and the transformation process (the physical side). Figure 6.1 is an important diagram which requires careful analysis. It shows that in order to purchase the resources required to undertake the transformation process, the organisation needs *cash*; the physical activities of the organisation depend for their existence upon the (prior) financial activities. Cash generation and disbursement is the hub around which the organisation revolves.

Four sources of cash are identified in Figure 6.1 (i.e. there are four broken lines entering the cash 'box'). In practice it is possible for the organisation to draw on many various sources but, for ease of exposition, we shall confine ourselves to four only: cash received from customers, who are termed 'debtors' if, as is usual in most manufacturing businesses, sales are made on credit rather than for cash; cash received from the owners of the organisation; and cash received from both short-term and long-term lenders (we shall explain the difference between those two sources in Section 6.4).

The two-way broken lines leading from the cash box to both owners and lenders require some explanation. As we noted in Chapter 1, in order to induce 'capital' contributions from owners and lenders, the organisation must usually offer some inducement, or reward, for the use of their cash in the form of regular annual, or semi-annual, payments. Thus lenders are rewarded by the payment of annual *interest* on the funds they have loaned, and owners are rewarded by the payment of *dividends* if the organisation is a limited company, or other agreed cash amounts which will depend upon the nature of the organisation and its relationship with its owners. (We explore these areas in detail in Chapter 11.)

Figure 6.1, as well as showing the physical resources existing at the balance sheet date, suggests that the organisation's photograph (balance sheet) may also reveal the existence of certain monetary resources—in particular that the organisation may possess as yet unspent amounts of cash and have outstanding debts due from customers (debtors), to whom sales have already been made. Both unspent cash and amounts due from debtors are treated as current assets and thus a more complete listing of the organisation's assets might appear as in Table 6.2. The assets shown in Table 6.2 represent the total amount of resources available to the organisation with which to undertake future transformation processes.

6.3   The Categorisation of Assets

In practice, the listing of assets in the balance sheet is carried out in an ordered, systematic way so as to convey information in a readily understandable and comparable manner. What constitutes an appropriate ordering

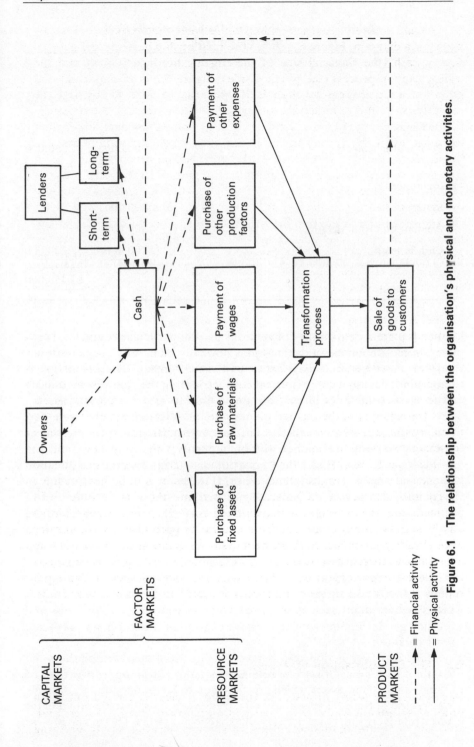

Figure 6.1   The relationship between the organisation's physical and monetary activities.

Table 6.2   Assets shown on the balance sheet as at
31 December 19X0

	£	£
Fixed assets		
Land	250,000	
Buildings	100,000	
Plant and machinery	900,000	1,250,000
Current assets		
Stocks	1,200,000	
Amount due from debtors	800,000	
Cash in hand	200,000	2,200,000
		£3,450,000

depends a great deal on the conventions used in particular countries. However, in most countries a distinction is normally made in an organisation's balance sheet between *fixed assets* and *current assets*. The distinction is important because under historical cost accounting the rules for measuring fixed assets sometimes differ from those used to measure current assets.

Unfortunately, there is no unique rule for determining whether a particular asset should be classified as fixed or current. Broadly speaking, one or both of two tests are applied (often implicitly): the *usage* test and the *turnover period* test. Under the (more popular) usage test, the classification of an asset depends on its intended use. If the asset is to be held within an organisation and used to generate revenue and there is no intention of immediate resale, it is classified as a fixed asset. If, on the other hand, the asset is to be used to generate revenue by being sold in its present or a modified form, or if it is to be converted into cash in some other way, then it should be classified as a current asset. According to the usage test, examples of fixed assets are plant and machinery, land and buildings, office equipment, fixtures and fittings, and motor vehicles. By the same test, current assets include items such as stocks of raw materials, work in progress and finished goods, amounts owing to the organisation (debtors), and cash and bank balances.

The turnover period test, a favourite of economists, emphasises the length of time an asset is to be retained by an organisation, rather than its intended use. Thus assets which are expected to be retained for a relatively long period of time are classified as fixed assets, and those to be retained for only a relatively short time are classified as current assets. There is no precise rule for defining 'relatively long' and 'relatively short' periods of time: in many cases, however, a relatively short time is taken to be one year.

For most assets, the classifications given by the usage and turnover period tests coincide. Nevertheless, unusual situations can arise where the two tests lead to different classifications. For example, consider the case of a manufacturing organisation that holds a stock of oil or coal to be used for heating its factorieș. The stock of fuel is used up, and replaced, every three months. According to the usage test, the fuel is a fixed asset—it is a resource which contributes to revenue-earning activities and is not intended to be resold. Applying the turnover test, however, suggests that the fuel is a current asset—it is expected to be kept for only a relatively short period of time. This example illustrates the sort of dilemma that is sometimes faced when attempting to classify assets. There is no 'right' answer; the accountant must use his judgment to decide which classification is preferable in a particular case. His decision should depend on the sort of information to be provided by the accounts; his task will be complicated if no clear criteria exist for making that decision. (The problem of conflicts between criteria for assessing different accounting methods was discussed in Chapter 4.)

Even if we ignore the possibility of conflict between the usage and turnover period tests, the classification of a particular asset *should always be related to the nature of the firm's operations*. Classification may depend on the nature of the organisation owning the asset or on the purpose to which it is to be put. For example, a motor vehicle owned by a retail firm and used to make deliveries to customers is a fixed asset. The same vehicle, owned by a motor trader who intends to sell it as soon as possible, is a current asset. Similarly, a company which owns shares in another company could treat such an investment in either of two ways: on the one hand the shares should be classed as a fixed asset if the investor company owns the shares (and intends to continue owning them) so as to have some *control* over the decisions of the investee company. On the other hand, if the shares have been purchased as a means of investing a temporary surplus of funds, and are likely to be sold in the near future, the shares should be classified as a current asset.

Having been classified as fixed or current, assets are then listed within the two main headings in terms of their *liquidity*, but here the possibilities of ordering are more varied. In the UK the list of balance sheet assets is as shown in Table 6.2, beginning with the least liquid fixed asset (land) and ending with the most liquid current asset (cash). In the USA the reverse is true. The actual method of listing is unimportant in itself—it is simply the result of conventions adopted by the accounting and legal professions in previous years—but consistency of application is important. It aids understandability and this prevents noise at the semantic level of communication. For ease of understanding we will list balance sheet assets in the manner used in the UK.

6.4   Claims on the Organisation's Assets

We have seen how the organisation must raise cash to finance the purchase of the factors of production, to pay the expenses of running the business, and to reward the providers of funds. In most cases this cash will come from the regular operations of the organisation in the form of cash receipts from customers. In other cases the cash will be raised, at irregular intervals, from external sources, i.e. from 'capital' contributions from owners and lenders. (We will deal in Chapter 11 with the advantages and disadvantages of raising cash from different sources.) Thus the total amount of the claims on an organisation's assets are, for balance sheet purposes, categorised as being due to the owners (the ownership interest in the organisation) or to other claimants (lenders or debt holders). The difference is of great practical importance. Claims which belong to the owners (in a limited company these owners are called shareholders), comprising the subscribed capital and the undistributed or 'retained' profits, will (generally speaking) be paid directly to them only if the organisation ceases trading. We should here distinguish between the capital subscribed by the shareholders and any dividends declared and payable by the company on such capital. Dividends represent claims due and are classified as current liabilities (see below)—whereas the subscribed capital will, in most cases, be repaid only on liquidation of the company. If, however, there is an active market in the organisation's shares, which allows them to be traded freely, the owners may sell their shares on the (stock) market at a price determined by forces operating within the market (i.e. at the market price).

Claims belonging to debt holders are of a different order. These claims must be satisfied by particular dates, both as to the capital repayment of the debt and as to the interest on the debt. Repayment dates, and thus the very nature of debts themselves, may vary greatly. For example, an organisation may borrow money which does not require repayment for ten or twenty years. This borrowing is classified for balance sheet purposes as a long-term debt. Alternatively, it may negotiate an overdraft with its bank, or an agreement of the time limit within which it must pay its suppliers of raw materials, both of which might be of the order of say three months. These debts are of a very short-term nature. Within these more extreme repayment dates exists a wide variety of other possibilities. The underlying point of importance is that the date of debt repayment determines its balance sheet classification. Thus, debts which are due for payment within one year are termed *current liabilities*; debts due for payment after periods longer than one year are termed either medium-term or long-term capital, depending upon the time period involved. There is no hard and fast rule which differentiates the medium from the long term.

The above possible forms of claim upon the organisation's resources are either of a permanent or a temporary nature (at least in relation to the life of the organisation). Figure 6.2 gives a diagrammatic representation of these forms. As all resources of the organisation are, by definition, provided by some party, whether shareholders or debt holders, the total of the balance sheet assets must always equal the total of claims on such assets. (We will see shortly how this equality is preserved by means of the book-keeping system.) We stress that this equality of assets and claims holds whatever method is used to 'value' the assets and liabilities. We can now present a more complete view of the organisation's balance sheet, which shows not only the resources available, but also their means of financing, and thus the claims upon them.

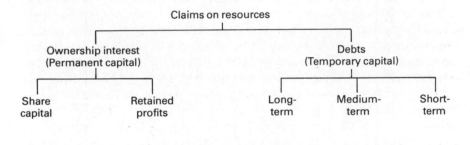

Figure 6.2   Forms of claims upon the organisation's resources.

Tables 6.3 and 6.4 offer two different balance sheet forms for a limited company. Table 6.3 shows a balance sheet in the more traditional 'horizontal' form, which, in the UK only, shows claims on the left and assets on the right. (Do not be confused about this. As we shall soon see, assets are *always* recorded on the left-hand side in the books of account. It is simply a quirk of UK accounting practice that, to report the position of the organisation, assets appear on the right-hand side of a balance sheet.) Table 6.4 shows exactly the same information in a vertical form, beginning with a listing of the organisation's net assets, and then showing below how these assets have been financed. We prefer the vertical format on the grounds that it is easier to read and thus more understandable. It also obviates any difficulties in understanding why assets should appear as left-hand entries in the books of account and on the right-hand side of the balance sheet!

6.5   The Preparation of the Balance Sheet

The importance of historical costs

Having discussed the content, layout and purpose of the balance sheet, we are now in a position to show how it might be constructed. Most balance

Table 6.3   Balance sheet in horizontal form—as at 31 December 19X0

	£	£		£	£
Ownership interest			*Fixed assets*		
Share capital	100,000		Land and buildings		100,000
Retained profits	150,000		Plant and machinery		210,000
		250,000			310,000
Long-term debt			*Current assets*		
10% loan (repayable in 19X8)		80,000	Stocks	100,000	
			Debtors	50,000	
Medium-term debt			Cash in hand	10,000	
8% loan (repayable in 19X3)		50,000			160,000
Current liabilities					
Taxation due on profits	30,000				
Trade creditors	40,000				
Bank overdraft	20,000				
		90,000			
		£470,000			£470,000

Table 6.4   Balance sheet in vertical form—as at 31 December 19X0

	£	£	£
Fixed assets			
Land and buildings			100,000
Plant and machinery			210,000
			310,000
Current assets			
Stocks		100,000	
Debtors		50,000	
Cash in hand		10,000	
		160,000	
less: *Current liabilities*			
Taxation due on profits	30,000		
Trade creditors	40,000		
Bank overdraft	20,000	90,000	70,000
Net assets			£380,000
Represented by:			
Ownership interest			
Share capital			100,000
Retained profits			150,000
			250,000
Long-term debt			
10% loan (repayable in 19X8)			80,000
Medium-term debt			
8% loan (repayable in 19X3)			50,000
			£380,000

sheets are, in practice, constructed on the basis of actual events which have occurred and which affect the organisation—that is to say, they are constructed on the basis of *transactions* undertaken by the organisation. Thus, the contents of balance sheets and, as we shall see in the following chapter, those of income statements also, are in most cases measured in terms of the transaction's actual or 'historical' cost. From the introduction of double-entry book-keeping (in the fifteenth century), until the last ten or twenty years, historical costs have been accepted, with little counter-argument, as the most appropriate basis for compiling balance sheets and income statements. The possible need to include the current costs of resources (i.e. today's costs) has been recognised only recently, as rates of inflation have increased to levels far greater than have been experienced previously. Thus, a conventional system of accounting has evolved, generally known as *historical cost accounting*, which is widely used throughout the Western world. However, it is important to recognise that historical cost accounting is not the only transactions-based approach to the measurement of income and value, nor is it the only system of accounting that can be implemented within a book-keeping framework. Alternatives exist which involve the use of measures of the current, rather than the historical, costs of resources, and which continue to be the subject of much debate in accounting circles. However, both for the purposes of explaining and illustrating the book-keeping framework and also to show how assets appear in balance sheets and expenses appear in income statements, we shall, in the following few chapters, remain with historical costs. We do this for two reasons. First, historical cost accounting remains the most widely used method of preparing accounting reports, and second, the adjustments required to convert historical cost figures to current costs are not very difficult—as we shall see in Chapters 14 and 15—although they may have a significant impact on measures of income and position.

The basis of double-entry book-keeping

Because the initial construction of a balance sheet represents our first sortie into the financial accountant's most traditional field—the field of book-keeping—we will deal only with a very simple series of transactions. In later chapters we will increase the degree of complexity such that we will be able ultimately to prepare a full set of accounts (balance sheet and income statement) from a more detailed set of transactions.

Let us, however, begin our explanation of book-keeping techniques by reiterating some basic relationships. We have suggested previously that each resource of the organisation is the subject of a counter-claim, i.e. that it is owned by some third party. This in turn suggests that all transactions affecting the organisation have two aspects, one recording the *acquisition* of a resource, the other recording the *source* used to finance the acquisition. These twin aspects of any transaction are represented by twin (or double) entries in the books of account—hence the term double-entry book-keeping. The technique of double-entry book-keeping bears a certain resemblance to the Newtonian law of physics, which states that for every action there is an opposite and equal reaction. One side of the entry is recorded on the left-hand side of the appropriate account and is termed a *debit* entry, the other side of the entry is recorded on the right-hand side of (usually) a different account and is termed a *credit* entry. It is most important to realise that the terms debit and credit, when applied to the technique of book-keeping, mean neither more nor less than left-hand side (debit) and right-hand side (credit) respectively. In no way does debit denote or imply anything 'bad' nor credit anything 'good'. What types of entry appear on the debit and credit sides we shall explain shortly. Of course, one major benefit of recognising this duality of transactions, and using it as the basis of the recording system, is its provision of an automatic check on the arithmetical accuracy of the entries in the accounting books. This automatic check greatly helps any third party, for example the auditor, who wishes to verify the accuracy of the accounting records.

We can now see how the organisation's assets and the claims on its assets are affected by particular types of transactions. For the remainder of this chapter we will examine only transactions which do *not* affect the wealth of the organisation, i.e. transactions which have no impact on the income statement.

Four distinct sets of such transactions are possible, each of which represents a flow of value from one account to another. These are as follows:

1. *Transactions involving an **increase in assets** accompanied by an identical decrease in assets*
   Suppose that an organisation buys raw material for £1,000 for which it pays in cash. Two aspects of the transaction are relevant. The organisation has both increased its assets (stock of raw materials) by £1,000, and decreased its assets (fall in the cash balance) by £1,000. In effect a swap of assets has taken place.

2. *Transactions involving an **increase in assets** accompanied by an identical increase in claims*
   Suppose that the organisation finances the purchase of raw materials by obtaining a loan of £1,000. Once again the transaction has two aspects. As in the previous case, the organisation has increased its assets (raw materials) by £1,000, but here no corresponding decrease in assets has ensued. The organisation has not used its own funds to buy the materials but rather has contracted a liability of £1,000 due to be repaid to the lender at some agreed future date, i.e. it has increased the claims on its assets.

3. *Transactions involving a **decrease in assets** accompanied by an identical decrease in claims*
   Suppose now that the organisation repays the £1,000 loan originally granted to purchase the raw materials. This transaction constitutes the reverse of that in (2) above. Its dual aspects represent the reduction of £1,000 in the organisation's cash balance, and an equivalent reduction in the amount due to the lender of £1,000.

4. *Transactions involving an **increase in claims** accompanied by an identical decrease in claims*
   Suppose finally that the organisation borrows £1,000 from its bank in order to repay the existing loan of £1,000. None of the organisation's assets is involved in this particular transaction—it is simply exchanging one liability (the bank overdraft) for another liability (the loan) of an equal amount.

We can summarise the above four sets of transactions as follows:

1. An **increase in assets** accompanied by an identical **decrease in assets**
2. An **increase in assets** accompanied by an identical **increase in claims**
3. A **decrease in assets** accompanied by an identical **decrease in claims**
4. An **increase in claims** accompanied by an identical **decrease in claims**

6.6   The Accounting Equation

It should now be apparent that the effect of any transaction which does not give rise to a change of wealth is to increase (or decrease) assets and claims by the same amount. It follows that, at any point in time, after a number of transactions have occurred, total assets must equal total claims—in other words, all of the assets of the business, at any point in time, are subject to the claims of debt holders or owners. This relationship, which is commonly known as the *accounting equation*, may be expressed in the following form:

Assets= Liabilities+ Ownership interest

The 'debits' and 'credits' previously referred to now come into play. The left-hand (or debit) side of the accounting equation is represented by the organisation's assets, the right-hand (or credit) side by the ownership inter- est and liabilities. This leads us to a simple rule. Assets (or *uses* of funds) always appear on the debit side of the account; ownership interest and liabilities (or *sources* of funds) always appear on the credit side. This identity is expanded upon in the following chapter when we consider a wider variety of uses and sources of funds than that considered so far, but we cannot stress too strongly that the underlying principle remains exactly the same. We will repeat it once again, as follows:

Left-hand side   = **Debit** = **Uses of funds**
Right-hand side= **Credit**= **Sources of funds**

This basic form of the accounting equation provides a first guide to the foundations of double-entry book-keeping. The following example of Mr Elm shows how the accounting equation can be used to illustrate the effect of transactions which do not involve any changes in wealth. In the next chapter the example is enlarged to accommodate transactions which affect the income statement and thus the wealth of the organisation.

6.7   Illustration of Double-entry Book-keeping

Mr Elm started business on 1 January 19X0. He undertook the following transactions during his first week of business.

1.   1 January: Paid £2,000 into the business bank account from his per-
     sonal savings.
2.   3 January: Borrowed £1,000 at an interest rate of 12% p.a. repayable
     on 30 June and paid it into the business bank account.
3.   4 January: Bought a machine for £1,800, paying for it from the business
     bank account. The machine is expected to give service for 3
     years, at the end of which it will be worthless.
4.   5 January: Bought 1,000 units of stock at £1 per unit, paying for them
     from the business bank account.

The accounting entries reflecting the above set of transactions are shown in
Table 6.5.

Table 6.5   Mr Elm—Accounting entries: transactions (1)–(4)

Transaction	Assets £	=	Ownership interest + £	Liabilities £
(1)	2,000 (Bank)		2,000	
(2)	1,000 (Bank)			1,000
(3)	1,800 (Machine)			
	(1,800) (Bank)			
(4)	1,000 (Stock)			
	(1,000) (Bank)			
	3,000	=	2,000	+ 1,000

Bank	200	
Machine	1,800	
Stock	1,000	

N.B. Numbers in brackets signify negative amounts (i.e. decreases in assets).

Transaction (1) involves an introduction of £2,000 into the business
bank account. Because the cash comes from Mr Elm's personal savings, and
because Mr Elm is the owner of the business, the credit entry appears under
Ownership interest. The term 'Capital account' is most commonly used in
practice to describe the individual's 'Ownership interest'. If we were to draw
up a balance sheet on 2 January it would show the following:

Current assets
  Cash   £2,000

represented by:
  Ownership interest (Capital account)   £2,000

Succeeding adjustments to this balance sheet are provided by transactions (2) to (4). Transaction (2) increases further the cash balance, while correspondingly creating a liability in respect of the repayment of the loan. The entry for transaction (3) reflects a swap of assets, the purchase of the machine being financed from the business's own resources. Similarly, transaction (4) swaps cash of £1,000 for stock of £1,000. The final line of the accounting equation represents the position of Mr Elm's business (i.e. his updated balance sheet) after his first four transactions. The business has assets of £3,000 (bank balance £200, machine £1,800 and stock £1,000) represented by ownership interest of £2,000 and liabilities of £1,000. This is in accordance with the basic principle of the accounting equation, i.e. entries involving the uses of funds are recorded on the left-hand side, and entries involving the sources of funds are recorded on the right-hand side of the equation.

However, for purposes other than recording transactions, the accounting equation can be rearranged, for example so as to define the residual interest of Mr Elm in the business:

Ownership interest = Assets − Liabilities
£2,000   £3,000− £1,000

In other words, the interest of the owners in a business is equal to the assets of the business less the amounts owing to third parties. Adopting this approach Mr Elm's balance sheet at 6 January would appear in vertical form as follows:

Mr Elm's balance sheet at 6 January

	£	£
Fixed assets		
Machine		1,800
Current assets		
Stock	1,000	
Cash	200	
	1,200	
less: *Current liabilities*		
Loan	1,000	200
	Net assets	£2,000
represented by:		
Ownership interest (Capital account)		£2,000

Before we look at the preparation of a more detailed balance sheet we must understand more fully how wealth is created by the organisation's activities. We thus turn our attention in the following chapter to the basis and compilation of the income statement.

Discussion Topics

1 Describe how assets are classified in a UK balance sheet. Can you think of any assets which do not fall easily into the 'fixed' and 'current' categories?

2 Why do particular organisations prepare their balance sheets on particular dates? What factors are likely to determine the choice of balance sheet date?

3 Why is it important to balance the amounts of physical and monetary assets owned by a manufacturing company? What are some of the possible effects of an imbalance?

4 Distinguish between the claims of owners and lenders. Why are the distinctions so important?

5 Why do you suppose that historical cost accounting has remained for so long as the basis for preparing accounting statements?

6 Why is the term 'double-entry' used to describe the accountant's recording process? What is the likely derivation of the terms debit and credit? Why do you suppose they refer to left-hand side and right-hand side respectively?

Further Reading

See end of Chapter 8 for reading for Part 2.

Exercises

6.1 Show how the following transactions would be recorded in an organisation's accounting equation.

(a) A payment of £10,000 by the owner of the organisation into its bank account.

(b) The purchase of 1,000 units of stock at a price of £5 per unit. Payment is made from the business bank account.

(c) The receipt of a loan of £20,000 from the organisation's bank. The proceeds are paid into the business bank account.

(d) The purchase of a machine for £30,000 of which £5,000 is paid immediately from the business bank account. The balance is payable at a later date.

(e) The repayment from the business bank account of £5,000 of the bank loan.

(f) The exchange of 400 units of stock at £5 per unit for a second-hand motor van valued at £2,000.

6.2   The following balances appear at the foot of Mr Angelotti's accounting equation on 31 December 19X5:

	£
Assets	
Plant and machinery	72,300
Land and buildings	48,800
Cash at bank	4,100
Stock	26,600
Motor vehicles	18,900
Debtors (amounts owed by customers)	16,700
	£187,400
Ownership Interest and Liabilities	
Creditors (amounts owed to suppliers)	22,900
Long-term loan from Spoletta Finance Ltd	75,000
Mr Angelotti—ownership interest	43,800
Taxation due to the Inland Revenue	22,400
Bank overdraft	23,300
	£187,400

- Prepare Mr Angelotti's balance sheet at 31 December 19X5.

Chapter 7

The Income Statement

In this chapter we will look at the second major component of the accounting model of the organisation—its income statement or profit and loss account. The two terms are synonymous but we prefer, and will continue to use, the former. It also seems to us a little incongruous that an account can apparently show both a profit *and* a loss at the same time! (However we should stress that the term 'profit and loss account' is used widely in practice. Indeed the Companies Act 1981 refers to Profit and Loss Accounts rather than Income Statements.) The purpose of the income statement is to provide information on the success (or failure) of the organisation's operations for the period under review. In recent years the income statement has assumed a position of great prominence with users of published accounts. For example, one of the statistics which is widely used to encapsulate a large company's performance for a period is its earnings (or income) per share; hence the primary emphasis given by users to the income statement, rather than to the balance sheet.

In Chapter 5 we suggested that the results of the organisation's operations were determined by its *accomplishments* for the period less the *efforts expended*. We defined accomplishments in terms of sales revenue generated during the period and efforts in terms of expenses incurred during the period. The two guiding principles to be used in determining whether revenue or expense should enter the income statement we explained to be the *realisation* principle and the *matching* principle respectively. A major purpose of this chapter will be to look in detail at some of the many different issues raised by the application of these two overriding principles to be used in determining income. The chapter has three major sections. The first section deals with the measurement of accomplishment for the period; the second deals with the measurement of effort; and the final section applies to the income statement some of the book-keeping ideas introduced in the last chapter. However before we examine each of these important issues we briefly turn our attention to an important underlying concept in the construction of an income statement—the relevant *accounting period*.

7.1   The Accounting Period

As we have noted previously, an income statement is a financial report of the result of an organisation's operating activities over a specified period of time. We may, intuitively, think of such a period as comprising one year and, indeed, most organisations do present *annual* reports of their performance and financial position. Yet there is no obvious reason why this should be so. The benefits to be derived from the use of such assets as buildings, machinery and, in some cases, stocks, last well beyond one year and in certain industries, for example heavy engineering and chemicals, the production process itself may last for over a year.

In former times accounts were not prepared annually, but rather at the end of the major activity or venture(s) undertaken by the organisation. We explained this initially in Chapter 4. The organisation of today cannot, however, wait until the completion of particular activities or ventures before accounts are prepared. Regular and timely information is required by owners and others to monitor the performance of the organisation, to assess the efficiency of its management, to make decisions on the granting or withdrawal of funds and, in particular, to compare the performance of the organisation over time and against other organisations. Thus an accounting period of uniform length (i.e. one year) is chosen. This uniformity does not, of course, extend to a common *date* for the determination of annual performance. Not all organisations report their performance on a calendar year basis (i.e. with a year-end of 31 December) and thus a variety of accounting year-ends exists. For example, the income statement of ICI plc is prepared for the year to 31 December; that of Sainsburys plc for the year to 31 March and that of Bass plc for the year to 30 September. Very large organisations are also required to produce semi-annual information, so that their owners do not have to wait until after the end of the accounting year before they learn of the firm's progress. We should note here also that the published accounts of most organisations do not appear until some time after the end of their accounting year—a three month time lapse is not unusual—to allow compilation and checking (by the auditors) of the accounting records.

7.2   Measurement of Accomplishment

In Chapter 5 we defined a (manufacturing) organisation's accomplishment for the period as relating to the number of units of finished goods which had been delivered and invoiced (or billed) to customers. Some justification for this definition is needed. It is by no means intuitively obvious that this is the only possible way of measuring accomplishment, and thus of determining revenue. Figure 7.1 suggests that at least two other alternative measures of accomplishment might be used; for example the total number of units

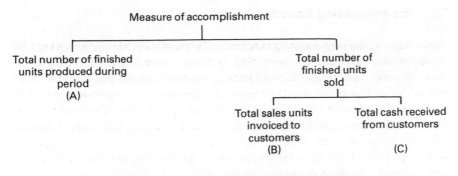

Figure 7.1   Measures of accomplishment.

produced (or even partly produced) during the period might be regarded as an appropriate measure of accomplishment or, alternatively, the total amount of cash collected from customers might seem to be an appropriate measure. In order to decide how to measure accomplishment, and thus how to recognise revenue, certain criteria are needed. Two criteria in practice dominate all others and thus determine the recognition of revenue:

(a)   all the work to be performed on the finished goods has been completed;

(b)   the finished goods have been accepted by the customer, such that the organisation has received an asset either in cash or as a promise to pay cash.

The application of these two criteria makes it easier to understand why revenue is recognised at the point of sale (point B in Figure 7.1) rather than at the time of production (point A) or the date of the receipt of cash (point C). In other words the physical act of invoicing (and in most cases delivering) goods to the customer indicates that all work on, and all services relating to, the finished goods have been performed and that the buyer has accepted the goods, either by a cash payment or a promise to pay at some future date. Many business transactions are conducted on the latter basis, i.e. a certain period of credit is granted to the customer (say 30 days) at the end of which payment for the goods is required. Earlier payment can often result in the customer paying less than the face value of the invoice. In this case the customer receives a discount for early settlement. It is at the point of sale that an objective measurement of the amount of revenue to be realised can first be made. This revenue constitutes the agreed price for the sale of the goods between the buyer and the seller. We will return later in this chapter to the problem which arises when the expected revenue is not in fact received, i.e. when customers do not pay in full for the goods they have bought.

7.3   Revenue Recognition at the Date of Production

Based upon the arguments presented above, it would in most cases be inappropriate for the organisation to measure its accomplishments in terms of units produced. This is because the organisation cannot be certain that the work involved in production of the goods constitutes all the work or services necessary to place them into a saleable condition; nor can it be sure that the finished production will be accepted by customers, either in terms of quantity or of agreed price.

There are, however, certain *specific* instances in which production may be deemed to be the critical event in revenue recognition. The most common of these instances relates to particular 'one-off' projects undertaken by organisations at the request of individual customers. For example, major long-term engineering and construction projects (the building of an oilrig or a sports stadium) will likely take place over a long period of time and be the subject of an agreed advance price between constructor and customer. Such long-term contracts are of particular significance to organisations which contract with the government for the supply of military, electronic and defence equipment. In these cases revenue is often recognised in stages as the contract proceeds, rather than as a lump sum at the termination of the project. The most usual method of recognising revenue in stages is via the 'percentage of completion' method, under which a proportion of the contract price, determined by the degree of completeness of the project, is recognised as revenue in each period of the project's life. This method is not as arbitrary as it might initially appear. The degree to which a contract is complete will usually be assessed by an independent party, for example an architect or surveyor, and in the later stages of a contract it is normal for an organisation to be able to predict with some degree of accuracy the levels of future costs to be incurred. The following example of Brunton Ltd shows how revenue might be recognised under a long-term contract.

Illustration

Brunton Ltd is engaged in a long-term contract to build a bridge. The following information relates to the contract:

	£
Total contract price	4,000,000
Work certified (by architect) to 31 December 19X1	2,500,000
Costs incurred on the contract to 31 December 19X1	2,050,000
Estimated further costs to completion	1,150,000

Assuming that no profit has been taken on the contract in previous years, we can estimate the proportion of the (likely) total profit on the contract which is applicable to the year to 31 December 19X1. The calculation of the applicable profit is as follows:

(a) *Estimated total profit on the contract*   £
Contract price   4,000,000
less: Estimated total costs
(2,050,000+1,150,000)   3,200,000

Estimated total profit   £ 800,000

(b) *Proportion applicable to the period to 31 December 19X1*

$$\frac{\text{Work certified to 31 December 19X1}}{\text{Total contract price}} \times \text{Estimated total profit}$$

$$= \frac{2,500,000 \times 800,000}{4,000,000} = £500,000$$

In practice the applicable profit of £500,000 may be reduced by some further percentage, perhaps to allow for the eventuality that the estimated further costs may increase, or that the customer may not be willing to pay the full price due to poor workmanship. In this case the profit of £500,000 might be reduced by, say, one-quarter, to give a profit for the year of £500,000×0.75=£375,000. This final reduction, in this case 25%, is an arbitrary adjustment. It is an example of the accountant's concept of prudence. Many companies in the UK calculate the profit earned on long-term contracts in a manner similar to that illustrated above. These include GEC, Plessey, Tarmac, and Taylor Woodrow. In 1983, £5.6m of Plessey's operating profit of £119m was calculated in this manner.

7.4   Revenue Recognition at the Date of Cash Receipt

The third alternative method of recognising revenue is to wait until the cash relating to the sale has been received from the customer. This method has some appeal. After all it is the receipt of cash from the sale of its products which largely determines the organisation's ability to continue its operations. The reasons for its rejection within the income statement as the basis of recognising revenue are probably two-fold[1]. In the first place the experience which the organisation has gathered over previous years will provide a good basis for predicting the amount of cash to be received from customers, such that recognition of revenue at the point of sale constitutes an objective basis for its inclusion in the income statement. Secondly, and more importantly, the accountant's income statement serves the function of identifying causes and effects. One such cause represents the sale of goods to customers, the effect of which is to generate in the same, or future, periods a receipt of cash from the same customers. If the organisation recognised its sales

---

[1] See Chapter 4 for a more general discussion of the relative merits of cash flow and accrual accounting.

revenue in cash terms such a relationship would be lost. For example, if cash received from customers during one period relates to sales made in the current and in preceding periods, then cash received from sales will not be 'matched' with the sales to which it relates. The following example of St James Ltd will help to make this clear.

Illustration

During the year to 31 December 19X2, St James Ltd sells 100,000 units of product X at £2 each, and 50,000 units of product Y at £3 each. Receipts during 19X2 were £325,000 which were made up as follows:

		£
Cash from sales of product X during 19X1		
20,000 units×£1.50 (19X1 price)		30,000
Cash from sales of product Y during 19X1		
10,000 units×£2.50 (19X1 price)		25,000
Cash from sales of product X during 19X2		
75,000 units×£2		150,000
Cash from sales of product Y during 19X2		
40,000 units×£3		120,000
Total cash received		£325,000

If the amount of £325,000 is shown as sales revenue in St James Ltd's income statement for 19X2 the effect will be to mismatch the sales with the cash received, by including in sales revenue cash received from the previous year's sales (£55,000) and excluding from sales revenue cash receivable from the current year's sales of £80,000 (i.e. 25,000 units of product X at £2 and 10,000 units of product Y at £3). Thus the correct matching of cause and effect in respect of sales would recognise for 19X2 sales revenue of £350,000, as follows:

	£
Revenue from product X (100,000 units at £2 per unit)	200,000
Revenue from product Y (50,000 units at £3 per unit)	150,000
Total revenue	£350,000

7.5   Some Problems in Revenue Recognition

The recognition of revenue at the point of sale is not without its problems. Few organisations are lucky enough to transact all their business with customers who pay in full at the due date. Most organisations have experience of customers who fail to meet their debts, either in full or in part. It is therefore normal to anticipate the likelihood of some default in payment by customers, and to provide against the current year's revenue for such a possibility. If provision is not made against the current year's revenue, future periods may be charged with the effects of actions taken earlier—in this case actions concerning the granting of credit to unreliable customers. In other words there would be a mismatching of costs with revenues, such that the performance of the organisation for the particular period would not mirror the results of actions taken in that period. If, for example, St James Ltd anticipates that 5% of the sales revenue recognised in 19X2 from the sale of product X may prove to be uncollectable, it will reduce its net income for 19X2 by 5% of £200,000, or £10,000, and classify this amount in its income statement as a 'provision for doubtful debts'.

7.6   Measurement of Effort

In Chapter 5 we defined the net result of the organisation's operations as being the difference between its accomplishments (the amount of revenue recognised during the period) and its efforts (the expenses incurred in earning revenue for the period). In other words, the periodic income of the organisation is the difference between revenues and expenses. Having looked at how we might determine the amount of revenue to be recognised, we now turn to the other, more tricky, side of the income statement—the measurement and recognition of expenses. We should here draw a distinction between the often used but often misunderstood terms expenditure and expense. An item of *expenditure* is any cash payment made by the organisation; an item of *expense* is any cost used up in earning revenue. Thus, not all items of expenditure are, as we shall see, treated as expenses, nor are all expenses necessarily represented by cash expenditure. For example, the purchase of shares in another company is an expenditure, though not an expense; depreciation of an asset is an expense though not an expenditure.

In principle, the recognition of periodic expenses is straightforward—just as efforts are matched with accomplishments, so are expenses matched with their associated revenues. For manufacturing organisations in particular, the practicalities of this matching may be far from easy. The difficulty most frequently arises in cases where the manufacturing organisation's level or volume of production does not equal its level or volume of sales, i.e. where the efforts associated with the production function do not correspond to those linked with sales. If, for example, production exceeds sales in any period, it becomes necessary to determine how much of the expenditure incurred in production (e.g. how much raw materials, labour, use of machinery, etc.) is to be matched against the sales revenue for the period and how much is to be carried forward to future periods to be matched against the sales of those periods. The problem is thus one of determining the production or product costs for the period. Recognition of costs which do not attach to products is less difficult, and thus the determination of such periodic costs as general and administrative expenses does not usually present the accountant with too many problems.

The determination of product costs represents one of the accountant's major problems. It is an important issue because it can significantly affect both the organisation's income (via the charge for the cost of goods sold in the income statement) and also the value of stock shown in the balance sheet. We thus devote most of Chapter 10 to its consideration. However, we offer at this stage a brief introduction to the nature of the accountant's problem. Suppose, as is likely, that the total number of finished units in stock at the start of the year plus the number of units produced during the year is greater than the number of units sold for the year. How should the accountant deal with the problems caused by this situation?

The following simple example should help to clarify the issues at stake.

Illustration

During the year to 31 December 19X0 (its first year of operation) Roker Ltd undertakes the following transactions with attendant costs and revenues:

Production   12,000 units of finished goods
Sales   10,000 units at £11 per unit

Production expenses:
    Variable costs per unit (i.e. costs identifiable with
                            units of production)   £3 per unit
    Fixed costs for the year (i.e. costs identifiable with
                            total production)   £24,000

Selling expenses:
    Variable costs per unit (i.e. costs identifiable with
                            units of sales)   £1 per unit
    Fixed costs for the year (i.e. costs identifiable with
                            total sales)   £30,000

If we assume that there is no work in progress on 31 December 19X0, the nature of the accountant's problem is somewhat easier to comprehend. The problem is this. How does the accountant *allocate* the production expenses of £60,000 (variable costs (12,000×£3)=£36,000, plus fixed costs of £24,000) over the finished products sold (10,000 units) and finished products unsold (2,000 units)? Selling expenses do not present a similar problem, as they are identifiable, both in terms of unit sales and total sales, with the period in which sales are made. Thus the whole of the selling expenses will always be charged in the period in which sales take place. To allocate production expenses the accountant needs a *rule*—one which allows him to relate the efforts linked to the production function (labour, materials, use of machinery, etc.) to the outputs of production (finished goods in stock, work in progress and finished goods sold), and to relate the efforts linked with other functions (sales, administration, finance, etc.) to the outputs of these functions (goods sold to customers). Expressed diagrammatically the accountant needs an allocation rule which allows him to identify the different efforts and outputs as shown in Figure 7.2.

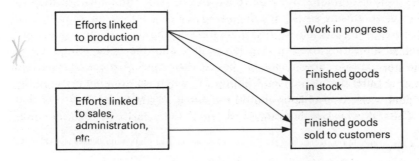

Figure 7.2   Efforts and outputs

By inserting the data for Roker Ltd into the appropriate boxes, the position appears as shown in Figure 7.3. The only box lacking a monetary value is the top right-hand box representing 'finished goods in stock', and it is to the valuation of finished goods that the allocation rule is directed. The accountant must devise some method of allocating the total production costs

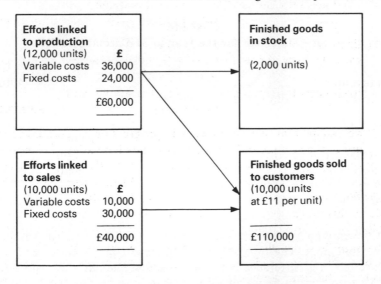

Figure 7.3   Efforts and outputs for Roker Ltd

of £60,000 such that a monetary value is placed upon the finished goods. This allocation problem has two dimensions. First, should the accountant allocate the fixed costs of production to closing stock? Second, if fixed costs are to be allocated, what basis should be used to allocate them? Phrased somewhat differently, the first question asks the accountant to decide whether closing stock is to be valued under either of two very different costing systems; either *direct costing* which does not entail an allocation of fixed costs to closing stock, or *full costing* which involves an allocation of fixed production costs. The second question asks the accountant to develop a method of allocating fixed production costs within the full costing system. We do not explore these issues further at this stage. A more appropriate place for a fuller discussion is in Chapter 10, when we examine in detail the many issues involved in the valuation of stock. We will also return in that chapter to the example of Roker Ltd.

7.7   The Layout of the Income Statement

Income statements, which, unlike balance sheets, relate to periods of time rather than points in time, are usually constructed on a functional basis, i.e. the efforts involved in generating sales revenue are linked, and classified, according to their respective functions (for example, production, sales, administration and finance). Thus a traditional (summarised) income statement of a limited company might appear as follows:

Oval Ltd
Income Statement for the year to 31 December 19X0

	£	£
Sales revenue		400,000
less: Cost of goods sold (production costs)		250,000
Gross profit		150,000
less: Selling costs	40,000	
Administrative costs	50,000	
Financing costs	30,000	120,000
Net income		£ 30,000

Conventionally, two income or profit figures are struck within the income statement. The first of these is the *'gross profit'* or *'gross margin'* which reflects the difference between sales revenue and the cost of goods sold. The gross profit figure gives an indication of profit available to meet non-production expenses. The second, and more important, figure is that of the *'net income'* or *'net profit'* which reflects the difference between sales revenue and all expenses incurred during the period. As we will see later in this chapter, the net income belongs to the owners of the organisation and is added to their ownership interest (i.e. it increases the value of their stake in the organisation) in the closing (end of period) balance sheet.

7.8   Dividends and Taxation

In the case of a limited company it is usual practice to appropriate or distribute some of the income to the owners and to retain the balance within the company. Such a distribution is termed a *dividend*. If a dividend is to be paid the net income added to ownership interest will be reduced by the amount of the dividend. The net income figure will also be reduced by an amount reflecting the charge for *taxation* on the year's income. It is a feature of most economic structures that a tax is levied on the income of organisations, computed in a way determined by legislation. It is rarely the case that any organisation's net income represents its taxable profit. Tax law prescribes a very detailed list of expenses and allowances which can be charged or claimed by organisations in computing the amount of tax payable to the government.

Thus taxation will appear in the income statement as a charge against net income and, because taxes on organisations are not usually paid until after the period to which they relate, tax will also appear in the balance sheet as a current liability. Limited companies (both public and private) pay *Corporation Tax* on their profits; individuals and partnerships pay *Income Tax*. The tax rules and rates applicable to the different business structures change constantly. Yearly adjustments to the rules and rates appear in the Finance Acts passed by Parliament. The subject of business and personal taxation is a complex matter beyond the scope of an introductory text, and we discuss it no further in this book.

To give a little more flesh to the rather bare income statement shown above, Figure 7.4 gives some indication of the types of expenses which might appear under each of the functional headings. The list is by no means exhaustive but should give some clues to the different types of expense within the income statement.

7.9   The Relationship Between Assets and Expenses

It should be stressed at this stage that assets (which appear in the balance sheet) and expenses (which appear in the income statement) are inextricably linked. Consider, for example, depreciation of factory equipment, raw materials used or depreciation of office machinery. Each of these expenses represents economic services which have been used up during the period, i.e.

Production costs
  Raw materials used
  Wages of factory workers and foremen
  Depreciation of factory equipment
  Insurance and rent of factory
  Factory heating and lighting

Selling costs
  Advertising
  Salesmen's salaries and commissions
  Distribution and transport costs

Administrative costs
  Salaries of managing director, accountant and office staff
  Computing facilities
  Office heating, lighting and telephone
  Depreciation of office machinery

Financing costs
  Interest payable on loans
  Bank overdraft charges
  Bad debt provisions

Figure 7.4   Types of expense appearing in the income statement

each represents a proportion of the organisation's stock of assets which has expired. The asset (balance sheet) amounts for factory equipment, raw materials and office machinery will thus be reduced by the charges appearing in the income statement. Some services are bought and used up instantaneously and thus never appear in the balance sheet as assets—examples from Figure 7.4 might include bank charges, salesmen's salaries and telephone charges. Thus when the organisation pays its salesmen's salaries, the amount paid will appear directly in the income statement as an expense. Whether resources are used over a period of time (as with raw materials or machinery) or are used instantaneously (as with salesmen's salaries) the underlying general principle is the same—expenses represent used-up or expired resources and, conversely, most assets represent unexpired costs which await transfer to the income statement during future years. There are, of course, exceptions to this rule. Land is rarely used up, and thus no charge for its use appears in the income statement. Nor does the ownership of shares in another organisation constitute an asset which is used up in earning revenue. This distinction between assets and expenses is also fundamental in understanding why both assets and expenses appear as left-hand side (debit) entries in the books. Each represents a *use* of funds, the difference being simply that assets benefit the organisation over a longer time period.

7.10   The Income Statement and the Accounting Equation

In the previous chapter we introduced the basic accounting equation as being:

Assets = Liabilities + Ownership interest

and we showed, with a very simple set of transactions, how a new balance sheet is struck after each transaction. Because none of these transactions involved any change in the organisation's wealth, we did not need to consider how the income statement (which measures changes in wealth) and the accounting equation are linked. This link will now be explored via the example of Mr Elm, introduced in Chapter 6. Before dealing with a further set of transactions, a more general analysis of the accounting equation is necessary.

We have explained in Chapter 6 that the ownership interest of the organisation comprises two elements—the amount of capital subscribed by the owners and the amount of profit or income which has been retained in the business (i.e. which has not been distributed as dividend). Thus we can extend the basic equation as follows:

$$\text{Assets} = \text{Liabilities} + \overbrace{\text{Subscribed capital} + \text{Retained income}}^{\text{Ownership interest}}$$

This chapter has shown that an organisation's net income is simply the excess of revenues over expenses. Therefore the retained income portion of the ownership interest may be rephrased to represent the (retained) excess of revenues over expenses. This allows the basic equation to be further expanded to show:

$$\text{Assets} = \text{Liabilities} + \overbrace{\text{Subscribed capital} + \text{Revenues} - \text{Expenses}}^{\text{Ownership interest}}$$

This 'final' equation shows clearly that the changes in wealth of the organisation, generated by the excess of revenues over expenses, belong to the owners and that, in consequence, the revenue and expense accounts are merely (important) subdivisions of the ownership interest account. Let us now return to the illustration of Mr Elm to see how a set of transactions involving changes in wealth is treated in the new, expanded accounting equation.

Chapter 6 showed that the balance sheet of Mr Elm, after four transactions, was as follows:

Assets = Liabilities + Subscribed capital
£3,000   £1,000   £2,000

Mr Elm now undertakes the following additional transactions, all conducted in January:

5.   10 January: Sells 100 units of stock for £2 per unit, paying the proceeds into the bank account.
6.   31 January: Uses the machine to modify the remaining 900 units of stock, which are sold for £5 per unit. Pays the proceeds into the bank.

7.   31 January: Pays the following expenses from the bank account:
                 Wages   £1,500
                 Advertising £   100
                 Insurance   £   500
                 Interest   £   10

The accounting entries reflecting the above transactions are shown in Table 7.1.

The first line of the equation comprises the closing balance sheet arising from transactions (1) to (4). Transaction (5), the sale of 100 units of unmodified stock on 10 January for £2 per unit, generates a profit to the business. Applying the accounting convention of matching, the historical cost of the stock is matched with the revenue realised from its sale, giving a profit of £100 (sales revenue of £200 less the historical cost of the stock sold of £100). How should the transaction be recorded? Receipt of the sale proceeds causes an increase in the asset 'bank balance' of £200. Disposal of the 100 units of stock, used up in generating sales, causes a reduction in the asset 'stock' of £100—the historical cost of the stock sold. The difference of £100 represents a profit to the business resulting from its trading activities and belongs to whoever is legally entitled to receive the profits of the business; in this case Mr Elm. In the accounting equation, revenues are increased by £200 (the amount of the sale) and expenses by £100 (the cost of the stock sold), thus increasing Mr Elm's ownership interest by a net amount of £100, the profit on the transaction.

Transaction (6), involving the modification and sale of the remaining stock, has a number of aspects. The sale itself results in an increase of £4,500 both in the bank balance and in sales revenue. We must also recognise the cost of the modified stock that has been sold. The cost of the unmodified stock was £900 and this amount should be subtracted from stock and treated as an expense. The cost of using the machine to process the stock is less straightforward. The cost of acquiring the machine is £1,800. However, in return for this expenditure the business expects to receive productive ser-vices for three years. The nub of the problem is this. The business has paid £1,800 to acquire machine services which span more than one accounting period and, in order to calculate that part of the total cost to be matched with current revenues, some procedure is needed to allocate the total cost of the machine between all periods which are expected to benefit from its services. That part of the total cost which is treated as an expense of the period under consideration is called the *depreciation charge* for the period. Alternative methods of calculating depreciation were mentioned briefly in Chapter 4 and will be considered in more detail in Chapter 9. At this stage, we adopt the most common method of allocating the cost of a fixed asset, which is known as the 'straight line' method. This method involves spreading the cost of the asset in equal parts over its estimated total life. In the case of Mr Elm's

Table 7.1   Mr Elm—Accounting entries (5)–(7)

	Assets				Claims			
Transaction	Bank	+ Machine	+ Stock	= Liabilities	+ Subscribed capital	+ Revenues	− Expenses	
Opening balances (from entries (1)–(4))	200	1,800	1,000	1,000	2,000			
(5)	200		(100)			200	(100)	Stock
(6)	4,500	(50)	(900)			4,500	(900)	Stock
							(50)	Depreciation
(7)	(1,500)						(1,500)	Wages
	(100)						(100)	Advertising
	(500)						(500)	Insurance
	(10)						(10)	Interest
						4,700	(3,160)	
Transfer of net income					1,540	(4,700)	(3,160)	
	2,790	1,750	0	1,000	3,540	0	0	

machine, the straight line method gives an annual depreciation charge of
£600 (£1,800 divided by 3), and thus a monthly charge of £600 divided by
12 = £50. This amount is deducted from the asset 'machine' and is also
treated as an expense. Transaction (7) involves the payment of four items of
expense; wages, advertising, insurance and interest for the month of January. In each case, the amount of the payment is subtracted from the bank
balance and treated as an expense.

All transactions for the period have now been entered in the accounting
equation. It remains to transfer net income (the difference between the
revenue and expense columns) to ownership interest. Net income for the
period is £1,540 and this amount is added to ownership interest. The totals of
the columns in the accounting equation now represent the position of Mr
Elm's business on 31 January. The business has assets of £4,540 (a bank
balance of £2,790 and a machine with a depreciated cost of £1,750) represented by ownership interest of £3,540 and a loan of £1,000. The ownership interest balance comprises capital paid in of £2,000 and the net income
for the period of £1,540.

**Table 7.2   Mr Elm—Accounting statements for the
month ended 31 January**

	£	£
Income statement for the month to 31 January		
Sales		4,700
less: Cost of stock used	1,000	
Depreciation of machine	50	
Wages	1,500	
Insurance	500	
Interest	10	
Advertising	100	3,160
Net income for the month		£1,540
Balance sheet on 31 January		
Assets		
Machine		1,750
Bank balance		2,790
		£4,540
Represented by:		
Ownership interest		
Balance on 1 January		2,000
add: Net income for the month		1,540
		3,540
Liabilities		
Loan		1,000
		£4,540

Finally we can present the accounting statements for Mr Elm which portray his performance for the month of January and his position as at 31 January. The income statement for the month (a restatement of the revenue and expense columns of the accounting equation) and the balance sheet at the end of the month (a restatement of the totals of each column of the accounting equation) are presented in Table 7.2.

Discussion Topics

1   Explain the importance of the 'accounting period' concept.

2   Explain the 'revenue recognition' principle and discuss the alternative ways in which revenue might be recognised.

3   What problems, if any, are inherent in the recognition of revenue at the time of sale? How might such problems be alleviated?

4   Distinguish between product costs and period costs. Why does the proper determination of product costs present so many problems to the accountant?

5   Distinguish between expense and expenditure. Give examples, in addition to those discussed in the text, of particular items which do not fall into both categories.

6   Explain the difference between dividends, taxation and the major types of income statement expense.

7   What is the relationship between asset and expense? Explain the difference between the two terms by way of particular examples.

Further Reading

See end of Chapter 8 for reading for Part 2.

Exercises

7.1   Mr Daland commences business on 1 March 19X7. During March 19X7 he undertakes the following transactions.
1.   Pays £20,000 into the business bank account from his own resources.
2.   Borrows £25,000 from Mrs Senta at an interest rate of 1% per month. Pays the proceeds into the business bank account.
3.   Purchases machinery for £25,000. He pays £10,000 from the business bank account and agrees to pay the balance on 31 May 19X7.
4.   Rents premises for an annual rent of £7,200, payable monthly.
5.   Purchases 100 units of raw materials for £100 per unit. He pays for these units immediately from the business bank account.
6.   Pays the following expenses from the business bank account:

Interest to Mrs Senta	£250
Rent	£600
Wages	£1,000
Lighting and heating	£300
Other expenses	£350

7. Provides for a depreciation charge of £400 on the machinery.
8. Uses the labour and machinery to convert 50 units of raw materials into finished goods, which he sells for £200 each. Pays the proceeds into the business bank account.

- (a)   Show Mr Daland's accounting equation entries for March 19X7.
- (b)   Prepare Mr Daland's income statement for the month of March 19X7 and his balance sheet at 31 March 19X7.

7.2   Countess Almaviva commenced business as a Basilio retailer on 1 January 19X9. During 19X9 she undertook the following transactions:

1 January 19X9
(a)   Paid £45,000 into the business bank account, of which £30,000 was from personal savings and £15,000 was a loan from Don Curzio at 15% p.a. interest.
(b)   Purchased a lease on a shop for £12,000 which she paid from the business bank account. The lease was for a period of 8 years and provided for an annual rent of £3,500, including rates.
(c)   Purchased fixtures and fittings for £7,500, paid from the business bank account. The fixtures and fittings had an estimated life of 10 years, and an expected resale value of £1,000 at the end of that time.
(d)   Bought from the business bank account 10,000 Basilios at a price of £2.00 per Basilio.

30 June 19X9
(e)   Sold 4,000 Basilios at £4.50 each and paid the proceeds into the business bank account.
(f)   Paid the following expenses from the business bank account:

Interest to Don Curzio	£1,125
Rent	£1,750
Assistant's salary	£2,100
Lighting and heating	£900
Telephone	£75
Other expenses	£1,200

31 December 19X9
(g)   Sold 5,000 Basilios at £5.00 each and paid the proceeds into the business bank account.
(h)   Paid the following expenses from the business bank account:

Interest to Don Curzio	£1,125
Rent	£1,750
Assistant's salary	£2,200
Lighting and heating	£1,250
Telephone	£85
Other expenses	£1,700

Countess Almaviva wishes to provide for depreciation on the lease and on the fixtures and fittings by the straight line method (i.e. by writing off, for each asset, an equal amount each year over the life of the asset).

- Prepare an income statement for Countess Almaviva for the year ended 31 December 19X9, and a balance sheet as at that date.

7.3   Sextus was a Roman entrepreneur who earned his living by sending ships to import spices and silks from the Far East. We shall use a little artistic licence in describing his activities. At the time that interests us, Sextus already has seven ships engaged in trade. He expects, however, that there will be a shortage of oriental goods in one year's time and he therefore resolves to buy an extra ship for one voyage. He expects to be able to buy a new ship for 10,000d, 7,500d payable immediately and the balance payable in six months' time. He would hire a team of oarsmen (since he disapproves of slavery) and they would be paid a wage of 1,000d on completion of the voyage. The voyage would take exactly one year, six months outwards to the oriental port and six months on the return. Sextus would have to spend 300d on provisions for the outward journey. He would also spend 4,000d on goods to be traded for silks and spices at the destination and 400d on goods to be traded at the destination for provisions for the return journey. On completion of the return journey, he would sell the silks and spices immediately for 8,500d but would have to spend 200d on selling expenses (transport and so on). He would also sell the ship at this time for an expected price of 8,000d. Sextus employs a clerk to keep the records and help with the administrative arrangements connected with the voyages of his seven ships already owned. This clerk, who receives a salary of 240d p.a., has enough idle time to be able to deal with the administration for the extra ship.

●   Prepare a calculation showing what gain Sextus would make from the extra ship.

Suppose that Sextus purchases the extra ship and that all the financial estimates given above prove exactly correct. He finds, however, that he has insufficient cash available to meet the second instalment of the price of the ship due six months after the start of the voyage. It is agreed that his friend Annius will provide the required amount and become a partner in the venture for the second six month period. Sextus will repay Annius at the end of the voyage and also pay him one half of the gain from the voyage during the second period of six months. Unfortunately they neglect to agree how this gain should be calculated.

●   Prepare a calculation showing what you consider to be an equitable apportionment of the gain. You may assume (if you think it relevant) that the market price of six-month-old ships is 9,200d.

Chapter 8

Accruals, Prepayments and Accounting Records

In the previous two chapters we introduced and explained the principles of conventional accounting recording via the double-entry system. A basic feature of conventional accounting is that revenues for a period are identified and *matched* with the costs incurred in earning them. In subsequent chapters we will discuss many of the features of the historical cost application of the double-entry framework; in particular we will look at the application of the matching concept to fixed and intangible assets, stock, and the treatment of ownership interest and long-term loan capital. Before doing so we consider one main feature of the double-entry framework—the treatment of accruals. Having done this, we then devote the remainder of this chapter to a comprehensive example of double-entry book-keeping, using both the accounting equation approach and the more conventional method of recording via 'T' accounts.

8.1 The Meaning of Accruals

The concept of accruals is central to the transactions-based approach to the measurement of net income and the determination of financial position. This approach, as we have explained, involves matching costs and revenues to determine net income. In consequence, it is only necessary to understand how to incorporate the following types of adjustments into the measurement of performance:

1. Costs and expenses incurred which have not yet been paid (*creditors* or *accrued expenses*).
2. Revenues earned for which payment has not yet been received (*debtors*).
3. Costs or expenses paid, the benefits from which will not arise until a subsequent period (*prepayments* or *payments in advance*).

These different types of adjustments will now be illustrated by means of a numerical example, relating to the activities of Mr Anfield for the year to 31 December 19X0. These activities, which represent a part only of Mr Anfield's total activities for the year, are listed in Table 8.1.

Table 8.1   Mr Anfield's transactions

During the year to 31 December 19X0, his first year of business, Mr Anfield engages in the following transactions:

1. Purchases 1,000 units of raw material at £11 per unit.
2. Pays suppliers £8,800 in respect of raw material purchases.
3. Pays lighting and heating costs of £2,000. An additional amount of £300, relating to the year to 31 December 19X0, is due but unpaid at the end of the year.
4. Pays six months loan interest to Mr Trafford. The loan of £10,000 was contracted on 1 January 19X0 and bears interest at 12% p.a.
5. Sells 800 finished units at £50 per unit.
6. Receives £35,000 from customers in respect of sales of finished goods.
7. Pays rent of £7,500 covering a period of fifteen months from 1 January 19X0.
8. Pays rates of £1,250 covering a period of fifteen months from 1 January 19X0.

Creditors and accrued expenses

Although very similar in principle, a distinction is sometimes drawn in practice between creditors and accrued expenses. The term 'creditors' is generally used to refer to amounts owing to, and billed by, suppliers of raw materials, whereas 'accrued expenses' is used to indicate amounts owing in respect of other items of expenditure which may not yet have been billed. In the case of Mr Anfield, examples concerning creditors arise from transactions (1) and (2). Mr Anfield buys raw materials during the year for £11,000 and pays his suppliers only £8,800 by the end of the year. Thus the amount he still owes at 31 December 19X0 (creditors in respect of raw material purchases) is £2,200. Transactions (3) and (4) provide examples of accrued expenses. Both the amount of £300 owing for lighting and heating and the £600 owing for interest are accrued expenses at 31 December.

Debtors

An example of the treatment of debtors is provided by transactions (5) and (6). Mr Anfield sells 800 finished units for a total of £40,000 and receives £35,000 from customers by 31 December. The balance still owing to him at that date (debtors in respect of sales) is therefore £5,000.

Prepayments

Transactions (7) and (8) provide examples of prepayments. The payments of both rent and rates cover a period beyond the end of the year under consideration. For example, the rent payment of £7,500 covers the period of fifteen months from 1 January 19X0. Hence £6,000 ($^{12}/_{15}$ of £7,500) relates to the current year (19X0) and £1,500 ($^{3}/_{15}$ of £7,500) relates to the next year (19X1). The same consideration applies to the payment for rates. The three months' portions of rent and rates which relate to the next accounting period (£1,500 for rent, £250 for rates) are classed as prepayments.

8.2   The Accounting Treatment of Accruals

In this section we describe the accounting treatment of each type of accrual. Note that we use only the appropriate headings within the accounting equation (i.e. Assets/Liabilities/Ownership interest/Revenues/Expenses) to explain each transaction.

1.   Creditors

In order that the accounting records reflect accurately the cost of all the stock bought during the year, it is necessary to ensure that both purchases made and paid for, as well as purchases made and not yet paid for (at the end of the year) are included in the total cost. This is achieved in two stages:

(a)   Increase stock of raw materials (assets) and increase creditors (liabilities) by the total amount of purchases (cash and credit) for the year. Thus, taking the figures from transaction (1), we have:

Assets (stock)=Liabilities (creditors)+ ... +Revenues−Expenses
        £11,000   £11,000

(b)   Decrease cash (assets) and decrease creditors (liabilities) by the payments made to suppliers during the year. Thus, using the figures in transaction (2), we have:

Assets (cash)=Liabilities (creditors)+ ... +Revenues−Expenses
     −£8,800   −£8,800

Note that these transactions have no impact on the income statement and that the amount appearing in Mr Anfield's balance sheet at 31 December 19X0 for creditors will be £11,000−£8,800=£2,200.

2.   Accrued expenses

The matching of costs and revenues to arrive at a net income figure for the year dictates that the income statement should be charged with all expenses which relate to the particular year, irrespective of their date of payment. The treatment of accrued expenses *per se* is no different; it is simply necessary to increase the expense in the income statement by the amount due but as yet unpaid, and to create a liability for the same amount. Thus using the figures in transaction (3) which relate to the amount accrued we have:

Assets=Liabilities+ ... +Revenues−Expenses
            £300   −   £300

The entry in respect of the costs actually paid of £2,000 is:

Assets (cash)= ... +Revenues−Expenses
  −£2,000   − £2,000

Thus the total charge in the income statement for lighting and heating costs is £2,300. The balance sheet at 31 December 19X0 will show £300 as accrued expenses, within the current liabilities section.

A similar procedure is adopted for the treatment of the six months' interest due on the loan from Mr Trafford as per transaction (4). Mr Anfield owes £600 for the period July–December 19X0. This gives:

$$\text{Assets (cash)} = \text{Liabilities} + \ldots + \text{Revenues} - \text{Expenses}$$
$$\text{£600} \qquad\qquad\qquad - \quad \text{£600}$$

The entry in respect of the loan interest already paid of £600 is:

$$\text{Assets (cash)} = \ldots + \text{Revenues} - \text{Expenses}$$
$$-\text{£600} \qquad\qquad - \quad \text{£600}$$

Thus the total charge in the income statement for loan interest is what we would expect for a loan of £10,000 at an annual interest rate of 12%, i.e. £1,200. The balance sheet will show £600 as an accrued expense.

3. Debtors
To ensure that the income statement reflects the full amount of sales for the year it is necessary, as we explained in relation to the treatment of creditors, to make two entries in the accounting records, as follows:

(a)   Increase debtors (assets) and increase sales revenue by the full amount of goods sold during the year. Taking the figures from transaction (5) gives:

$$\text{Assets (debtors)} = \ldots + \text{Revenues} - \text{Expenses}$$
$$\text{£40,000} \qquad\qquad \text{£40,000}$$

(b)   Increase cash (assets) and reduce debtors (assets) by the amount paid by debtors. Taking the figures from transaction (6) gives:

$$\text{Assets}$$
$$\text{Debtors} \quad \text{Cash}$$
$$-\text{£35,000} + \text{£35,000}$$

Thus the amount appearing in Mr Anfield's balance sheet at 31 December 19X0 for debtors will be £40,000−£35,000=£5,000.

4. Prepayments
The requirements of the matching concept apply equally to prepayments as to accrued expenses. In this case it is necessary to exclude from the income statement any expenses which have been paid in advance of the period to which they relate. Thus the following entries would be made for the rental expense (transaction (7)):

Assets   = ... + Revenues – Expenses
–£7,500 (Cash)   – £7,500 (Rent)
+£1,500 (Prepayment)   + £1,500 (Rent)

The cash paid reduces assets by £7,500 and increases expenses by the same amount, but because £1,500 of the payment relates to the following period (i.e. the yearly charge is £6,000) a second entry is necessary to reduce the expense and to create a prepayment, which is treated for balance sheet purposes as a current asset.

Similar arguments hold for the payment of rates as per transaction (8). The entries are as follows:

Assets   = ... + Revenues – Expenses
–£1,250 (Cash)   – £1,250 (Rates)
+£ 250 (Prepayment)   + £ 250 (Rates)

8.3   Accruals: Some Further Considerations

We now pursue further the question of accruals, and consider what happens in the next accounting period to the closing balances for creditors, accrued expenses, debtors and prepayments. Together with all the other balances on the bottom line of the accounting equation (arising from the other transactions undertaken by the organisation) they form the basis for the balance sheet at the end of the current period. *Together with the other balances, they also provide the first line of the accounting equation entries for the next accounting period.* We illustrate this general procedure later in this chapter. As far as accruals are concerned, their subsequent impact is as follows. In the next period, the amount of the cash paid to suppliers will not relate wholly to purchases made in that period, i.e. some of the cash paid will be used to reduce, or eliminate, the amount owing to suppliers (the opening creditor) at the beginning of the period. Similar considerations apply to accrued expenses, debtors and prepayments. The impact of one period's closing accruals on the costs and revenues of the next period is perhaps most clearly explained by considering the general relationships between costs and revenues, on the one hand, and cash payments and receipts on the other. A study of these relationships also serves to clarify further the nature of the accrued costs and revenues which are matched in conventional accounting income statements.

The relationship between the cost of raw materials acquired (purchases) and cash payments to suppliers is:

Purchases = Cash paid to suppliers + Closing creditors
           – Opening creditors

In Mr Anfield's case, purchases for 19X0 are:

Purchases $= 8,000 + 2,200 - 0 = £11,000$

The same type of relationship holds with accrued expenses. Hence the charge for an expense in an accounting period is:

$$\frac{\text{Expense}}{\text{charge}} = \frac{\text{Cash paid for}}{\text{expense item}} + \frac{\text{Closing accrued}}{\text{expense}} - \frac{\text{Opening accrued}}{\text{expense}}$$

In other words, the charge against income for a period is the cash payment during the period plus amounts incurred but not yet paid at the end of the period, minus amounts paid during the period that were owing at the start of the periods (i.e. that relate to the previous period). For example, Mr Anfield's lighting and heating expense for 19X0 is:

Lighting and heating expense $= 2,000 + 300 - 0 = £2,300$

Suppose that, in 19X1, Mr Anfield pays lighting and heating costs of £2,700, and an additional amount of £100 relating to the year to 31 December 19X1 is due but unpaid at the end of the year. It is clear that £300 of the cash payment relates to the amount outstanding from the previous year and that £2,400 of the cash payment relates to the lighting and heating expense incurred in 19X1. Thus Mr Anfield's lighting and heating expense for 19X1 is:

$$\frac{\text{Lighting and}}{\text{heating expense}} = \frac{\text{Cash}}{\text{paid}} + \frac{\text{Closing accrued}}{\text{expense}} - \frac{\text{Opening accrued}}{\text{expense}}$$

$$£2,500 \quad = £2,700 + \quad £100 \quad - \quad £300$$

Similar considerations apply to debtors and prepayments. Thus the sales revenue for a period is:

Sales revenue $=$ Cash received $+$ Closing debtors $-$ Opening debtors

For Mr Anfield, sales revenue for his first year of business is:

Sales revenue $= 35,000 + 5,000 - 0 = £40,000$

Finally, the expense charge for an item subject to prepayments is:

$$\frac{\text{Expense}}{\text{charge}} = \frac{\text{Cash paid for}}{\text{expense item}} + \frac{\text{Opening}}{\text{prepayment}} - \frac{\text{Closing}}{\text{prepayment}}$$

Note in this final case that the opening (prepayment) balance increases the charge for the year while the closing balance decreases it. So, for example, Mr Anfield's rent cost (expense charge) for 19X0 is:

$$\frac{\text{Expense}}{\text{charge}} = \frac{\text{Cash paid}}{\text{for expense}} + \frac{\text{Closing}}{\text{accrued}} - \frac{\text{Opening}}{\text{accrued}} + \frac{\text{Opening}}{\text{prepayment}} - \frac{\text{Closing}}{\text{prepayment}}$$

The above expressions are of great importance. As we have noted, they describe the relationship between cash receipts and payments and the amounts appearing in income statements as revenues and expenses.

8.4   Double-entry Book-keeping—A Simple Example

Up to now we have used the expanded accounting equation to record accounting transactions and to reflect their dual nature. We believe that this is the clearest way of demonstrating the structure of transactions-based recording systems. In practice, this method of double-entry recording is rarely used. The problem with the accounting equation approach, as we have used it, is simply that it is too cumbersome as a means of maintaining all the accounting records of actual organisations. Our examples have been sim- plified—a real organisation may have many different assets, liabilities and expenses, necessitating, strictly, a very large number of columns in any accounting equation.

   We now turn our attention to the method of double-entry recording used almost universally; for convenience we refer to this method as 'conven- tional double-entry recording'. It is widely known as the 'T' Account approach, for reasons which will become evident as we progress. We also reconcile this method with the accounting equation approach. It should be stressed that identical principles underlie the two methods, and that both lead to the same figures in income statements and balance sheets.

Main differences between the conventional and accounting equation approaches

The differences between the conventional and accounting equation approaches are no more than differences in the method of recording the same information. They may be summarised as follows:

1.   Under the accounting equation approach each asset, liability, etc. has its own column. Under the conventional approach, the accounting equa- tion is replaced by a book (called a *ledger*) and each accounting equation column is replaced by a page in this ledger. Each page is called an *account*, so, for example, the ledger will include a Cash at bank account, a Machine account, a Stock account, a Capital account, a Long-term loan account, an Income account, and so on.
2.   Each column of the accounting equation may include both positive and negative amounts, as for example we showed in our treatment of debtors and prepayments in the last section. In a ledger account, 'positive' amounts are shown on one side of the page and 'negative' amounts on the other. At the end of a period, each side of the account is summed, and the difference between the two sides is the *balance* on the account.
3.   Under the conventional approach a list of the balances on each account is prepared at the end of each period. This is known as a *trial balance*. An illustrative trial balance is given in Table 8.2. Each balance is equivalent to the balance at the foot of an accounting equation column. The balances in the trial balance are listed vertically (compared with the horizontal presentation of the accounting equation) in two columns.

Table 8.2   Illustration of (simplified) trial balance

	£	£
Land and buildings	XX	
Plant and machinery	XX	
Stock	XX	
Debtors	XX	
Cash	XX	
Share capital } Ownership interest		XX
Retained profits }		XX
Creditors		XX
Sales		XX
Cost of goods sold	XX	
Expenses	XX	
	XX	XX

One column contains the balances on accounts where the sum of the entries on the left-hand side exceeds the sum of those on the right; the other column contains the balances on other accounts. The two columns should have equal totals, like the two sides of the accounting equation. The trial balance provides an arithmetic check that two aspects of each transaction have been recorded. It does not, however, indicate whether they have been entered in the correct accounts.

Reconciliation of the conventional and accounting equation approaches

We shall now show that, in spite of their different procedures, the conventional and accounting equation approaches are in fact based on identical principles and lead to identical measures of income and position. Recall the accounting equation which has formed the basis of our double-entry recording:

Assets = Liabilities + Ownership interest + Revenues − Expenses

Rearranging the equation gives:

Assets + Expenses = Liabilities + Ownership interest + Revenues

Entries on the left of the accounting equation relate to either assets or expenses, and those on the right to liabilities, ownership interest or revenues. *Balances* on the left of the accounting equation are either assets or expenses, and those on the right are liabilities, ownership interest or revenues.

Similar rules apply to the conventional method. For example, amounts that would be added to the left of the accounting equation or subtracted from the right (remembering that 'negative' entries are not made under the conventional method) are placed on the left-hand side of the account, and amounts that would be added to the right-hand side of the accounting equation (or subtracted from the left-hand side) are put on the right-hand side of the account.

The conventional method avoids the terms left- and right-hand side in favour of the terms *'debit'* and *'credit'*, often abbreviated to *Dr* and *Cr*. As we noted earlier, a debit entry is one made on the left of an account, and a credit entry is made on the right. These are the *only* meanings which accounting attaches to the terms 'debit' and 'credit'.

Accounting entries should therefore be made as follows:

Entries for	Left-hand side Debit (Dr)	Right-hand side Credit (Cr)
Assets	Increase	Decrease
Expenses	Increase	Decrease
Liabilities	Decrease	Increase
Ownership interest	Decrease	Increase
Revenues	Decrease	Increase

As far as *balances* on accounts at the end of a period are concerned, the following rules hold:

1. If the sum of the entries on the left-hand side of the account is greater than the sum of the entries on the right, the difference is a *debit balance*, and is either an asset or an expense.
2. If the sum of the entries on the right-hand side is greater than the sum of the entries on the left, the difference is a *credit balance*, and is represented by a liability, ownership interest or revenue.

In the remainder of this chapter we shall work through the recording of a short series of transactions using both the accounting equation and conventional approaches. Readers wishing to practice the conventional approach further may use it to rework the accounting illustrations we have given in previous chapters. We provide a more detailed book-keeping example in Appendix B on pages 222–247.

Illustration

Mr Stamford owns and manages a retail business. His balance sheet on 1 January 19X0 is given in Table 8.3. During the year to 31 December 19X0 he undertakes the following transactions:

1. Obtains an additional long-term loan of £4,000 at 10% p.a. interest.
2. Purchases on credit 3,200 units of stock at £20 per unit.
3. Sells on credit 3,000 units of stock at £30 per unit.
4. Receives £85,000 from debtors.
5. Pays £56,000 to creditors.

Table 8.3   Mr Stamford—Balance sheet on 1 January 19X0

	£	£	£
Fixed assets at cost		27,000	
less: Accumulated depreciation		10,000	17,000
Current assets			
Stock (500 units at £16 per unit)	8,000		
Debtors	6,000		
Cash at bank	2,000	16,000	
less: *Current liabilities*			
Creditors	5,000		
Accrued expenses	1,000	6,000	
Net current assets			10,000
Net assets			£27,000
Represented by:			
Ownership interest			16,000
Long-term loan at 10% p.a.			11,000
Long-term funds employed			£27,000

6. Pays other expenses (excluding depreciation and loan interest) of £9,000, including accrued expenses owing on 1 January 19X0.
7. Accrued expenses at the end of the year amount to £2,000.
8. Charges depreciation of £5,000 on fixed assets.
9. Pays one year's interest on the long-term loans, amounting to £1,500.
10. Withdraws £8,000 from the business bank account for his personal use.

Accounting equation approach

Mr Stamford's accounting equation entries and balances are shown in Table 8.4. The treatment of transactions undertaken during the year has been dealt with fully in previous chapters and we do not need to discuss it further here. The first row of figures in the accounting equation deserves some comment, however. The figures are taken from the balance sheet in Table 8.3 and represent the bottom line of Mr Stamford's accounting equation for the last year. Similarly, the last line of the accounting equation in Table 8.4 forms the basis of the balance sheet at the end of the current year, and will form the first row of next year's accounting equation.

Conventional accounting approach

Use of 'T' accounts.   The first stage in the conventional approach is to enter each of the transactions in individual accounts. To illustrate the entries we use·'T' accounts, so called because of their design, each one of which

Table 8.4 Mr Stamford—Accounting equation entries

	Fixed assets £	+ Stock £	+ Debtors £	+ Cash at bank £	= Ownership interest £	+ Loans £	+ Creditors £	+ Accrued expenses £	+ Revenues £	− Expenses £
Balance at 1 January 19X0	27,000 (10,000)	8,000	6,000	2,000	16,000	11,000	5,000	1,000		
Transactions during the year:										
(1)				4,000		4,000				
(2)		64,000					64,000			
(3)		(58,000)*	90,000						90,000 Sales	(58,000) Cost of goods sold
(4)			(85,000)	85,000						
(5)				(56,000)			(56,000)			
(6)				(9,000)				(1,000)		(8,000) Expenses
(7)								2,000		(2,000) Expenses
(8)	(5,000)									(5,000) Depreciation
(9)				(1,500)						(1,500) Interest
(10)				(8,000)	(8,000)					
					8,000				90,000	(74,500)
Transfer of net income to ownership interest					15,500					(15,500)
	12,000 +	14,000 +	11,000 +	16,500 =	23,500 +	15,000 +	13,000 +	2,000 +	90,000 −	90,000

*(500×£16)+(2,500×£20)=£58,000 using the assumption that the materials bought first are used first.

represents a page or account in the organisation's books of accounts. Each 'T' account is equivalent to an accounting equation column, and the balance on the account at the end of the period is the same as for the equivalent accounting equation column. There is, however, an expansion beyond the accounting equation approach as we have used it so far. Instead of simply having two columns for revenues and expenses, a separate account is kept for *each* item of revenue and expense. The balances on these accounts are transferred to the income statement, usually described in the books as the 'profit and loss account', at the end of the period. The 'T' accounts for Mr Stamford are shown in Table 8.5. Note that the positive and negative items which were entered in the same accounting equation column are placed on opposite sides of the 'T' accounts. Transactions are referred to by their numbers, and the rules outlined earlier in this chapter are followed to determine on which side of the 'T' account a particular item is entered. We have used abbreviations in our examples ('Bal.' for Balance, 'c/d' for carried down, and so on) whereas in the actual books of account, each account would contain fuller descriptions. For example, the creditors account might appear as follows:

Creditors

		£			£
31 December 19X0	Cash paid	56,000	1 January 19X0	Balance brought down	5,000
31 December 19X0	Balance carried down	13,000	31 December 19X0	Purchases	64,000
		£69,000			£69,000
			1 January 19X1	Balance brought down	13,000

The amount described as 'balance carried down' at the end of a period is a balancing figure. It is entered again (as 'balance brought down') on the opposite side of the account. This treatment is simply a matter of style, used conventionally to determine and record the balance on each account at the end of a period. Note that the balance on each account corresponds to the equivalent figure in the accounting equation in Table 8.4 before net income is transferred to ownership interest.

One further point, illustrated by the entries appearing on the creditors' account, deserves mention. It is unlikely that the amounts for cash paid and for purchases will represent single transactions. It is more likely that cash will have been paid to a number of different creditors at various times during the year for purchases made at different times. Hence the figures for cash paid and purchases in the creditors' account represent the *total* payments and purchases during the year. If Mr Stamford's transactions had been recorded periodically (e.g. monthly) throughout the year, the creditors' account would

Table 8.5   Mr Stamford—'T' accounts

Fixed assets (net)

Bal. 1 Jan.	17,000	(8)	5,000
		Bal. c/d	12,000
	17,000		17,000
Bal. 31 Dec.	12,000		

Stock

Bal. 1 Jan.	8,000	(3)	58,000
(2)	64,000	Bal. c/d	14,000
	72,000		72,000
Bal. 31 Dec.	14,000		

Debtors

Bal. 1 Jan.	6,000	(4)	85,000
(3)	90,000	Bal. c/d	11,000
	96,000		96,000
Bal. 31 Dec.	11,000		

Cash at bank

Bal. 1 Jan.	2,000	(5)	56,000
(1)	4,000	(6)	9,000
(4)	85,000	(9)	1,500
		(10)	8,000
		Bal. c/d	16,500
	91,000		91,000
Bal. 31 Dec.	16,500		

Ownership interest

(10)	8,000	Bal. 1 Jan.	16,000
Bal. c/d	8,000		
	16,000		16,000
Bal. 31 Dec.	8,000		

Creditors

(5)	56,000	Bal. 1 Jan.	5,000
Bal. c/d	13,000	(2)	64,000
	69,000		69,000
Bal. 31 Dec.	13,000		

Sales

		(3)	90,000

Expenses

(6)	8,000
(7)	2,000

Interest

(9)	1,500

Long-term loans

Bal. c/d	15,000	Bal. 1 Jan.	11,000
		(1)	4,000
	15,000		15,000
		Bal. 31 Dec.	15,000

Accrued expenses

(6)	1,000	Bal. 1 Jan.	1,000
Bal. c/d	2,000	(7)	2,000
	3,000		3,000
		Bal. 31 Dec.	2,000

Cost of goods sold

(3)	58,000

Depreciation expense

(8)	5,000

include twelve entries each for 'cash paid' and for 'purchases'. The balance on the account will still be £13,000 of course. Similar considerations apply to the other accounts.

Preparation of trial balance. The next stage in the conventional approach is to check the arithmetical accuracy of the entries. This procedure is equivalent to checking that the two sides of the bottom line of the accounting equation have equal totals. The check is made by preparing a trial balance, which is a listing of the balances on individual accounts, with debit (Dr) balances in the left column and credit (Cr) balances in the right. The sums of the debit and credit balances should be equal. If the totals do not agree, the trial balance will not balance, and the causes of the difference must be traced. Mr Stamford's trial balance is shown in Table 8.6. The balances represented by the first eight items (i.e. down to, and including, accrued expenses) are placed directly in the balance sheet, because they represent assets, liabilities or ownership interest. The remaining five items comprise income statement entries. The balance of these entries, representing net income for the period, is transferred to ownership interest.

Preparation of the final accounts. The income statement, or profit and loss account, is another 'T' account, and forms part of the organisation's

Table 8.6   Mr Stamford—Trial balance at 31 December 19X0

	Dr £	Cr £
Fixed assets (cost £27,000 – accumulated depreciation £15,000)	12,000	
Stock	14,000	
Debtors	11,000	
Cash at bank	16,500	
Ownership interest		8,000
Long-term loans		15,000
Creditors		13,000
Accrued expenses		2,000
Sales		90,000
Cost of goods sold	58,000	
Expenses	10,000	
Depreciation expense	5,000	
Interest	1,500	
	£128,000	£128,000

Table 8.7   Mr Stamford—'Transferring' entries

Sales

Profit and loss account	90,000	(3)	90,000

Cost of goods sold

(3)	58,000	Profit and loss account	58,000

Expenses

(6)	10,000	Profit and loss account	10,000

Depreciation expense

(7)	5,000	Profit and loss account	5,000

Interest

(8)	1,500	Profit and loss account	1,500

Profit and loss account

Cost of goods sold	58,000	Sales	90,000
Expenses	10,000		
Depreciation expense	5,000		
Interest	1,500		
Balance c/d	15,500		
	90,000		90,000
		Balance b/d	15,500

double-entry records. The next stage in the preparation of final accounts using the conventional method is to transfer the balances on the various 'expense' and 'revenue' accounts to the profit and loss account. The last five 'T' accounts are affected, and the 'transferring' entries are shown in Table 8.7.

The closing balance on the profit and loss account of £15,500 represents net income for the year, and is transferred to ownership interest as follows:

Profit and loss account

Ownership interest	15,500	Balance b/d	15,500

Ownership interest

		Balance c/d	8,000
		Profit and	
Balance c/d	23,500	loss account	15,500
	23,500		23,500
		Balance b/d	23,500

The final accounts may now be prepared. The income statement (Table 8.8) is a summary of the figures contained in the profit and loss account in the organisation's books. The balance sheet (Table 8.9) is a summary of the balances remaining in the books after the profit and loss account balance has been transferred to ownership interest. Note that details of changes in ownership interest since the last balance sheet are shown, that the original cost of, and accumulated depreciation on, fixed assets are disclosed separately, and that assets and claims are categorised under the main headings of fixed assets, current assets, ownership interest, long-term loans and current liabilities. The income statement and balance sheet prepared from conventional records are identical to those that would have been obtained using the accounting equation information in Table 8.4.

Table 8.8   Mr Stamford—Income statement for the year ended 31 December 19X0

	£	£
Sales		90,000
less: Cost of goods sold		58,000
Gross profit		32,000
less: Expenses	10,000	
Depreciation	5,000	
Interest	1,500	
		16,500
Net income for the year		£15,500

Table 8.9   Mr Stamford—Balance sheet at 31 December 19X0

	£	£	£
Fixed assets at cost		27,000	
less: Accumulated depreciation		15,000	12,000
Current assets			
Stock	14,000		
Debtors	11,000		
Cash	16,500	41,500	
less: *Current liabilities*			
Creditors	13,000		
Accrued expenses	2,000	15,000	
Net current assets			26,500
Net assets			£38,500
Represented by:			
Ownership interest			
Balance at 1 January		16,000	
add: Net income for the year		15,500	
		31,500	
less: Drawings		8,000	23,500
Long-term loans at 10% p.a.			15,000
Long-term funds			£38,500

Discussion Topics

1 Distinguish between creditors and accrued expenses. What items would you expect to see classified under these two headings in the balance sheet?

2 Distinguish between debtors and prepayments. What items would you expect to see classified under these headings in the balance sheet?

3 Describe the main features of, and differences between, the accounting equation and the 'T' account approaches to recording transactions. Why is the latter more popular in practice?

4 Explain the purpose and usefulness of the trial balance.

5 Explain via equations the relationships which exist between cash payments and expense charges appearing in the income statement.

6 What items would you expect to see appearing on the debit side of the trial balance? On the credit side? What determines the nature of these balances?

7 Explain (in terms of 'debit' and 'credit' entries) how the following items would
   be recorded using conventional double-entry book-keeping:
   (a) Purchase of stock on credit.
   (b) Purchase of productive machinery for cash.
   (c) Receipts from customers in respect of credit sales.
   (d) Repayment of a loan.
   (e) Payment in respect of research and development expenditure.
   (f) Sale of goods on credit.
   (g) Payments to suppliers in respect of credit purchases.
   (h) Payment of wages to clerical assistants.
   (i) Payment of wages to labour involved in production.
   (j) Amounts received in respect of ordinary shares issued at a premium.
   (k) Payment of loan interest.
   (l) Provision of an annual depreciation charge on shop fittings and fixtures.
   (m) Payment of an electricity bill.
   (n) Withdrawal of cash from a business by the owner.
   (o) Payment of cash into a business by the owner.

Further Reading

Hendriksen, E.S., *Accounting Theory,* Irwin 1970, Chapters 4–6.

Mace, J.R., 'Accounting as a basis for taxation', in Carsberg, B. and Hope, A: (eds),
   Current Issues in Accounting, Philip Allan, 1984.

Nobes, C., *Introduction to Financial Accounting,* George Allen and Unwin, 1983.

Exercises

8.1 The following information relates to various transactions of Yamadori Ltd for
   the year ended 31 December 19X8.

   1. *Lighting and heating*
   Amount owing for electricity at 1 January, £750; payments for electricity
   during the year, £3,700; payments for gas during the year, £4,900; amount
   owing for electricity at 31 December, £920; amount owing for gas at 31
   December, £630.
   2. *Rent and rates*
   Rent owing at 1 January, £1,000; rates paid in advance at 1 January, £1,700;
   payments for rent during the year, £11,000; payments for rates during the
   year, £7,200; rent owing at 31 December, £2,000; rates paid in advance at 31
   December, £1,800.
   3. *Trade creditors*
   Amount owing to creditors at 1 January, £28,600; purchases during the year,
   £186,200; cash paid during the year, £171,900; discounts received during the
   year, £7,400.
   4. *Trade debtors*
   Amount owing by debtors at 1 January, £39,100; sales during the year,
   £302,800; cash received during the year, £288,700; discounts allowed during
   the year, £14,500; bad debts written off during the year, £3,500; goods
   returned by customers during the year, £1,800.

● Prepare the ledger accounts ('T' accounts) of Yamadori Ltd for the year ended 31 December 19X8 in respect of:
(1) Lighting and heating
(2) Rent and rates
(3) Trade creditors
(4) Trade debtors.
Show the balances brought down at 1 January 19X9.

8.2 On 1 July 19X1, Count Almaviva paid £2,000 into his business as capital. The following transactions then took place:

3 July	Purchased motor van for £800
6 July	Purchased goods on credit from Cherubino, £700
8 July	Paid rent, £40
14 July	Purchased goods on credit from Antonio, £300
16 July	Sold goods for cash, £200
18 July	Sold goods on credit to Marcellina, £400
21 July	Paid for petrol and oil, £20
23 July	Sold goods on credit to Barbarina, £600
25 July	Paid Cherubino £680 in full settlement
30 July	Received £350 from Marcellina but was informed that it would not be possible to collect any more of the debt
31 July	Paid salaries, £100
	Goods, invoice price £80, were returned by Barbarina
	Provided for depreciation on the motor van, £20.

● Write up the necessary entries in the ledger accounts of Count Almaviva and prepare a trial balance at 31 July 19X1.

8.3 Miss Brunnhilde runs a management consultancy business. Her trial balance at 30 April 19X7 is as follows:

	Dr £	Cr £
Bank overdraft		16,100
Debtors	17,400	
Fees earned		118,900
Freehold property at cost	80,000	
Interest paid	4,500	
Long term loan		50,000
Office expenses paid	16,200	
Ownership interest at 1 May 19X6		22,800
Salaries paid	73,600	
Withdrawals by Miss Brunnhilde during the year	16,100	
	£207,800	£207,800

The following additional information is available:
(a) Miss Brunnhilde owes a further £500 interest at 30 April 19X7.
(b) Office expenses include a payament for rates of £2,400 covering the period from 1 April 19X7 to 30 September 19X7.
(c) Office expenses amounting to £1,500 have been incurred but not entered in the books at 30 April 19X7.

● Prepare Miss Brunnhilde's income statement for the year ended 30 April 19X7 and her balance sheet as at that date.

Part 3

Asset Valuation and Long-term Financing

Chapter 9

Fixed and Intangible Assets

In this and the following chapter we consider the problems involved in defining and measuring assets (for inclusion in the balance sheet) and in determining the costs of using assets (for inclusion in the income statement). We begin, however, by reiterating the distinction between expenses and assets (first outlined in Chapter 7) since much of this chapter depends on an understanding of this distinction. We then consider the accounting treatment of *fixed* assets and the methods available for calculating that part of their cost which should be charged to each period's income statement. Finally we examine some of the problems inherent in the definition and measurement of *intangible* assets.

9.1 Distinction Between Expenses and Assets—A Review

We have seen in previous chapters how historical cost accounting involves the preparation of an income statement and a balance sheet, and we have explained that the organisation's net income is measured by matching the revenues earned for the period with the costs incurred in earning them. The balance sheet includes costs incurred which have not, at the balance sheet date, been matched with revenues. This procedure gives rise to the problem of deciding which items of expenditure should be matched against revenue in the income statement (expenses) and which should be shown in the balance sheet (assets). Let us now remind ourselves of the principles.

Suppose that an organisation purchases an item for cash or on credit (i.e. it incurs an item of expenditure). The item may be tangible, for example raw materials, oil, coal, stationery, machinery or property, or it may be a service, for example a person's labour, the use of a telephone, the expertise of a consultant, the use of accommodation or the hire of equipment. Whatever the nature of the purchase, one aspect of the transaction will be recorded by reducing the enterprise's cash balance (if purchase is by cash) or by increasing liabilities (if purchase is on credit). Because of the dual nature of all transactions, the second aspect will be either to increase assets by the amount of the transaction *or* to increase expenses (and hence reduce net income). The question is how to decide which items of expenditure are assets and which are expenses. The decision is of fundamental importance because it affects both the reported net income and the reported financial position of an organisation, and thus the decisions of those who use its accounting reports, i.e. the decisions of the participant groups first discussed in Chapter 3.

Within the conventional transactions-based approach, the following guidelines indicate a general answer to the question:

- If the *full* benefits from the expenditure arise *during* the accounting period in which the expenditure is incurred, *the expenditure should be treated as an expense.*
- If *some* benefits from the expenditure arise *after* the accounting period in which the expenditure is incurred, *that proportion of the expenditure relating to those benefits should be treated as an asset.*

In the latter case, where the expenditure is treated as an asset, an appropriate part of the cost of the asset will be transferred to expense during each period in which benefits arise. Thus, under the historical cost approach, *the amount of assets in the balance sheet is represented by costs which have not yet been matched against revenues.* Most expenditures are matched against revenues eventually; the problem of the accruals-based approach is one of allocating the costs of assets between the accounting periods that benefit from their use. Different patterns of allocation lead to different patterns of net income through time, and it may be that different information will be conveyed to participants by one pattern of income than by another.

9.2   Fixed Assets and Depreciation

Under historical cost accounting, the cost of a fixed asset is charged to the income statement over a number of accounting periods, generally equal to the number of years of the asset's productive life. Thus the cost of plant and machinery will be charged over fewer years than will the cost of buildings. We can now look in greater detail at the calculation of the proportion of an asset's cost (the periodic depreciation charge), and the consequent calculation of the written-down cost (or 'book value') of the asset for inclusion in the balance sheet. In other words, the depreciation charge and the asset's book value are simply two sides of the same coin—the charge determines the book value. It should be stressed from the outset that the terms 'depreciation' and 'book value' as conventionally used by accountants in preparing income statements and balance sheets have very specific meanings. These meanings may not accord with those used by non-accountants. A non-accountant asked to define depreciation might respond with a definition that referred in some way to *diminution of value.* The same person, if asked to provide a definition of value, might attempt to relate it to such concepts as 'worth', 'utility', or desirability'. Regrettably, such definitions do not coincide with those implied by the historical cost accounting treatment of depreciation. As we have seen, the purpose of the accountant's depreciation charge is one of cost allocation; depreciation is that part of the cost of an asset which has been or is being written off to the income statement, and the balance sheet amount is that part of the original cost of an asset that has not yet been charged against revenues. In neither case does the balance sheet asset amount necessarily bear any resemblance to such notions of 'current value' as current replacement cost or selling price, except by accident.

Other meanings of depreciation have been suggested. For example, depreciation is often referred to as a source of funds for the replacement of assets. Depreciation, however, does not generate any funds *per se*. It is *cash inflow,* in the form of sales revenue, which produces funds for the replacement of assets. A more charitable interpretation of the 'funds generation' view of depreciation might be that, by charging depreciation to the income statement, and thereby reducing income, the possible distribution of funds, equal to the depreciation charge, is prevented. (The relationship between depreciation and cash flow is explored further in Chapter 18, Flow of Funds Statement.)

The accounting entries necessary to record fixed assets and associated depreciation are straightforward, and are illustrated later in this chapter. Broadly speaking, when an organisation buys a fixed asset, the amount of its total assets is increased by the acquisition cost and the amount of cash held is reduced by the same amount. If the asset purchase is on credit, the other side of the entry is to increase liabilities rather than to reduce cash. Subsequently in each future accounting period, the amount to be written off the cost of the asset (the depreciation charge) is calculated. This amount is then deducted from the previous written down value of the asset (appearing in the last balance sheet) and is added to expenses (i.e. deducted from current year revenues). Thus the balance sheet will, at any time, show both the cost of the asset and the accumulated depreciation to date. This figure for accumulated depreciation represents the total of all the charges passed through the income statement. All fixed assets are treated in this way, with one exception. The exception lies in the treatment of land. Land is not expected to be used up in production in the same way as other fixed assets and thus, under historical cost accounting, is normally recorded as an asset at cost, the amount of which is unchanged from period to period.

9.3 Methods of Depreciation

A variety of methods may be used to calculate periodic depreciation charges. Under historical cost accounting, all are essentially methods of allocating the original cost of an asset, less its expected eventual residual value, between the accounting periods in which the asset is expected to be used. For example, the UK professional accountancy bodies commenting on depreciation, say that:[1]

> Provision for depreciation of fixed assets having a finite useful life should be made by allocating the cost... less estimated residual values of the assets as fairly as possible to the periods expected to benefit from their use.

Most assets depreciate as a result of both *use* and the *passage of time. Ceteris paribus,* a machine which has never been used would still have a finite life—it may be the victim of technological advances, or it may simply deteriorate physically over time. Of those assets which are used, it is normally the case that the more intensively an asset is worked, the shorter is its productive life. Some methods of depreciation emphasise the passage of time in allocating the cost of an asset over its useful life; other methods emphasise the pattern of use.

In this section we describe the three most frequently used depreciation methods: the *straight line* method; the *reducing balance* (or declining balance or fixed percentage of declining balance) method; and the *sum-of-the-years-digits* method. The first of these three is by far the most widely used in practice. For example, the *Survey of Published Accounts*[2] which reports the accounting practices of 300 large UK companies shows that, for the year ended 30 June 1982, 252 of these companies chose the straight line method of depreciation. The popularity of the straight line method rests largely on its simplicity of operation and its understandability.

Consider the case of an organisation that purchases an asset, details of which are given in Table 9.1. The life expectation is based normally on the expected economic life of the asset rather than on its physical life, i.e. the expected life is the number of years the organisation expects to retain and use the asset. Such an estimate may be provided by the organisation's engineers. The prediction of the expected economic life of the asset is of great practical importance. This figure, which represents the basis of the allocation of cost, determines both the periodic charge to the income statement and also the balance sheet book value. For example, if the depreciation charge is very high relative to the net income figure, as is the case in highly capital intensive organisations, the choice of asset life can greatly influence the organisation's net income. The expected scrap or resale value represents the organisation's best estimate of the amount it will receive for the asset at the end of its economic life. The difference between the cost of the asset and

---

[1]Statement of Standard Accounting Practice No. 12 *Accounting for Depreciation,* The Institute of Chartered Accountants in England and Wales, December 1977, paragraph 16.

[2]*Financial Reporting 1982–83: A Survey of UK Published Accounts,* The Institute of Chartered Accountants in England and Wales, 1983.

Table 9.1   Details of asset

Cost	$C=£15,000$
Expected life	$N=3$ years
Expected scrap (or resale) value at end of life	$S=£3,000$

its expected residual value represents the total amount to be depreciated over the asset's economic life. We should, however, note that the original cost and expected residual value, although both expressed in money terms, are qualitatively different because of the dates at which they arise; the former is an observed payment whereas the latter is an uncertain estimate. The accounting problem is how to spread the depreciable cost of £12,000 (£15,000–£3,000) between the three years of the asset's expected life.

The *straight line* method spreads the total depreciation cost evenly over the expected life of the asset. The income statement of each accounting period (assuming each is of equal length, say one year) is charged with the same depreciation amount, calculated from the following simple expression:

$$D=\frac{C-S}{N}$$

where D is the annual (or periodic) depreciation charge, and C, S and N are as defined in Table 9.1. Thus for the asset described in Table 9.1, the annual depreciation charge is:

$$D=\frac{15,000-3,000}{3}=£4,000$$

The *reducing balance* method charges as depreciation each period a constant percentage of the written down value (cost less accumulated depreciation) of the asset at the start of the period. The periodic depreciation *rate* may be calculated from the following expression:[3]

$$d=1-N\sqrt{\frac{S}{C}}$$

where d is the periodic rate of depreciation (expressed as a decimal of one)

---

[3]The depreciation rate, d, is calculated so as to reduce the original cost of the asset to its residual value over its expected life, i.e. a value for d must be found to satisfy the equation:

$C(1-d)^N=S$

Rearranging gives:

$(1-d)^N=S/C$

$(1-d)=\sqrt[N]{(S/C)}$

$d=1-\sqrt[N]{(S/C)}$

and N, S and C are as defined previously. For the asset described in Table 9.1, the annual depreciation rate is:

$$d = 1 - 3\sqrt{\frac{3,000}{15,000}} = 0.415 \text{ or } 41.5\%$$

To calculate the depreciation *charge* for each year, the depreciation *rate* must be applied to the reducing book value of the asset as follows:

		£
Time 0	Cost	15,000
Time 1	First year's depreciation	
	(41.5% × 15,000)	6,225
Time 1	Written down value	8,775
Time 2	Second year's depreciation	
	(41.5% × 8,775)	3,640
Time 2	Written down value	5,135
Time 3	Third year's depreciation	
	(41.5% × 5,135)	2,135
Time 3	Written down value	3,000

The depreciation charges are £6,225 for the first year of the asset's life, £3,640 for the second, and £2,135 for the third.

Although the *sum-of-the-years-digits* (SYD) method is rarely found in the UK, it is used in the United States and elsewhere. It often gives results similar to those obtained from the reducing balance method and is easier to calculate. The depreciation charge for a particular year is found by multiplying the net cost of the asset (original cost minus expected residual value) by a fraction. The numerator of the fraction is the number of years of the asset's life remaining at the beginning of the year under consideration. The denominator, which is the same each year, is the sum of an arithmetic progression, whose first term is the life of the asset and whose final term is one. Each intermediate term is equal to the previous term minus one. This rather cumbersome description masks an essentially simple process, which can be illustrated by the example of the asset in Table 9.1. Annual depreciation charges under the SYD method are as follows:

	Depreciation charge £
Year 1 $\dfrac{3}{(3+2+1)} \times (15,000 - 3,000) =$	6,000

Year 2 $\dfrac{2}{(3+2+1)} \times (15,000-3,000)=$ 4,000

Year 3 $\dfrac{1}{(3+2+1)} \times (15,000-3,000)=$ 2,000

The numbers thrown up by the above examples illustrate some interesting characteristics of conventional depreciation calculations. The first concerns the objectivity and verifiability of the figures. These two criteria are frequently used in defence of historical cost accounting methods and we discussed their merits in Chapter 4. Yet in the above examples two of the three basic numbers used in calculating depreciation (expected life and expected residual value) are estimates and, in consequence, are not necessarily objective, nor can they be verified. We consider later in this section the adjustments that might be required if estimates of future life and residual value change during the asset's economic life.

The second interesting characteristic is that all three methods of depreciation provide the same total depreciation over the life of the asset and, consequently, if actual life and residual value are as estimted, all three have the effect of writing down the book value of the asset to its residual value by the end of its economic life. This is illustrated in Table 9.2 which shows the declining book value pattern of the asset under each depreciation method. The figures in Table 9.2 are expressed graphically in Figure 9.1.

Table 9.2 and Figure 9.1 also illustrate a third characteristic of the depreciation methods. Each method produces a different *pattern* of book value for the asset over its life and a different pattern of annual depreciation charges, even though the *total* depreciation charge is the same under each method. These different patterns of depreciation charges contribute to different annual figures for net income. If we assume that the organisation acquiring the asset in our example has net income before depreciation of £7,000 p.a. for each of the three years of the asset's life, we can calculate its income under each method, net of depreciation, for each year. The figures are shown in Table 9.3 and Figure 9.2. If income before depreciation is constant each year, the application of straight line depreciation results in a similarly constant stream of net income figures. Application of either of the other two methods results in a lower net income figure during the early years of the asset's life and increasing net income during the later years.

We noted earlier that the UK professional accountancy bodies recommend that the cost of fixed assets should be allocated "as fairly as possible to the periods expected to benefit from their life". This begs the question as to what is meant by "as fairly as possible", but it appears that the straight line method of depreciation would be a suitable method for those assets which are expected to depreciate primarily on a *time* basis, and/or which produce benefits *evenly* over their useful life (e.g. buildings). The reducing balance and SYD methods might allocate more fairly the cost of assets which are expected to produce greater benefits (are used more intensively) in the

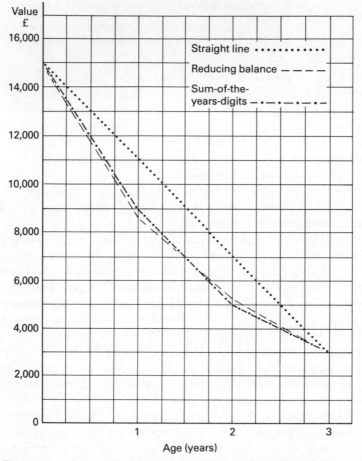

Figure 9.1   Asset value patterns using various depreciation methods.

earlier years of their life. Because these latter two methods charge a greater amount of depreciation in the earlier years of an asset's life, they are sometimes referred to as methods of 'accelerated depreciation'.

Which pattern of depreciation book value and net income is preferable depends on the criteria selected for choosing between accounting methods. However, we should note at this stage that the differences between the patterns of depreciation and net income observed when one asset is owned, may be reduced or even eliminated if an enterprise owns a large number of assets and replaces some each year. Differences between book value patterns may also be reduced, though by a lesser amount. Suppose that the firm in our example owns three assets similar to the one described in Table 9.1 and replaces one of the assets each year. At the start of the year it will own one new asset, one one-year-old asset and one two-year-old asset. The depreciation figures in Table 9.2 show that whichever method of depreciation is used (provided the same method is applied to all three assets) the total

Table 9.2   Asset 'book' value patterns using various depreciation methods

		Straight line £	Reducing balance £	Sum-of-the-years-digits £
Time 0	Cost	15,000	15,000	15,000
Time 1	Depreciation (Income statement)	4,000	6,225	6,000
Time 1	Balance sheet 'Book value'	11,000	8,775	9,000
Time 2	Depreciation (Income statement)	4,000	3,640	4,000
Time 2·	Balance sheet 'Book value'	7,000	5,135	5,000
Time 3	Depreciation (Income statement)	4,000	2,135	2,000
Time 3	Balance sheet 'Book value'	3,000	3,000	3,000
Total depreciation		12,000	12,000	12,000

depreciation charge each year will be £12,000. For example, the annual reducing balance charge of £12,000 will be made up as follows:

	£
Asset 1 (1 year old)	6,225
Asset 2 (2 years old)	3,640
Asset 3 (3 years old)	2,135
	£12,000

This is because the total depreciation charge for one asset over its life is the same whichever depreciation method is used. The total written-down values of the three assets at the end of the year will be as follows (based on the figures in Table 9.2):

Method of depreciation	Straight line £	Reducing balance £	Sum of the years digits £
Asset 1 (1 year old)	11,000	8,775	9,000
Asset 2 (2 years old)	7,000	5,135	5,000
Asset 3 (3 years old) —prior to resale	3,000	3,000	3,000
Total written-down value	£21,000	£16,910	£17,000

The preceding analysis is directed primarily at fundamental differences between different depreciation methods. Three further aspects of historical cost depreciation deserve mention.

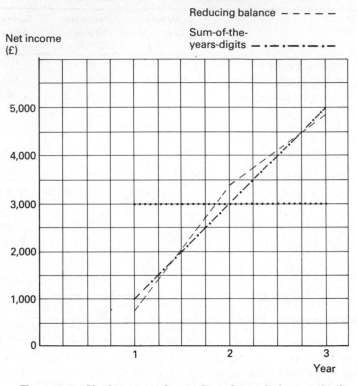

Figure 9.2   Net income using various depreciation methods.

1. Asset depreciation entirely through use

There exists a small group of assets that depreciate entirely as a result of use,
i.e. independently of their age. A good example of such an asset is a freehold
mine. For such an asset, a depreciation method that allocates the cost of the
asset between the periods of its expected life according to one of the
time-related procedures discussed so far may be inappropriate, particularly
if, as may be quite likely, the quantities mined vary greatly from year to year.
It may be better to relate the depreciation charge to the number of units of
output produced by the asset during an accounting period. For example,
suppose that an organisation purchases for £550,000 a mine which is
expected to produce a total of 100,000 tons of metal and to have a residual
value after so doing of £50,000. A *unit-based* depreciation charge can be
calculated from the formula:

$$D_U = \frac{C - S}{N_U}$$

Table 9.3   Net income using various depreciation methods

	Straight line £	£	Reducing balance £	£	Sum-of-the-years-digits £	£
Year 1 Income before depreciation	7,000		7,000		7,000	
less: Depreciation	4,000		6,225		6,000	
Net income		3,000		775		1,000
Year 2 Income before depreciation	7,000		7,000		7,000	
less: Depreciation	4,000		3,640		4,000	
Net income		3,000		3,360		3,000
Year 3 Income before depreciation	7,000		7,000		7,000	
less: Depreciation	4,000		2,135		2,000	
Net income		3,000		4,865		5,000
Total net income years 1–3		£9,000		£9,000		£9,000

where D_U is the depreciation charge per unit of output, N_U is the total number of units of output expected from the asset, and C and S are as defined previously. The figures above give a depreciation charge *per ton* of metal mined (D_U) as follows:

$$D_U = \frac{550,000 - 50,000}{100,000} = £5$$

The depreciation charge for a particular period will be £5 multiplied by the number of units of output produced during the period.

2.   Repair and maintenance costs

A second important and allied aspect of depreciation concerns the treatment of repair and maintenance costs. If these costs are expected to arise evenly throughout an asset's life it may be sufficient to charge them as expenses in the years in which they are incurred. Typically, however, repair costs for many assets tend to increase as the asset gets older. In addition, major overhauls or maintenance may be required at intervals less frequent than once a year. If in such circumstances these costs are written off as incurred, the total cost of using an asset will be much higher in some years than in others, resulting in a volatile pattern of net income. Such a result may violate the matching principle if the revenue generating potential of the asset is constant from year to year. Suppose for example, that the asset described previously in Table 9.1 requires a major overhaul, costing £3,000, at the end of the second year of its life. Assuming that straight line depreciation is used, the total cost of using the asset during each year of its life will be as follows:

	Year 1 £	Year 2 £	Year 3 £
Depreciation	4,000	4,000	4,000
Cost of overhaul	–	3,000	–
Total cost	4,000	7,000	4,000

The 'hump' in the second year may be eliminated by spreading the cost of the overhaul over the asset's life, e.g. at the rate of £1,000 each year, giving a total cost per annum of £5,000. Under this method, some part of the cost of major repairs is allocated to years prior to the expenditure being incurred. Consequently, the charges in the years prior to the expenditure are based on an estimate of the cost of the overhaul. The accounting entries required to record this treatment are illustrated in the next section.

3.   Reassessments of asset life

Finally we consider the adjustments that should be made if original estimates of asset life or residual value are revised. A major factor affecting the expected economic life of an asset is the possibility of obsolescence. An asset is made obsolete when alternative, more efficient assets become available and it is economically worthwhile for the owner of the asset to replace it with a newer model. This is particularly the case with high-technology assets such as computers. The original estimate of an asset's life should include a provision for obsolesence. By its nature, however, this provision may prove to be inaccurate. Similarly it is quite likely that the residual value of an asset, estimated when the asset is acquired, will turn out to be different from the original expectation. If the change in estimated life or residual value is substantial, it may be necessary to revise depreciation calculations to incorporate the new estimates, for example by increasing or decreasing the future annual depreciation charge or by a single adjustment to the written down book value of the asset. However, it is more common under historical cost accounting for adjustments arising from changed expectations to be dealt with when the asset is disposed of. Thus if, for example, in the case of the asset described in Table 9.1, the actual residual value is £4,000, rather than the estimated £3,000, a surplus or 'profit on sale' or £1,000 will be reported in the year in which the asset is sold. The accounting entries associated with this treatment are described below.

9.4   Accounting Entries for Depreciation

We now illustrate the accounting entries required to record fixed assets and depreciation, together with the treatment of irregular repair and mainte-

Table 9.4 Details of machine

Cost (paid in cash)	£15,000
Expected life	3 years
Actual life	3 years
Expected scrap value at end of life	£3,000
Actual scrap value at end of life (received in cash)	£4,000
Maintenance cost, paid in cash at the end of the second year of life	£3,000

nance costs and profits or losses on disposal of assets. Details of the relevant asset, a machine, are given in Table 9.4. The purchaser of the machine decides to adopt the straight line method of depreciation and to spread the maintenance cost over the life of the asset. Thus the annual depreciation and maintenance charge is as follows:

$$£$$

Depreciation $\dfrac{15,000-3,000}{3}$ 4,000

Maintenance $\dfrac{3,000}{3}$ 1,000

5,000

The accounting entries necessary to record the purchase, use and sale of the asset are shown in Table 9.5. The 'accounting equation' format used is the one described in earlier chapters.

For each year of the machine's life net income is reduced by £5,000, the charge for depreciation and maintenance. For presentation purposes, the two components of this charge are shown separately in the income statement. The double entry is completed each year by reducing the asset 'machine' by £4,000 (the annual depreciation charge) and by increasing the 'provision for maintenance' column by £1,000 (the allocated maintenance charge). The 'provision for maintenance' balance may be thought of as an expense incurred but not yet paid (an accrued expense) until the end of year 2 of the asset's life when the payment is made, and thereafter as a payment made for which the benefit has not yet been received (a prepayment). The proceeds from selling the machine are added to the bank balance. The double entry is completed by reducing the machine balance by the amount needed to decrease it to zero (i.e. by £3,000, the *expected* scrap value) and by increasing revenue by the difference between actual and expected sale proceeds (£1,000). Had actual sale proceeds been less than expected, the difference would have been entered as an expense.

Table 9.5   Accounting entries for recording fixed assets, depreciation and planned maintenance

	Assets		= Provision for maintenance	+ Revenue	− Expenses
	Cash £	Machine £	£	£	£
Transaction					
Time 0 Purchase of asset	(15,000)	15,000			
Time 1 Year 1 depreciation and maintenance		(4,000)	1,000		(5,000) Depreciation and maintenance
Time 1 Book value		11,000	1,000		
Time 2 Year 2 depreciation and maintenance		(4,000)	1,000		(5,000) Depreciation and maintenance
Time 2 Maintenance payment	(3,000)		(3,000)		
Time 2 Book value		7,000	(1,000)		
Time 3 Year 3 depreciation and maintenance		(4,000)	1,000		(5,000) Depreciation and maintenance
Time 3 Sale of asset	4,000	(3,000)		1,000 Profit on sale of asset	
		0	0		

As we noted earlier, fixed asset information in the balance sheet is normally presented to show separately the original cost of assets and the attendant accumulated depreciation. In order to facilitate this process, the two components of written-down value are usually recorded in separate columns. To transform the entries for accumulated depreciation from negative to positive figures, the column is switched from the left to the right side of the equation. Extracts of the relevant entries in our example would be as follows:

		$...+\dfrac{\text{Machine}}{\text{at cost}}+...=...+\dfrac{\text{Accumulated}}{\text{depreciation}}+...$	
		£	£
Time 0	Cost	15,000	
Time 1	Depreciation		4,000
Time 1	Balances	15,000	4,000
Time 2	Depreciation		4,000
Time 2	Balances	15,000	8,000
Time 3	Depreciation		4,000
Time 3	Balances	15,000	12,000
Time 3	Sale	(15,000)	(12,000)
		0	0

At each point in time, the difference between the totals in the two columns is equal to the net book value shown in Table 9.5.

9.5   Intangible Assets

The fixed assets discussed earlier in this chapter fall into a category known as *tangible assets*, i.e. assets that have physical substance and can be 'touched'. There is another category, known as *intangible assets*, which may be defined as expenditure incurred by an organisation, in return for which it receives nothing immediately tangible or physical, but which *may* result in the receipt of benefits beyond the accounting period in which the expenditure arises. In other words, apart from their lack of physical substance, intangible assets exhibit very similar characteristics to their tangible counterparts. We now consider briefly the accounting treatment of these intangible assets.

Types of Intangible Assets
There are three main types of intangible assets: research and development; goodwill; and patents, trademarks and copyrights.

Research and development.   Many organisations incur expenditure on research and development (R&D). Indeed, science and technology based companies (for example, those involved in the manufacture of computers and other electronic products, engineering companies, and firms dealing with chemical products) often spend considerable sums on R&D. For example, in the year to 31 December 1983, ICI plc spent £276 million on R&D, which was equivalent to 3% of its turnover and approximately 45% of its historical cost pre-tax income. R&D expenditure is usually categorised in a threefold way, as comprising pure research, applied research and development expenditure. Expenditure on pure research is undertaken to advance knowledge with no specific application in mind concerning the results of the research. Applied research involves expenditure to apply the results of pure research to broad areas of an organisation's activities. Development expenditure is undertaken to adapt the results of applied research to the improvement of specific processes and products. Although the distinctions between the three categories are often blurred in practice, they are nevertheless relevant because, as we explain shortly, different accounting treatments are sometimes adopted for the different categories. This is especially the case in the UK.

Goodwill

Goodwill may be regarded in broad terms as the difference between the total value of an organisation as a single entity, and the sum of the value of its individual net assets (i.e. assets less liabilities) excluding goodwill. It derives from factors such as reputation, expertise and the quality of relationships with customers, suppliers and others with whom the organisation transacts. It may be thought of as reflecting the *excess* value of future returns over and above those that would normally be expected from the particular collection of assets owned by the organisation. Companies such as Marks and Spencer, Coca Cola, Heinz, Sainsburys and Mercedes-Benz may expect to derive substantial benefits from the reputations they have built up over a number of years. However, in spite of its importance to many organisations goodwill is very difficult to measure. This is largely because the measurement of such attributes as reputation, expertise and prestige is very subjective and not easily quantifiable. For this reason, goodwill is usually recognised in conventional accounting as an asset only when it is purchased. This occurs most frequently when one organisation purchases or 'takes over' another at a price above the sum of the values of the assets of the acquired organisation. For example, if one company buys another company for £2 million, and the company being purchased owns net assets valued individually at a total of £1.5 million, goodwill on acquisition is taken as £500,000.

Patents, trademarks and copyrights

Expenditure on items such as patents, trademarks and copyrights allows an organisation the exclusive use of the process or material covered by the patent, trademark or copyright, usually for a predetermined number of years. So long as the process or material concerned is not superseded by another that is more efficient or otherwise worthwhile, it has some value to the organisation. Once this ceases to be the case, the patent, trademark or copyright has reached the end of its effective life, even if the legal protection it accords has not expired.

9.6   Accounting Treatment of Intangible Assets

The choice of appropriate accounting treatments for intangible assets within the conventional accounting framework produces a classic conflict between the concepts of accruals (or matching) and conservatism (or prudence). On the one hand, intangible assets represent expenditures, the benefits from which are expected to span a number of accounting periods. The matching concept suggests that the expenditures should be matched with the revenues towards which they contribute, implying a treatment similar to that of fixed assets, whereby an item of expenditure should be viewed initially as an asset, and shown as such in the balance sheet, and subsequently be written off to the income statement over the periods during which it produces benefits. Where intangible assets are concerned, amounts written off are normally referred to as *amortization* rather than depreciation. The alternative methods of amortization (depreciation) and their relative characteristics and merits are as described for fixed assets.

On the other hand, there is often a fundamental difference between intangible and tangible assets. With the possible exception of patents, trademarks and copyrights and certain items of R&D, intangible assets generally have no value if separated from the organisation owning them. For example, the goodwill attached to the name of Marks and Spencer could not easily be transferred to another company. This characteristic creates considerable uncertainty about the value of intangible assets relative to the value of tangible assets. For this reason, the concept of prudence suggests that they should be written-off at the earliest opportunity. Indeed they are frequently not treated as assets at all but rather as immediate expenses. For example, the current statement of UK professional accountancy bodies on the treatment of research and development expenditure requires that expenditure on pure and applied research should be written off in the year of expenditure and that the same treatment should be applied to development expenditure unless a stringent set of conditions is satisfied.[4]

Where intangible assets are to be written-off over a number of periods, two particular problems arise. The first problem is to identify the cost of the

---

[4]Statement of Standard Accounting Practice No. 13, *Accounting for Research and Development*, The Institute of Chartered Accountants in England and Wales, December 1977, paragraphs 20 and 21.

asset. If the asset is bought from a third party, for example the purchase of goodwill on the acquisition of another organisation or the purchase of patents, the identification of cost poses few problems. Many intangible assets are not acquired in this way, however. Rather they are created within the enterprise (as, for example, is the case with reputation and expertise), and it may be difficult or impossible to identify the particular costs contributing to their creation. This difficulty is so great that only rarely are internally created intangible assets carried forward in the balance sheet. The second problem is to estimate the time period over which intangible assets are to be amortized. Although this is also a problem with tangible assets, there exist more complications with intangible assets, where the length of time during which an asset will produce net benefits is particularly difficult to identify.

To summarise, expenditure on intangible assets may either be written-off in the period in which it is incurred or be dealt with in the same way as expenditure on fixed assets, i.e. placed initially in the balance sheet and amortized as an expense over its effective life, subject to any limitations imposed by legislation or by accounting standards.

9.7   Illustrations of the Accounting Treatment of Intangible Assets

We now provide an example of each main type of intangible asset and describe its accounting treatment.

Research and development

Pittodrie Ltd manufactures a range of chemical products. During year 1, it incurs the following expenditure on research and development:

Development of project Easter. (This has already proved successful. 10,000 units of the associated product were sold in year 1 and future sales are estimated at 30,000 units in year 2, 20,000 units in year 3, and no units thereafter)	£120,000
General research	£50,000
	£170,000

The expenditure of £120,000 incurred on the development of project Easter results in benefits (future sales) that can be identified. Provided that sales are expected to generate surpluses greater than the development costs, an appropriate accounting treatment could be to 'spread' the development expenditure over the life of the product in proportion to the number of product units sold each year. Hence the amount of £120,000 would in the first instance be treated as an asset. It would subsequently be transferred as a cost to the income statement (i.e. matched with revenues) as follows:

$$£$$

Year 1 $\left(\dfrac{10,000}{60,000} \times £120,000\right)$ 20,000

Year 2 $\left(\dfrac{30,000}{60,000} \times £120,000\right)$ 60,000

Year 3 $\left(\dfrac{20,000}{60,000} \times £120,000\right)$ 40,000

$$£120,000$$

The unallocated cost at the end of each year (£100,000 at the end of year 1 and £40,000 at the end of year 2) would be shown as an intangible asset in the balance sheet of Pittodrie Ltd. (Although such a treatment is currently possible in the UK, the vast majority of organisations write off all their R&D in the year of its incurrence.)

There is no specific project revenue against which the general research expenditure of £50,000 can be matched. Although it is presumably expected to result at some time in increased net revenues, there is considerable uncertainty attached to both their timing and their amount. In this situation, the concept of prudence would predominate, and the expenditure of £50,000 would be charged as an expense to the income statement in year 1.

Goodwill

Parkhead Ltd takes over the entire share capital of Boghead Ltd on 1 January. The net assets of Boghead Ltd, excluding goodwill, are valued at £3.8 million. The agreed takeover price, payable in cash on 1 January, is £4.5 million.

The implied value of the goodwill of Boghead Ltd at 1 January is £700,000 (the excess of the purchase price over the value of net assets). Initially it will be recorded in the books of Parkhead Ltd as an asset. The question then arises as to the period over which the goodwill should be written-off against income. As the goodwill is unlikely to have any resale value in isolation from the other assets acquired, the prudence concept suggests that it should be written-off as soon as possible. On the other hand, the factors of reputation, expertise and so on, which underlie goodwill, are likely to result in benefits for many years, and the matching concept suggests that the cost of goodwill should be spread over the number of accounting periods likely to benefit from its existence. The number of such periods may be very large—indeed it could be so large that no writing-off of goodwill may seem necessary in the foreseeable future. In practice, it is likely that a compromise between the prudence and matching concepts will result in the goodwill of £700,000 being amortized over a finite number of years. The precise period will probably be chosen arbitrarily, where no reasonable guess can be made of the 'life' of goodwill, and may vary between as little as 5 years and as much as 50 years. Recent legislation, as embodied in the 1981 Companies Act, states only that the period over which goodwill is to be written-off may not exceed the useful economic life of the goodwill in question.

Patents, trademarks and copyrights

Suppose that Goldstone Ltd manufactures novelties. It acquires for £150,000 a patent to produce a particular novelty good, the cappielow. When it is acquired by Goldstone Ltd, the patent has a further twelve years to run. Production of cappielows is expected to be profitable during the remaining life of the patent.

On acquisition, the cost of the patent will be treated as an asset. It will then be written-off (amortized) over its remaining life of twelve years. The method of amortization chosen may depend on the patterns of benefits expected from production of cappielows. If the benefits are expected to be similar from year to year, the straight line method will probably be used. Under this method, the annual amortization charge will be £12,500 (£150,000 ÷ 12) and the balance sheet value of the patent will be decreased by £12,500 each year (i.e. it will be £137,500 at the end of the first year). A different pattern of benefits may suggest the use of a different amortization method; for example, the expectation of declining benefits over time may lead to the use of the reducing balance method.

We conclude with a general comment on the question as to whether expenditure on intangible assets should be written off immediately or over a number of periods. Most professional accountancy bodies, in the UK and elsewhere, recommend that certain intangible assets, in particular research and development, should be written off immediately. This recommendation is generally based on the difficulty of identifying, and the uncertainty attaching to, future benefits arising from the possession of such assets. Nevertheless, it is presumably the case that organisations undertaking expenditure on intangible assets do so because they expect the expenditure to give rise to future benefits having a present value at least equal to the amount of the expenditure. The immediate amortization of the expenditure, particularly if the amount spent varies considerably over time, may result in wide fluctuations in reported performance from period to period and in the omission from balance sheets of assets having positive values. Such a treatment may be misleading to users of accounting reports who wish to make predictions of an enterprise's likely future performance.

Discussion Topics

1   Outline the main methods of calculating depreciation, and discuss their basic differences.

2   What does the term 'depreciation' mean when used by accountants? Explain other possible meanings of the term and discuss why these meanings may not be acceptable to accountants.

3   What do the terms 'use' and 'time' depreciation mean? Can you think of any assets which depreciate purely through time, or purely because of use?

4   What is the difference between depreciation and maintenance cost? What justification is there for including them together?

5   What are the principal types of intangible assets?

6   What distinguishes intangible assets from other fixed assets?

7   Why do you suppose that most professional accountancy bodies recommend that research and development be written-off immediately to the income statement? Why is goodwill not treated in the same way?

8   On 1 November 1967, AEI Ltd forecast that its profit for the year to 31 December 1967 would amount to £10 million. The company was taken over by GEC Ltd which later announced that AEI Ltd had incurred a loss of £4.5 million in 1967. Two firms of auditors (one of which had reviewed the original forecast) issued a joint statement which included the following sentence:

> Broadly speaking, of the difference of £14.5 million, we would attribute £5 million to adverse differences which are matters substantially of fact rather than of judgment, and the balance of £9.5 million to adjustments which remain substantially matters of judgment.

Discuss the matters of accounting judgment which might have produced a difference of £9.5 million in the profit figures.

Further Reading

Baxter, W.T. *Depreciation*, Sweet and Maxwell, 1971.

Bierman, H. and Dukes, R.E. 'Accounting for research and development costs', *Journal of Accountancy*, April 1975.

Gynther, R.S., 'Some "conceptualizing" on goodwill', *The Accounting Review*, April 1969.

Hendriksen, E.S., *Accounting Theory*, Irwin 1970, Chapter 13.

Lee, T.A., 'Goodwill: an example of will-o'-the-wisp accounting', *Accounting and Business Research*, Autumn 1971.

Morris, R., 'Distribution policy: an economic rationale', *Accountancy*, October 1982.

Sherwood, K., 'Depreciation, residual values and revaluations', *Accountancy*, February 1983.

Exercises

9.1   Figaro purchases a machine for £6,000. He estimates that the machine will last eight years and its scrap value will then be £1,000.

- (a)   Prepare the ledger accounts for the first three years of the machine's life and show the balance sheet extract at the end of each year, charging depreciation using the straight line method.
- (b)   What would be the net book value of the machine at the end of the third year if depreciation was charged at 20% p.a. using the reducing balance method?

9.2   Mr Carlos, a manufacturer, purchases a motor van on 1 January 19X3 for £10,000. He intends to keep the motor van for four years, at the end of which time he expects to be able to sell it for £4,000. Mr Carlos expects to spend £2,000 on a major overhaul during 19X5 and wishes to spread the cost of the overhaul *equally* over the asset's life.

- (a)   For each of the years 19X3, 19X4, 19X5 and 19X6, calculate the expected total annual cost (depreciation plus overhaul) of the motor van and its expected written-down book value at the end of the year, based on the following methods of depreciation:
  - (i)   straight line
  - (ii) reducing balance
  - (iii) sum-of-the-years-digits.
- (b)   Explain the accounting entries which will be needed to record the cost of the overhaul.

9.3   Zerlina Ltd commenced business on 1 September 19X0. It purchased and sold plant and machinery during the three years ended 31 August 19X3, as follows:

1 Sept. 19X0	Purchased Mk I Blender	for	£10,000
	Purchased Mk I Mixer	for	£12,000
1 Sept. 19X1	Purchased Mk II Blender	for	£11,000
1 Sept. 19X2	Purchased Mk II Mixer	for	£14,000
	Sold Mk I Mixer	for	£ 6,000
31 Aug. 19X3	Purchased Mk III Blender	for	£13,000
	and received £5,000 trade-in allowance		
	against the Mk I Blender		

- Show the accounting entries for Zerlina Ltd, necessary to record the above transactions, if depreciation is to be provided:
- (a)   using the straight line method at an annual rate of 20%;
- (b)   using the reducing balance method at an annual rate of 30%.

9.4   On 1 July 19X2, Mr Alfredo buys a microcomputer for £4,000. He expects that its economic life will be 5 years, and that it will have a resale value of £500 at the end of that time. He decides to use the straight line method for providing depreciation on the microcomputer.

On 30 June 19X4, Mr Alfredo realises that his estimate of the microcomputer's economic life was optimistic and that it is unlikely to last beyond 30 June 19X6. He also believes that it will have no scrap or resale value at that time. In consequence, he decides to amend *future* annual depreciation charges so as to write-off its entire cost by 30 June 19X6. He does not wish to adjust the written-down book value of the asset at 30 June 19X4.

On 30 June 19X6, Mr Alfredo disposes of the microcomputer by selling it to a scrap metal dealer for £100.

● Show the accounting entries relating to the microcomputer for the period from 1 July 19X2 to 30 June 19X6, under the following assumptions:
(a)   That Mr Alfredo prepares accounts annually to 30 June.
(b)   That Mr Alfredo prepares accounts annually to 31 December.

9.5   Inez Ltd bought a machine for £500,000 on 1 January 19X3 and sold it for £100,000 on 1 January 19X6. The machine was replaced immediately by an identical new model costing £700,000. The market values of the machine at the end of 19X3, 19X4 and 19X5 were estimated as follows:

31 December 19X3	£300,000
31 December 19X4	£150,000
31 December 19X5	£100,000

Inez Ltd prepares accounts annually to 31 December.

● (a)   Prepare a statement showing the amounts to be entered in the company's profit and loss accounts and balance sheets for 19X3, 19X4, 19X5 and 19X6 in respect of the machine bought on 1 January 19X3, for annual depreciation charges, profit or loss on sale of the machine and written-down value at the end of each year, under each of the following assumptions:
  (i)   that depreciation is calculated by the straight line method, at an annual rate of 25%.
  (ii)   that depreciation is calculated by the reducing balance method, at an annual rate of 50%.
  (iii)   that depreciation is calculated each year as the fall in the market value of the machine during the year.
(b)   Using the figures you have calculated in (a), discuss the relative merits of the above three methods of providing depreciation.

Chapter 10

Stock

In this chapter we explain the different possible accounting treatments of stock, or as the asset is sometimes termed 'inventory'. Our explanations of the alternative treatments available for valuing stock will be conducted within the historical cost framework.

As with fixed assets, the accounting entries associated with stock are, in principle, straightforward. The original cost of the stock is treated initially as an asset and subsequently the cost is transferred to the income statement as the asset is used up. Thus, the income statement for a period includes the cost of stock sold during the period, usually termed *cost of sales* or *cost of goods sold,* and the balance sheet at the end of the period shows the cost of stock unsold at the balance sheet date. The accounting entries are illustrated later in the chapter.

Stock is a tangible asset which is used up in order to generate revenue. Many enterprises, for example retail stores such as Marks and Spencer and Sainsburys, sell stock in the form in which it is purchased, without undertaking any productive or manufacturing operations. For such enterprises all stock is in a similar form—available immediately for resale. Other organisations, for example manufacturing companies such as the Ford Motor Co., buy raw materials and convert them in some way before reselling them. As we saw in Chapter 5, the conversion (or transformation) process involves the use of such factors as labour, machines, power and factory space. In consequence, manufacturing companies hold stock in three different forms:

1. *Raw materials*—representing stock that has been purchased but which has not yet entered the transformation process.
2. *Work in progress*—representing raw materials on which some transformation work has taken place, but which have not yet been converted into a final resaleable form.
3. *Finished goods*—representing items which have been fully transformed and are in a form suitable for resale.

The process whereby raw material stock is converted to finished goods is shown diagrammatically in Figure 10.1. Each of the three upper boxes represents one of the different forms of stock described above. At any time, a manufacturing organisation will likely hold stock in each of the three forms. Broadly speaking, the cost of raw materials is the amount paid for those raw materials which have not entered the transformation process; the

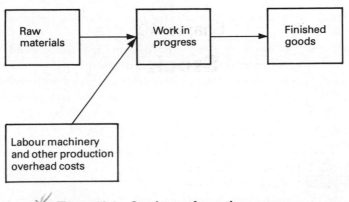

Figure 10.1   Stock transformation process.

cost of work in progress is the cost of raw materials on which some conversion work has been undertaken (but which are not yet in a final resaleable form) plus the cost of other inputs, such as labour, machinery and production overheads, which have been incurred in (partially) converting the raw materials; and the cost of finished goods is the raw materials cost plus all costs to convert the stock into a form suitable for resale.

In this chapter we devote our primary intention to the treatment of stocks of raw materials and finished goods. The particular problems involved in determining the cost of long-term work in progress were mentioned in Chapter 7, and will be reviewed later in this chapter. Having stated earlier that the cost of stock, in whatever form, is treated initially as an asset, and is subsequently transferred as an expense to the income statement, the major problem faced by the organisation lies in deciding what is meant by the 'cost' of stock. Much of the chapter is concerned with this problem. Two particular problems arise in identifying the historical cost of stock; the choice of *costing method* and the *stock flow assumption* to be used.

10.1   Stock Costing Methods

The problem of choosing a costing method arises only where an organisation undertakes a manufacturing or production process. The problem is to determine whether work in progress and finished goods should be valued at *direct cost* or *full cost*. We first introduced the different possible costing methods in Chapter 7, when determining the appropriate charge for the amount of effort used up in the production process. The aim of the costing method is to reflect how *traceable* are costs to units of finished product. Certain costs such as direct labour and raw materials, which are usually combined in a particular proportion into the finished product, are termed *directly traceable,* or simply, *direct costs*. This 'directness' suggests that there is a causal link between costs incurred and output produced. The aggregation of direct labour and raw material cost is often termed the *prime cost of production*.

Other costs, although incurred in producing the finished good, are not directly traceable to individual units of production or, if traceable, may possess a very tenuous relationship. These costs comprise both variable and fixed manufacturing overheads. Because of their indirect traceability to production, these costs are commonly termed *indirect costs*. Examples of indirect costs are rent payable, insurance, depreciation, foreman's salary, etc. Indirect costs often form the most substantial element of product costs.

The make-up of the cost of a particular product using the criterion of traceability might be as follows:

			£
Direct costs:	Direct labour	(2 hours at £3 per hour)	6
	Raw materials	(4 kg at £1.50 per kg)	6
		Prime cost	12
Indirect costs:	Total manufacturing overheads, allocated		
	on the basis of		14
		Full cost=Total product cost	£26

10.2   The Allocation of Manufacturing Overhead Costs

The above illustration of a total product cost shows an element of total manufacturing overheads, allocated on some, as yet unspecified, basis. The allocation of total manufacturing overhead, i.e. both variable and fixed overhead, to units of product is termed *full* or *absorption costing*. The word 'allocation' implies the dividing-up of a single whole into individual parts, and so entails the use of a dividing mechanism—or an allocation or absorption rate. Full costing, therefore, involves the choice of an appropriate mechanism or rate to allocate the total overheads to products. The rate is determined usually by dividing the period's overheads by some measure of the organisation's level of productive activity.

Typically, a single rate is not used to allocate all the organisation's manufacturing overheads. Overheads are more usually split into their fixed and variable components, and a different allocation rate is applied to each type of overhead. The calculation of the variable overhead per unit is the easier task; variable overhead is normally related to the number of labour hours (or in rarer cases the number of machine hours) taken to produce one unit. The calculation of the amount of fixed overhead to be allocated to each production unit is much less easy.

At its most basic level, the fixed overhead allocation rate is expressed in the following form:

$$\text{Fixed overhead rate} = \frac{\text{Budgeted fixed overhead for the period}}{\text{Measure of productive activity (estimate)}}$$

The resultant rate is an *average* rate, based on the assumption that units produced in one period of the year will take up a similar proportion of fixed overhead costs as units produced in other periods. The rate itself depends on two factors; a numerator representing the expected money amount to be incurred for overheads for the period, and a denominator representing the level of productive activity expected during the period which may be expressed in money terms, in hours, or in production units. Because of these different possible methods of measuring productive activity, fixed overhead rates may be expressed as percentages, or as £s per hour, or as £s per unit of production.

Two fundamental problems are thus presented by the choice of a fixed overhead allocation rate. First, how should the organisation select the measure of productive activity to be used as the denominator, i.e. as the basis for allocating overheads; and, following sequentially, how should it interpret any differences arising if the actual number of hours, or units of production, or money amounts comprising the denominator are different from expectations? We now look in turn at each of these two problems.

1. The basis for fixed overhead allocation

Many different bases are used to allocate fixed overheads to products. If the organisation produces only one product, the allocation is most often determined simply by dividing fixed overheads by the number of units produced. If, however, the organisation produces many different products, one single multipurpose allocation rate may be inappropriate, and different rates (and bases) of allocation may be used for each of the different products. All of this can make for great difficulties in the interpretation of the results of fixed overhead allocation and thus of stock valuation. The following example illustrates some of the issues which can arise when fixed overheads are allocated to production on the basis of different activity measures.

Example   Priestfield Ltd produces two products. Budgeted data for the year are as follows:

	Product A		Product B	
Direct costs per unit:		£		£
Material	(5 kg×£5)	25.00	(3 kg×£7.50)	22.50
Labour	(2 hr×£3.75)	7.50	(3 hr×£5)	15.00
Machine cost	(½ hr×£15)	7.50	(1½ hr×£20)	30.00
Total direct cost per unit		40.00		67.50
Budgeted output (units)		25,000		20,000
Total budgeted overheads (all fixed)			£1,000,000	

The following bases for allocation will be used to illustrate the procedures involved in assigning the total amount for overheads (£1,000,000) to products A and B.

1.   Direct labour hours
2.   Direct labour cost
3.   Machine hours
4.   Machine cost
5.   Total variable cost
6.   Budgeted output

Applying the six different methods gives overhead allocations as shown in Table 10.1. The application of the six different bases of overhead allocation gives six different solutions. In five of the six cases, product B bears the greater proportion of fixed overheads, whereas if budgeted output is used as the allocation basis, product A, because of its greater output, bears the greater proportion. Which of the methods should be chosen? It is a difficult question to answer. All the methods give answers which, it can be argued, are equally right and, by the same token, are equally wrong—because all the methods are equally *arbitrary*. And in one sense each of the answers produced by these book-keeping adjustments is acceptable for stock costing purposes as long as it is understood that the results are purely a function of the arbitrary bases used, and as long as the chosen method is applied consistently.

We might argue that it may be more sensible to relate such allocations to the *nature* of the individual product, and thus to the nature of the overhead costs to be allocated. For example, if the product in question is produced by the use of capital intensive methods, so that the bulk of fixed overhead costs reflects this situation, then machine hours might represent the most suitable allocation basis. In our example this would entail the use of method 3, under which the greater proportion of overhead costs would be allocated to product B, each unit of which uses three times as much machine time as does product A.

If, however, the production process is more dependent on the use of labour, and thus the attendant fixed overhead costs are more likely to be a function of labour intensiveness, it seems more appropriate to use either labour costs or labour hours as the allocation base. In practice, labour hours are more widely used as an allocation basis than labour costs. In our example method 1 would be used.

2.   Changes during the period in the basis of overhead allocation
In the previous example we have used predetermined (determined before the time of incurrence) rates to allocate overheads to products. The use of predetermined rates to cost products is necessary, as it is obviously not advisable to wait until the end of an accounting period before preparing

Table 10.1   Priestfield Ltd—Different methods of fixed overhead allocation

		Product A £	Product B £
Labour hours: Total A (2×25,000)	50,000		
B (3×20,000)	60,000		
	110,000 hr		
Allocation rate $\frac{£1,000,000}{110,000\ hr} = \frac{£9.0909\ per}{labour\ hour}$		454,550	545,450
Labour cost: Total A (£7.50×25,000)	£187,500		
B (£15.00×20,000)	£300,000		
	£487,500		
Allocation rate $\frac{£1,000,000}{£487,500} = \frac{205\%\ of}{labour\ cost}$		384,600	615,400
Machine hours: Total A (½×25,000)	12,500		
B (1½×20,000)	30,000		
	42,500 hr		
Allocation rate $\frac{£1,000,000}{42,000\ hr} = \frac{£23.529\ per}{machine\ hour}$		294,120	705,880
Machine cost: Total A (£7.50×25,000)	£187,500		
B (£30.00×20,000)	£600,000		
	£787,500		
Allocation rate $\frac{£1,000,000}{£787,000} = 127\%$		238,100	761,900
Total direct Total A (£40.00×25,000)	£1,000,000		
cost: B (£67.50×20,000)	£1,350,000		
	£2,350,000		
Allocation rate $\frac{£1,000,000}{£2,350,000} = 42.55\%$		425,500	574,500
Budgeted Total A	25,000		
output: B	20,000		
	45,000 units		
Allocation rate $\frac{£1,000,000}{45,000\ units} = \frac{£22.222}{per\ unit}$		555,560	444,440

stock valuations. For example, large companies must produce interim reports which necessitate interim stock valuations. But the use of estimated overhead rates presents certain interpretational difficulties if the *actual* level of activity (labour hours, production units, etc.) differs from the estimated level used to determine the rate.

We can best explain this situation by way of an example. Suppose that the expected (budgeted) fixed overhead for the forthcoming period is £15,000 and suppose that the firm expects to produce 15,000 units. Production units are to be taken as the basis for overhead allocation. The overhead allocation rate is thus:

$$\text{Allocation rate} = \frac{\text{Budgeted overhead}}{\text{Level of activity}} = \frac{\text{£15,000}}{\text{15,000 units}} = \text{£1 per unit}$$

This situation is illustrated graphically in Figure 10.2.

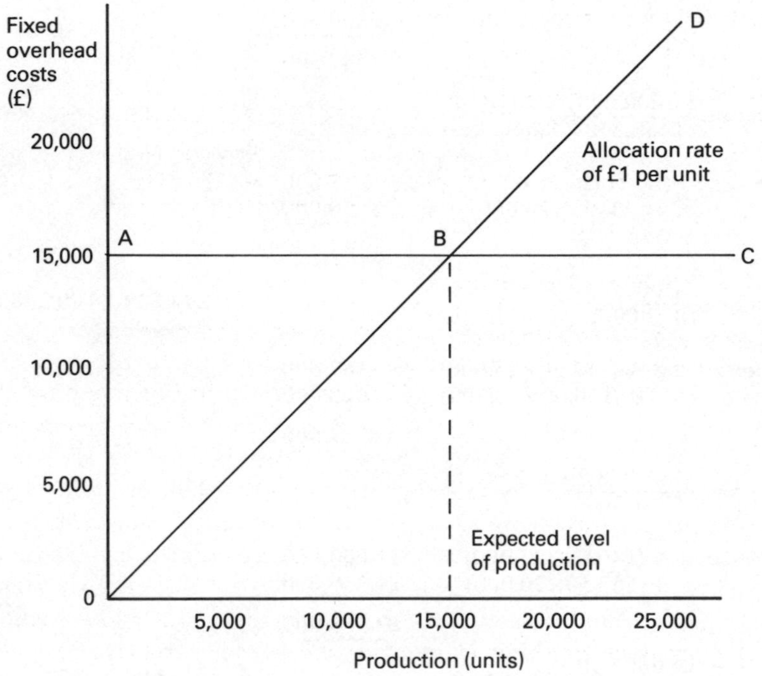

AC represents the budgeted fixed overhead line, which is constant (£15,000) at all levels of production
OD represents the overhead allocation line on the basis of an allocation rate of £1 per unit
B represents the point at which the overhead allocation line is expected to intersect the budgeted overhead line (i.e. the level of production at which the expected overhead of £15,000 is fully allocated to production units)

Figure 10.2   Graphical representation of overhead allocation (1).

Now, suppose that the actual level of activity for the period falls short of the expected level by 5,000 units, so that actual production is only 10,000 units. Figure 10.3 shows the impact of this decrease in volume. Because of the decline in volume from 15,000 units to 10,000 units of production there

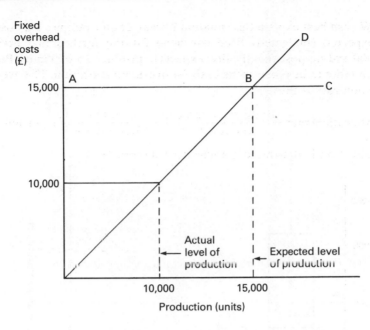

Figure 10.3   Graphical representation of overhead allocation (2).

is a difference between the level of costs expected to be allocated to production (the budgeted figure of £15,000) and the costs actually allocated (10,000 units at £1 per unit equals £10,000). This difference of £5,000 is termed a *volume variance,* because its cause is a change in the volume of production. Volume variances may be favourable or unfavourable. If, as in this example, budgeted fixed overheads (£15,000) are greater than the total of fixed overheads allocated to production (£10,000), then obviously some fixed overheads (£5,000) remain unallocated for the period. These unallocated fixed overheads represent an *unfavourable* volume variance and *in the period's income statement this unfavourable variance is usually treated as an adjustment to the cost of goods sold.* Conversely, if the volume of production had exceeded expectations and therefore the firm had allocated all its fixed costs (and more) to production, the resultant difference would be termed a *favourable* volume variance. Similar variances will arise if actual overhead costs differ from budgeted costs.

10.3   Full Costing vs Direct Costing

We can now illustrate the differences between the two main methods of stock costing, initially by means of a diagram and then by means of a numerical example. Figure 10.4 shows the flows of costs associated with

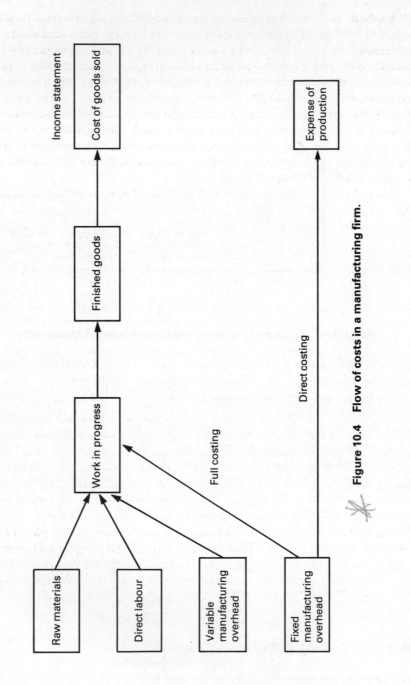

Figure 10.4   Flow of costs in a manufacturing firm.

each method. It is the treatment of fixed manufacturing overhead costs which differentiates the two systems. Under full costing, fixed manufacturing overhead costs are allocated to work in progress, and subsequently to finished goods, and are included as an element of cost of goods sold in the income statement when the finished goods are sold. Under direct costing, fixed manufacturing overhead costs are treated as an expense of the period rather than as an expense of the product, and are written off to the income statement in the period in which they are incurred. The significance of the differences revealed by applying both full and direct costing methods to the same set of data are now explained via the example of Roker Ltd which was first introduced in Chapter 7 (page 112).

The following data relate to Roker Ltd's level of activity for the years 19X0, 19X1 and 19X2.

		19X0	*19X1*	*19X2*
(a)	Sales (in units)	10,000	12,000	2,000
(b)	Selling price (per unit)	£11	£11	£11
(c)	Production (in units)	12,000	12,000	–
(d)	Production costs			
	Direct (per unit)	£3	£3	–
	Fixed (per period)	£24,000	£24,000	–
(e)	Selling and administrative costs			
	Direct (per unit)	£1	£1	£1
	Fixed (per period)	£30,000	£30,000	–
	Opening stock (in units)	0	2,000	2,000

Some comments on the above data are necessary before we begin our analysis. First, for illustrative purposes only, selling price per unit, direct costs per unit, and fixed costs per period are assumed to be constant over the three year period. Second, no production takes place in 19X2 and no fixed costs are incurred in that year. Finally, the full and direct costs per unit of stock are calculated on the basis of production costs only (i.e. all selling and administrative costs are excluded from the stock cost calculation).

Our analysis initially takes the form of income statements prepared for each of the three years under both costing methods. To prepare an income statement under full costing we need first to calculate the full cost per unit of stock. This is done as follows, using production units as the allocation base:

$$\text{Full cost per unit} = \frac{\text{Direct cost}}{\text{per unit}} + \frac{\text{Total fixed costs}}{\text{Production units}}$$

$$= \quad £3 \quad + \quad \frac{£24,000}{12,000 \text{ units}}$$

$$= \quad £5$$

The cost per unit of stock under direct costing is represented by the direct production cost per unit of £3.

Table 10.2   Roker Ltd—Income statements under full costing

	19X0		19X1		19X2	
	£	£	£	£	£	£
Sales revenue		(10,000×£11) 110,000		(12,000×£11) 132,000		(2,000×£11) 22,000
less: Cost of goods sold						
Opening stock		0		10,000		10,000
add: Cost of production						
Direct	36,000		36,000		0	
Fixed	24,000		24,000		0	
	(12,000×£5) 60,000		(14,000×£5) 70,000		(2,000×£5) 10,000	
less: Closing stock	(2,000×£5) 10,000	50,000	(2,000×£5) 10,000	60,000	0	10,000
Gross profit		60,000		72,000		12,000
less: Selling costs						
Direct	(10,000×£1) 10,000		(12,000×£1) 12,000		(2,000×£1) 2,000	
Fixed	30,000		30,000		0	
		40,000		42,000		2,000
Net income		£20,000		£30,000		£10,000

Table 10.3   Roker Ltd—Income statements under direct costing

	19X0		19X1		19X2	
	£	£	£	£	£	£
Sales revenue		(10,000×£11) 110,000		(12,000×£11) 132,000		(2,000×£11) 22,000
less: Direct costs						
Cost of goods sold						
Opening stock	0		(2,000×£3) 6,000		(2,000×£3) 6,000	
Production costs	(12,000×£3) 36,000		(12,000×£3) 36,000		0	
	36,000		42,000		6,000	
less: Closing stock	(2,000×£3) 6,000		(2,000×£3) 6,000		0	
		30,000		36,000		6,000
Selling costs	(10,000×£1) 10,000	40,000	(12,000×£1) 12,000	48,000	(2,000×£1) 2,000	8,000
		70,000		84,000		14,000
Contribution margin (£7 per unit)		70,000		84,000		14,000
less: Fixed costs for the period						
Production	24,000		24,000			
Selling	30,000	54,000	30,000	54,000	0	0
Net income		£16,000		£30,000		£14,000

Table 10.2 shows income statements for 19X0, 19X1 and 19X2 prepared under full costing. The format of the full costing income statement reflects Roker Ltd's particular functional activities; thus costs are classified in terms of the functions of production and selling, rather than in terms of their behaviour with respect to the firm's activities. Direct and fixed costs of production are grouped together to determine the total cost of goods sold, and direct and fixed costs of selling are grouped together to determine the total selling costs.

Table 10.3 shows income statements for 19X0, 19X1 and 19X2 prepared under direct costing. Here the format is very different. It reflects the way costs behave with respect to Roker Ltd's production and sales activities, i.e. whether costs are variable (direct) or fixed. Thus, all direct costs are grouped together and deducted from sales revenue to show the *contribution margin*. The contribution margin per unit is £7, being the difference between the sales revenue per unit of £11 and the direct production, selling and administrative cost per unit of £4. Fixed production and selling costs are then deducted from the contribution margin to determine the firm's net income.

The likely differences arising from the application of each costing method should now be clear. Full costing carries forward some of the firm's fixed production costs into closing stock, via a higher cost per unit. (Note that fixed *selling* costs do not affect stock valuation.) Thus, if we examine the net income for 19X0 under each method we see that the full costing income is £4,000 higher than the income under direct costing. This is explained by the treatment of the fixed production costs as shown in Table 10.4. The total production costs for 19X0 (fixed and direct) are £60,000 and are the same for each method. However, under full costing £10,000 of these costs are carried forward to the following period, thus increasing closing stock and increasing income; under the direct costing approach only £6,000 of these total costs are carried forward and all fixed costs are immediately written-off as expenses. The difference of £4,000 represents the difference in income for the year as between the two methods.

In 19X1 the net income of £30,000 is identical for each method. Why is this? After all, Roker Ltd is still using a full costing method which costs stock at £5 per unit, which is £2 per unit higher than the direct cost method. The reason is that in 19X1, unlike 19X0, production and sales are equal at 12,000 units, and in consequence opening and closing stocks must be the same (i.e. at the start and end of 19X1, Roker Ltd had 2,000 units in stock). Because opening and closing stocks are the same in terms of units, and there is no difference in the cost per unit, *there cannot be any difference in the income arising from the different methods of stock valuation.*

Finally, in 19X2, when the opening stock of the year is sold and no further production takes place, the direct costing method shows the higher income figure by £4,000. We would expect this to happen as the direct costing approach charges £4,000 *less* against revenue in 19X2 than the full

Table 10.4   Roker Ltd—Treatment of total production costs for 19X0

	Full costing £	Direct costing £
Production costs incurred		
Direct	36,000	36,000
Fixed	24,000	24,000
Total	£60,000	£60,000
Split as to:		
Costs assigned to closing stock		
2,000 units×£5 per unit	£10,000	
2,000 units×£3 per unit		£6,000
Costs expensed to income statement	£50,000	£54,000

costing approach, because the opening stock under direct cost is lower by £4,000. In 19X2 the previous 'advantages' of using full costing, in terms of showing higher income, have been eliminated.

The disposition of accounting net income over the three years is as follows:

	Full costing £	Direct costing £
19X0 Income	20,000	16,000
19X1 Income	30,000	30,000
19X2 Income	10,000	14,000
Total Income	£60,000	£60,000

Some comments and conclusions from the above analysis follow:

1. In 19X0 the full costing method generates the higher income figure. This occurs because the production level of 12,000 units is greater than the level of sales of 10,000 units. Thus, some production overheads (£4,000) are not written-off to the income statement but are carried forward to 19X1. We can therefore state as a general rule that—*if stock levels are rising, full costing will generate the higher income.*

2. In 19X1 the two methods produce the same income figures. We can therefore state that—*if production and sales are equal, and there are no changes in the method of stock valuation, full and direct costing will produce similar figures.*

3. In 19X2, when the opening stock of 2,000 units is sold, and no further production takes place, the variable costing method shows the higher income figure. We can therefore state that—*if stock levels are falling, direct costing will show the higher income.*

10.4   Stock Flow Assumptions

In many organisations it is not possible to identify which particular items of stock have in fact been sold. For example, a retail tobacconist may buy and sell substantial quantities of a particular brand of pipe tobacco. Suppose he has in stock 200 tins purchased at different times in the past. If he sells 10 tins during a period, he is unlikely to be able to identify from which batch or batches of purchases the tins have come. This would not matter if each tin in stock had cost the same amount. But suppose that the 200 tins had been bought at different prices—the question for the accountant is to decide which prices should be transferred to the income statement as the cost of the 10 tins sold. This problem is resolved by making an *assumption* about the physical flow of stock in a business. Various assumptions are possible, of which the three most common are *first in first out* (FIFO), *last in first out* (LIFO) and *weighted average.* Under FIFO, it is assumed that when an item of stock is sold or used, that item is the oldest one of its kind held (i.e. the one which first came into stock). Hence, under FIFO the charge for cost of goods sold represents the cost of the first available purchases, and the balance sheet amount of stock still held is assumed to represent the cost of those items purchased most recently. Under LIFO, the opposite assumption is made, i.e. that when a stock item is sold or used, that item is the one of its kind most recently purchased. Hence, under LIFO the charge for cost of goods sold represents the last of the available purchases and the balance sheet value of stock is assumed to be the cost of the earliest purchases. Under the weighted average method, stock sold or used is assumed to be drawn proportionately from the units held at the time of sale or use. Hence stock on hand at any time is assumed to represent a weighted average of stock available during the preceding period.

Each of the above stock flow assumptions may be applied in one of two ways. The first involves the calculation of the cost of stock sold and the consequent stock balance each time a sale is made. This is known as the *perpetual* method, and is used in the main illustration in the following section. The alternative, but less exact procedure, involves a single calculation of the cost of goods sold and value of each type of stock at the end of each period—the *periodic* method. This method is also illustrated in the next section.

The stock flow assumptions described above are made in order to allocate the total cost of stock during a period between the income statement and the balance sheet. They need not necessarily represent the actual physical movement of stock. Indeed the need for a stock flow assumption arises because the actual movement of stock cannot be precisely identified. Nevertheless, it may be that one assumption seems more likely than others to reflect actual stock movements. In a later section of this chapter we consider the importance of this characteristic in the selection of a stock flow assumption.

10.5   Illustration of Alternative Methods

A manufacturing company, Hampden Ltd, produces and sells glebes as shown in Table 10.5. The company has no stock of either glebes or raw materials at the start of the year. The direct costs per unit (of £3, £4 and £5) include the costs of raw materials and of all other direct expenses. In addition, Hampden Ltd incurs fixed production overhead costs of £5,000 during the year. All 2,000 units of raw material are fully converted to finished goods by the end of the year. Thus the company incurs total costs of £12,500 during the year, consisting of £7,500 direct costs and £5,000 fixed overhead costs. The basic problem, using the historial cost framework, is to decide how much of these total costs should be charged as expenses to the income statement and how much should be carried forward as the cost of stock held at the end of the period.

Table 10.5   Hampden Ltd—Details of glebe production and sales

			£
1 January	Costs of raw materials and other direct expenses	1,000 units at £3 =	3,000
1 May	do.	500 units at £4 =	2,000
1 October	do.	500 units at £5 =	2,500
Total units produced during year		2,000	7,500
31 March	Sales of finished goods	700 units at £10=	7,000
31 October	do.	900 units at £10=	9,000
Total sales during year		1,600	16,000

Notes: 1. All raw materials are converted to finished goods during the year.
   2. Production overhead costs amount to £5,000 for the year.

Table 10.6 shows six alternative methods of calculating cost of goods sold (the amount to be charged to the income statement as the cost of stock used) and the balance sheet value of stock (the cost of stock held at the end of the period). Each method is a combination of one of the two costing methods (direct or full costing) and one of the three stock flow assumptions (FIFO, LIFO and weighted average cost) described previously. For each of the three full cost methods, fixed overheads are allocated by dividing the total cost of £5,000 by the number of units converted to finished goods (2,000), giving a cost of £2.50 per unit. This is only one of a number of methods available for allocating fixed overhead costs, as we saw earlier in this chapter. Each 'full cost' figure in Table 10.6 is thus equal to the equivalent 'direct cost' figure plus an allocated overhead cost of £2.50 per stock unit.

Table 10.6   Hampden Ltd—Cost of goods sold and balance sheet value calculations for glebe stock: perpetual basis

Costing method:	Direct cost			Full cost		
Stock flow assumption:	FIFO	LIFO	Weighted average cost	FIFO	LIFO	Weighted average cost
	£	£	£	£	£	£
Cost of goods sold (COGS)						
31 March 700 at £3	2,100	2,100	2,100			
700 at £(3+2.50)				3,850	3,850	3,850
31 October 900 : 300 at £3						
500 at £4						
(Balance) 100 at £5	3,400					
900 500 at £5						
(Balance) 400 at £4		4,100				
900 at £4.154*			3,739			
900 at direct cost plus £2.50 per unit				5,650	6,350	5,989
Cost of goods sold	5,500	6,200	5,839	9,500	10,200	9,839
Balance sheet values						
31 December 400 at £5	2,000					
400 : 300 at £3						
100 at £4		1,300				
400 at £4.154			1,661			
400 at direct cost plus £2.50 per unit				3,000	2,300	2,661
Total cost	7,500	7,500	7,500	12,500	12,500	12,500
(COGS+Balance sheet value)						

*[(300×£3)+(500×£4)+(500×£5)]÷1,300=£4.154

The figures relating to alternative stock flow assumptions are calculated as follows. Using FIFO, the cost of goods sold is calculated each time sales are made on the assumption that the units sold are those which have been longest in stock. Thus, in relation to the sale of 900 units on 31 October, the units sold are assumed to be the 300 remaining from the batch produced on 1 January at £3 per unit (the other 700 having been sold on 31 March), the 500 produced on 1 May at £4 per unit, and the remainder, 100 units, from the production of 500 units at £5 on 1 October. The closing stock of 400 units is assumed to be drawn from the batch produced most recently (on 1 October) at £5 per unit.

Under LIFO, each batch of glebes sold is assumed to be drawn from the most recently produced units in stock at the date of sale. Hence the units sold on 31 October are assumed to consist of the 500 units produced on 1 October at £5 per unit plus the balance (400 units) from those produced on

1 May at £4 per unit. The units held in stock at the end of the year are assumed to be represented by the 300 units at £3 from the batch produced on 1 January and the 100 units at £4 from the batch produced on 1 May.

Using the weighted average method of costing stock we assume that stock sold is drawn proportionately from the units held at the time of sale. Thus before the sale on 31 October, Hampden Ltd has in stock:

	£
300 units at £3 (the balance of the 1 January production) =	900
500 units at £4 (produced on 1 May) =	2,000
500 units at £5 (produced on 1 October) =	2,500
1,300 units costing a total of	£5,400

The weighted average cost per unit is £4.154 (£5,400 ÷ 1,300 units), and this figure is applied both to the stock sold on 31 October and to the stock remaining at that date which is retained until the end of the year.

Whichever stock flow assumption and costing method are chosen, the following equation (a variant of those introduced in Chapter 8) holds:

$$\text{Opening stock} + \text{Cost of production} = \text{Cost of goods sold} + \text{Closing stock}$$

This may be demonstrated by using the figures in Table 10.6, as follows:

Costing method	Stock flow assumption	Opening stock	+	Cost of production	=	Cost of goods sold	+	Closing stock
Direct cost	FIFO	0	+	7,500	=	5,500	+	2,000
Direct cost	LIFO	0	+	7,500	=	6,200	+	1,300
Direct cost	Weighted average	0	+	7,500	=	5,839	+	1,661
Full cost	FIFO	0	+	12,500	=	9,500	+	3,000
Full cost	LIFO	0	+	12,500	=	10,200	+	2,300
Full cost	Weighted average	0	+	12,500	=	9,839	+	2,661

In the case of Hampden Ltd, the 'total cost' of glebes (i.e. the cost of goods sold plus the cost of closing stock) is the same whichever stock flow assumption is adopted, provided that the same costing method is used. This is so because the cost of opening stock is the same in each case (zero). Had opening stocks been costed on different bases, the totals would differ, although the equation would still hold for each method. The equation demonstrates clearly that the problem is one of allocation; specifically of allocating the total cost of stock available between the income statement and the balance sheet.

The figures calculated in Table 10.6 may be used to help to calculate Hampden Ltd's net income and to determine its balance sheet for the year.

For simplicity, we assume that the glebe is the only product manufactured by the company; that all costs and sales are on a *cash* basis; that the company owns no assets other than stock and cash; and that the company started business on 1 January. Summarised income statements and balance sheets are given in Table 10.7. The differences between the net income figures derive solely from the different costing methods and the different stock flow assumptions. Hence, for a particular costing method, the income under each stock flow assumption differs solely because of the different cost of goods sold figure. For a particular stock flow assumption, income figures differ between direct cost and full cost by £1,000 in each case. This is because under the full cost method overhead costs of £1,000 (400 units at £2.50 each) are carried forward as part of the cost of closing stock.

Table 10.7   Hampden Ltd—Summarised income statements and balance sheets

Costing method:	Direct cost			Full cost		
	FIFO	LIFO	Weighted average cost	FIFO	LIFO	Weighted average cost
Stock flow assumption:	£	£	£	£	£	£
Income statement						
Sales	16,000	16,000	16,000	16,000	16,000	16,000
less: Cost of goods sold	5,500	6,200	5,839	9,500	10,200	9,839
	10,500	9,800	10,161	6,500	5,800	6,161
less: Overheads	5,000	5,000	5,000	0	0	0
Net income	5,500	4,800	5,161	6,500	5,800	6,161
Balance sheet						
Ownership interest*	5,500	4,800	5,161	6,500	5,800	6,161
Stock of finished goods	2,000	1,300	1,661	3,000	2,300	2,661
Cash†	3,500	3,500	3,500	3,500	3,500	3,500
	5,500	4,800	5,161	6,500	5,800	6,161

*Equal to net income for the year as the balance at the start of the year is assumed to be zero.
†Sales revenue (£16,000) minus direct cost of stock produced (£7,500) and cost of overheads (£5,000) equals £3,500.

The figures in Table 10.7 illustrate general differences between alternative stock flow assumptions and costing methods. Other things being equal, cost of goods sold is generally smallest (and income consequently greatest) when FIFO is used, if *stock costs* increase during an accounting period. LIFO generally leads to the highest cost of goods sold and the lowest income figure, and the weighted average cost method produces answers between those given by FIFO and LIFO. As we have seen in the previous section, for any given stock flow assumption, the full cost method generally produces higher income figures when *stock levels* are rising (as in the case of Hampden Ltd). This is because part of fixed overhead costs is effectively deferred until a subsequent period. If stock levels fall, however, the 'benefit' from such deferral disappears.

We now turn to the *periodic* basis of stock calculation. This method is widely used in practice. Its basis can be most clearly seen from the equation introduced above. Rearranging that equation enables us to define cost of goods sold as follows:

$$\text{Cost of goods sold} = \text{Opening stock} + \text{Cost of production} - \text{Closing stock}$$

In other words, stock used during a period equals stock held at the start of the period plus stock produced during the period, minus stock held at the end of the period. Hence, cost of goods sold may be calculated by estimating closing stock directly (rather than as a by-product of the cost of goods sold calculation) and subtracting this figure from the sum total of opening stock and cost of production. The relevant figures for Hampden Ltd are shown in Table 10.8.

Table 10.8   Hampden Ltd—Alternative calculations of cost of goods sold

Costing method:	Direct cost			Full cost		
	FIFO	LIFO	Weighted average cost	FIFO	LIFO	Weighted average cost
Stock flow assumption:	£	£	£	£	£	£
Opening stock	0	0	0	0	0	0
Cost of stock produced (including overheads if appropriate)	7,500	7,500	7,500	12,500	12,500	12,500
	7,500	7,500	7,500	12,500	12,500	12,500
less: Closing stock (Table 10.6)	2,000	1,300	1,661	3,000	2,300	2,661
Cost of goods sold	5,500	6,200	5,839	9,500	10,200	9,839

The periodic basis may produce different answers from those given by the perpetual basis. Consider the case of Hampden Ltd. For each combination of costing method and stock flow assumption a single calculation of cost of goods sold and closing balance sheet value is undertaken at the end of the year. Details are given in Table 10.9. The main difference between the figures in this table and those in Table 10.6 is the omission from the analysis of the different dates of sale and of the particular stock available at each such date. So, for example, under LIFO the 1,600 glebes sold during the period are assumed to comprise the 500 units produced on 1 October, the 500 units produced on 1 May and 600 units (the balance) of those produced on

Table 10.9   Hampden Ltd—Cost of goods sold and balance sheet value calculations: periodic basis

Costing method:						
	Direct cost			Full cost		
Stock flow assumption:	FIFO	LIFO	Weighted average cost	FIFO	LIFO	Weighted average cost
	£	£	£	£	£	£
Cost of goods sold—1,600 glebes						
1,000 at £3						
500 at £4						
(Balance) 100 at £5						
1,600	5,500					
500 at £5						
500 at £4						
(Balance) 600 at £3						
1,600		6,300				
1,600 at £3.75*			6,000			
1,600 at direct cost plus £2.50 per unit				9,500	10,300	10,000
Cost of goods sold	5,500	6,300	6,000	9,500	10,300	10,000
Balance sheet values—400 glebes						
400 at £5	2,000					
400 at £3		1,200				
400 at £3.75			1,500			
400 at direct cost plus £2.50 per unit				3,000	2,200	2,500
Total cost (COGS+Balance sheet value)	7,500	7,500	7,500	12,500	12.500	12,500

*[(1,000×£3)+(500×£4)+(500×£5)]÷2,000=£3.75

1 January. This clearly ignores the fact that none of the 500 units produced on 1 May was available for sale on 31 March—indeed it implies that at least 100 of those units were sold on 31 March as no more than 900 of the 1,000 units produced on 1 May and 1 October could have been sold on 31 October. Despite this obvious 'inaccuracy', the method does enjoy the advantage that it avoids the cost of maintaining detailed cost records. Use of the method depends on the relationship between the costs associated with this 'inaccuracy' and the costs of keeping perpetual stock records.

10.6   The Choice of a Stock Flow Assumption

Having described the main stock flow assumptions, we now consider their relative merits and the rationale for choice between them. In times of changing prices FIFO gives the most outdated figure for cost of goods sold in the income statement but produces the most up-to-date balance sheet figures for closing stock. LIFO gives the opposite results, i.e. it provides an up-to-date figure for cost of goods sold but an outdated figure for closing stock. Weighted average cost gives intermediary results. The choice of stock flow assumption ultimately depends on the information required by users and, in particular, on their preference for information in either the income statement (LIFO) or the balance sheet (FIFO).

It might also be argued that the method chosen should help a business to make decisions which provide funds for the replacement of stock. Suppose that Mr Parade, a retailer, commences business on 1 January by paying £1,000 into a business bank account. During the following year he buys 50 units of stock at £8 per unit (on 1 February) and 50 units at £12 per unit (on 1 June) and sells 50 units at £15 per unit on 31 December, at which time the current buying price of the stock is £13 per unit. On 31 December he withdraws for personal purposes an amount equal to the business income for the year. He incurs no other expenses and receives no other revenues. Mr Parade's income statement and balance sheet, using alternative stock flow

Table 10.10   Mr Parade—Income statements and balance sheets using alternative stock flow assumptions

	FIFO £	LIFO £	Weighted average cost £
Income statements			
Sales (50 units at £15)	750	750	750
less: Cost of goods sold			
(50 units at £8)	400		
(50 units at £12)		600	
(50 units at £10)			500
Net income	£350	£150	£250
Balance sheets			
Ownership interest:			
Cash paid in	1,000	1,000	1,000
add: Net income	350	150	250
	1,350	1,150	1,250
less: Amount withdrawn	350	150	250
	£1,000	£1,000	£1,000
Stock:			
(50 units at £12)	600		
(50 units at £8)		400	
(50 units at £10)			500
Cash	400	600	500
	£1,000	£1,000	£1,000

assumptions, are given in Table 10.10. Cash balances at 31 December are comprised of cash paid in (£1,000) plus sales receipts (£750) less cost of stock purchased (£400+£600=£1,000) less the amount withdrawn (equal to the income according to the particular stock flow assumption adopted). If Mr Parade wishes to replace the 50 units of stock sold on 31 December, it will cost him £650 (50×£13). All of the stock flow assumptions show that there is insufficient cash left in the business to make the replacement. LIFO enables the most units to be replaced, FIFO the least.

10.7 Accounting Entries

In this section we illustrate the accounting entries necessary to record the acquisition, conversion and sale of stock. We use the example of Hampden Ltd and make the FIFO perpetual stock flow assumption. Details are as shown in the first and fourth columns of Tables 10.6 and 10.7. We assume that production overheads are paid quarterly, i.e. that £1,250 is paid on 31 March, 30 June, 30 September and 31 December. The accounting equation entries using direct cost are given in Table 10.11, and those using full cost in Table 10.12. In both cases the costs of stock (including production overheads under full costing) are added initially to the asset 'stock' and, on sale, are transferred to the income column (which here represents a condensation of the revenue and the expense columns). The only difference between the two tables relates to the treatment of production overheads. These are deducted directly from revenue where direct costing is used, and indirectly, via cost of goods sold, where full costing is adopted. In the latter case, some of the production overheads are carried forward to the next period as part of the closing stock value.

10.8 The Lower of Cost and Net Realisable Value Rule
COMAR RULE

We have discussed earlier how conventional accounting practice is heavily influenced by certain accounting concepts including the accruals (or matching) and prudence concepts. The matching concept has determined the treatment of stock described so far in this chapter. The prudence concept is also relevant, however. According to conventional practice, once the 'cost' of each item of closing stock has been determined it must be compared with the net realisable value of the stock. The net realisable value is the estimated sale proceeds of the stock less any costs still to be incurred in converting the stock to a suitable form for sale and in actually selling it. If the net realisable value of closing stock is lower than its cost, then the value of closing stock must be written down from cost to net realisable value. This treatment satisfies both the prudence concept (it recognises foreseeable 'losses') and the matching concept (if net realisable value is less than cost, there will be insufficient future revenues against which cost can be 'matched').

Table 10.11 Hampden Ltd—Accounting entries for recording stock using FIFO and direct cost

		Assets				*Ownership interest + Liabilities + Income*	
		Stock	+	*Cash*	=	*Income*	(transferred to ownership interest)
		£		£		£	
Transaction							
1 Jan.	Production of 1,000 units	3,000		(3,000)			
31 March	Production overheads			(1,250)		(1,250)	(Production overheads)
	Sales of 700 units			7,000		7,000	(Sales)
		(2,100)				(2,100)	(Cost of goods sold)
1 May	Production of 500 units	2,000		(2,000)			
30 June	Production overheads			(1,250)		(1,250)	(Production overheads)
30 Sept.	Production overheads			(1,250)		(1,250)	(Production overheads)
1 Oct.	Production of 500 units	2,500		(2,500)			
31 Oct.	Sale of 900 units			9,000		9,000	(Sales)
		(3,400)				(3,400)	(Cost of goods sold)
31 Dec.	Production overheads			(1,250)		(1,250)	(Production overheads)
31 Dec.	Balances	2,000	+	3,500	=	5,500	

Table 10.12   Hampden Ltd—Accounting entries for recording stock using FIFO and full cost

Transaction	Assets		=	Ownership interest + Liabilities + Income	
	Stock £	Cash £	=	Income £	(transferred to ownership interest)
Transaction					
1 Jan. Production of 1,000 units	3,000	(3,000)			
31 March Production overheads	1,250	(1,250)			
31 March Sales of 700 units		7,000		7,000	(Sales)
	(3,850)			(3,850)	(Cost of goods sold)
1 May Production of 500 units	2,000	(2,000)			
30 June Production overheads	1,250	(1,250)			
30 Sept. Production overheads	1,250	(1,250)			
1 Oct. Production of 500 units	2,500	(2,500)			
31 Oct. Sale of 900 units		9,000		9,000	(Sales)
	(5,650)			(5,650)	(Cost of goods sold)
31 Dec. Production overheads	1,250	(1,250)			
31 Dec. Balances	3,000	3,500	=	6,500	

The accounting entry required to implement the lower of cost and net realisable value rule on an item-by-item basis is as follows:

If the net realisable value of closing stock is less than its cost, reduce the asset 'stock' by the difference between cost and net realisable value, and increase cost of goods sold by the same figure.

The effect of this entry is that, for balance sheet purposes, stock is valued at the lower of cost and net realisable value.

Finally, we should return briefly to the issue of the valuation of long-term contracts. As we saw in Chapter 7, long-term contracts may present particular problems if they are subject to the application of the normal 'lower of cost and net realisable value' rule. As an extreme example, consider the case of a builder whose only business is the construction of one factory every three years. Application of conventional historical cost accounting rules would value his work in progress at *cost* at the end of two years in every three, thus showing zero income in each of those two years. The entire surplus from building each factory would be recognised in the third year of each contract. Such a treatment might result in volatile reported annual income figures, and may be misleading to users. For this reason, it is sometimes regarded as acceptable to abate the prudence concept in favour of the matching concept and to recognise a part of the profit on long-term contracts in advance of their completion, along the lines illustrated in Chapter 7 (pages 108–109).

We conclude this chapter by reiterating that in most manufacturing organisations stock forms a large percentage of the assets existing at the balance sheet date. For example, stock (in its three forms) represented 18% of ICI's *total* assets, and 38% of ICI's *current* assets in its 1983 balance sheet. Examination of ICI's 1983 income statement shows that the charge for cost of goods sold (use of stock during the year) represents 65% of ICI's total expenses and 800% (!) of its pre-tax income for the year. Thus a knowledge of the available methods of stock valuation and their respective characteristics (ICI uses full costing and the FIFO cost flow assumption) is critical to an understanding of their significance in determining both an organisation's net income and the level of its current assets.

Discussion Topics

1 Describe the stock conversion process that takes place in a manufacturing enterprise and explain the differences between raw materials, work in progress and finished goods.

2 Explain what you understand by the choice of a 'costing method'. Outline the main alternative methods and discuss their relative merits.

3 Explain what you understand by the choice of a 'stock flow assumption'. Outline the main alternative assumptions and evaluate them.

4 What is the 'lower of cost and net realisable value' rule? Why is it applied?

5 Analyse the relationship between opening stock, closing stock, cost of production and cost of goods sold.

6 Explain, with illustrations, the extent to which historical cost based stock treatments result in the provision of sufficient funds to replace stock as it is used up.

7 Distinguish between the 'perpetual' and 'periodic' bases of stock calculation.

8 How might cost of goods sold be estimated by an enterprise that does not keep detailed stock records?

9 What particular problems of stock treatment are associated with long-term contracts?

Further Reading

Hendriksen, E.S., *Accounting Theory,* Irwin, 1970, Chapter 11.

Exercises

10.1 Ruiz Ltd buys and sells sarastros. The company prepares accounts annually to 31 October. On 1 November 19X5 Ruiz Ltd had no stock of sarastros.

  On 1 December 19X5 the company purchased 10,000 sarastros at 15p each, and on 1 January 19X6 it purchased a further 5,000 at 18p each. 5,000 sarastros were sold on 1 March 19X6 at a price of 30p each. On 1 May 19X6, 10,000 sarastros were purchased at 20p each and on 1 September 19X6 the company sold 4,000 sarastros at a price of 35p each.

● (a) Calculate the gross profit made on the sale of sarastros during the year ended 31 October 19X6 and the value of the stock of sarastros held at 31 October 19X6, under each of the following stock flow assumptions:
      (i) last in, first out (LIFO)
      (ii) first in, first out (FIFO)
      (iii) weighted average cost.
   (b) Comment on the relative merits of the above three assumptions for costing stock.

10.2 Mr Aida commences business as a manufacturer of Anninas on 1 January 19X1. On that date he pays £200,000 into the business bank account from his personal resources. Each Annina requires 2 kg of raw material. Mr Aida purchases the following quantities of raw materials during the two years to 31 December 19X2.

1 Jan. 19X1	10,000 kg at £2.00 per kg=£20,000
30 June 19X1	10,000 kg at £2.50 per kg=£25,000
30 Sept. 19X1	5,000 kg at £2.75 per kg=£13,750
31 Jan. 19X2	10,000 kg at £3.00 per kg=£30,000
31 July 19X2	8,000 kg at £3.30 per kg=£26,400
	43,000 kg

During 19X1, 24,000 kg of raw material are converted to 12,000 Anninas. The remaining 1,000 kg held at 31 December 19X1 are in stock at that date. During 19X2 these units, together with the 18,000 kg purchased during 19X2 are converted to 9,500 Anninas. Throughout the two-year period, each Annina manufactured requires 3 hours of direct labour time. Each hour of direct labour costs £4 during 19X1 and £5 during 19X2. In addition, conversion of raw materials to Anninas requires the use of a machine which Mr Aida purchases for £60,000 on 1 January 19X1. The machine has a two-year life and no residual value at the end of that time. Mr Aida wishes to depreciate the machine using the straight line method of depreciation. Manufacturing overheads (excluding machine depreciation, direct labour costs and raw material costs) amount to £30,000 in 19X1 and £27,000 in 19X2. Other expenses are £28,000 for 19X1 and £32,000 for 19X2.

Sales of Anninas are as follows:

31 July 19X1	4,000 units at £24.00 per unit=	£96,000
31 Oct. 19X1	3,000 units at £25.00 per unit=	£75,000
31 Dec. 19X1	2,000 units at £27.00 per unit=	£54,000
31 March 19X2	4,000 units at £27.00 per unit=£108,000	
30 Sept. 19X2	5,000 units at £30.00 per unit=£150,000	
31 Dec. 19X2	3,500 units at £32.00 per unit=£112,000	

21,500 units

All revenues and payments are made in cash during the year in which they arise. Mr Aida wishes to adopt the FIFO stock flow assumption.

- (a)   Prepare Mr Aida's income statements for 19X1 and 19X2, and his balance sheets at 31 December 19X1 and 31 December 19X2, under each of the following costing methods:
     (i) direct cost
     (ii) full cost (allocating appropriate overhead costs on the basis of the number of units produced).
  (b)   Show Mr Aida's accounting equation entries for 19X1 and 19X2, assuming that the direct costing method is adopted.
  (c)   Comment on the figures revealed by your answer to (a) above.

10.3   Mr Hermann is a shopkeeper who specialises in the purchase and sale of four product lines—riccardos, mantuas, lunas and leonoras. He does not maintain continual stock records, but provides the following information regarding his most recent year's trading:

	Riccardos	Mantuas	Lunas	Leonoras
	£	£	£	£
Stock at start of year	2,000	6,500	3,200	8,700
Purchase of stock during year	47,800	35,100	63,900	98,200
Estimated cost of stock held at end of year	3,100	12,300	3,300	6,900
Estimated net realisable value of stock held at end of year	3,500	11,600	4,400	8,200

- Calculate the cost of goods sold for Mr Hermann's business for his most recent year's trading. Explain and justify your calculations.

10.4   Mr Giorgio commences business as a retailer of violettas on 1 January. During his first year of trading he buys and sells violettas as follows:

1 Jan.	Buys 500 at £75 each
28 Feb.	Buys 500 at £80 each
31 March	Sells 700 at £100 each
31 May	Buys 500 at £70 each
30 June	Sells 400 at £95 each
31 Aug.	Sells 200 at £85 each
1 Sept.	Buys 800 at £65 each
30 Nov.	Sells 600 at £105 each

- (a)   Calculate Mr Giorgio's gross profit from selling violettas during the year and the balance sheet value of violettas at the end of the year under the FIFO, LIFO and weighted average cost stock flow assumptions, assuming that the calculations are based on:
    (i) the *perpetual* basis
    (ii) the *periodic* basis.
  (b)   How would your answers to (a) above change if the net realisable value of violettas at 31 December was £68 each?

10.5   Vitellia Ltd was incorporated on 1 January 19X6, with a paid up capital of £8,000,000, to design, develop and manufacture a revolutionary sports motor cycle. During 19X6 the company built up its organisation, leased premises, purchased plant and recruited a development team. An amount of £3,000,000 was spent on plant and machinery, whilst the cost of materials, labour and overhead expenses (including depreciation) recorded in the books amounted to £500,000 during the year.

In 19X7, development work on a prototype continued, while the company prepared production facilities against the day when development would be complete. Expenditure of £1,000,000 on tooling costs was incurred, a further £500,000 was spent on an advertising campaign, and the cost of materials used, labour and overhead expenses amounted to £1,000,000. When the company was incorporated, the directors discussed depreciation of fixed assets and settled on a rate of 5% on cost during the development years, and 10% on cost thereafter.

At 31 December 19X7, stocks of raw materials were valued at £200,000. There was no income of any sort during 19X6 and 19X7, and the directors decided to treat development costs as intangible assets in the balance sheet at 31 December 19X7.

On 1 January 19X8, development of the prototype was satisfactorily completed and it was decided to retain the vehicle as a demonstration model. At this time the factory was prepared to produce motor cycles at the rate of 400 per year to be sold direct to the consumer for cash at £2,500 each. However, teething troubles at the factory reduced production for the year to 80 vehicles, of which only 40 were sold. Rigorous economy in the face of this situation reduced labour costs to £50,000 for the year, whilst materials purchased cost £45,000. Advertising and other overhead costs amounted to £450,000. The stock of raw materials on 31 December 19X8, was £95,000, there was no stock of work in progress, and closing stocks of finished goods were valued at direct cost. The directors decided to treat the loss for 19X8 as deferred expenditure (i.e. as an intangible asset).

During 19X9, 320 motor cycles were produced, and 200 sold. Direct costs were reduced to £2,000 per vehicle, whilst advertising and overhead expenses were held at £450,000 for the year. Stocks of raw material remained at the same level throughout the year, and stocks of finished goods were accounted for on the FIFO basis. The directors proposed once more to treat the loss as deferred expenditure, arguing that whilst prototype development was completed in 19X7, their market had developed at a slower rate than anticipated. They hope that expanding sales in the future will make it possible to set off development expenditure against revenue in later years when the project has matured.

- (a) Prepare draft balance sheets for Vitellia Ltd as at 31 December 19X7, 19X8 and 19X9, in accordance with the directors' decisions.
- (b) Comment on the manner in which the circumstances outlined above have been treated in the accounts for the last three years, and suggest a course of future actions.

10.6 Ms Ilia and Ms Electra both started business as retailers on 1 January 19X7. During the year to 31 December 19X7, the two ladies undertook identical business transactions as follows:

- (i) Purchased equipment on 1 January 19X7 for £100,000. The equipment has an estimated life of 5 years, at which time it will be worth £10,000.
- (ii) Paid research and development expenditure of £50,000.
- (iii) Purchased stock as follows:

   1 January 19X7   2,000 units at £50 each
   1 May 19X7   2,000 units at £100 each.

- (iv) Sold stock as follows:

   30 September 19X7   2,000 units at £150 each.

- (v) Incurred other expenses of £50,000.

The two retailers use different accounting conventions for the purpose of calculating profit, as follows:

   Depreciation: Ms Ilia uses straight line depreciation. Ms Electra uses the reducing balance method.
   Research and development: Ms Ilia writes off R&D expenditure over a 10 year period, using the straight line method. Ms Electra writes off the expenditure in the year in which it is incurred.
   Stock: Ms Ilia uses the FIFO method for valuing stock. Ms Electra uses LIFO.

- (a) Prepare income statements for Ms Ilia and Ms Electra for the year ended 31 December 19X7.
- (b) Discuss the implications of the income figures in the accounts you have prepared.

Chapter 11

Financing

In the previous two chapters we have looked at the accounting treatment of the major classes of assets, and examined some possible ways in which depreciation and cost of goods sold might be calculated. We now turn our attention to the other side of the balance sheet—to the ways in which organisations raise finance—and look at how the receipt of finance, and the payment of rewards to the providers of finance, are dealt with in accounting statements.

Finance includes both ownership interest (sums provided by the owners of an enterprise) and liabilities (sums provided by other parties). The finance raised by an organisation is frequently described as its *capital*. We shall henceforth use the terms 'finance' and 'capital' interchangeably. In this chapter we identify the main sources of finance, describe their chief characteristics and explain why it is important to distinguish between them. The three most significant forms of private sector organisation—individuals, partnerships and limited liability companies—are differentiated throughout the chapter.

11.1 Long-term and Short-term Financing

Organisations raise capital to finance the acquisition of assets. As we have seen in previous chapters, assets are acquired for different purposes. Broadly speaking, fixed assets represent the productive long-term capacity of the organisation; current assets are held for early resale, or for early conversion into cash in some other way. In consequence, the type of capital required to finance assets varies with the nature of the particular assets. In general, assets that are to be held for a long period should be financed by a stable, long-term source of finance, whereas assets with short or unpredictable lives should be financed by a more flexible, short-term source. For example, an organisation would be unwise to raise a 20-year loan to finance an asset to be held for only six months; interest charges will have to be paid for $19\frac{1}{2}$ years after the end of the asset's life. Similarly, it would be risky to finance a long-term investment (e.g. the purchase of plant and machinery) by a bank overdraft that might have to be repaid at short notice.

For many organisations, a substantial part of current assets (stocks and debtors) is financed by current liabilities (primarily trade creditors and bank overdrafts). This is usually a convenient and sensible arrangement, as fluctuations in the level of both current assets and current liabilities tend to be influenced by the level of an organisation's activity. The intention in this chapter is to concentrate on long-term capital, which is needed primarily to finance the acquisition of fixed assets and any *permanent* surplus of current assets over current liabilities, i.e. permanent *working capital*. We have discussed the treatment of debtors and creditors in Chapter 8.

11.2   Sources of Long-term Capital: Individuals

A business run by an individual raises its long-term capital from two main sources:

1. *Long-term loans,* which comprise loans from banks and other organisations and individuals and which are not repayable in the near future.[1]
2. *Ownership interest,* which includes both funds paid into the business by the owner from his personal resources, and net income of the business which has not been distributed to the owner (i.e. retained income or retained profits).

Other sources are also used, for example the owner may lease assets, or raise funds via business expansion schemes.

There are three distinguishing characteristics of the two main sources of long-term capital:

(a)   the returns they offer
(b)   the provisions relating to the repayment of capital
(c)   their relative degrees of security.

We shall look at each of these in turn.

Returns
The returns payable on long-term loans are usually fixed by contract at the time the loan is advanced. Loan contracts normally demand a periodic payment of a fixed amount (termed *interest*), often once or twice each year. In most cases interest is payable whether or not the organisation makes a profit. Thus a contract to loan £100,000 at 10% per annum over 10 years, interest being due at half-yearly intervals, would entail semi-annual interest payments to the lender of £5,000.

---

[1] The distinction between a long-term and a short-term loan is not clear cut. As a rough rule of thumb, a short-term loan might be regarded as one repayable within two or three years of the granting of the loan and a long-term loan as one payable after a longer period of time.

The periodic returns to the individual himself are represented by the organisation's net income for the period, calculated after the deduction of fixed interest and other expenses. Thus returns to the owner may fluctuate from year to year and indeed may be negative in some years if the business makes a loss. In many cases, the amounts actually withdrawn from the business by its owner (called *drawings*) will not equal the income available. The amount of drawings depends on the availability of cash and on the extent to which funds are needed by the business to purchase new or replacement assets. As we illustrate later, drawings are not treated as an expense under conventional accounting practice, but rather as a deduction from ownership interest.

The above descriptions suggest that the returns on ownership interest are likely to be much more volatile than those on long-term loans; the former will fluctuate with the level of the organisation's income whereas the latter are fixed by contract. Volatility is often regarded as a measure of the risk borne by the providers of long-term capital; other things being equal, a risk-averse provider of capital will prefer less volatile to more volatile returns. Thus the owner of a business bears more risk (in relation to his returns) than do the providers of long-term capital. He may also, of course, receive greater rewards.

Repayment of capital

When a long-term loan is made to an individual it is usual for a date (or series of dates) to be fixed for repayment of the loan. The amount to be paid at each repayment date is also normally agreed in advance.

Ownership interest is, however, not usually repaid until the activities of the business cease, although there is no legal restriction to stop the individual withdrawing some, or even all, of his capital at any time. The amount of capital to be repaid to the owner when the business ceases depends entirely on the position of the business at that time. It is equal to the proceeds from selling assets less the amounts needed to pay all liabilities, including the repayment of long-term loan capital.

Security

Long-term loans are often secured by a *charge* (in favour of the lender) on particular assets of the business. Thus if interest is not paid, or capital is not repaid on the due date, the lender may take possession of the charged assets and dispose of them. He may retain from the disposal proceeds sufficient to pay outstanding interest and repay the amount of the loan. The balance is returned to the owner of the business. If the loan is not secured, or if the proceeds from selling charged assets are insufficient to pay the amounts due to the lender, he may take action against the owner personally to recover sums owing to him. Thus the liability of an individual for his enterprise's financial obligations is *unlimited*. On the cessation of the business, long-term lenders have a prior claim over the owner on the funds available, in respect of both the payment of interest and the repayment of capital due to them.

The individual is thus the ultimate risk bearer. In respect of both returns and capital repayment he has no security—he must ensure that the business continues to generate surpluses. His rewards from owning the business comprise the residue after all other claims have been satisfied.

11.3 Sources of Long-term Capital: Partnerships

Partnerships are business structures that are owned, and often managed, by a group of individuals called partners. Many large professional organisations, for example firms of accountants, solicitors, doctors and dentists, are partnerships. Partnerships raise their long-term capital from the same types of sources as individuals, and have very similar rights and obligations. These rights and obligations are determined largely by the requirements of the Partnership Act, 1890. Partners differ from individuals in two main respects. First, if the partnership's resources are insufficient to pay its liabilities, the individual partners are jointly and severally liable for them. In other words, any party to whom the partnership owes money has the right to take action against some or all of the partners in respect of amounts owing to him. For example, if all but one of the partners are without personal resources, the remaining partner is liable in full for all liabilities of the partnership. This can be a heavy burden.

Partnerships also differ from individuals in respect of the partners' joint ownership of the enterprise. It is necessary to divide between the partners both the net income of the partnership and any surplus remaining on its cessation. The division is normally made in accordance with a *partnership agreement* which defines the entitlement of each partner to his share in income and capital surpluses. As with individuals, each partner's share of income is not usually treated as an expense. Instead it is added directly to his share of ownership interest—specifically to his capital account. The arrangement for allocating net income between partners may be quite complex, and may include provision for payment of 'salary', 'interest on capital', and 'share of residual income'. The total amount due to each partner as his allocation of income, however determined, is added to his capital account. Withdrawals by partners are called drawings and are deducted directly from the capital account of the partner. These accounting treatments are illustrated later in the chapter.

11.4 Sources of Long-term Capital: Limited Companies

Ownership interest

We explained in Chapter 2 that limited liability companies were created in response to the need for organisations to raise very large amounts of finance.

Thus, in order to persuade investors to accept some of the risks associated with an organisation's activities, without at the same time expecting them to jeopardise their entire personal fortunes, the right to create limited companies was granted. As the name suggests, the important distinction between limited liability companies and other types of organisation relates to the potential liability of the owners. The liability of the owners of limited companies for company debts is limited to the amount of capital they have provided or agreed to provide to the company. The owners cannot generally be compelled to find further capital from their private resources if the company has insufficient funds to meet its obligations. Individuals and partners, on the other hand, have unlimited liability for the debts contracted by their business. It is, however, often the case that the owners of *small* limited companies are required by lenders to provide personal guarantees as security for debts. In these cases the practical differences between small companies and partnerships are lessened considerably.

A second major difference between limited companies and other organisations is that the former have a legal identity separate from the identities of their owners. Like individuals and partnerships, limited companies raise long-term finance from two main sources—ownership interest and long-term loans. Ownership interest is created by limited companies selling *shares* in themselves to individuals and organisations. These shares are known as *ordinary* or *equity* shares. The total capital raised in this way is called ordinary share capital or equity capital. Each share has a *nominal* or *par* value of, for example, 25p or £1. This value has little significance other than as a means of describing the share—*it does not necessarily correspond either with the value of the share (e.g. as determined by the assets of the organisation) or even with the price at which it is issued (sold) by the company*. Shares, like many other goods, are usually sold (issued) at the highest price the market will bear. This price is invariably greater than the nominal value and the resultant surplus is called a *share premium,* and is recorded separately in the company's accounts. Both the nominal value of shares and the share premium are treated as part of a company's ownership interest, i.e. both belong to the owners. The share premium account is often termed a 'capital reserve' and, like the share capital account, cannot be distributed to the owners except on liquidation or in other very limited circumstances.

The other part of ownership interest is termed 'retained profits', i.e. profits that have not been distributed. These are also known as 'revenue reserves'. The distinction between capital and revenue reserves is important. As stated in the previous paragraph, capital reserves are not distributable, and although revenue reserves represent *undistributed* profits, they do not necessarily represent funds available for distribution. It cannot automatically be assumed that if the organisation wished to distribute its retained profits sufficient cash would be available for this purpose. It is quite possible for an organisation to show both a high level of reserves and a low (or non-existent) level of cash because profits have been tied up in non-cash assets.

Distributions made by a company to its shareholders (owners), equivalent to the 'drawings' of individuals and partners, are called *dividends*. Unlike the drawings of individuals and partners, dividends are not deducted directly from ownership interest, but rather are treated as an appropriation of the company's net income (i.e. they are deducted from net income). The balance of net income is then added to retained profits.

If a company ceases to trade (i.e. in the event of its liquidation), ordinary shareholders are in much the same position as individuals or partners. They are entitled to share in the distribution of any funds remaining after all other claims have been satisfied. Ordinary shareholders are in fact entitled to the residue of both periodic income and amounts available on liquidation, and are thus the ultimate risk bearers, except in so far as their risk is restricted by their limited liability. This explains why equity capital is often termed 'risk capital'.

Except in special circumstances, ordinary share capital that has been paid to a company cannot be repaid until the company is liquidated. However, this does not mean that the owners of the share capital cannot disinvest before the liquidation of the company: shareholders may sell their shares to other individuals or organisations. Being able to buy and sell shares freely and thus invest in different companies at different times is one of the major attractions to investing shareholders. The price at which shares are traded at any point in time is known as their *market value* at the time, and should not be confused with their nominal value, or indeed with any other figure relating to the shares in the financial statements. It is vital to understand that the sale of shares from one shareholder to another does not affect in any way the accounting transactions of the company. It is a private sale between two parties external to the company, and simply represents a change of ownership. The company 'owes' the same amount to the owners, *whoever they may be*.

The shares of many companies, particularly large companies, are traded in a specialised market, called the Stock Exchange.[2] This is primarily a market for 'second hand' shares and securities, although a company wishing to issue additional shares will have regard to the price at which its existing shares are being traded, when deciding on a price for the additional issue. A company that wishes to have its shares traded on the Stock Exchange must apply for its shares to be 'listed' (or 'quoted'). Companies that have applied successfully for a listing are known as *listed companies* (or *quoted companies*). Special accounting requirements apply to listed companies, for example the need to produce semi-annual interim reports. Other companies,

---

[2]It is outside the scope of this book to provide a detailed discussion of the role and workings of the Stock Exchange. A good description is contained in R.J. Briston, *The Stock Exchange and Investment Analysis,* 3rd Ed, George Allen and Unwin, 1975, Part

which constitute the vast majority of companies in the UK, are called unlisted (or unquoted) companies. Shares in unquoted companies are not so readily marketable, and ownership interest is not spread among so many shareholders.

Loan capital

The basic characteristics of long-term loan capital, in terms of returns, repayment of capital and security, are similar for all types of business structure. There are, however, two main differences in this respect between limited companies and other organisations. The first relates to the terminology used to describe such capital. Long-term loans to limited companies are known variously as *debentures, loan stock* and *debt capital,* all of which mean essentially the same thing. The second difference is that long-term loans to limited companies may be either *redeemable* or *irredeemable.* Redeemable loans are those under which a date is fixed for repayment of the capital at the time the loan is given. Almost all long-term loans to organisations other than limited companies are of this kind. Irredeemable loans are those where no date is fixed for repayment. The lender may require repayment only if the company defaults on the payment of interest or on some other condition of the loan. The company may usually choose to repay an irredeemable loan when it wishes.

Preference capital

A third source of long-term capital is available to limited companies—*preference shares.* These are a hybrid of equity and debt capital. Legally, they are part of the ownership interest of a company. In most other respects, however, they resemble long-term loan capital more closely than equity capital. The return on such shares (the preference dividend) is usually stated as a maximum rate, and arrangements for repayment of capital are normally determined when the shares are issued.

To summarise, the sources of long-term capital available to limited liability companies are, in essence, very similar to those available to other organisations. Their accounting treatment tends to be more complex because of the greater formality that is attached to their issue, returns and redemption.

11.5   Capital Structure

An organisation's *capital structure* is the relationship between its various sources of capital. The definition is usually restricted to long-term sources of finance. It is beyond the scope of this book to evaluate the relative merits of alternative sources of finance[3]; the present chapter is concerned rather with the ways in which such alternatives are recorded and reported. Nevertheless, one particular aspect of capital structure is of great interest to those who use accounting reports—the level of the organisation's *gearing*. Gearing (or *leverage* as it is termed in the USA) is the relationship between the loan capital and equity capital of an enterprise. It may be defined in a number of ways, of which the most common is:

$$\text{Gearing ratio} = \frac{\text{Value of fixed interest capital}}{\text{Total value of the organisation}}$$

The total value of the organisation is defined as the value of ownership interest plus the value of loan capital. (Note that for the purpose of the gearing definition preference shares are often treated as loan capital.) An organisation's gearing is higher, the greater is the proportion of loan capital in its capital structure. To calculate the gearing ratio, 'value' may be taken to refer to either market value or book value. In general, the former is the better measure of the current position of the organisation, and is to be preferred.

For example, consider the case of two quoted companies, Grosvenor plc and Brandywell plc. Details of the long-term capital of each company are given in Table 11.1.

The gearing ratios of each company, based on market values, are:

$$\text{Grosvenor plc} = \frac{3,000,000(1.25)}{2,000,000(1.50) + 3,000,000(1.25)} = 0.556 \text{ or } 55.6\%$$

$$\text{Brandywell plc} = \frac{1,000,000(0.98)}{10,000,000(0.75) + 1,000,000(0.98)} = 0.116 \text{ or } 11.6\%$$

Gearing ratios based on book values are:

$$\text{Grosvenor plc} = \frac{3,000,000}{(2,000,000 + 600,000) + 3,000,000} = 0.536 \text{ or } 53.6\%$$

$$\text{Brandywell plc} = \frac{1,000,000}{(2,500,000 + 3,200,000) + 1,000,000} = 0.149 \text{ or } 14.9\%$$

Whether the gearing ratio is based on market or book values, Grosvenor is the more highly geared of the two companies.

The importance of the gearing ratio is that it provides information about one aspect of an organisation's risk, its *financial risk*. If an organisation increases its gearing, the average return expected by its owners should increase, as a result of the acquisition of 'cheaper' loan financing. In other

---

[3]For an excellent discussion of this topic see for example R. Brealey and S. Myers, *Principles of Corporate Finance,* McGraw–Hill, 1981, especially Chapter 14.

Table 11.1   Grosvenor plc and Brandywell plc—Long-term capital details

	Grosvenor plc £	Brandywell plc £
Ordinary shares:		
2,000,000, each having a nominal value of £1	2,000,000	
10,000,000, each having a nominal value of 25p		2,500,000
Retained profits:	600,000	3,200,000
Long-term loans:		
£3,000,000 10% debentures, redeemable in 1999	3,000,000	
£1,000,000 irredeemable 8% loan stock		1,000,000
Market value per ordinary share	£1.50	75p
Market value per £100 debenture/loan stock	£125	£98

words, the prior right to income and capital enjoyed by preference shareholders and the lenders of loan capital determines that their required return is generally less than that required by equity owners. On the other hand, the financial risk of owners is increased with higher gearing because of:

(a)   the increased risk of loss of control and (possibly) liquidation, if fixed interest payments cannot be met in any year, and
(b)   the increased variability of returns to owners.

As an example of the second point, consider the case of two companies, Broomfield Ltd and Cliftonhill Ltd, each of which pays an ordinary dividend each year equal to its income after interest. Broomfield Ltd has no loan capital. Cliftonhill Ltd makes fixed interest payments of £1,000 each year. Annual income before interest and dividends is presently £1,000 for Broomfield Ltd and £2,000 for Cliftonhill Ltd. The figures in Table 11.2 show the effects on the ordinary dividends of each company if income (i) increases by

Table 11.2   Broomfield Ltd and Cliftonhill Ltd—Effects on ordinary dividends of changes in income

	Broomfield Ltd			Cliftonhill Ltd		
	Present income £	+10% £	−10% £	Present income £	+10% £	−10% £
Income before interest and dividends	1,000	1,100	900	2,000	2,200	1,800
Fixed interest payments	0	0	0	1,000	1,000	1,000
Ordinary dividend	1,000	1,100	900	1,000	1,200	800
Percentage change in ordinary dividend	–	+10%	−10%	–	+20%	−20%

10%, and (ii) decreases by 10%. The ordinary dividend of Cliftonhill Ltd (the geared company) is more sensitive to changes in pre-interest income than is the ordinary dividend of Broomfield Ltd.

11.6   Accounting Treatment of Long-term Sources of Capital

We now illustrate the recording and presentation of transactions relating to long-term capital for individuals, partnerships and limited companies.

Individuals

Mr Gayfield commences business on 1 January 19X0 by paying £8,000 from his personal resources into a business account. On the same day he receives a loan from Mrs Somerset of £3,000 which he also pays into the bank. Interest at 15% is payable on the loan annually in arrears (i.e. the interest is payable at the *end* of each year). The loan is repayable after five years. During the year to 31 December 19X0 Mr Gayfield's business makes sales of £21,260 and incurs expenses, excluding interest, of £14,380. Sales are all for cash and are paid into the bank account. All expenses are paid from the bank account. On 31 December the interest due on the loan, amounting to £450, is paid. During the year, Mr Gayfield withdraws £5,200 from the business bank account for his personal use. This amount includes transfers to Mr Gayfield's personal bank account and invoices paid by the business that relate to Mr Gayfield's personal affairs.

The accounting equation entries necessary to reflect the above transactions are shown in Table 11.3. The information in Table 11.3 is presented in the form of an income statement and balance sheet in Table 11.4. Note the different treatments accorded to interest paid on the long-term loan (which is regarded as an expense) and payments made to, or on behalf of, the owner (the drawings charged directly to ownership interest). Note also that net income for the year, after interest, is added to ownership interest, and represents Mr Gayfield's return for the year. The treatment adopted in Tables 11.3 and 11.4 would be the same whether or not the owner worked in the business himself. In other words, net income represents both the return on capital paid in *and* the reward paid to Mr Gayfield for his labour.

Partnerships

Miss Sealand and Miss Meadow commence business in partnership on 1 January 19X1. On that date they pay into the business bank account capital from their personal resources as follows: Miss Sealand £12,000, Miss Meadow £9,000. They also receive a loan of £5,000 from Mr Dean which is paid into the bank. The loan is repayable after 10 years, and carries interest at the rate of 10% per annum, payable in arrears. During the following year they receive sales revenue of £32,900 and pay expenses, excluding interest,

Table 11.3   Mr Gayfield—Accounting entries

	Assets		Ownership interest + Liabilities + Net income					
	Cash at bank £	=	Ownership interest £	+	Loan from Mrs Somerset £	+	Net income £	
Transaction								
Capital paid in	8,000		8,000					
Loan from Mrs Somerset	3,000				3,000			
Sales	21,260						21,260	(Sales)
Expenses excluding interest	(14,380)						(14,380)	(Expenses)
Interest to Mrs Somerset	(450)						(450)	(Interest)
Drawings	(5,200)		(5,200)					
							6,430	(Net income)
Transfer of net income to ownership interest			6,430				(6,430)	
Balances at end of year	12,230	=	9,230	+	3,000	+	0	

Table 11.4   Mr Gayfield—Accounting statements

	£	£
Income statement for the year ended 31 December 19X0		
Sales		21,260
less: Expenses	14,380	
Interest paid	450	14,830
Net income for the year		£6,430
Balance sheet on 31 December 19X0		
Assets		
Cash at bank		£12,230
Ownership interest		
Capital paid in	8,000	
add: Net income for the year	6,430	
	14,430	
less: Drawings	5,200	9,230
Liabilities		
Loan from Mrs Somerset		3,000
		£12,230

of £17,600. These amounts are paid into or from the bank account as appropriate. They also withdraw from the partnership bank account the following personal drawings: Miss Sealand £7,300, Miss Meadow £5,800. On 31 December they pay Mr Dean the interest due of £500. Their partnership agreement provides for each partner to be credited at the end of each year with 5% interest on her capital balance at the start of the year. In addition, each partner is to receive an annual salary of £5,000. Any balance of income is to be shared in a 2-to-1 ratio, Miss Sealand to Miss Meadow.

Accounting equation entries to record the above transactions are shown in Table 11.5. The information is presented in the form of accounting statements in Table 11.6. Two elements of the statements in Table 11.6 differ from those given in Table 11.4 and deserve closer attention. The first is that a separate *appropriation statement* is provided, showing how income for the year is divided between Miss Sealand and Miss Meadow in accordance with the details of the partnership agreement. Thus the appropriation statement shows how available income is shared between the owners. Such a statement is not needed for an individual because all income belongs to the (sole) owner. Each partner's share of income is added to her ownership interest. The second differentiating element is that partners' ownership interests are described as capital accounts. (This terminology may also be used for individuals.) In practice, a partner's ownership interest is sometimes subdivided into a *capital account* (the amount of which is usually

Table 11.5   Miss Sealand and Miss Meadow—Partnership accounting entries

| Transaction | Assets | = | Ownership interest + Liabilities + Net income | | | |
	Cash at bank £		Ownership interest Miss Sealand £	Ownership interest Miss Meadow £	Loan from Mr Dean £	Net income £
Capital paid in	21,000		12,000	9,000		
Loan from Mr Dean	5,000				5,000	
Sales	32,900					32,900 (Sales)
Expenses excluding interest	(17,600)					(17,600) (Expenses)
Interest to Mr Dean	(500)					(500) (Interest)
Drawings	(13,100)		(7,300)	(5,800)		
						14,800 (Income)
Transfer of net income to ownership interest (see Table 11.6 for details)			8,100	6,700		(14,800)
Balances at end of year	27,700	=	12,800	9,900	+ 5,000	+ 0

Table 11.6   Miss Sealand and Miss Meadow—Accounting statements

Income statement for the year ended 31 December 19X1

	£	£
Sales		32,900
less: Expenses	17,600	
Interest paid	500	18,100
Income for the year		£14,800

Appropriation statement for the year ended 31 December 19X1

	Miss Sealand	Miss Meadow	Total
	£	£	£
Interest on capital (at 5%)	600	450	1,050
Salaries	5,000	5,000	10,000
Balance (shared 2:1)	2,500	1,250	3,750
	8,100	6,700	14,800

Balance sheet on 31st December 19X1

			£
Assets			
Cash at bank			£27,700

Capital accounts	Miss Sealand	Miss Meadow	
Capital paid in	12,000	9,000	
add: Share of net income for the year	8,100	6,700	
	20,100	15,700	
less: Drawings	7,300	5,800	
	12,800	9,900	22,700
Liabilities			
Loan from Mr Dean			5,000
			£27,700

unchanged from year to year, and represents the 'permanent' long-term capital provided by the partner) and a *current account* (in which all other transactions, including share of income and drawings, are shown).

Limited companies

Plainmoor Ltd is incorporated (i.e. created) on 1 January 19X2 with *authorised share capital* as follows:[4]

1,000,000	50p ordinary shares
200,000	£1 irredeemable 12% preference shares

[4]Authorised share capital is the *maximum* amount of share capital a particular company may issue, as agreed by the original promoters of the company. The amount of authorised capital may subsequently be changed if the shareholders so agree.

On 1 January, the following capital is *issued* for cash:[5]

    500,000   50p ordinary shares at a price of £1.50 each
    100,000   £1 irredeemable preference shares at par (i.e. at the
                    nominal value of £1 each)
   £200,000   Irredeemable 10% debentures at par

During the following year, Plainmoor Ltd makes sales of £175,000 and incurs expenses, excluding interest, of £75,000. Sales revenue and expenses are paid into or out of the company bank account as appropriate. On 31 December, the company pays debenture interest (of £20,000), the preference dividend (of £12,000) and an ordinary dividend of 10p per share (£50,000).[6]

Accounting equation entries for the above transactions are given in Table 11.7. Accounting statements for Plainmoor Ltd, reflecting the information in Table 11.7, are shown in Table 11.8. The principles involved in presenting the income statement are similar to those applied in presenting the accounts of individuals and partnerships; interest on long-term loans (debentures) is treated as an expense, whereas payments to owners (dividends to ordinary and preference shareholders) are treated as appropriations of income. Dividends are equivalent to owners' drawings except that, as we noted earlier, they are not deducted directly from ownership interest, but rather subtracted from net income. The balance sheet is also drawn up on similar lines to those adopted for other organisations except that its content (and that of the income statement) is determined largely by legal requirements. Two particular features of long-term capital are specific to limited companies. The first is the inclusion of *authorised* share capital. This inclusion is demanded by company law. It is important to recognise that this figure (£700,000) does not form part of the company's double-entry records—it is a memorandum entry to indicate the maximum share capital the company is empowered to issue. Hence it is not included in the figure for total share capital and reserves. Second, capital paid in by owners (£750,000 from ordinary shareholders and £100,000 from preference shareholders) is subdivided between issued capital (the nominal value of the shares issued) and share premium (the difference between the amount received and the nominal value). In this case, the share premium is £1 per ordinary share (the issue price of £1.50 minus the nominal value of 50p), giving a total of £500,000. As we noted earlier, a share's nominal value is of no particular significance other than as a means of describing and identifying the share.

---

[5]Issued capital is that part of its authorised share capital issued by a company.

[6]In this case, the amount of dividends is described as an amount per share. This is the usual method of showing dividends. They are sometimes described as percentages, for example as a dividend of 10% or 20%. In such cases, the percentage relates to the *nominal* value of *issued* capital. Thus for Plainmoor Ltd, the ordinary dividend could be described as a dividend of 20%, i.e. 20% of the nominal value of the ordinary shares issued, £250,000 (500,000×50p), which equals £50,000.

Table 11.7 Plainmoor Ltd—Accounting entries

Transaction	Assets Cash at bank £	=	Ordinary share capital £	Preference share capital £	Share premium £	Reserves £	Debentures £	Net income £	
Ordinary shares issued	750,000	=	250,000		500,000				
Preference shares issued	100,000			100,000					
Debentures issued	200,000						200,000		
Sales	175,000							175,000	(Sales)
Expenses excluding interest	(75,000)							(75,000)	(Expenses)
Debenture interest	(20,000)							(20,000)	(Interest)
								80,000	(Income)
Preference dividend	(12,000)							(12,000)	(Preference dividend)
Ordinary dividend	(50,000)							(50,000)	(Ordinary dividend)
								18,000	(Retained net income)
Transfer of retained net income to reserves						18,000		(18,000)	
Balances at end	1,068,000	=	250,000	+ 100,000	+ 500,000	+ 18,000	+ 200,000	+ 0	

Table 11.8   Plainmoor Ltd—Accounting statements

	£	£
Income statement for the year ended 31 December 19X2		
Sales		175,000
less: Expenses excluding interest	75,000	
Debenture interest	20,000	95,000
Income for the year		80,000
less: Appropriations:		
Dividends—preference	12,000	
ordinary	50,000	62,000
Retained income, added to reserves		£18,000
Balance sheet on 31 December 19X2		
Assets		
Cash at bank		£1,068,000
Share capital and reserves		
Authorised 1,000,000 50p Ordinary shares	500,000	
200,000 £1 irredeemable 12% preference shares	200,000	
	700,000	
Issued 500,000 50p Ordinary shares	250,000	
100,000 £1 irredeemable 12% preference shares	100,000	350,000
Share premium		500,000
Reserves		18,000
Total share capital and reserves		868,000
Long-term loans		
Irredeemable 10% debentures		200,000
Capital employed		£1,068,000

This chapter completes our review and explanation of the constituent elements of the balance sheet and income statement prepared under historical cost accounting. You should now be in a position to understand the nature, purpose and the limitations of both these financial statements, and, in particular, you should be able to comprehend the way in which the double-entry book-keeping system serves as the basis for the compilation of all entries appearing in each of the two statements. The appendix following this chapter brings together, by way of a detailed book-keeping example, most aspects of an organisation's transactions, and draws on the ideas and examples used in this and previous chapters.

Discussion Topics

1 Outline and explain the relationships you might expect to observe on an enterprise's balance sheet between fixed and current assets on the one hand, and long-term and short-term sources of finance on the other.

2 Describe the main respects in which the financial characteristics of individuals, partnerships and limited companies differ.

3 Discuss the major differences between ownership interest (or equity capital) and long-term loans (or loan capital).

4 Distinguish between 'drawings' and 'dividends'. To what extent does either measure the returns to an organisation's owners?

5 What do you understand by a company's 'gearing ratio'? Why is it important?

6 Distinguish between 'appropriations' and 'expenses'.

7 Each of the following terms might be found in a set of accounts. In respect of each, state where it would be found, what it means and which accounting entries it reflects.

   (a)   Capital account
   (b)   Ordinary share dividends
   (c)   Loan interest paid
   (d)   Authorised share capital
   (e)   Share premium
   (f)   Current account
   (g)   20,000 £1 redeemable 7% preference shares
   (h)   Reserves
   (i)   Debenture interest paid
   (j)   Retained income
   (k)   Drawings
   (l)   Preference share dividends
   (m)   Long-term loan
   (n)   Balance of partnership profit (share 2:1:1)
   (o)   10 million 25p ordinary shares
   (p)   Irredeemable 13% debentures.

Further Reading

Armitage, B., 'Raising equity capital: Is the BES right for you?' *Accountancy,* June 1984.

Briston, R.J., *The Stock Exchange and Investment Analysis,* 3rd Edn, Allen and Unwin, 1975.

Peasnell, K.V. and Ward, C.W.R., *British Financial Markets and Institutions,* Prentice-Hall International, 1985.

Exercises

11.1 Mr Ramphis, a grocer, has prepared the following accounts for his first year's trading from 1 January 19X7.

Profit and loss account for the year ended 31 December 19X7

	£		£
Purchases	24,860	Sales	40,950
Gross profit c/d	16,090		
	40,950		40,950
Wages	14,040	Gross profit b/d	16,090
Sundry shop expenses	7,690	Net loss for the year	7,410
Van expenses	1,770		
	23,500		23,500

Balance sheet on 31 December 19X7

Capital:			
Cash paid in	10,000	Van	5,000
less: Net loss for the year	7,410	Cash at bank	90
	2,590		5,090

Mr Ramphis is perturbed that the accounts do not balance and asks for your assistance. He gives you the following information:

(i) Mr Ramphis has taken groceries to the value of £30 per week for his personal consumption for which no adjustment has been made.

(ii) Included in the purchases figures of £24,860 are goods to the value of £3,500 which were held in stock at 31 December 19X7.

(iii) All sales and purchases were for cash. On 31 December 19X7, Mr Ramphis made sales amounting to £2,500 to a local restaurant. He received payment for these sales on that date, and paid the amount received into the bank account. As yet, no other entry has been made in the records in respect of these sales.

(iv) There was no cash in hand at the end of the year.

(v) The figure for wages is made up as follows:

	£
Mr Ramphis, £150 per week	7,800
Employees' wages, £120 per week	6,240
	14,040

(vi) Sundry shop expenses include £2,000 which was paid on 1 January 19X7, for the purchase of equipment to be used in the shop. Mr Ramphis estimates the life of this equipment at 10 years, and its scrap value at the end of that period at zero.

(vii) The van was purchased on 1 January 19X7. Mr Ramphis estimates that he will keep it until 31 December 19X9, when its value will be about £1,700.

(viii) Depreciation is to be provided on fixed assets using the straight line method of calculation.

- (a) Prepare a statement with brief explanatory notes showing any adjustments which you think are necessary to the accounts prepared by Mr Ramphis.
- (b) Prepare a revised profit and loss account for the year ended 31 December 19X7 and balance sheet as at that date.

11.2 Amonasro and Radames formed a partnership on 1 September 19X2, to buy and sell annas. The terms of the partnership were as follows:

(i) Profits were to be shared $\frac{2}{3}$ to Amonasro and $\frac{1}{3}$ to Radames.
(ii) In addition, Radames was to receive a salary of £2,000 p.a.
(iii) On 31 August in each year, interest was to be credited at the rate of 10% on the balance of each partner's capital account on the previous 1 September.

The balances shown below appeared in the books of the partnership on 31 August 19X3. Amonasro and Radames maintain separate accounts for each item of revenue and expense contributing to income.

	Dr Assets and expenses £	Cr Ownership interest, liabilities and revenues £
Capital accounts (capital introduced on 1 September 19X2):		
Amonasro		40,000
Radames		20,000
Drawings:		
Amonasro	12,000	
Radames (including salary)	10,800	
Lease on premises at cost	24,000	
Motor vehicles at cost	7,200	
Office furniture and equipment at cost	2,400	
Cash at bank	20,660	
Sales		133,600
Purchases	87,000	
Discounts allowed to customers	1,940	
Discounts received from suppliers		3,520
Office salaries	11,160	
Rent and rates	7,600	
Insurance	960	
Repairs	660	
Lighting and heating	1,740	
Motor vehicle expenses (excluding depreciation)	3,480	
Carriage and postage	3,620	
General expenses	1,900	
	197,120	197,120

The following additional information is available:

(i)   Straight line depreciation is to be provided at the following rates on cost:

Motor vehicles   25%
Office furniture and equipment   10%

(ii)   The value of stock at 31 August 19X3 is estimated at £11,200.

(iii) A provision of £3,000 for amortization of the lease is to be made.

(iv)   No interest is to be charged on partners' drawings.

• Prepare the partnership profit and loss account for the year ended 31 August 19X3, and balance sheet as at that date.

11.3   Giovanni is a long established public limited company. In the year ended 31 December 19X1 it issued 10,000 shares of £1 nominal value at a premium of £1. Cash was received on 30 December 19X1 and banked on 31 December 19X1. The allotment of shares was made on 31 December 19X1. No entries for either of these transactions have been made in the trial balance which appears below:

| | £'000s | |
	Dr	Cr
Sales		2,500
Sales returns	100	
Purchases	1,800	
Trade creditors		150
Trade debtors	250	
Bad debts provision at 1 January 19X1		50
Share capital		650
Revenue reserves at 1 January 19X1		400
Fixed assets	300	
Accumulated depreciation 31 December 19X1		150
Depreciation charge for the year	50	
Stock at 1 January 19X1	1,300	
Expenses	100	
	3,900	3,900

Stock at 31 December 19X1 was valued at £1,100,000. The bad debts provision is to be adjusted to £25,000.

• Prepare the profit and loss account of Giovanni plc for the year ended 31 December 19X1 and the balance sheet as at that date.

11.4   Amneris Ltd was incorporated on 1 May 19X0 with authorised share capital as follows:

5,000,000   50p ordinary shares
1,000,000   £1 irredeemable 14% preference shares

On 1 May 19X0, the following capital was issued for cash:

3,000,000   50p ordinary shares at a price of £1.25 each
700,000   £1 irredeemable preference shares at a price of £1.10 each
£1,000,000   12% debentures at par, redeemable on 30 April 19X9 at par.

During the year ended 30 April 19X1, Amneris Ltd acquired fixed assets at a cost of £4,500,000, made sales of £3,200,000 and incurred expenses of £2,400,000 (excluding interest but including £900,000 depreciation on fixed assets). Sales revenue, the cost of fixed assets and expenses (excluding depreciation) were paid into or out of the company bank account, as appropriate. On 30 April 19X1, Amneris Ltd paid one year's interest on the debentures, an annual preference dividend of 14% and an ordinary dividend of 10p per share.

- (a)   Prepare Amneris Ltd's profit and loss account for the year ended 30 April 19X1 and its balance sheet on that date, in a form suitable for publication.
- (b)   Outline the main characteristics of the various types of capital issued by Amneris Ltd.

11.5   Lescaut plc is a listed company whose major activity is retailing. The company prepares accounts annually to 31 March. The following is a summary of the balances extracted from the books of Lescaut plc for the year ended 31 March 19X6:

	£millions
Bank overdraft	38.1
Reserves	110.0
Creditors	76.7
Debentures (10%—repayable 19Y5)	800.0
Debtors	8.1
Depreciation: Accumulated provisions at 1 April 19X5:	
Fittings and equipment	372.8
Freehold land and buildings	263.5
Directors' remuneration	0.8
Fittings and equipment, at cost	780.0
Freehold land and buildings, at cost	1,486.0
Goodwill	112.6
Interest payable	82.4
Interim dividend paid (5%)	25.0
Investment income	10.3
Issued share capital	500.0
Overhead expenses	85.5
Profit and loss account	
(credit balance at 1 April 19X5)	275.0
Purchases	432.8
Sales	920.5
Stock (balance at 1 April 19X5)	227.3
Investments in shares	126.4

The following information is also available:

- (i)   The authorised share capital of Lescaut plc is £700 million.
- (ii)   Stock at 31 March 19X6 is estimated at £282.9 million.
- (iii)   Depreciation is to be provided, using the straight line method, at the following rates:
  - Fittings and equipment   25%
  - Freehold land and buildings   5%
- (iv)   No provision has yet been made for audit charges for the year, which are estimated at £500,000.

    (v) The directors wish to provide for a final dividend of 10% of the issued
        share capital, in addition to the interim dividend already paid.
  (vi) Interest payable includes debenture interest (£60 million) and bank
        overdraft interest (£22.4 million). Debenture interest is payable on 30
        June and 31 December each year.

- (a) Prepare the trial balance of Lescaut plc at 31 March 19X6, *before*
        taking account of points (i) to (vi) above.
   (b) Prepare the profit and loss account of Lescaut plc for the year ended
        31 March 19X6 and its balance sheet as at that date.

APPENDIX B
A Detailed Example of Double-entry Book-keeping

B.1   Book-keeping and accounting activities

In the previous seven chapters we have examined the procedures necessary
to prepare the income statement and the balance sheet. To produce meaningful statements of performance (income statement) and position (balance
sheet) the accounting process should record all transactions and events
which affect the organisation's business activities. Further, as we have
explained in Chapters 6 and 7, the accounting process must allocate
revenues and expenses to the period in which they are generated and
incurred.

    The preparation of meaningful financial statements thus comprises two
distinct stages; first the recording and classification of a variety of transactions and events, and secondly the allocation of revenues and expenses to
specific time periods. The first stage is purely mechanical—the accountant
acts as a book-keeper. The second stage is less mechanical—it involves
adjustments to the accounting records and requires the accountant to exercise his judgment. We shall examine each stage in turn.

B.2   Stage one: book-keeping activities

    (*i*) *Source documents, journals and ledgers.* Most business transac-
tions are supported by some documentary evidence. Raw material purchases
are normally accompanied by suppliers' invoices; the local electricity board
sends regular bills for the cost of heating and lighting; when a company sells
goods it usually sends a sales invoice to the customer and retains a copy for its
own records; cheque payments are evidenced by cheque stubs or cheque
copies, and receipts by completed paying-in slips. Such documents are called
source documents and represent the raw material from which financial
statements are produced.

    At regular interals (daily, weekly or monthly depending upon the
volume of transactions and the managers' efficiency) the financial data

contained in the source documents are entered into the accounting records.[1] In the illustration which follows (Section B.4) the data are entered directly into the company's ledger accounts. We have previously referred to these ledger accounts as 'T' accounts. In large organisations the volume of transactions is too great to allow for individual recording in the ledger accounts. Instead, the individual transactions are recorded in *journals*, or *day books*, and only the monthly or quarterly totals are entered into the ledger accounts.

The number of separate journals kept by the organisation will depend upon the nature of its business, but large organisations normally maintain a sales journal, a purchases journal, a cash receipts journal and a cash payments journal. It is worth emphasising that these journals do *not* form part of the double-entry book-keeping system—they simply store the data to be transferred or 'posted' later, in aggregate, to the ledger accounts.

However, the management of a business requires much more information about debtors and creditors than the aggregate total of credit sales and purchases made during an accounting period. Specifically, management should know the exact amount owed to the business by each *individual* customer; know when a *specific* customer has reached his limit of credit; and for *control* purposes, have a general history of the purchase and payment patterns of each customer. In addition, managers need to know the exact amounts owing to individual suppliers, so that purchases can be controlled and payments made on time. Details extracted from purchase invoices, copies of sales invoices, cheque stubs and paying-in slips can be used to maintain an updated 'balance outstanding' for each customer and supplier. These records, called *subsidiary ledgers*, are also outside the double-entry book-keeping system.

In the example which follows the number of transactions is insufficient to warrant the use of either journals or subsidiary ledgers. Instead, information is recorded directly in the organisation's *general ledger* which contains a 'T' account for each classification of asset, equity, liability, revenue and expense. Whether or not journals are maintained, the financial data become part of the double-entry book-keeping system only when they are entered into the accounts of the general ledger.

(ii)   Trial balance. Each business transaction gives rise to a debit entry and an equivalent credit entry. Hence, the sum of all debit balances must equal the sum of all credit balances at any given time. This can be checked by extracting the balances and listing them in a trial balance. We discussed the nature and usefulness of the trial balance in Chapter 8. However, the fact that the sum of the debit balances equals the sum of the credit balances is not proof that the book-keeping procedures have been free from error. For

---

[1]In most large organisations these accounting records are maintained on a computer. However, the principles discussed in this appendix are effectively the same whether records are kept manually or on a computer.

example, although the matching of equal debit and credit entries will result in a trial balance which balances, the composition of the trial balance will be incorrect if an item has been posted incorrectly to the debit of, say, the cash account instead of, say, the depreciation expense account.

B.3   Stage two: from trial balance to financial statements

(*i*)   *Accounting adjustments.*   Even in the absence of book-keeping errors the financial statements cannot normally be prepared directly from the trial balance. We have seen in previous chapters that the accountant must make a series of adjustments in order to match revenues and expenses of particular periods. Matching normally involves the recognition of pre-payments, accruals, depreciation and closing stock. These adjustments must be recorded in the relevant general ledger accounts.

The final adjustment prior to the preparation of the financial statements is to transfer the balances on the various 'expense' and 'revenue' accounts to the profit and loss account. The profit and loss account is a 'T' account in the general ledger like the other 'T' accounts referred to above. This transfer of balances means that, apart from the balance on the profit and loss account, no balance remains on any expense or revenue account—there are no balances on these accounts to be carried forward to the next accounting period.

(*ii*)   *Income statement and balance sheet.*   The final accounts may now be prepared. The income statement is a summary of the figures contained in the profit and loss account in the general ledger. The balance sheet is a summary of the balances remaining (i.e. a sheet of balances) in the ledger after the profit and loss account balance has been transferred to ownership interest.

In the following sections we illustrate these procedures by means of a comprehensive review example.

B.4   The Camera Shop Ltd—an illustration

The Camera Shop sells camera equipment, films and processing chemicals to professional photographers. Its balance sheet at 31 July 19X4 is presented opposite.

All sales and purchases are on credit. The company's fixed assets consist of shop fittings and office equipment, all of which are depreciated on a straight line basis at an annual rate of 10% on cost. The bank loan was taken out three years ago. Interest is charged at a rate of 15% p.a. payable on 31 March and 30 September; no capital repayments are due until 19X7. The shop is rented at an annual cost of £7,200 and the rent is paid quarterly in advance on 1 March, June, September and December. A stock count and valuation is undertaken at the end of each month so that monthly accounting

The Camera Shop Ltd—Balance sheet at 31 July 19X4

	£	£	£
Assets employed			
Fixed assets			
Shop and office equipment at cost			26,400
less: Accumulated depreciation			12,600
			13,800
Current assets			
Stock		43,670	
Debtors	34,000		
less: Provision for bad debts	1,700	32,300	
Prepaid rent		600	
Cash at bank		1,550	
		78,120	
Current liabilities			
Trade creditors		24,070	
Interest accrued		1,200	
Miscellaneous accruals		740	
		26,010	
Net current assets			52,110
Total assets less current liabilities			65,910
Creditors due after more than one year			
Bank loan			24,000
			£41,910
Capital and reserves			
Share capital			25,000
Retained profit			16,910
			£41,910

statements can be prepared. At the end of each month the provision for bad debts is adjusted to an amount equal to 5% of the debtors' balance.

The following is a record of the transactions and events which took place in August 19X4:

Transaction/ event	Date	
1	2/8	Received a cheque for £7,000 from Edgbaston Studios in respect of goods sold in July.
2	3/8	Took delivery of film and chemicals costing £1,800 from Headingley Film and Equipment Company; details are recorded on their invoice no. H42.
3	3/8	Paid £2,500 to Trafford Camera Equipment Ltd on cheque no. 6210.

4	5/8	Sold cameras and darkroom equipment to Trent Photographers for £6,600 on invoice no. 801.
5	9/8	Wrote cheque no. 6211 for £280 to pay an electricity bill accrued at the end of July.
6	11/8	Bought a new electric typewriter for £850 on cheque no. 6212.
7	12/8	Received supplies of cameras costing £3,600 from Oval Photographic Equipment Ltd; details are recorded on their invoice no. 081.
8	16/8	Sold darkroom equipment, cameras and film to Mr Lord for £5,850 on invoice no. 802.
9	17/8	Cashed cheque no. 6213 to pay wages of £1,230.
10	18/8	Paid £4,000 to Oval Photographic Equipment Ltd on cheque no. 6214.
11	19/8	Paid transport costs of £460, accrued in July, on cheque no. 6215.
12	24/8	Paid dividend of £800 on cheque no. 6216.
13	25/8	Received a cheque for £4,750 from Mr Lord.
14	31/8	Received an electricity bill for £390 for electricity used in August. Owed wages of £1,120 at the end of the month. A stock count established that the cost of the stock on hand was £44,100.

Our task is to prepare an income statement for the month of August and a balance sheet at 31 August 19X4. We shall adopt the following framework:

Section B.5   check that the opening balances on the accounts in the general ledger are consistent with those on the balance sheet at 31 July.

Section B.6   using the double-entry system of book-keeping, record all transactions for August in the relevant accounts in the general ledger.

Section B.7   extract a trial balance from the accounts in the general ledger.

Section B.8   make any necessary adjustments to the figures in order to match correctly the period's revenues and expenses.

Section B.9   close off the accounts in the general ledger ready for next month's transactions and prepare an income statement and balance sheet.

B.5   The opening balances

At the end of July the Camera Shop prepared an income statement for the period 1 July to 31 July (not shown here) and a balance sheet at 31 July (reproduced in Section B.4). The figures included in those two financial statements are represented by the balances extracted from the general ledger accounts. The balances on the various revenue and expense accounts have been transferred to the profit and loss account; thus the only balances remaining in the general ledger should be those appearing in the balance sheet at 31 July. We must check that this is so.

The accounts appear in the general ledger sequenced by account number (Table B.1). The numerical ordering, for ease of understanding, is as follows:

   (i)   all assets in the order they appear in the balance sheet;
  (ii)   all liabilities in the order they appear in the balance sheet;
 (iii)   all ownership interest accounts;
 (iv)   all revenues;
  (v)   all expenses and appropriations in the order they appear in the income statement.

Table B.1   The Camera Shop Ltd—Chart of general ledger accounts

Account name	Account number
Shop and office equipment—cost	100
Shop and office equipment—accumulated depreciation	101
Stock	110
Debtors	115
Provision for bad debts	116
Prepaid rent	120
Cash at bank	130
Trade creditors	200
Interest accrued	220
Miscellaneous accruals	230
Bank loan	240
Share capital	300
Retained profit	310
Sales revenue	400
Purchases	420
Cost of goods sold	425
Rent expense	430
Wages expense	431
Heat and light expense	432
Bad debts expense	440
Depreciation expense	450
Interest expense	460
Dividends	500
Profit and loss	600

The accounts are not numbered consecutively because other accounts may be added later and these will require new numbers. This system of ordering is only one of many available (for example, an alternative system is to order the accounts alphabetically).

The ledger accounts presented on pages 239–247 are as they would appear at 31 August and not 31 July (i.e. they comprise part of the solution to this review problem). To see how they would have appeared at 31 July we must ignore all items which have an August date. For example, the accounts numbered 100, 101, 120 and 431 would have appeared at 31 July as follows:

Shop and office equipment: cost	No. 100		Shop and office equipment: accumulated depreciation	No. 101
31 July Balance 26,400			31 July Balance 12,600	

Prepaid rent	No. 120		Wages expense	No. 431
31 July Balance 600				

(Check all the accounts to satisfy yourself that each balance sheet figure, and no other, has been 'brought forward' correctly in the general ledger.)

B.6   Recording the transactions in the general ledger

The Camera Shop does not maintain journals. Instead all transactions are entered directly into the general ledger. In this section we shall explain the book-keeping entries which are necessary to record the August transactions in the general ledger.

Transaction 1

2 August. Received a cheque for £7,000 from Edgbaston Studios in respect of goods sold in July.

The receipt of a cheque for £7,000 increases the cash balance of the Camera Shop and we record this by debiting the Cash at Bank account (Account number 130, hereinafter referred to as AC130). This cash receipt is the result of a sales transaction which occurred at an earlier date. We are informed that the Camera Shop sold goods to Edgbaston Studios for £7,000 in July. No cash changed hands at the time of the transaction and this *credit sale* was recorded in the general ledger by crediting Sales Revenue (AC400) and debiting Debtors (AC115) with £7,000 each. As Edgbaston Studios had not settled their account by 31 July, the £7,000 posted to the Debtors account was included in the balance of £34,000 on that account at 31 July. On 2 August Edgbaston Studios settled its account and its debt is extinguished by making a credit entry of £7,000 in the Debtors account.

Accounting entry:			£	£
2 August	Cash (130)	Debit	7,000	
	Debtors (115)	Credit		7,000

Transaction 2

3 August. Took delivery of film and chemicals costing £1,800 from Headingley Film and Equipment Company; details are recorded on their invoice no. H42.

The Camera Shop has received a consignment of film and chemicals from a supplier. The shop has not paid cash on delivery (COD) but has purchased the goods on credit and will pay the supplier at a later date. Although no cash has been paid, the legal title to the goods has passed to the Camera Shop and the transaction must be recorded in the account. As the goods are items of stock which are to be resold at a future date, £1,800 is debited to the Purchases account (AC420). The supplier is now a creditor of the business, and this is recognised by crediting the Trade creditors account (AC200) with £1,800.

Accounting entry:			£	£
3 August	Purchases (420)	Debit	1,800	
	Trade creditors (200)	Credit		1,800

Transaction 3

3 August. Paid £2,500 to Trafford Camera Equipment Ltd on cheque no. 6210.

At an earlier date the Camera Shop purchased goods on credit from Trafford Camera Equipment Ltd. At the time of that transaction the purchase value was debited to the Purchases account and credited to the Trade creditors account (as in Transaction 2 above). The Camera Shop is now eliminating its liability to a trade creditor by settling its account. Hence both the balance of Trade creditors (AC200) outstanding and the balance of Cash at bank (AC130) are reduced by £7,000.

Accounting entry:			£	£
3 August	Trade creditors (200)	Debit	7,000	
	Cash at bank (130)	Credit		7,000

Transaction 4

5 August. Sold cameras and darkroom equipment to Trent Photographers for £6,600 on invoice no. 801.

No cash was received at the date of sale. However, the goods became the property of Trent Photographers at that date and the sale must be recorded in the accounts of the Camera Shop. Sales revenue (AC400) is credited with £6,600 and as Trent Photographers owes money to the shop we recognise this by debiting the Debtors' account (AC115) with £6,600.

Accounting entry:			£	£
5 August	Debtors (115)	Debit	6,600	
	Sales revenue (400)	Credit		6,600

Transaction 5

9 August. Wrote cheque no. 6211 for £280 to pay an electricity bill accrued at the end of July.

An electricity bill for £280 was received on 5 August. The bill referred to the cost of electricity used by the Camera Shop up to 31 July. At 31 July the Camera Shop recognised that it had used, but not paid for, electricity during the month. It estimated (accurately) that the cost was £280 and this amount was debited to Heat and light expense (AC432) and crediting Miscellaneous accruals (AC230). The transaction on 9 August refers to the settlement of the account. Cash (AC130) is credited with £280 and the liability to the Electricity Board is extinguished by debiting Miscellaneous accruals (AC230) with £280.

Accounting entry:			£	£
9 August	Misc. accruals (230)	Debit	280	
	Cash (130)	Credit		280

Transaction 6

11 August. Bought a new electric typewriter for £850 on cheque no. 6212.

This is a cash transaction—cash was paid at the time of purchase. The typewriter has not been purchased with the intention of resale. It is not, therefore, part of the Camera Shop's stock-in-trade and the cost is *not* entered in the Purchases account. Rather the typewriter is a fixed asset which will last, and provide benefits, for several years. It is categorised as Shop and office equipment, and will be depreciated over its useful life.

Accounting entry:			£	£
11 August	Shop and office equipment:			
	cost (100)	Debit	850	
	Cash (130)	Credit		850

Transaction 7

12 August. Received supplies of cameras costing £3,600 from Oval Photographic Equipment Ltd; details are recorded on their invoice no. 081.

This transaction is similar to that described as Transaction 2 above. It is a purchase of stock on credit.

Accounting entry:			£	£
12 August	Purchases (420)	Debit	3,600	
	Trade creditors (200)	Credit		3,600

Transaction 8

16 August. Sold darkroom equipment, cameras and film to Mr Lord for £5,850 on invoice no. 802.

This transaction is similar to that described as Transaction 4 above. It is a sale of goods on credit.

Accounting entry:			£	£
16 August	Debtors (115)	Debit	5,850	
	Sales revenue (400)	Credit		5,850

Transaction 9

17 August. Cashed cheque no. 6213 to pay wages of £1,230.

The Camera Shop pays staff wages twice a month. Strictly, the wages have been accruing daily over the first 17 days, but as both the expense and the cash settlement occur within the same accounting period the transaction can be recorded as a straightforward cash transaction.

Accounting entry:			£	£
17 August	Wages expense (431)	Debit	1,230	
	Cash (130)	Credit		1,230

Transaction 10

18 August. Paid £4,000 to Oval Photographic Equipment Ltd on cheque no. 6214.

This transaction is similar to that described as Transaction 3 above. It is the cash settlement of a supplier's account. As the amount paid (£4,000) is greater than the amount purchased from Oval Ltd in August (£3,600, Transaction 7) it is likely that this payment is in respect of goods purchased in July.

Accounting entry:			£	£
18 August	Trade creditors (200)	Debit	4,000	
	Cash at bank (130)	Credit		4,000

Transaction 11

19 August. Paid transport costs of £460, accrued in July, on cheque no. 6215.

This transaction is similar to that described as Transaction 5 above. It is the cash settlement of a bill which refers to an expense incurred in a previous period.

Accounting entry:			£	£
19 August	Misc. accruals (230)	Debit	460	
	Cash (130)	Credit		460

Transaction 12

24 August. Paid dividend of £800 on cheque no. 6216.

This transaction involves a cash payment and consequently £800 is credited to the Cash at bank account (AC130). The debit is posted to the Dividends

account (AC500) which will be shown as a deduction in the income statement. However, there is an important distinction between the payment of
dividends and, say, the payment of wages (see Transaction 9 above). Wages
are an *expense* of running the business. They are deducted as part of the
calculation of net profit for the period. Dividends are a *distribution* or
appropriation of the profit for the period and appear in the income statement *after* net profit has been calculated.

Accounting entry:			£	£
24 August	Dividends (500)	Debit	3,000	
	Cash (130)	Credit		3,000

Transaction 13

25 August. Received a cheque for £4,750 from Mr Lord. This transaction is similar to that described as Transaction 1.

Accounting entry:			£	£
25 August	Cash (130)	Debit	4,750	
	Debtors (115)	Credit		4,750

Events 14 and 15

31 August. Estimated that the cost of electricity used during August was
£390.
Owed wages of £1,120 at the end of the month.
A stock count established that the cost of the stock on hand was
£44,100.

These three items of information do not refer to transactions. They are,
however, important in the calculation of accrued expenses at the end of the
month and of cost of goods sold for the month and as such will be taken into
account in Section B.8.

B.7   The trial balance

The trial balance is a list of all the accounts used by the business and the
balance on each account at a specific date. The fact that the sum of all debit
balances equals the sum of all credit balances does not ensure the book-
keeping process has been error-free (see section B.2 above). However, a
lack of balance does indicate the existence of one or more errors. These
errors should be identified before proceeding further.

The trial balance of the accounts of the Camera Shop at 31 August is
presented in the first two columns of Table B.2. *The figures in the trial
balance represent the balances in the accounts in the general ledger after
recording Transactions 1–13 but before making any end of period adjustments.* The sum of all the debit balances amounts to £116,830 and is equal to
the sum of all the credit balances.

Table B.2 The Camera Shop Ltd—Worksheet for the month ended 31 August 19X1

Account no.	Account title	Trial balance Debit	Trial balance Credit	Adjustments Debit	Adjustments Credit	Adjusted trial balance Debit	Adjusted trial balance Credit	Income statement Debit	Income statement Credit	Balance sheet Debit	Balance sheet Credit
100	Shop and office equipment—cost	27,250				27,250				27,250	
101	Shop and office equipment—accumulated depreciation		12,600		(1) 227		12,827				12,827
110	Stock	43,670		(7c) 44,100	(7a) 43,670	44,100				44,100	
115	Debtors	34,700				34,700				34,700	
116	Provision for bad debts		1,700		(4) 35		1,735				1,735
120	Prepaid rent	600			(3) 600						
130	Cash at bank	3,180				3,180				3,180	
200	Trade creditors		22,970				22,970				22,970
220	Interest accrued		1,200		(2) 300		1,500				1,500
230	Miscellaneous accruals				(5) 390 (6) 1,120		1,510				1,510
240	Bank loan		24,000				24,000				24,000
300	Share capital		25,000				25,000				25,000
310	Retained profit		16,910				16,910				16,910
400	Sales revenue		12,450				12,450		12,450		
420	Purchases	5,400			(7b) 5,400						
425	Cost of goods sold			(7a) 43,670 (7b) 5,400	(7c) 44,100	4,970		4,970			
430	Rent expense			(3) 600		600		600			
431	Wages expense	1,230		(6) 1,120		2,350		2,350			
432	Heat and light expense			(5) 390		390		390			
440	Bad debts expense			(4) 35		35		35			
450	Depreciation expense			(1) 227		227		227			
460	Interest expense			(2) 300		300		300			
500	Dividends	800				800		800			
	Subtotals	116,830	116,830	95,842	95,842	118,902	118,902	9,672	12,450	109,230	
	Transfer retained profit to ownership interest							2,778			2,778
	Totals	116,830	116,830	95,842	95,842	118,902	118,902	12,450	12,450	109,230	109,230

B.8   Accounting adjustments and worksheets

Table B.2 is an illustration of an end-of-period accounting worksheet. The major advantage of a worksheet is its comprehensiveness. All 'post trial balance' adjustments can be entered on, and 'draft' financial statements prepared from, the worksheet. Given the chaos that often exists in the accounting departments of business organisations after the financial year end and prior to the completion of the financial statements, accounting adjustments are not usually entered in the general ledger until the financial statements have been agreed. We shall adopt this approach also by completing the accounting process on the worksheet before entering the adjustments in the general ledger. The sequence of steps is as follows:

 (i)   record the accounting adjustments in the 'Adjustments' columns on the worksheet;
 (ii) refer to the original trial balance and to the adjustments to produce an 'Adjusted trial balance'; and
 (iii) produce a draft income statement and balance sheet in the final four columns of the worksheet.

If we are satisfied with the correctness of the draft financial statements, we can record the accounting adjustments in the general ledger and close off each account in readiness for the next accounting period.

The adjustments to be made at 31 August can be ascertained from the information provided in Section B.4. The numbers assigned to the adjustments below can be used to identify the entries made on the worksheet.

Adjustment 1.   The Camera Shop depreciates its fixed assets on a straight line basis at an annual rate of 10% on cost. At 31 August the cost of shop and office equipment was £27,250 and thus one month's depreciation amounts to £27,250 × 0.01 ÷ 12 = £227.

Accounting entry:			£	£
31 August	Deprec'n expense (450)	Debit	227	
	Shop and office equipment			
	—accum. deprec'n (101)	Credit		227

Adjustment 2.   Interest on the bank loan is charged at a rate of 15% p.a., payable on 31 March and 30 September. No interest need be *paid* in August but we should *accrue* for one month's interest, i.e. £24,000 × 0.15 ÷ 12 = £300.

Accounting entry:			£	£
31 August	Interest expense (460)	Debit	300	
	Interest accrued (220)	Credit		300

Adjustment 3.   The shop is rented at an annual cost of £7,200 and the rent is paid quarterly in advance on 1 March, June, September and December. The rent for the month of August was thus prepaid on 1 June.

We must now recognise as an expense that part of the rental payment which relates to August.

Accounting entry:			£	£
31 August	Rent expense (430)	Debit	600	
	Prepaid rent (120)	Credit		600

Adjustment 4.   At the end of each month the provision for bad debts is adjusted to an amount equal to 5% of the debtors' balance. At 31 August the balance on the Debtors' account is £34,700, which requires a provision for bad debts of £34,700×0.05=£1,735. As the provision at the beginning of the month was £1,700, a further £35 must be provided against possible bad debts.

Accounting entry:			£	£
31 August	Bad debts expense (440)	Debit	35	
	Prov'n for bad debts (116)	Credit		35

Adjustment 5.   On 31 August the Camera Shop estimated that the cost of electricity used in August was £390. We must record this expense in August and recognise that the Camera Shop owes £390 to the Electricity Board at the end of the month.

Accounting entry:			£	£
31 August	Heat and light expense (432)	Debit	390	
	Misc. accruals (230)	Credit		390

Adjustment 6.   The Camera Shop owed wages of £1,120 at the end of the month. The accruals principle applies here in the same way as in Adjustment 5.

Accounting entry:			£	£
31 August	Wages expense (431)	Debit	1,120	
	Misc. accruals (230)	Credit		1,120

Adjustment 7.   A stock count established that the cost of the stock on hand at the end of the month was £44,100.

The Camera Shop has adopted a periodic stock costing system. Under this system an *individual* cost of goods sold figure is not calculated for each transaction. Instead a *total* cost of goods sold figure is calculated at the end of the period. This figure forms the basis of the adjusting entries relating to stock. We explained in Chapter 10 that the cost of goods sold figure is calculated as follows:

>   opening stock
> +purchases for the period
> =cost of goods available for sale in the period
> −closing stock
> =cost of goods sold for the period.

These calculations affect both the Cost of goods sold account (AC425) in the general ledger and the worksheet as follows:

Adjustment 7a.   The opening stock figure is transferred from the Stock account (AC110) to the Cost of goods sold account (AC425).

			£	£
Accounting entry:				
31 August	Cost of goods sold (425)	Debit	43,670	
	Stock (110)	Credit		43,670

Adjustment 7b.   The purchases figure is transferred from the Purchases account (AC420) to the Cost of goods sold account (AC425).

			£	£
Accounting entry:				
31 August	Cost of goods sold (425)	Debit	5,400	
	Purchases (420)	Credit		5,400

Adjustment 7c.   At this stage there is no closing stock figure in the accounting records. However, the stock at 31 August has been counted and its cost determined at £44,100. This amount must be deducted from the figure for the cost of goods available for sale, i.e. the Cost of goods sold account (AC425) is credited with £44,100. In addition, as the stock on hand at 31 August appears in the balance sheet at that date, £44,100 should be debited to the Stock account (AC110). (Note that the opening stock figure of £43,670 has already been transferred out of this account as part of Adjustment 7a.)

			£	£
Accounting entry:				
31 August	Stock (110)	Debit	44,100	
	Cost of goods sold (425)	Credit		44,100

The net effect of these three adjustments is to produce a cost of goods sold figure of £4,970 and a closing stock figure of £44,100.

We can now check the arithmetical accuracy of our book-keeping. The total of these debit adjustments should equal the total of the credit adjustments. As both columns sum to £95,842, we can now produce an 'Adjusted trial balance' on the worksheet by adding (or subtracting) the various adjustments to (or from) the balances on the original trial balance. Again the sum total of the adjusted debit balances (of £118,902) is equal to the sum total of the adjusted credit balances.

Each of the above adjustments should also be entered in the general ledger. The entries can be identified by reference to the 'Accounting entries' described above and to the 'Adjustments' column on the worksheet.

B.9   Closing off the accounts and preparing the financial statements
The balances shown in the 'Adjusted trial balance' on the worksheet are now entered in the columns headed 'Income statement' and 'Balance sheet'. The

balances from accounts numbered 100 to 310 are balance sheet items because they represent either assets, liabilities or ownership interest. Those balances from accounts numbered 400 to 500 consist of income statement items. The balance of revenues over expenses and appropriations, representing 'retained profit for the period' is transferred from the income statement to ownership interest in the balance sheet.

Once again these worksheet entries are reflected by corresponding entries in the general ledger accounts. The balances on the various revenue, expense and appropriation accounts (AC400–500) are transferred to the Profit and Loss account (AC600). The balance on the Profit and Loss account is then transferred to the Retained Profit account (AC310). Having 'closed off' all the revenue, expense and appropriation accounts in this way, only the 'balance sheet' accounts (AC100–310) show outstanding balances. These balances are carried forward to form the opening balances for the September transactions.

The financial statements can be prepared from the worksheet or the general ledger. If the figures are taken from the ledger, the *balances carried forward* are used to prepare the balance sheet at 31 August, and the *entries in the Profit and loss account* (AC600) are used to prepare the income statement. The completed financial statements are presented in Tables B.3 and B.4.

Table B.3   The Camera Shop Ltd—Income statement for the month ended 31 August 19X4

	£	£
Sales revenue		12,450
Cost of goods sold		4,970
Gross profit		7,480
Rent	600	
Wages	2,350	
Heat and light	390	
Bad debts	35	
Depreciation	227	
Interest	300	
		3,902
Net profit		3,578
Dividends		800
Profit for the year, retained		£2,778

Table B.4   The Camera Shop Ltd—Balance sheet at 31 August 19X4

	£	£	£
Assets employed			
Fixed assets			
Shop and office equipment at cost			27,250
less: Accumulated depreciation			12,827
			14,423
Current assets			
Stock		44,100	
Debtors	34,700		
less: Provision for bad debts	1,735	32,965	
Cash at bank		3,180	
		80,245	
Current liabilities			
Trade creditors		22,970	
Interest accrued		1,500	
Miscellaneous accruals		1,510	
		25,980	
Net current assets			54,265
Total assets less current liabilities			68,688
Creditors due after more than one year			
Bank loan			24,000
			£44,688
Capital and reserves			
Share capital			25,000
Retained profit			19,688
			£44,688

The Camera Shop Ltd—General ledger accounts

Shop and office equipment—cost   No. 100

DATE		REF	DEBIT	DATE		REF	CREDIT
31 July	Balance		26,400				
11 Aug	Cash	130	850				
				31 Aug	Balance		27,250
			27,250				27,250
31 Aug	Balance		27,250				

Shop and office equipment—accumulated depreciation   No. 101

DATE		REF	DEBIT	DATE		REF	CREDIT
				31 July	Balance		12,600
				31 Aug	Depreciation expense	450	227
31 Aug	Balance		12,827				
			12,827				12,827
				31 Aug	Balance		12,827

Stock   No. 110

DATE		REF	DEBIT	DATE		REF	CREDIT
31 July	Balance		43,670	31 Aug	Cost of goods sold	425	43,670
31 Aug	Cost of goods sold	425	44,100				
				31 Aug	Balance		44,100
			87,770				87,770
31 Aug	Balance		44,100				

Debtors   No. 115

DATE		REF	DEBIT	DATE		REF	CREDIT
31 July	Balance		34,000	2 Aug	Cash	130	7,000
3 Aug	Sales revenue	400	6,600	25 Aug	Cash	130	4,750
16 Aug	Sales revenue	400	5,850				
				31 Aug	Balance		34,700
			46,450				46,450
31 Aug	Balance		34,700				

Provision for bad debts   No. 116

DATE		REF	DEBIT	DATE		REF	CREDIT
				31 July	Balance		1,700
				31 Aug	Bad debts expense	440	35
31 Aug	Balance		1,735				
			1,735				1,735
				31 Aug	Balance		1,735

Prepaid rent   No. 120

DATE		REF	DEBIT	DATE		REF	CREDIT
31 July	Balance		600	31 Aug	Rent expense	430	600
			600				600

Cash at bank No. 130

DATE		REF	DEBIT	DATE		REF	CREDIT
31 July	Balance		1,550	3 Aug	Trade creditors	200	2,500
2 Aug	Debtors	115	7,000	9 Aug	Misc. accruals	230	280
25 Aug	Debtors	115	4,750	11 Aug	Equipment—cost	100	850
				17 Aug	Wages expense	431	1,230
				18 Aug	Trade creditors	200	4,000
				19 Aug	Misc. accruals	230	460
				24 Aug	Dividends	500	800
				31 Aug	Balance		3,180
			13,300				13,300
31 Aug	Balance		3,180				

Trade creditors No. 200

DATE		REF	DEBIT	DATE		REF	CREDIT
3 Aug	Cash	130	2,500	31 July	Balance		24,070
18 Aug	Cash	130	4,000	3 Aug	Purchases	420	1,800
				12 Aug	Purchases	420	3,600
31 Aug	Balance		22,970				
			29,470				29,470
				31 Aug	Balance		22,970

Interest accrued   No. 220

DATE		REF	DEBIT	DATE		REF	CREDIT
				31 July	Balance		1,200
				31 Aug	Interest exp.	460	300
31 Aug	Balance		1,500				
			1,500				1,500
				31 Aug	Balance		1,500

Miscellaneous accruals   No. 230

DATE		REF	DEBIT	DATE		REF	CREDIT
9 Aug	Cash	130	280	31 July	Balance		740
19 Aug	Cash	130	460	31 Aug	Heat & light expense	432	390
				31 Aug	Wages expense	431	1,120
31 Aug	Balance		1,510				
			2,250				2,250
				31 Aug	Balance		1,510

Bank loan   No. 240

DATE		REF	DEBIT	DATE		REF	CREDIT
				31 July	Balance		24,000
31 Aug	Balance		24,000				
			24,000				24,000
				31 Aug	Balance		24,000

Share capital   No. 300

DATE		REF	DEBIT	DATE		REF	CREDIT
				31 July	Balance		25,000
31 Aug	Balance		25,000				
			25,000				25,000
				31 Aug	Balance		25,000

Retained profit   No. 310

DATE		REF	DEBIT	DATE		REF	CREDIT
				31 July	Balance		16,910
				31 Aug	Profit & loss	600	2,778
31 Aug	Balance		19,688				
			19,688				19,688
				31 Aug	Balance		19,688

Sales revenue   No. 400

DATE		REF	DEBIT	DATE		REF	CREDIT
				3 Aug	Debtors	115	6,600
				16 Aug	Debtors	115	5,850
31 Aug	Profit & loss	600	12,450				
			12,450				12,450

Purchases No. 420

DATE		REF	DEBIT	DATE		REF	CREDIT
3 Aug	Trade creditors	200	1,800	31 Aug	Cost of goods sold	425	5,400
12 Aug	Trade creditors	200	3,600				
			5,400				5,400

Cost of goods sold No. 425

DATE		REF	DEBIT	DATE		REF	CREDIT
31 Aug	Stock	110	43,670	31 Aug	Stock	110	44,100
31 Aug	Purchases	420	5,400				
				31 Aug	Profit & loss	600	4,970
			49,070				49,070

Rent expense No. 430

DATE		REF	DEBIT	DATE		REF	CREDIT
31 Aug	Prepaid rent	120	600				
				31 Aug	Profit & loss	600	600
			600				600

Wages expense No. 431

DATE		REF	DEBIT	DATE		REF	CREDIT
17 Aug	Cash	130	1,230				
31 Aug	Misc. accruals	230	1,120				
				31 Aug	Profit & loss	600	2,350
			2,350				2,350

Heat and light expenses   No. 432

DATE		REF	DEBIT	DATE		REF	CREDIT
31 Aug	Misc. accruals	230	390				
				31 Aug	Profit & loss	600	,390
			390				390

Bad debts expense   No. 440

DATE		REF	DEBIT	DATE		REF	CREDIT
31 Aug	Provision for bad debts	116	35				
				31 Aug	Profit & loss	600	35
			35				35

Depreciation expense   No. 450

DATE		REF	DEBIT	DATE		REF	CREDIT
31 Aug	Shop & office equipment—accumulated depreciation	101	227				
				31 Aug	Profit & loss	600	227
			227				227

Interest expense   No. 460

DATE		REF	DEBIT	DATE		REF	CREDIT
31 Aug	Interest accrued	220	300				
				31 Aug	Profit & loss	600	300
			300				300

Dividends   No. 500

DATE		REF	DEBIT	DATE		REF	CREDIT
24 Aug	Cash	130	800				
				31 Aug	Profit & loss	600	800
			800				800

Profit and loss   No. 600

DATE		REF	DEBIT	DATE		REF	CREDIT
31 Aug	Cost of goods sold	425	4,970	31 Aug	Sales revenue	400	12,450
	Rent expense	430	600				
	Wages expense	431	2,350				
	Heat & light expense	432	390				
	Bad debts expense	440	35				
	Depreciation expense	450	227				
	Interest expense	460	300				
	Dividends	500	800				
31 Aug	Balance to retained profit	310	2,778				
			12,450				12,450

Appendix B—Exercises

B.1 You are given the following information relating to the year ended 31 December 19X1 of Fenena, who commenced business on 1 January 19X1:

	£
Creditors	6,400
Debtors	5,060
Purchases	16,100
Sales	28,400
Motor van	1,700
Drawings	5,100
Insurance	174
General expenses	1,596
Rent and rates	2,130

Salaries	4,162
Stock at 31 December 19X1	2,050
Sale returns	200
Cash at bank	2,628
Cash in hand	50
Capital introduced	4,100

● Prepare Fenena's income statement for the year ended 31 December 19X1 and her balance sheet as at that date.

B.2 The 'T' accounts below show the transactions of Abigaille during the month of April:

Cash			Trade creditors			Stock		
(d) 22,500	(a)	8,200	(g) 19,300	(b) 20,000		(b) 20,000	(j)	500
(i) 40,000	(e)	1,200	(j) 500	(f) 4,400				
(k) 5,200	(g)	19,300						

Salaries and wages			Debtors			Sales		
(a) 8,200			(c) 27,500	(d) 22,500			(c)	27,500
(l) 400							(k)	5,200

Furniture and fixtures			Accrued wages			Rent expenses		
(f) 4,400	(h)	100		(l)	400	(m)	200	

Depreciation			Bank loan			Prepaid rent		
(h) 100				(i)	40,000	(e) 1,200	(m)	200

● For each of the above entries (a) to (m) describe the nature of the underlying economic event. Be as specific as possible.

B.3 Below is the rough draft of the final accounts of Manon Wholesalers Ltd:

Profit and loss account as at 31 December 19X1

Sales			184,910
less: Opening stock		22,000	
Purchases		91,060	
		113,060	
Closing stock		23,520	136,580
Warehouse expenses			25,390
Rent		4,500	
less: Paid in advance		750	3,750
Wages			7,690
Bad debts			820
Directors' fees			4,000
General expenses			19,000
Debenture interest			7,500
Depreciation on van			800
Dividends received			(3,250)
Retained profits b/f			(18,140)	184,140
Retained profits c/f			770

Balance sheet for year ended 31 December 19X1

250,000 Ordinary shares		250,000	Cash at bank		530
£200,000 5% Debentures		200,000	Debtors (less bad £820)	55,210	
Creditors:			Gov'ment securities (cost)	16,930	
Trade creditors	39,050		Goodwill	25,000	
Rent	750	39,800			97,140
			Van (cost)		2,600
Reserves:			Stocks (cost)		23,520
General	10,000		Premises (cost)		426,000
Van depreciation	800				
Bad debt provision at					
1 Jan. 19X1	2,880	13,680			
Profit		770			
		504,250			548,790

These accounts have been drafted by a clerk who has little knowledge of either book-keeping or presentation of accounts. You may assume that the accounting balances have been copied accurately, and that the errors that prevent the accounts from balancing can be discovered by inspection and arithmetical check etc.

- (a) Prepare a simple calculation ('reconciliation statement') to explain the difference between the two sides of the balance sheet. (If you cannot find all the errors, put in a balancing figure as a 'suspense account balance'. This same amount would then also be a necessary addition to the balance sheet in (b).)
- (b) Redraft the accounts in good form, giving effect to the following:
    - (i) Allowance has to be made for a final dividend of £12,500;
    - (ii) Debenture interest accrued at 31 December 19X1 was £2,500.

B.4 Mr Leporello commenced business as a retail chemist on 1 February 19X7, with an initial capital of £30,000, which he paid into his business bank account. He appointed Mr Masetto shop manager on 1 February 19X7, at an annual salary of £2,000. In addition, Mr Masetto is to receive commission of 20% of the net profit of the business, before charging commission.

During the year ended 31 January 19X8, Mr Leporello did not maintain proper books of account, but after an examination of the available records you ascertain the following:

1. An analysis of the bank statements for the year ended 31 January 19X1 is:

Receipts	£	Payments	£
Capital introduced	30,000	Lease	20,000
Takings banked	123,720	Shop fittings and equipment	8,800
Bank loan	20,000	Motor van	2,740
		Payments to suppliers	112,360
		Interest on bank loan	1,000
		General overhead expenses	8,335
		Rent	3,750
		Balance at 31 Jan. 19X8	16,735
	173,720		173,720

2. All sales were for cash and takings are banked daily, subject to the retention of a cash float of £100. The following payments were made out of cash takings:

	£
Salary—Mr Masetto	1,980
Drawings—Mr Leporello	4,000
Payments to suppliers	1,390
General overhead expenses	840

3. The premises are rented on a long lease, at an annual rental of £5,000.
4. At 31 January 19X8 cheques sent to suppliers, amounting to £2,500, have not been presented to the bank for payment.
5. Invoices from suppliers, amounting to £8,600, have not been paid.
6. Stock at 31 January 19X8 is valued at £36,500.
7. Depreciation is to be provided on the van at the rate of 25% on cost, and on the shop fittings and equipment at 10% on cost.
8. During the year Mr Leporello took goods which had cost £100 for his personal consumption.

● Prepare a profit and loss account for Mr Leporello for the year ended 31 January 19X8 and a balance sheet as at that date.

B.5 Susanna carries on the business of a self-employed ice cream vendor. The business is seasonal and all the sales are made from a van. Susanna has her accounts of the business prepared each year to 31 December. She has a contract with Gilda Ice Cream Limited whereby she buys all her goods for resale from them at selling price less 33⅓% and less 2½% for monthly settlement. Susanna always takes the 2½%. She also receives, at the end of the season, a rebate of 1% of the cost of her purchases before cash discount, if her sales for the season which runs from 1 April to 31 October exceed £5,000. In the year under review, she received £60.

The balances on Susanna's books at 31 December 19X0 were:

	£	£
Capital account		1,654
Van at cost	1,600	
Depreciation of van		800
Equipment at cost	350	
Depreciation of equipment		280
Garage rates in advance	9	
Accountancy		60
Balance at bank	840	
Garage rent due		5
	2,799	2,799

You obtain the following information concerning Susanna's transactions for the year to 31 December 19X1:

1. From cheque books, paying-in books and bank statements:

	£
Gilda Ice Cream Ltd—goods for sale	5,350
Wages	280
Van expenses	300
Laundry	104
Garage rent (52 weeks)	52

Garage rates (two half-years)	40
Accountancy	60
Rebate from Gilda Ice Cream Ltd	60
New van	1,100
Sundry business expenses	278
Private payments	320
Cash banked ex takings	7,574
Balance at bank 31 December 19X1	590

2. There is no record of takings and some goods for resale have apparently been paid for out of takings. The only cash payments recorded were:

	£
Petrol and oil	27
Casual wages	130
Sundry expenses	19

Any cash not accounted for is to be treated as drawings.

3. The old van was traded in for £700; it was used as a deposit on a new van costing £1,800.
4. Due to a power supply failure, stock with a resale value of £30 was damaged and had to be destroyed.
5. Depreciation is to be provided on a straight line basis at 25% on the van and 10% on the equipment, the new van to be depreciated as if in use on 1 January 19X1.
6. £64 is to be provided for accountancy.
7. At the year end the amounts for accrued rent and prepaid rates were £6 and £14 respectively.

● Prepare Susanna's income statement for the year ended 31 December 19X1 and her balance sheet as at that date.

B.6 You are provided with the following trial balance of Rigoletto as at 31 December 19X1:

	£	£
Capital account at 1 Jan. 19X1		22,607
Purchases	194,100	
Sales		261,450
Office wages and salaries	16,720	
Rent and rates	4,930	
Debtors	36,150	
Sundry expenses	2,071	
Bad debts written off	942	
Drawings	4,751	
Provision for doubtful debts		1,851
Cash at bank	1,408	
Creditors		17,154
Cash in hand	167	
Stock	41,062	
Motor car—cost	3,600	
Motor car—depreciation		
(at 31 Dec. 19X0)		1,050
Discounts received		974
Carriage inwards	436	
Commissions received		1,251
	306,337	306,337

You are provided with the following additional information for the purposes of preparing the final accounts:

1. Closing stock has been valued at £49,678.
2. The rent of the premises is £3,200 p.a. payable half-yearly in advance on 31 March and 30 September.
3. Rates for the year ending 31 March 19X2 amounting to £744 were paid on 11 April 19X1.
4. Depreciation on the car is to be provided using the straight line method at a rate of 20% p.a.
5. The provision for doubtful debts (£1,851) was the general provision which appeared in last year's accounts. During the current year, bad debts of £942 were written off against the accounts of specific customers. It has now been agreed that further debts amounting to £710 are to be written off against specific customers, and the closing provision is to be adjusted to 5% of the revised debtors figure.
6. Wages and salaries to be accrued amount to £1,506.

● Prepare the profit and loss account of Rigoletto for the year ended 31 December 19X1 and his balance sheet as at that date.

B.7   The following trial balance was extracted from the books of Ernani as at 31 December 19X1:

Trial balance

	£	£
Capital as at 1 Jan. 19X1		82,430
Freehold properties, at cost	59,000	
Motor vans:		
Balance, 1 Jan. 19X1 at cost	15,000	
Additions less sales in year	650	
Accumulated depreciation, 1 Jan. 19X1		6,750
Stock in trade, 1 Jan. 19X1	13,930	
Balance at bank	6,615	
Bad debts	1,075	
Provision for bad debts, 1 Jan. 19X1		275
Trade debtors and creditors	11,320	11,380
Drawings	4,000	
Wages and salaries	13,127	
Motor and delivery expenses	3,258	
Rates	700	
Purchases	108,440	
Sales		142,770
Legal expenses	644	
General expenses	5,846	
	243,605	243,605

Additional information:

1. Stock in trade at 31 December 19X1 was valued at £14,600.
2. Rates paid in advance as at 31 December 19X1 were £140.
3. The provision for bad debts is to be increased to £350.
4. On 1 January 19X1 a motor van which had cost £680 was sold for £125. Depreciation provided for this van up to 1 January 19X1 was £475.

5. Depreciation of motor vans (including additions) is to be provided at 20% of cost.
6. The balance on legal expenses account includes £380 in connection with the purchase of one of the freehold properties.
7. The manager is entitled to a commission of 5% of the net profit, *after* charging the commission.

● Prepare a profit and loss account for Ernani for the year ended 31 December 19X1 and a balance sheet as at that date.

B.8 Abdallo Ltd prepares accounts each year to 31 March, using conventional historical cost accounting methods. The following balances have been extracted from the books of Abdallo for the year ended 31 March 19X8:

	£'000
Issued shared capital	1,000
Reserves	286
Freehold property, at cost	560
Plant and equipment, at cost	724
Plant and equipment—accumulated	
depreciation at 1 April 19X7	324
Stock in hand at 1 April 19X7	735
Trade creditors	147
Trade debtors	345
Bank overdraft	182
Sales	1,971
Purchases of stock	1,256
Operating expenses (excluding depreciation)	290

The following additonal information is available:

1. Stock on hand at 31 March 19X8 has been estimated at £775,000.
2. Depreciation is to be provided on plant and equipment at a rate of 30% using the reducing balance method.
3. It is proposed to pay an ordinary dividend of £150,000 as soon as possible, in respect of the year ended 31 March 19X8.
4. Accrued operating expenses amounting to £8,000 have not yet been entered in the books.

● (a) Prepare the trial balance of Abdallo Ltd at 31 March 19X8, *before* taking account of the information in 1 to 4 above.
(b) Prepare the profit and loss account of Abdallo Ltd. for the year ended 31 March 19X8, and balance sheet at that date, *after* taking account of the information in 1 to 4 above.
(c) Comment briefly on the likely usefulness to shareholders of the accounts you have prepared.

B.9 The accountant of Ottavio Ltd has prepared a trial balance as at 31 December 19X7. From this he has already prepared a draft profit and loss account for 19X7 which reveals a profit for the year of £60,000. This and the remaining balances are listed below:

Profit for the year £60,000;   Bank overdraft £70,000;
General reserve £40,000;   Land and buildings £200,000;
Trade creditors £210,000;   Stock at 31 December 19X7 £110,000;
Share capital £170,000;
Plant and equipment, at cost, £200,000;

Rent, paid in advance, £20,000;   Share premium £80,000;
Debtors £250,000;   Accrued expenses £25,000;
Accumulated depreciation on plant and equipment £125,000.

However, the following points are brought to your attention:

1. No depreciation has been charged for 19X7. You discover that depreciation is calculated on a straight line basis and that all the plant and equipment was bought on 1 January 19X2.
2. The stock figure was taken directly from the company's records. A physical stock count has since taken place and has shown the stock at 31 December to be worth only £103,000.
3. The last electricity bill received by the company was for the three months up to 31 October 19X7. The next bill is not due until 31 January 19X8. You estimate that this next bill will amount to £3,000.
4. As a result of the company's performance in 19X7, the directors have announced that the company will pay a dividend of £20,000 to its shareholders.

- (a) Prepare the trial balance from the list of balances provided.
  (b) Taking account of all the information provided prepare a balance sheet for Ottavio Ltd as at 31 December 19X7.
  (c) Comment on the results revealed by the balance sheet.

B.10 Mr Zaccaria buys and sells ismaeles. His draft balance sheet on 31 March 19X0 was as follows:

	£		£
Capital account	134,500	Fixed assets at cost	160,000
		less: Depreciation	65,000
			95,000
Trade creditors	48,000	Stock of ismaeles	31,000
		Debtors	42,000
		Cash at bank	14,500
	182,500		182,500

Mr Zaccaria's transactions during the year ended 31 March 19X1 may be described as follows:

1. Sales amounted to £240,000.
2. The gross profit percentage was 20% of sales.
3. General expenses (excluding depreciation and the cost of ismaeles) amounted to £18,500, and were all paid in cash.
4. No fixed assets were bought or sold. Depreciation on fixed assets amounted to £16,000.
5. Mr Zaccaria withdrew £10,000 from the business for personal expenditure.
6. Debtors at the end of the year were equal to 3 months' sales.
7. Creditors at the end of the year were equal to 2 months' purchases.
8. Stock of ismaeles at the end of the year was sufficient to meet sales requirements for 4 months, assuming sales at the rate of £240,000 p.a.

- (a) Prepare Mr Zaccaria's income statement for the year ended 31 March 19X1 and his balance sheet on that date.
  (b) Mr Zaccaria has little knowledge of accounting. Write a report, explaining to him in simple terms why his income for the year is not equal to the change in his cash balance.

Part 4

Alternative Measurement Methods

Chapter 12

Changing Price Levels and Alternative Accounting Methods

Historical cost accounting has been used for almost five hundred years, and we have spent the last seven chapters explaining the principles underlying the preparation of historical cost financial statements. Does that mean that we (and others) consider historical cost to be the best method available for determining net income and financial position?

From the beginning of this book we have defined the primary purpose of accounting as identifying, measuring and communicating useful information to decision makers. Because there are several alternative ways of carrying out this process we introduced a set of evaluative criteria for alternative accounting methods. These criteria were categorised as relating either to the *usefulness* or to the *feasibility* of the various methods. In Chapter 3 we noted that management forecasts of future cash flows are potentially very relevant to users' decisions but that such forecasts are subjective, difficult to verify and may involve the disclosure of confidential information. Consequently, we concluded that it is most unlikely that cash forecasts will form the basis of published statements in the foreseeable future.

In Chapter 4 we noted that historical cash flows satisfy the criteria of objectivity and verifiability, but could, in certain circumstances, produce misleading figures, for example when entities trade extensively on credit, and/or incur large amounts of capital expenditure. Accrual accounting tries to avoid this problem by recording transactions at the time of sale and purchase rather than at the time of cash receipt and cash payment, and by spreading the cost of long-lived assets over their useful lives. Further, we noted that in times of stable prices historical cost accounting generates an income figure which is both a good measure of past performance and a good indicator of future performance. We concluded that this method of accounting 'produces an income or profit figure which, historically, has been deemed to be more useful and more understandable to the users of financial statements than the more erratic cash flow figures' (Chapter 4, page 59).

It would therefore seem that historical cost accounting satisfies both the usefulness and the feasibility criteria. However, the evaluation of the usefulness of historical cost figures in Chapter 4 assumed stable prices. But prices are rarely stable and over the past twenty years there have been frequent movements in price levels in most Western countries. Inflation, more than any other event, has caused accountants to question the suitability of historical cost accounting as a method of reporting business performance and to give serious consideration to alternative accounting methods. In this chapter we shall identify the problems encountered by historical cost accounting in times of changing prices, and in the following three chapters we shall describe and evaluate several alternative accounting methods according to the criteria introduced in Chapter 4. We begin by examining the impact of changing price levels upon accounting figures.

12.1 Changing Price Levels

In 1975 a professor at the University of Manchester purchased a house for £30,000. In 1984 he spent a sabbatical year in the USA and rented out the house for a sum that provided him with £6,000 after all expenses. He was delighted with the '20% return' on his investment. But was his return really so high? In 1984 houses similar to the professor's were being bought and sold for £100,000. Presumably the professor (we hasten to add that he was not a professor of accounting) could have sold his house for £100,000 prior to his depature to the USA. If so, perhaps his return from renting was only 6%—£6,000 on £100,000.

To the professor it did not matter which rate of return figure he used—it was important only that he received the highest rent possible. But the decisions of a business manager might be influenced by the reported rate of return. If one division of the business is showing a return of 20% the manager may be tempted to authorise the investment of more money in that particular division. If the division shows a return of only 6% he may be better advised to recommend closing it down and investing the money in a bank deposit account. Inflation is important to accountants because it can distort the accounting figures upon which decisions might be based. In particular, in inflationary times the historical costs of certain assets will be significantly below their current values, and the historical costs of assets 'consumed' will be lower than their current costs. As a result, the organisation's net assets figure may be understated and its net income figure overstated in historical cost accounts. For example, suppose the data relating to the house above referred to an industrial building with an estimated useful life of 50 years. Should the asset be disclosed in the balance sheet at £30,000 (historical cost) or £100,000 (current value) and should the depreciation charge in the income statement be £600 (based on historical cost) or £2,000 (based on current value)?

The existence of changing price levels has prompted accountants to reconsider two fundamental principles upon which conventional accounting is based—the use of historical cost as the method of asset valuation and the use of money as the unit of measurement. We have shown above how historical costs can become outdated, but to appreciate the recent attention given to the appropriateness of the unit of measurement we must clarify what we mean by 'changing price levels'.

It would not have been unusual in recent years to read that, over a twelve month period, the price of calculators had fallen by 25%, the price of a new car had risen by 15%, and the rate of inflation was 10%. The variety of figures may be confusing, and part of the confusion arises because two types of price changes are involved. Changes in *specific price levels* reflect the price changes of specific items such as calculators and cars. Changes in *general price levels* reflect the price changes of a group, or basket, of goods and services. Changes in specific price levels, which may vary widely, contribute to the overall price change as reflected in the general price level. *Inflation refers strictly to a change* in the general price level and, in the UK, inflation is most commonly measured by the increase in the retail price index (RPI) which consists of a weighted average of the changes in the prices of a variety of consumer goods and services.

The RPI is not a perfect consumer index because it does not take into account all items on which people spend money, nor does it cover spending by the whole community. Rather it is intended to measure a representative national basket of goods and services. The RPI is constructed monthly, when staff from unemployment benefit offices in 200 towns throughout the UK collect approximately 130,000 prices for more than 600 different goods and services. Each item in the index is given a 'weight' according to its comparative importance, and a weighted index is constructed. The base date for the current RPI is 15 January 1974 and a selection of RPI numbers is provided in Table 12.1. The percentage change from year to year is calculated as follows:

$$\frac{\text{Change in index}}{\text{Previous year's index}} = \text{Yearly percentage change}$$

which for 1983, for example, is

$$\frac{(342.8 - 325.5)}{325.5} = 5.3\%$$

When the general price level increases it takes more pounds to buy the same basket of goods and services than previously. As a result, the *purchasing power* of the pound declines, i.e. as the general price level changes, so the amount of goods and services that can be purchased with a pound also changes. This suggests that in terms of its ability to buy goods and services the pound is an unstable unit of measurement. The implication for accounting should now be obvious. In periods of significant changes in the general price level the pounds disclosed in financial statements represent past

Table 12.1   Index of Retail Prices: January 1974 = 100

	Retail Price Index	Annual percentage increase in retail prices
December 1960	50.2	
December 1965	59.5	
December 1970	75.6	
December 1971	82.4	9.0
December 1972	88.7	7.6
December 1973	98.1	10.6
December 1974	116.9	19.2
December 1975	146.0	24.9
December 1976	168.0	15.1
December 1977	188.4	12.1
December 1978	204.2	8.4
December 1979	239.4	17.2
December 1980	275.6	15.1
December 1981	308.8	12.0
December 1982	325.5	5.4
December 1983	342.8	5.3
December 1984	358.5	4.6

acquisition costs only. As different acquisitions take place at different times, these (different) pounds are not, strictly speaking, additive.

We stated earlier that, in times of rising prices, the income figure reported in historical cost accounts might be 'overstated'. This is not meant to imply that there is some 'correct' income figure which should be disclosed. There is no such thing! Income can be defined in several ways and, given the role which accounting plays in providing information to interested groups, we should not be surprised to learn that different users may wish to use different income figures for different decisions. Much of this and subsequent chapters is concerned not with determining which is the correct way to calculate income, but with identifying which methods of accounting produce income figures and asset values which are useful for decisions.

12.2   Income Determination

We begin our analysis of changing prices by illustrating the artificial nature of income figures.

Suppose that Mr Blundell commences trading on 1 January with £10 in cash. On that date he purchases one item of stock for £10. He holds the stock until 31 December, on which date he sells it for £25 cash. During the year the RPI increases by 20% and the replacement cost of the stock increases by 50% to £15.

Table 12.2 illustrates the financial statements which Mr Blundell would prepare by applying the principles explained in the previous seven chapters.

Table 12.2   Mr Blundell—Conventional financial statements

Income statement for the year	£
Sales	25
Cost of goods sold	10
Income	15

Balance sheet at 31 December	Prior to withdrawal of cash £	After withdrawal of cash £
Assets:		
Cash	25	10
Ownership interest:		
Initial capital	10	10
Income for the year	15	—
	25	10

The historical cost of the goods sold, £10, is matched against the sales revenue of £25 to produce an income of £15. At the year end the balance sheet reveals an asset, cash, of £25, and ownership interest of £25, comprising opening capital of £10 and income for the year of £15. Given a reported income figure of £15 it might not be unreasonable for Mr Blundell to assume that he could withdraw £15 from the business and spend it. If he does withdraw £15 for his personal use, the ownership interest will be reduced by £15, and the cash balance of £25 will be reduced by £15 to £10. At the end of the year the business appears to be in exactly the same position as it was at the beginning of the year—it possesses assets of £10 in cash, this amount having been supplied by the owner.

However, as he contemplates another year's trading Mr Blundell may not be totally convinced that the business is in the same position at the end of the year as it was at the beginning, and he may question the wisdom of withdrawing, and spending, all the first year's income. Part of the problem is that in determining the amount to be withdrawn from the business he has relied upon one income figure (that measured by historic cost), which is only one of several which could have been calculated. Let us consider how it is possible for several different income figures to be calculated from this simple set of transactions.

The *economic concept of income* has been defined by Hicks[1] as "the amount which a man can consume during a period and still remain as well off at the end of the period as he was at the beginning", and this definition has been used by some as a basis for defining accounting profit. For example, a company's profit can be defined as the amount it can distribute to its

---

[1] Hicks, J.R., *Value and Capital*, 2nd Ed, Oxford University Press, 1946.

shareholders and be as well off at the end of the year as it was at the beginning.[2] Neither of these definitions views income as the result of matching costs and revenues. Rather the process involves the valuation of assets at the end of a period and the setting aside of a sufficient amount to ensure that the organisation is as 'well off' at the end of the period as it was at the beginning, i.e. maintaining its capital. The surplus, if any, is income.

If no distributions have been made during the period this process can be expressed as follows:

$$I_{0 \to 1} = V_1 - V_0$$

where $I_{0 \to 1}$ is the income for the period from time 0 to time 1, and V_0, V_1 are the capital values at time 0 and time 1 respectively.

However, this approach raises two questions. First, how to value assets at the beginning and at the end of the year, and second, how to measure 'well offness'. The value of assets at the beginning of a period cannot be compared realistically with the value of assets at the end of a period because, by definition, they exist at different times. To compensate for this disparity one of the values must be adjusted to the time scale of the other. Accountants have, in general, preferred to adjust the opening valuation to make it comparable with the valuation at the end of the period.

It should now be clear that the calculation of income figures depends upon (at least) two factors:

(a) *Asset valuation*:   How should the entity's assets be valued at the beginning and the end of a period?

(b) *Capital maintenance*: What adjustment (if any) should be made to the opening capital (ownership interest) valuation to make it comparable with the closing valuation?

Initially we will examine these two distinct stages of income determination independently of each other. In the following section we begin by considering the rationale for three different concepts of capital maintenance.

12.3   Capital Maintenance Concepts

The situation described in Table 12.2 enables us to examine the impact of different concepts of capital maintenance upon reported income figures independently of the choice of an asset valuation method. In this particular example there is no need to choose a method of valuing assets because the business holds only cash at both the beginning and the end of the year. On 1 January the net assets of the business comprise £10 cash; on 31 December,

---

[2] Alexander, S.S., 'Income measurement in a dynamic economy' (revised by D. Solomons), in Baxter, W.T. and Davidson, S. (eds), *Studies in Accounting Theory*, Sweet and Maxwell, 1962.

prior to the decision to withdraw money from the business, they comprise £25 cash. The final income figure will therefore depend upon the capital maintenance concept adopted, i.e. how the value of net assets held at the beginning of the period is restated to make it comparable with the value of net assets at the end of the period.

The rationale for the capital maintenance concept adopted in Table 12.2 is simple. If the business possesses £25 on 31 December (the end of the period), and £10 on 1 January (the beginning of the period) then Mr Blundell must set aside only £10 to be as well off at the end of the period as at the beginning. Consequently, £15 can be 'consumed' as income. Under this concept of capital maintenance, Mr Blundell is deemed to be as well off *in money terms* on 31 December as he was on 1 January. His *money capital* (of £10) has been maintained and there is an implicit assumption that £10 at the beginning of the year can be compared with £10 at the end of the year.

It could be argued however that Mr Blundell is not as well off in terms of 'general purchasing power' at the end of the year as he was at the beginning. Holding cash of £10 on 31 December would not enable him to buy as many goods and services as holding £10 on 1 January. Given the rise of 20% in the RPI he would need £12 (£10×1.20) to buy the same basket of consumer goods at the end of the year that he could have bought with £10 at the beginning of the year. Thus, if he wishes to maintain the *general purchasing power* of his capital he must retain £12 in the business. The procedure is reflected in column (ii) of Table 12.3 where a *capital maintenance adjustment* of £2 is made, and income is calculated as the residual figure of £13.

The general purchasing power concept of capital maintenance uses an index which approximates the (general) spending habits of the owner. The owner is termed a 'proprietor', and this concept of capital maintenance is

Table 12.3   Mr Blundell—Effect on income of different concepts of capital maintenance

	£	£	£
Balance sheets at 31 December (prior to withdrawal of cash)			
Assets:			
Cash	25	25	25
Ownership interest:			
Initial capital	10	10	10
Capital maintenance adjustment	–	2	5
Income for the year	15	13	10
	25	25	25
Capital maintained in terms of:	money	general purchasing power	operating capacity
	(i)	(ii)	(iii)

often termed a 'proprietary' concept. An alternative approach is to consider 'well offness' from the point of view of the business entity. We noted in Chapter 4 that financial statements are prepared on the assumption that the entity is a going concern and in this example one would expect Mr Blundell to continue to buy and sell items of stock in the following year. Well offness at the year-end could be defined in terms of the entity's ability to operate at the same level of activity in the following year. Consequently, rather than seeking to maintain the purchasing power of the owner, we could select a capital maintenance concept which maintains the *operating capacity* of the business by setting aside sufficient funds to maintain the *physical* size of the entity. This approach to capital maintenance is often termed an 'entity' approach, to distinguish it from the proprietary approach explained earlier. At the beginning of the year the business had sufficient funds to buy one item of stock. In order to purchase one item of stock at the end of the year, i.e. in order to maintain the entity's operating capacity, £15 (the current cost of the stock) must be retained in the business. This procedure is reflected in column (iii) of Table 12.3 where a capital maintenance adjustment of £5 is made and income is calculated as the residual figure of £10. Note that although three different income figures are produced by the three methods, the asset amount (£25 in cash) is the same under each method.

12.4 Methods of Asset Valuation

We noted in Section 12.2 that methods of measuring income and position (which we call 'accounting methods') may be classified according to two main characteristics—an asset valuation method and a capital maintenance concept. The chosen asset valuation method determines the value of assets in the balance sheet and the operating costs in the income statement. The choice of capital maintenance concept determines how much income is set aside to maintain the value of opening capital.

The example set out in Table 12.3 was concerned primarily with showing the impact of different capital maintenance concepts on the net income figure. Because the example looked at assets held only at the beginning and end of the year (when the only asset possessed was *cash*), it ignored the problems presented when fixed assets or stock are held, either during the year (as is the case in the example itself) or at the end of the year. In other words, the example was kept deliberately simple. In practice any business which owns fixed assets or stock *at any time during the year* possesses assets to which alternative valuation methods could be applied. We return to this particular problem in Chapter 15.

One method of asset valuation is *historical cost*, the method which we have described so far in this book and which forms the primary basis of asset valuation in the UK and other countries. If this method is adopted, assets are 'valued' at their original purchase price (less any applicable depreciation). Thus land purchased on 1 January 1974 for £100,000 would be assigned a figure of £100,000 in the historical cost accounts prepared on 31 December 1984 (and on any other date also).

A fundamental weakness of the historical cost method during times of rising prices can be explained by reference to Table 12.4. Figures can be added together, or subtracted from one another only if they are expressed in a common measurement unit. For example, an international businessman who decides to count the cash in his wallet whilst flying between Frankfurt and New York might discover 120 dollars, 200 Deutschmarks and 100 pounds. Presumably he would not simply mutter that he was down to his 'last 420' and order another gin and tonic. He cannot meaningfully add together dollars, Deutschmarks and pounds because they represent different units of measurement. In particular they represent a different general purchasing power (e.g. one pound can currently—in 1985—purchase approximately 3.5 times as many goods as can one Deutschmark) and one would expect the businessman to convert his cash into one currency, representing one common measure of purchasing power, before adding together the three amounts. In Table 12.4 all the costs are expressed in pounds sterling, and yet it can be argued that the adding of 100,000 '1974 pounds' to 380,000 '1983 pounds' is as meaningless as adding pounds to dollars, and for the same reason—they represent a different general purchasing power. The Retail Price Index stood at 100 in January 1974 and 341.9 in November 1983. £1 in January 1974 could have purchased 3.42 times as many goods and services as £1 in November 1983.

Table 12.4   Extract from a balance sheet using the historical cost method of asset valuation

	£
Balance sheet at 31 December 1983	
Fixed assets:	
Land (purchased Jan. 1974)	100,000
Buildings, net (purchased Dec. 1976)	420,000
Plant and machinery, net (purchased June 1981)	650,000
	1,170,000
Current assets:	
Stock (purchased Nov. 1983)	380,000
Cash	80,000
	£1,630,000

One way of eliminating this problem is to convert the costs of all assets into pounds of *current purchasing power,* i.e. to express the costs of all assets in pounds possessing the same general purchasing power. This can be achieved by using the RPI. As the RPI stood at 100 in January 1974 and at 342.8 in December 1983, we could express the asset, land, in December 1983 pounds by converting the £100,000 from pounds of January 1974 to pounds of December 1983 as follows:

$$£100,000 \times \frac{342.8}{100} = £342,800$$

In general the conversion, or restatement, can be expressed as follows:

$$\text{Asset cost} \times \frac{\text{Index adjusting to}}{\text{Index adjusting from}} \qquad \text{i.e. } \frac{\text{Index at balance sheet date}}{\substack{\text{Index at date item first} \\ \text{recorded in books of account}}}$$

The restated costs of the assets of the company, all of which are presumed to have been bought at different times, are illustrated in Table 12.5. The *extent* of the difference between the figures presented in Table 12.4 and those in Table 12.5 is immediately apparent. Remember also that these different figures relate to exactly the same assets.

Table 12.5   Extract from a balance sheet using the 'pounds of current purchasing power' method of asset valuation

	£CPP
Balance sheet at 31 December 1983	
Fixed assets:	
Land (100,000 × 342.8/100)	342,800
Buildings, net (420,000 × 342.8/168.0)	857,000
Plant and machinery, net (650,000 × 342.8/295.8)	753,279
	1,953,079
Current assets:	
Stock (380,000 × 342.8/341.9)	381,000
Cash	80,000
	£2,414,079

By applying a general price index to the cost of assets, the current purchasing power method of accounting takes no account of the *specific* price changes affecting an entity's resources and consequently, as a means of updating asset values, it is unlikely to provide more than a rough approximation to the current values or costs of those resources. Methods of asset valuation which take account of the changes in cost or value of specific assets are called *current cost,* or *current value,* methods of asset valuation. These methods may be based upon replacement costs (i.e. current buying prices), on realisable values (i.e. current selling prices), or on a mixture of both.

Replacement costs might be obtained from several sources including suppliers' price lists, professional valuers or the entity's own costs of production. Table 12.6 illustrates how different sources might be used for different assets in order to produce a replacement cost balance sheet.

Table 12.6   Extract from a balance sheet using the replacement cost method of asset valuation

	£
Balance sheet at 31 December 1983	
Fixed assets:	
Land (valued by professional valuer)	400,000
Buildings, net (valued by a professional valuer)	1,500,000
Plant and machinery, net (from manufacturers' price lists)	820,000
	2,720,000
Current assets	
Stock (from up-to-date internal costings)	395,000
Cash	80,000
	£3,195,000

12.5   Classification of Reporting Methods

We stated above that methods of measuring net income and financial position could be classified according to two main characteristics—an asset valuation method and a capital maintenance concept. The asset valuation method determines the value of assets in the balance sheet and the operating costs shown in the income statement. The choice of capital maintenance concept determines how much income (however measured) is set aside to maintain the value of opening capital. We have introduced briefly three methods of asset valuation (historical cost, current purchasing power and current cost) and three methods of maintaining capital (in terms of money, purchasing power and operating capacity). The alternative reporting methods classified in accordance with these two characteristics are shown in Table 12.7.

Of the nine possible combinations of asset valuation and capital maintenance, five represent theoretical and practical possibilities and have been described for convenience by a letter. These letters have no significance other than as descriptive devices within this text. Method A describes conventional accounting practice which has been considered extensively in this book. Under method B the historical costs of assets are restated at the end of the accounting period by means of a general price index to express them in terms of pounds of current purchasing power. In addition, the

Table 12.7   Alternative methods of accounting

Capital maintenance \ Asset valuation	Historical cost	Historical cost × general price index	Current cost (e.g. replacement cost, realisable value)
Money capital	✓ (A)	✗	✓ (C)
Money capital × General price index (i.e. owners' general purchasing power)	✗	✓ (B)	✓ (D)
Operating capacity	✗	✗	✓ (E)

✓ = Possible combination
✗ = Unlikely combination
(A)…(E) = Classification of available method

money capital is restated by means of a general price index to maintain its general purchasing power. This method of accounting was introduced, briefly, into the UK in the mid-1970s as a supplement to the historical cost accounts of quoted companies and is still in use as a supplementary method in the USA. It is called 'current purchasing power' (CPP) accounting in the UK and 'constant dollar accounting' in the USA. We shall consider this method in Chapter 14.

Methods C, D and E use current costs or current values to value assets and differ only as to how much of the reported income should be set aside to maintain the value of capital. A variant of method E, called 'current cost accounting' (CCA) is currently reported in supplementary accounts in both the UK and the USA, although much debate has centred on its usefulness.

In the preceding seven chapters we have described and explained the accounting method used in conventional accounting practice. In this chapter we have considered what is meant by 'accounting method' and discovered that the term comprises both a method of valuing assets and a method of maintaining capital.

In times when price *levels* are stable and there are neither changes in relative prices nor major technological changes, the choice of accounting method is relatively unimportant because three of the asset valuation methods (historical cost, current purchasing power and current cost) produce identical cost figures, and the three concepts of capital maintenance produce similar results. This might explain why the historical cost method of accounting, which is relatively objective, understandable, and easily verified has been so widely accepted for so long. (Conventional accounting practice values assets at their historical cost and maintains capital in money terms.) However, in times of changing price levels the various asset valuation methods and capital maintenance concepts can produce widely differing results, and it is the existence of high rates of inflation in the last twenty years that has caused accountants to reconsider the principles upon which conventional accounting is based.

In the following chapters we shall evaluate the usefulness and feasibility of these alternative methods of accounting using the set of criteria introduced in Chapter 4.

Discussion Topics

1 Explain what is meant by 'capital maintenance' and outline the effect of capital maintenance adjustments on an organisation's income.

2 Distinguish between the maintenance of operating capacity and the maintenance of the general purchasing power of owners' equity. What views of the organisation do the two methods of capital maintenance imply?

3 Discuss the view that effort expended on evaluating alternative concepts of capital maintenance is wasted.

4 Why does the instability of the monetary unit present so many problems to accountants? What types of organisation are likely to be most affected by such instability?

Further Reading

Baxter, W.T. *Inflation Accounting*, Philip Allan, 1984, Chapter 4.

Hope, A., 'Accounting and changing prices', in Carsberg, B. and Hope, A. *Current Issues in Accounting*, 2nd Ed, Philip Allan, 1984.

Scapens, R.W., '*Accounting in an Inflationary Environment*', 2nd Ed, Macmillan, 1981, Chapters 1 and 2.

Whittington, G., *Inflation Accounting: An Introduction to the Debate*, Cambridge University Press, 1983, Chapter 3.

Chapter 13

Economic Measures of Income and Value

In the previous chapter we identified the two major components of income measurement—the valuation of assets and the maintenance of capital. Each of the methods described in Chapter 12 derives net income and financial position on the basis of *actual transactions*. An alternative method of income determination may be derived from the concepts of economics. This method is based on the discounted cash flow approach described in the appendix to Chapter 3, and relies on the use of forecasts (of future cash flows) rather than on past transactions. In this chapter we will explain this method and also discuss the role and usefulness of economic measures generally. Appendix C to this chapter contrasts the forecast-based and transactions-based approaches. First, however, a word of caution. Because of their dependence on forecasts, and their consequent high degree of subjectivity, economic measures have found little favour amongst accounting practitioners who seek to measure and report an organisation's past performance. Nevertheless, such measures may provide a benchmark against which various transactions-based approaches can be evaluated. It is for this reason that we devote a chapter to a consideration of economic measures.

13.1 The Nature of Economic Income and Value: Certainty

The economic value of an organisation at any point in time is usually defined as the discounted present value of all net cash distributions the organisation expects to make in the future. The economic income of the organisation for a particular period is described as the increase in its capital value during that period, after making suitable adjustments for dividends paid and capital introduced. Under conditions of certainty both the future cash distributions and the future discount rates are known in advance, i.e. *estimates of both future cash distributions and appropriate discount rates will not vary depending on the time at which estimates are made*. In consequence, the following expressions may be used to calculate economic value and economic income, if certainty is presumed:[1]

$$\text{Economic value} \quad EV_t = \sum_{j=t+1}^{n} \frac{D_j}{(1+i)^{j-t}} \tag{13.1}$$

where EV_t is the economic value at time t,

$\quad$ D_j is the cash distribution to be made at time j,

$\quad$ i is the appropriate discount rate (assumed to be constant from period to period),

$\quad$ n is the last time at which a cash distribution is expected.

$$\text{Economic income} \quad EI_{t-1 \to t} = EV_t - EV_{t-1} + D_t - CI_t \tag{13.2}$$

where $EI_{t-1 \to t}$ is the economic income for the period from time $t-1$ to time t,

$\quad$ EV_t, EV_{t-1} are the economic values at time t and time $t-1$ respectively,

$\quad$ D_t is the cash distribution made at time t, and

$\quad$ CI_t is capital introduced at time t.

In order to simplify the analysis in the remainder of this chapter, we shall treat capital introduced as a negative dividend payment. In consequence, the term CI_t disappears from expression (13.2). The following illustration explains the application of this method.

$\quad$ Ashton Ltd has been trading for many years. It is the company's policy to distribute all net cash inflows as dividends as they arise. The company's cost of capital is 20% p.a. The directors intend to pay dividends of £50,000 after one year (i.e. at time 1) and £60,000 at the end of all future years.

$\quad$ Using expression (13.1) we may calculate the present economic value of Ashton Ltd (EV_0) and its expected economic value at all subsequent points in time, as follows:[2]

$$EV_0 = \sum_{j=1}^{\infty} \frac{D_j}{(1.2)^j}$$

$$= \frac{50,000}{(1.2)} + \frac{60,000}{(1.2)^2} + \frac{60,000}{(1.2)^3} + \cdots$$

$$= \frac{50,000}{(1.2)} + \left[\frac{60,000}{0.2} \times \frac{1}{1.2} \right]$$

$$= 41,667 + 250,000$$

$$EV_0 = \underline{£291,667}$$

---

[1]See the appendix to Chapter 3 for an explanation of discounting methods and of the sigma ($\sum$) notation.

[2]The symbol ∞ means 'infinity'.

$$EV_1 = \sum_{j=2}^{\infty} \frac{D_j}{(1.2)^{j-1}}$$

$$= \frac{60,000}{(1.2)} + \frac{60,000}{(1.2)^2} + \frac{60,000}{(1.2)^3} + \ldots$$

$$= \frac{60,000}{0.2}$$

$$EV_1 = \underline{\underline{£300,000}}$$

The economic value at time 2 and all subsequent times will also be £300,000 because at any (annual) point in time after time 2 the company expects to receive £60,000 per annum indefinitely. Thus the economic value at any point in time after time 1 is the discounted present value, at 20% interest, of a perpetuity of £60,000, i.e. £300,000.

The economic income of Ashton Ltd for each future period may be calculated from expression (13.2), as follows:

$$EI_{0\rightarrow 1} = EV_1 - EV_0 + D_1$$
$$= 300,000 - 291,667 + 50,000$$
$$EI_{0\rightarrow 1} = £58,333$$
$$EI_{1\rightarrow 2} = EV_2 - EV_1 + D_2$$
$$= 300,000 - 300,000 + 60,000$$
$$EI_{1\rightarrow 2} = £60,000$$

The economic income for all subsequent periods will also be £60,000 as economic value does not change after time 2 and the constant annual distribution is £60,000. Under conditions of *certainty* the economic income of a period is equal to the economic value at the start of the period multiplied by the discount rate (i.e. $EI_{t-1\rightarrow t} = i \times EV_{t-1}$). Thus, in the case of Ashton Ltd, economic income for the period from time 0 to time 1 (£58,333) may, alternatively, be calculated as 20% of the value at time 0, i.e. as 20% of £291,667, and for each subsequent period as 20% of £300,000.

Let us now analyse the effect of the above on an individual shareholder in the company. This may lead to a clearer understanding of the principles underlying the economic value approach. Suppose that Mr Home owns 10% of Ashton Ltd. His share of the company's value at time 0 (t_0) and time 1 (t_1) and of the dividend paid by the company during the period from time 0 to time 1 is as follows:

	Ashton Ltd £	*Mr Home* (10%) £
Economic value, t_0	291,667	29,167
Economic value, t_1	300,000	30,000
Dividend paid by company, $t_0 \rightarrow t_1$	50,000	5,000

How much better off is Mr Home at the end of the period (t_1) than he was at the beginning (t_0), as a result of owning 10% of the company?

	£	£
At t_0 his share of the company was worth		29,167
At t_1 his share of the company is worth	30,000	
and he has cash from the dividend of	5,000	35,000
His 'gain' during the period is		5,833

We can now interpret the gain of £5,833 in capital maintenance terms as representing the maximum amount Mr Home could spend during the period from his share in Ashton Ltd, and still be as well off (in terms of money capital) at the end of the period as he was at the beginning. If he sold £833 of his share in the company and spent the proceeds, together with the cash distribution of £5,000, he would be left with a share in the company worth £29,167—the same as at the start of the period. As a result of his ownership of 10% of Ashton Ltd, Mr Home has gained £5,833 in the period from time 0 to time 1. Under the forecast-based approach to income and value measurement, this amount is called his income from the company.

13.2   The Nature of Economic Income and Value: Uncertainty

In the previous section we discussed the nature of economic measures of income and value using the simplifying assumption of certainty. In reality, organisations operate under conditions of uncertainty. In consequence, the estimated values of future cash distributions will normally depend on the information available at the time at which the estimate is made, i.e. *expectations may change as time passes*. In addition, different discount rates may be appropriate for different periods, and estimates of the appropriate discount rates may change over time. So, for example, at the end of 1985 the directors of a company might estimate a net cash inflow of £100,000 receivable at the end of 1990. The £100,000 is discounted at 20% p.a. for five years. It is possible that at the end of 1986 the directors may have revised their estimate of the net cash inflow in 1990 to, say, £80,000 *and* revised their estimate of the discount rates to be applied in the intervening four years. In order not to over-complicate our exposition, we shall assume that the appropriate discount rate is constant for each period, and that its estimated value is the same whenever the estimate is made. We shall concentrate, therefore, upon changes in the estimates of future cash flows. However, the principles involved in handling changing discount rate estimates are similar to those for dealing with changing cash flow estimates.

In expressions (13.1) and (13.2) we used subscripts to denote the time at which a cash flow is expected to arise. Under conditions of uncertainty, when expectations may change over time, it is necessary also to indicate the time at which the estimate is made. We use superscripts for this purpose. Thus D_t^s is the net cash flow an organisation expects to distribute at time t, as estimated at time s. In the example above $D_{90}^{85} = £100,000$ and $D_{90}^{86} = £80,000$. Using the subscript and superscript notation we may amend expressions (13.1) and (13.2) to incorporate uncertainty. Thus, the economic value of an enterprise at time t, as estimated at time s, may be estimated from the following amended version of expression (13.1):

$$EV_t^s = \sum_{j=t+1}^{n} \frac{D_j^s}{(1+i)^{j-t}} \tag{13.3}$$

where EV_t^s is the economic value at time t, estimated at time s,
  D_j^s is the cash distribution to be made at time j, estimated at time s,
  i is the discount rate appropriate for the risk of expected distributions, and
  n is the last time at which a cash distribution is expected.

Let us summarise the analysis so far and assess its implications. We have defined income as the amount one can consume during a period and still remain as well off at the end of the period as at the beginning. For example, for the year 1984–85:

$$I_{84 \to 85} = V_{85} - V_{84} + D_{85} \tag{13.4}$$

If we adopt economic value as the method of asset valuation this expression can be restated as:

$$EI_{84 \to 85} = EV_{85} - EV_{84} + D_{85} \tag{13.5}$$

As the balance sheet reports the value of the entity at the end of a period, as estimated at the end of a period, we can, using superscripts to indicate the date on which the estimate is made, restate expression (13.5) as:

$$EI_{84 \to 85}^{85} = EV_{85}^{85} - EV_{84}^{84} + D_{85}^{85} \tag{13.6}$$

If economic measures were to be the basis for reporting performance, an organisation might calculate its economic income for the period in accordance with expression (13.6), i.e. its economic value at the end of the year, estimated at the end of the year (the 1985 balance sheet) *less* its economic value at the beginning of the year, estimated at the beginning of the year (the 1984 balance sheet) *plus* any cash distribution made during the year. In general terms this can be expressed as:[3]

---

[3]This definition of economic income is often referred to as 'total economic income'.

$$\text{Reported } EI_{t-1\to t} = EV_t^t - EV_{t-1}^{t-1} + D_t^t \tag{13.7}$$

where EV_t^t is the economic value of the enterprise at time t, as estimated at time t,

    EV_{t-1}^{t-1} is the economic value of the enterprise at time $t-1$, as estimated at time $t-1$, and (presumably) as already reported at time $t-1$, and

    D_t^t is the actual distribution made at time t.

Income calculated in this way comprises distributions made by an organisation plus any increase in its economic value from one year to the next—and this increase could include increases which are the result simply of a *change in expectations concerning future cash flows*.

Remember that the final reported income figure would depend also upon the capital maintenance concept applied to the economic value at the beginning of the year. In this section, however, we are focusing only on the implications of using economic values as a method of asset valuation.

It is apparent from expression (13.7) that part of the reported economic income figure could be the result of changes in expectations over the year. We would be able to isolate this 'unexpected gain' (i.e. income arising in a period which was not expected at the start of the period) if we knew the expectations of the organisation's managers at the beginning of the year. In other words, at the beginning of the year what did the managers expect the economic value and the cash distribution to be at the end of the year, and hence what did they expect economic income to be?[4] Using superscripts to denote the time at which the estimate is made we can express *expected* economic income as:

$$\text{Expected } EI_{84\to85}^{84} = EV_{85}^{84} - EV_{84}^{84} + D_{85}^{84} \tag{13.8}$$

In general terms the expected economic income for the period $t-1$ to t, estimated at time s, may be estimated from the following amended version of expression (13.2):

$$EI_{t-1\to t}^{s} = EV_t^s - EV_{t-1}^s + D_t^s \tag{13.9}$$

where $EI_{t-1\to t}^s$ is the economic income for the period from time $t-1$ to time t, estimated at time s,

    EV_t^s and EV_{t-1}^s are the economic values at time t and time $t-1$, respectively, both estimated at time s, and

    D_t^s is the cash distribution, less capital introduced, at time t, estimated at time s.

---

[4]Strictly, expected income may be estimated either at the beginning of the period (when it is called *ex ante* income) or at the end (when it is called *ex post* income). To illustrate the distinction between expected income and windfall gain, we consider only *ex ante* income for the remainder of this chapter.

In a certain world, reported economic income, expression (13.7), and expected economic income, expression (13.9), would be identical. In an uncertain world each may give a different estimate of income. The difference between reported income and expected income must be 'unexpected' income (i.e. a gain or loss due to changes in expectations). This unexpected income is normally referred to as a 'windfall' gain or loss. (This term should be familiar. Such windfall gains as pools wins and gambling revenues are common features of British society.) From expressions (13.6) and (13.8) we can identify the difference between reported and expected income and hence the windfall gain or loss. Thus (expression (13.6) – expression (13.8)) becomes:

$$\text{Reported } EI^{85}_{84\to85} - \text{Expected } EI^{84}_{84\to85}$$

$$= \left[EV^{85}_{85} - EV^{84}_{84} + D^{85}_{85} \right] - \left[EV^{84}_{85} - EV^{84}_{84} + D^{84}_{85} \right]$$

$$\text{Therefore, Windfall gain}_{84\to85} = \left[EV^{85}_{85} - EV^{84}_{85} \right] + \left[D^{85}_{85} - D^{84}_{85} \right] \quad (13.10)$$

and generally:

$$\underline{\text{Windfall gain}_{t-1\to t} = \left[EV^{t}_{t} - EV^{t-1}_{t} \right] + \left[D^{t}_{t} - D^{t-1}_{t} \right]} \quad (13.11)$$

It is apparent from this expression that the windfall gain is based entirely on changes in expectations. The following illustration deals with the treatment of unexpected gains and losses.

Eastgate Ltd has been trading for many years. The company distributes all net cash inflows as dividends as they arise. The appropriate discount rate for the company's distributed cash flows is estimated at 20% per annum. At time 0, Eastgate Ltd pays an annual dividend of £87,000 and the directors estimate that future distributions will be £90,000 per annum indefinitely. At time 1, the company receives, and distributes, only £78,000 and the directors revise their estimate of future annual dividends to £84,000. At time 2, £96,000 is received and distributed and the directors estimate that future dividends will be £96,000.

Table 13.1 shows the economic value of Eastgate Ltd, estimated for and at different points in time. The figures are calculated from expression (13.3). For example, the company's economic value at time 0, estimated at time 0 (i.e. $t=0$, $s=0$) is:

$$EV^{0}_{0} = \sum_{j=1}^{\infty} \frac{D^{0}_{j}}{(1.2)^{j}}$$

$$= \frac{90,000}{(1.2)} + \frac{90,000}{(1.2)^{2}} + \frac{90,000}{(1.2)^{3}} + \cdots$$

$$= \frac{90,000}{0.2}$$

$$EV^{0}_{0} = \underline{£450,000}$$

**Table 13.1   Eastgate Ltd—Estimates of economic value
made at different points in time (£)**

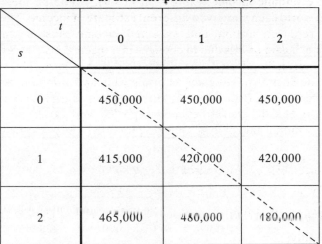

s \ t	0	1	2
0	450,000	450,000	450,000
1	415,000	420,000	420,000
2	465,000	480,000	480,000

s=time at which estimate is made
t=time to which value relates
Figures calculated using expression (13.3)

and its value at time 0, estimated at time 1 (i.e. $t=0$, $s=1$) is:

$$EV_0^1 = \frac{78,000}{(1.2)} + \frac{84,000}{(1.2)^2} + \frac{84,000}{(1.2)^3} + \cdots$$

$$= \frac{78,000}{(1.2)} + \left[\frac{84,000}{0.2} \times \frac{1}{1.2}\right]$$

$$EV_0^1 = £415,000$$

If Eastgate Ltd used economic measures in its published reports, it would, for each period, report its economic value at the end of the period, estimated at the end of the period, i.e. during the period considered in the illustration the company would report the value figures on the broken diagonal line shown in Table 13.1. It would also report its annual economic income, calculated by applying actual cash distributions together with the figures on the diagonal line in Table 13.1 to expression (13.7). For example, at time 1 the company would report its value (EV_1^1) as £420,000 (from Table 13.1). Reported economic income for the period ended at time 1 (EI_0^R, where superscript R signifies reported economic income) would be calculated using expression (13.7):

$$EI_{0\rightarrow1}^R = EV_1^1 - EV_0^0 + D_1^1$$

$$= 420,000 - 450,000 + 78,000$$

$$EI_{0\rightarrow1}^R = £48,000$$

Reported income figures for both periods are shown in column (a) of Table 13.2.

Table 13.2   Eastgate Ltd—Various measures of income and windfall gain, time 0 to time 2 (£)

Period	(a) Reported economic income	(b) Expected income	(c) Windfall gain/(loss)
0→1	48,000	90,000	(42,000)
1→2	156,000	84,000	72,000

(a)   Calculated using expression (13.7)
(b)   Calculated using expression (13.9)
(c)   Calculated using expression (13.11)

The economic income reported for each period may be split into two elements: expected income and windfall gain. For example, expected income for the period to time 1 ($EI_{0\rightarrow1}^0$) may be estimated using expression (13.9):

$$EI_{0\rightarrow1}^0 = EV_1^0 - EV_0^0 + D_1^0$$

$$= 450,000 - 450,000 + 90,000 = \underline{£90,000}$$

or by the expression:[5]

$$EI_{0\rightarrow1}^0 = i \times EV_0^0$$

$$= 0.2 \times 45,0000 \qquad\qquad = \underline{£90,000}$$

This figure together with an estimate of expected income for the second period, is shown in column (b) of Table 13.2. The windfall gain for the period to time 1 is the difference between reported economic income (£48,000) and expected income (£90,000), i.e. a windfall loss of £42,000 in this case. The figure may be calculated directly using expression (13.11):

[5]This calculation of expected income depends on our earlier assumption of a constant discount rate, and may be derived from expression (13.9), using the valuation relationship stated in expression (13.3). The algebra is not important to the present exposition and is omitted. In general terms it may be expressed as

$$EI_{t\rightarrow t-1}^t = i \times EV_t^t$$

$$WG_{0 \to 1} = (EV_1^1 - EV_1^0) + (D_1^1 - D_1^0)$$
$$= (420,000 - 450,000) + (78,000 - 90,000)$$
$$= -£42,000, \text{ i.e. a windfall loss.}$$

This windfall loss is comprised of two parts, both of which reflect changes in expectations during the period. The first (£30,000) is the reduction in the manager's estimate of the company's value at time 1. This value was estimated as £450,000 at the start of the period and as £420,000 at the end. The second (£12,000) is the amount by which the actual dividend paid during the period (£78,000), fell short of the manager's estimate of the dividend (£90,000) at the start of the period. Windfall gains for both periods are shown in column (c) of Table 13.2.

Reported economic income for the period from time 0 to time 1 is £48,000, consisting of expected income of £90,000 less a windfall loss of £42,000. Reported economic income for the period from time 1 to time 2 is £156,000, comprising expected income of £84,000 and a windfall gain of £72,000.

13.3 The Role and Usefulness of Economic Measures

We argued in Chapter 3 that, in general, most users of accounting reports have two main, interdependent information requirements:

(a) forecasts of some aspects of the future performance of the reporting entity, and
(b) regular reports explaining both differences between forecasted and actual performance, and changes in forecasts if expectations have changed.

We argued further that although the aspects of an organisation's performance for which forecasts are required may differ from user to user, most users are interested in its cash flows. Hence, it would seem sensible for organisations to provide two types of financial statement:

(a) a statement of forecasts of the entity's expected future cash flows, and
(b) a statement of the entity's actual cash flows together with an explanation of the differences between the forecasted and the actual cash flows.

In the light of our analysis in the previous section it would also seem to be appropriate for some estimate of the uncertainty associated with the expected future cash flows to be disclosed, to help the user select an appropriate discount rate.

We are now in a position to ask an important question. How far would a method of reporting, based on economic measures of income and value, go

towards satisfying the assumed information needs of an organisation's owners? The most powerful argument supporting economic income and value
measures is that they are based on the discounting of expected cash flows,
using a discount rate which is appropriate to the risk of the cash flows. These
data are essentially the same as those required by owners; estimated future
cash flows, a discount rate based on the risk of the estimated cash flows, and
actual cash flows of the period under consideration together with changes in
expectations during that period.

Suppose that for each period an organisation reported its estimated
economic income for the period, subdivided into expected income and
windfall gains. Expected income would indicate to the owner the management's estimate of the amount of cash flows which *could* be distributed in
each future period, without reducing the organisation's capital in money
terms. Economic value would indicate management's estimate of the discounted present value of expected future cash distributions.

The owner also requires an indication of how effective are the organisation's managers in setting estimates and achieving estimated performance.
In a reporting system based on economic measures, this indication would be
provided primarily by reported windfall gains, which reflect changes in
expectations about cash flows or discount rates. An organisation which
regularly reports relatively high windfall gains or losses may be operating in
particularly volatile markets, or may be employing managers who have poor
estimating ability, or who are deliberately distorting reported income and
value figures. If reported windfall gains or losses are consistently in the same
direction and of similar size, an owner may conclude that management's
current estimates are likely to be optimistic (if windfall losses are regularly
reported) or pessimistic (if windfall gains are regularly reported). If over a
number of periods a mixture of windfall gains and losses is reported, and if
their size is significant, an owner will need to weigh the possible causes and
modify his opinion of the managers' estimates accordingly.

The above analysis suggests that a reporting system based on economic
measures of income and value should not necessarily be regarded as ideal.
However, such a system would help owners to estimate the efficiency of an
organisation's managers in making predictions and in achieving predicted
performance. Consequently, it may provide owners with information for
their decision models at least as useful as would be provided by any alternative (transactions-based) method which involves reporting past performance
and current position.

However, the very relationship between economic value and future
cash flows which makes relevant the reporting of economic value and
income contains its own potential downfall, i.e. an accounting method based
upon economic value will be subject to criticisms similar to those levelled at
financial statements incorporating cash forecasts. Economic measures are
based on estimates of future cash flows and discount rates which are not

objective and cannot be verified; and changes in economic values, as a result of changes in expectations, may provide information which could be advantageous to competitors. In addition, the resulting pattern of income places undue emphasis on the recognition of the opportunities of realising gains rather than on the production or sale involved in their realisation.

For our present purposes, however, it does not matter that a reporting method based on economic measures of income and value is impractical. Even if it is, economic income and value provide *benchmarks* against which alternative, more practical accounting methods may be assessed. Let us explain the rationale of this argument.

We have noted a relevant method of reporting to be one which represents a good basis for predicting the expected value of, and the risk attached to, the organisation's future cash distributions. As part of the prediction process, the reporting method should also enable owners to explain both differences between estimated and actual distributions and changes in expectations regarding future distributions. For various reasons it is unlikely that the forecasted information will be provided directly, and hence published financial statements will continue to be based predominantly on transactions-based accounting methods. What we need is a way of assessing whether the information provided by practical, feasible accounting methods (based upon historical cost, adjusted historical cost or current cost methods of asset valuation) can be interpreted to provide the predictive and control information required by users.

Economic measures of income and value could help to provide the way. Economic value is based upon estimates of future cash flows and the risk associated with them. This is the sort of information required by users. In addition, economic values are reported in a format which allows easy comparison with values, or costs, generated by more practical methods of asset valuation. If a particular accounting method consistently enables good estimates of economic measures to be achieved, then that method is as useful as a method based on economic measures, subject to the costs of making the estimates and their degree of accuracy. Economic measures of income and value can therefore be used as a benchmark, or intermediate criterion, against which other (transactions-based) measures may be evaluated.

The case outlined above in favour of economic measures of income and value is made on *a priori* (i.e. theoretical) grounds. There exists little real-world evidence concerning the usefulness of economic measures. The *a priori* case suggests that economic measures should be used as benchmarks against which the usefulness of alternative reporting methods might be measured; its tentative nature suggests that such a use should not be the only criterion adopted. In subsequent chapters, where alternative transactions-based measures are evaluated, we apply other criteria in addition to the degree of association with economic measures.

APPENDIX C
Comparison Of and Relationship Between
Forecast-based and Transactions-based Approaches

This appendix contrasts the forecast-based and transactions-based approaches to the measurement of income and position discussed in Chapters 12 and 13. Under the forecast-based approach, the first step is to calculate the value of the organisation based on the discounted present value of the net cash inflows it expects to receive (and distribute to its owners) in the future. Periodic income is then calculated as the increase in the organisation's value between the beginning and end of the period plus any distributions made to the owners during the period. Using a transactions-based approach, income can be calculated in a similar manner (but using historical or current costs instead of discounted present values). However, it is more usually calculated by matching revenues with (historical or current) costs. The organisation's balance sheet at the end of the period includes the (historical or current) costs of resources which have been acquired, but which have not yet been matched with revenues. Thus forecast-based approaches emphasise future expectations, while transactions-based approaches emphasise past activities and resources presently owned. The following simple example addresses these issues and shows how the two approaches might be reconciled.

Mr Elland commenced business at the beginning of year 1. He immediately bought for £100,000 a machine that produces components. The machine has a life of five years, at the end of which time it has no scrap or resale value. Mr Elland receives net cash inflows of £40,000 at the end of each of the five years of the machine's life, from the production and sale of components. He ceases to trade at the end of year 5, when the machine has no further productive capacity. Mr Elland's required annual rate of return (discount rate) over the period is 20%.

Calculations of the income and position of Mr Elland's business for each of the five years are given in Tables 13.3, 13.4, 13.5, 13.6 and 13.7. Tables 13.3 and 13.4 show economic value and economic income calculations using the forecast-based approach. It is a characteristic of these measures that, under conditions of certainty, the economic income of a period is equal to the economic value at the start of the period multiplied by the discount rate. For example, the economic income of period 3, £16,852 equals 20% of £84,260. Tables 13.5 and 13.6 show transactions-based calculations of income and position ('value') for each period using historical cost as the method of asset valuation. We assume that the net cash inflows each period are equal to revenues less annual operating costs, excluding the purchase cost of the machine, and that the machine is depreciated on a straight line basis. The 'value' of the business at the end of each year is the original cost of the machine less the accumulated depreciation. In Table 13.7 we

Table 13.3   Mr Elland—Calculations of value of business using forecast-based approach

	£
Start of year 1 (before buying machine)	100,000
Start of year 1 (after buying machine)	
$40,000 \times a_{\overline{5}|} \, 20\% = 40,000(2.9906) =$	119,624
End of year 1 $\quad 40,000 \times a_{\overline{4}|} \, 20\% = 40,000(2.5887) =$	103,548
End of year 2 $\quad 40,000 \times a_{\overline{3}|} \, 20\% = 40,000(2.1065) =$	84,260
End of year 3 $\quad 40,000 \times a_{\overline{2}|} \, 20\% = 40,000(1.5278) =$	61,112
End of year 4 $\quad 40,000 \times a_{\overline{1}|} \, 20\% = 40,000(0.8333) =$	33,332
End of year 5	0

Value at each point in time is calculated as the discounted present value of future net cash inflows.

Table 13.4   Mr Elland—Calculations of income of business using forecast-based approach

			£
Start of year 1 (gain from			
buying machine)	$119,624 - 100,000$	$=$	19,624
Year 1	$103,548 - 119,624 + 40,000 =$		23,924
Year 2	$84,260 - 103,548 + 40,000 =$		20,712
Year 3	$61,112 - 84,260 + 40,000 =$		16,852
Year 4	$33,332 - 61,112 + 40,000 =$		12,220
Year 5	$0 - 33,332 + 40,000 =$		6,668
			100,000

Income each period is calculated as: Value at end of period – value at start of period + cash distributed to owner during period, from expression (13.2) on page 271.

Table 13.5   Mr Elland—Calculations of income of business using transactions-based approach

		£
Year 1	$40,000 - 20,000 =$	20,000
Year 2	$40,000 - 20,000 =$	20,000
Year 3	$40,000 - 20,000 =$	20,000
Year 4	$40,000 - 20,000 =$	20,000
Year 5	$40,000 - 20,000 =$	20,000
		100,000

Income each period is calculated as:
Revenues earned less operating costs incurred (assumed to be equal to annual net cash inflows)   40,000

less: Part of original cost of machine written-off each year
$(1/5 \times 100,000)$ 20,000

    20,000

Table 13.6   Mr Elland—Calculations of 'value' of business using transactions-based approach

		£
Start of year 1	100,000− 0 =	100,000
End of year 1	100,000− 20,000 =	80,000
End of year 2	100,000− 40,000 =	60,000
End of year 3	100,000− 60,000 =	40,000
End of year 4	100,000− 80,000 =	20,000
End of year 5	100,000−100,000 =	0

'Value' at each point in time is the original cost of the machine less that part of the original cost which has been written-off in calculating the income of previous periods.

Table 13.7   Mr Elland—Alternative calculations of income of business under transactions-based approach, using general formula as in Table 13.4

		£
Year 1	80,000−100,000+40,000 =	20,000
Year 2	60,000− 80,000+40,000 =	20,000
Year 3	40,000− 60,000+40,000 =	20,000
Year 4	20,000− 40,000+40,000 =	20,000
Year 5	0− 20,000+40,000 =	20,000
		100,000

Income each period is calculated as: Value at end of period−value at start of period+cash distributed to owner during period, basing values on the transactions-based 'values' calculated in Table 13.6

demonstrate that conventional accounting figures of net income, like their forecast-based counterparts, may be calculated from the general formula in expression (13.2). Of course, the resultant income figures differ from those obtained using the forecast-based approach because we have used different methods to determine value.

Under both forecast-based and transactions-based approaches, *the total income over the whole life of the organisation is the same* (£100,000 in our illustration—see Tables 13.4 and 13.5), and is equal to the sum of cash inflows minus the sum of cash outflows during the enterprise's entire life. However, *a crucial difference is that the pattern of income (and value) from year to year is different under each approach*. The central problem facing accountants is how to *allocate* this net cash flow between accounting periods in a way which is as helpful as possible to users. The two approaches lead to the same pattern of income *only* if one approach produces an identical measure of value to the other at each and every point in time during an organisation's life. Of course, the 'final' reported income figure will depend also upon the capital maintenance concept adopted.

Discussion Topics

1 In what respects does the existence of uncertainty complicate economic measurements of income and value?.

2 Explain the distinction between 'expected income' and 'windfall gains' in economic income measurement.

3 Discuss why the distinction between 'expected income' and 'windfall gains' may be important to users of the measurements, particularly insofar as the users wish to make predictions.

4 Discuss the objections to the use of economic measures as means of reporting organisational performance.

5 Do you think that a study of economic measures of income and value is helpful to an accounting student? Why (or why not)?

Further Reading

Alexander, S., 'Income measurement in a dynamic economy' (revised by Solomon, D.), in Baxter, W.T. and Davidson, S. (eds), *Studies in Accounting*, Institute of Chartered Accountants in England and Wales, 1977.

Arnold, J. and El-Azma, M., *A Study of the Relative Usefulness of Six Accounting Measure of Income*, Institute of Chartered Accountants in England and Wales, Research Committee Occasional Paper No. 13, 1978, Section III.

Barton, A., 'Expectations and achievements in income theory', *The Accounting Review*, October 1974.

Hicks, J.R., *Value and Capital*, 2nd Ed, Oxford University Press, 1946, Chapter 14.

Lee, T.A., *Income and Value Measurement*, 2nd Ed, Nelson, 1981.

Parker, R.H. and Harcourt, G.C. (eds), *Readings in the Concept of Measurement of Income*, Cambridge University Press, 1969, Parts I, II and III.

Revsine, L., 'On the correspondence between replacement cost income and economic income', *The Accounting Review*, July 1970.

Shwayder, K., 'A critique of economic income as an accounting concept', *Abacus*, August 1967.

Solomons, D., 'Economic and accounting concepts of income', *The Accounting Review*, July 1961.

Whittington, G., 'Accounting and economics', in Carsberg, B. and Hope, A. (eds), *Current Issues in Accounting*, 2nd Ed, Philip Allan, 1984.

Exercises

13.1 Ferrando Ltd was incorporated on 1 January 19X4 with initial capital subscribed of £75,000. The whole of the initial capital was invested in a project which was expected to produce net cash inflows of £15,000 p.a. indefinitely, the first receipt being expected on 31 December 19X4. On incorporation, the directors of Ferrando Ltd declared their intention of distributing all net cash inflows to the company's owners (shareholders) as dividends, and of investing in no projects other than the one described above.

On 31 December 19X4, the company received and distributed the first cash inflow from the project, which amounted to £13,000. At the same time the directors estimated that future net cash inflows would be £14,000 p.a.

On 31 December 19X5, £16,000 was received from the project and distributed, and the directors revised their estimate of the future annual net inflow to £16,000.

The cost of capital of Ferrando Ltd (i.e. the return required by its shareholders) was estimated at 20% p.a. on incorporation, and has since remained at that level.

● On the basis of the directors' estimates, calculate the following for each of the years 19X4 and 19X5:
(a)   the company's economic value at the end of the year, as estimated at the end of the year;
(b)   the company's '*reported*' economic income for the year;
(c)   the company's '*expected*' economic income for the year;
(d)   the company's windfall gain for the year.

13.2   Dorabella plc is incorporated on 1 January 19X0 with an initial capital of £3 million. It invests all its initial capital immediately in a fixed asset with an expected life of four years and no scrap value. As a result of this investment, the directors of Dorabella plc expect to receive net cash inflows of £1 million per annum for four years, the first receipt being expected on 31 December 19X0. The directors expect no cash flows after 31 December 19X3 and the company will cease operations on 1 January 19X4. The directors intend to distribute all net cash inflows as dividends (or return of capital) on 31 December of the year in which they arise. They estimate the appropriate discount rate at 10% p.a.

As the company evolves, the directors' estimates of future cash flows change as follows:

Time at which estimate is made	Time at which cash flow is expected to arise	31/12/X0 £000	31/12/X1 £000	31/12/X2 £000	31/12/X3 £000
1/1/X0		1,000	1,000	1,000	1,000
1/1/X1		1,000	1,300	1,300	1,300
1/1/X2		1,000	1,200	1,200	1,200
1/1/X3		1,000	1,200	1,400	1,400
1/1/X4 (cash flows actually received)		1,000	1,200	1,400	1,500

● (a)   For each year of the company's life, calculate its income for the year and its position at the end of the year using the historical cost transactions-based approach.

(b)   For each year of the company's life, calculate:
    (i)   the company's economic value, as estimated at the end of the year;
    (ii)   the company's '*reported*' economic income for the year;
    (iii)   the company's '*expected*' economic income for the year;
    (iv)   the company's windfall gain for the year.

(c)   Comment on the likely usefulness of the various measures of income and value you have calculated; deal particularly with differences between your answers to (a) and (b).

Chapter 14

Current Purchasing Power Accounting

In Chapter 13 we made a distinction between 'forecast-based' and 'transactions-based' approaches to asset valuation. Forecast-based approaches use the discounted cash flow approach to the measurement of wealth, and we have described and evaluated one such method, based on measures of 'economic value' and 'economic income'. We concluded that although economic measures of income and value provide information relevant to the needs of an organisation's participants (i.e. economic value is based upon estimates of future cash flows and their associated risk) the dependence of the measures on forecasts, and their consequent high degree of subjectivity, mean that they are unlikely to be reported in practice. Nevertheless their close association with 'relevant information' suggests they might provide a benchmark, or intermediate criterion, against which various, more practical approaches can be evaluated. In this chapter and in Chapter 15 we turn our attention once again to transactions-based approaches to the measurement of income and value when price levels are changing.

14.1 Transactions-based Approaches

Under transactions-based approaches net income is derived from actual transactions and represents the difference between revenues and associated costs. Traditionally, these costs have been the original, or historical, costs of the resources used. In an environment where prices are stable and are not expected to change, measures of income and financial position obtained by using historical costs will, self evidently, be identical to those obtained by using current costs.

However, the existence of changing prices creates problems when measurements are based upon historical costs (see Chapter 12). We have suggested that if financial statements are to provide information useful to participants, such information should be based, as far as possible, upon current prices. The professional accountancy bodies in several countries (including Australia, Canada, New Zealand, the UK and the USA) have at various times put forward proposals to incorporate the impact of changing prices into published financial statements.

However, it is one thing to accept in principle that financial statements should report the impact of changing prices, and quite another to develop a method which is acceptable in practice. Several methods of accounting can be claimed to incorporate the effects of changing price levels, but the choice of the most appropriate method will depend upon the answers to the following three questions:

(a)   Which price level changes should be accounted for? Should the accounting method report the impact of changes in the general price level or changes in specific price levels? Or both?

(b)   Which assets' values should be adjusted to take account of changing prices? Should all assets (and all liabilities) be adjusted, or should the adjustment be restricted to non-monetary assets such as fixed assets and stocks?

(c)   Which method of capital maintenance should be adopted—money, general purchasing power, or operating capacity?

These three questions represent the three stages necessary to construct an accounting method to account for changing price levels. If we bear them in mind during our analysis and evaluation of alternative methods, we may be better able to identify not only the alternative selected, but also the alternatives rejected at each stage. This may then help us to understand the objective of, and the rationale for, the method selected.

In Chapter 12 we introduced five alternative accounting methods (Table 12.7, page 268). Under method B a general price index is applied to an entity's assets, and capital is maintained in terms of general purchasing power. The effect of applying a general price index to an entity's assets is to express the cost of each asset in terms of 'current purchasing power'. In the UK this method of accounting is called 'general price level' accounting or, more commonly, 'current purchasing power' (CPP) accounting. CPP accounting is the subject of the remainder of this chapter.

14.2   Current Purchasing Power Accounting

In this section we illustrate the application of CPP accounting to a set of business transactions. Details of Mr Villa's business transactions for his first two years of trading are given in Table 14.1 (for simplicity we presume that all transactions take place on the first or last day of the accounting year). The same transactions will be used in Chapter 15 to illustrate the application of replacement cost accounting. However, not all the information provided in Table 14.1 is required to prepare a set of CPP accounts. In Table 14.2 we show the accounting equation entries required to record Mr Villa's

Table 14.1   Mr Villa—Business transactions

Mr Villa commences business as a retailer on 1 January, 19X1. He undertakes the following transactions during the subsequent two years. All transactions are for cash.

1 January 19X1
1. Pays £30,000 into the business bank account.
2. Buys equipment for £15,000. The equipment has an expected life of 10 years, at the end of which it will have no scrap or resale value. Mr Villa wishes to apply the straight line method of depreciation to the equipment.
3. Buys 2,000 units of stock at £5 per unit.

31 December 19X1
4. Sells 2,000 units of stock for £10 per unit.
5. Pays expenses of £5,000.
6. Buys 2,500 units of stock for £15,000 (i.e. at £6 per unit, representing a 20% price increase during the year).
    (Note: The price of *new* equipment like Mr Villa's is now £16,500, representing a 10% price increase during the year.)

31 December 19X2
7. Sells 2,000 units of stock for £11.50 per unit.
8. Pays expenses of £6,500.
9. Replaces stock for £14,400 (i.e. 2,000 units at £7.20 per unit, representing a 20% price increase during the year).
    (Note: The price of *new* equipment like Mr Villa's is now £18,150, representing a 10% price increase during the year.)

transactions using the historical cost method, and in Table 14.3 we present his historical cost income statements and balance sheets for the two years. (Readers wishing to obtain further practice of the conventional double-entry recording procedures using 'T' accounts introduced in Chapter 8 might wish to rework the accounting equation entries in Table 14.2—the same income statements and balance sheets should result!)

CPP accounting does not involve a fundamental departure from historical cost accounting. We noted in Chapter 12 that accounting figures can be added or subtacted in a meaningful way only if they are expressed in a common measurement unit. In times of changing prices the pound (or any other currency) is no longer a stable unit of measurement and CPP accounting substitutes pounds of current purchasing power for pounds of original purchasing power as the measurement unit, i.e. the unit of measurement becomes purchasing power units rather than money. All other conventional historical cost accounting principles remain unchanged.

CPP accounting allows us to restate the historical cost accounts of Mr Villa (Table 14.3) in pounds of current purchasing power at the balance sheet dates. In general, the restatement, or conversion, factor can be expressed as:

$$\frac{\text{Index at balance sheet date}}{\text{Index at date the item was first recorded in the books of account}}$$

Table 14.2   Mr Villa—Accounting equation entries: Historical cost

	Equipment £	+	Stock £	+	Cash at bank £	=	Ownership interest £	+	Income £	
19X1										
1 Jan.:										
Transaction (1)					30,000		30,000			
Transaction (2)	15,000				(15,000)					
Transaction (3)			10,000		(10,000)					
31 Dec.: Transaction (4)					20,000				20,000	Sales
			(10,000)						(10,000)	Cost of goods sold
Transaction (5)					(5,000)				(5,000)	Expenses
Transaction (6)			15,000		(15,000)					
Depreciation (15,000÷10)	(1,500)								(1,500)	Depreciation
									3,500	Income
Transfer income to ownership interest							3,500		(3,500)	
Balances	15,000 (1,500)	+	15,000	+	5,000	=	33,500	+	0	
19X2										
31 Dec.: Transaction (7)					23,000				23,000	Sales
			(12,000)						(12,000)	Cost of goods sold
Transaction (8)					(6,500)				(6,500)	Expenses
Transaction (9)			14,400		(14,400)					
Depreciation	(1,500)								(1,500)	Depreciation
									3,000	
Transfer income to ownership interest							3,000		(3,000)	
Balances	15,000 (3,000)	+	17,400	+	7,100	=	36,500	+	0	

Table 14.3   Mr Villa—Historical cost income statements and balance sheets

	19X1	19X1	19X2	19X2
	£	£	£	£
Income statements				
Sales		20,000		23,000
less: Cost of goods sold		10,000		12,000
Gross profit		10,000		11,000
less: Expenses	5,000		6,500	
Depreciation	1,500		1,500	
		6,500		8,000
Net profit		3,500		3,000
Balance sheets				
Ownership interest:				
Opening balance		30,000		33,500
add: Net profit for the year		3,500		3,000
		33,500		36,500
Equipment at cost		15,000		15,000
less: Accumulated depreciation		1,500		3,000
		13,500		12,000
Current assets: Stock	15,000		17,400	
Cash at bank	5,000		7,100	
		20,000		24,500
		33,500		36,500

In the UK the index generally used is the retail price index (RPI). The CPP financial statements for year 1 of Mr Villa's business are presented in Table 14.4, and we explain below the principles underlying their preparation. We assume that the RPI was 100 on 1 January 19X1, 105 on 31 December 19X1 and 110 on 31 December 19X2.

In the income statement, both the sales revenue and the attendant expenses arose (and were first recorded in the books) on the last day of the year, and are therefore already expressed in year-end pounds. The numerator and the denominator of the conversion factor are identical numbers, representing the RPI number on 31 December. If, however, sales revenue had arisen at the mid-point of the year the conversion factor would be 105/102.5, and revenue would be shown at 20,000×105/102.5= £20,444. Each item in the income statement which did not arise on the last day of the year must be restated in year-end pounds, i.e. the impact of changing price levels is felt most keenly when there is a time lag between

Table 14.4   Mr Villa—Income statements and balance sheets, 19X1

	HC £			CPP £
Income statements				
Sales		20,000	×105/105	20,000
less: Cost of goods sold		10,000	×105/100	10,500
Gross profit		10,000		9,500
less: Expenses	5,000		×105/105 5,000	
Depreciation	1,500		×105/100 1,575	
		6,500		6,575
Operating profit		3,500		2,925
Loss on holding net monetary assets			(5,000×5/100)	250
Net profit		3,500		2,675
Balance sheets				
Equipment at cost		15,000	×105/100	15,750
less: Accumulated depreciation		1,500	×105/100	1,575
		13,500		14,175
Current assets:				
Stock	15,000		×105/105 15,000	
Cash at bank	5,000		5,000	
		20,000		20,000
		33,500		34,175
Ownership interest:				
Opening balance		30,000		30,000
Capital maintenance reserve		–	(30,000×5/100)	1,500
		30,000		31,500
Retained profit		3,500		2,675
		33,500		34,175

purchase and use of an asset. As the goods sold on 31 December were purchased on 1 January, the cost of goods sold figure of £10,000 in the historical cost accounts is expressed in '1 January pounds', when the RPI stood at 100. This figure must be restated to CPP £10,500 (£10,000×105/ 100) to reflect the change in purchasing power of the £10,000 invested in stock twelve months previously. The historical cost depreciation charge of £1,500 refers to the equipment purchased on 1 January. As the historical cost of equipment, £15,000, is expressed in 1 January pounds, so the depreciation charge of £1,500 ($1/10 \times$ £15,000) is also expressed in 1 January pounds, and must be restated into pounds of current purchasing power (£1,500 $\times$ 105/100=£1,575). At this stage the CPP operating income figure amounts to £2,925, compared with the historical cost figure of £3,500. The remaining item in the CPP income statement (loss on holding net monetary assets) is complex and we shall be able to explain it more easily after we have considered the balance sheet adjustments.

CPP accounting requires that a distinction be made in the balance sheet between monetary items and non-monetary items. *Non-monetary items* (e.g. fixed assets and stock) can maintain their general purchasing power during a period of inflation because it is possible for an increase in their prices to compensate for a fall in the value of money. Consequently, the historical costs of non-monetary items are restated in year-end pounds. The equipment, purchased on 1 January is restated using the factor 105/100, whereas the stock on hand at the year end, purchased on 31 December is already expressed in year-end pounds.

Monetary items are those assets and liabilities which are fixed in money terms regardless of changes in the general price level. They cannot maintain their general purchasing power during a period of inflation because their prices cannot increase. Cash is one such asset. Suppose an individual keeps £10,000 in his bank current account for one year during which time the RPI increases by 10%. Suppose also that no interest accrues on the amount. At the end of the year he still has £10,000 in the account but the purchasing power of this asset has fallen. He now needs £10,000 $\times$ 110/100=£11,000 to buy the same amount of goods. He has incurred a *loss of purchasing power* of £1,000 by holding a monetary asset during a period of rising prices. The same would be true had he sold an item of stock for £10,000 on credit and allowed the debtor one year to pay. Conversely, a purchaser who buys an item on credit experiences a purchasing power gain as the eventual payment to his creditor will be worth less than the equivalent amount at the time of purchase. Some further examples of monetary items are given in Table 14.5.

Because their amounts are fixed, monetary items must be disclosed at their money, or face, value in the balance sheet, and any loss of general purchasing power suffered by holding monetary assets is recognised as an

Table 14.5   Examples of monetary items

Assets	*Liabilities*
Advances to suppliers, employees, etc.	Accrued expenses
Bank deposits	Bank overdrafts
Bills receivable	Creditors
Cash	Debentures
Debtors, and provision for doubtful debts	Dividends and interest payable
Prepaid expenses	Loans

expense in the income statement. Mr Villa held a cash balance of £5,000 from 1 January to 31 December. On 31 December he required £5,250 (i.e. £5,000×105/100) to maintain the general purchasing power of his opening cash balance and hence suffered a *loss* in purchasing power of £250. This loss is deducted from the CPP operating income and added to the ownership interest as part of the capital maintenance reserve. We explain below the reason for this treatment. The cash balance is shown at face value in the balance sheet. Had Mr Villa held *net monetary liabilities* (for example, if he had a bank overdraft and trade creditors and if the total of these was greater than the sum of his trade debtors and cash balances) the reverse situation would apply, and he would record a general purchasing power *gain* for holding net monetary liabilities.

Finally, we consider the capital maintenance concept adopted under CPP accounting. From Table 12.7 (page 268) we see that CPP accounting maintains the general purchasing power of capital by applying a general price index to money capital. The opening capital (ownership interest) of Mr Villa is £30,000. At the year end £31,500 (£30,000×105/100) is required to maintain the general purchasing power of Mr Villa's stake in the business and a capital maintenance reserve of £1,500 is included in ownership interest for this purpose. This capital maintenance reserve can also be viewed as representing the total of all the individual adjustments made to restate the historical cost (HC) figures into CPP figures, and therefore to maintain Mr Villa's purchasing power. Thus from Table 14.4 we can see that the £1,500 is made up of:

	£
Increase in assets (34,175−33,500)	675
Increase in cost of goods sold (10,500−10,000)	500
Increase in depreciation (6,575−6,500)	75
Loss on holding net monetary assets	250
	£1,500

Compared to the historical cost figures, the CPP statements show higher net asset and ownership interest figures and a lower income figure. During a period of rising prices, increases in the net asset and the ownership interest figures are inevitable, but it may not always be the case that CPP net income is lower than HC net income. The relationship between the CPP and HC income figures will depend upon not only the restatement of the cost of goods sold and depreciation figures but also on whether the organisation held net monetary assets or net monetary liabilities. We discuss this matter further in the next section.

As CPP accounting applies a single index to the historical cost figures, entities need not maintain separate accounting records. It is sufficient to prepare historical cost accounts in the usual manner and convert them to accounts of current purchasing power at the year end. The ease with which

HC accounts can be restated in subsequent years is illustrated in Table 14.6. Table 14.6 reproduces the HC accounts for Mr Villa's second year of trading and presents the CPP accounts alongside. During the year, the RPI increased from 105 to 110, representing an annual inflation rate of 4.76% (5/105). The principles underlying the restatement procedure are the same as those for the previous year.

As all items are to be expressed in year-end pounds the numerator of the conversion factor is 110 for each item restated. (In the first year it was 105 for each comparable item.) The cost of goods sold figure is restated from 31 December 19X1 (the date on which the goods were purchased) to 31 December 19X2, and the depreciation figure is restated from 1 January 19X1 to 31 December 19X2 (i.e. the £1,500 depreciation charge is one-tenth of the original £15,000 which first appeared in the historical cost records at the beginning of 19X1 when the RPI stood at 100). Mr Villa again held £5,000 cash for the whole year and suffered a loss in purchasing power of £238 (£5,000×5/105).

The historical cost of stock in the balance sheet comprises two amounts bought on different dates. Stock costing £14,400 was purchased on 31 December 19X2 and is already expressed in year-end pounds, but the remaining stock, costing £3,000, was purchased at the end of 19X1 and must be restated. Finally, the balance of ownership interest in CPP terms at the end of 19X1 was £34,175 (i.e. Table 14.4 shows the make-up of ownership interest as representing capital introduced+capital maintenance reserve+retained profit) and hence £35,802 (£34,175×110/105) is required to maintain the general purchasing power of Mr Villa's stake in the business at the end of 19X2. This involves an additional capital maintenance adjustment of £1,627 (£35,802−£34,175). This is made up of:

	£	£
Increase in fixed assets at 31/12/X2 (13,200−12,000)	1,200	
less: Increase applicable to, and taken in, in 19X1	675	525
Increase in stock (17,543−17,400)		143
Increase in cost of goods sold (12,571−12,000)		571
Increase in depreciation (1,650−1,500)		150
Loss on holding net monetary assets		238
		£1,627

14.3   Current Purchasing Power in Practice

Applying the restatement procedures of CPP accounting to the historical cost accounts of Mr Villa we find that the asset values are increased and the net profit is reduced in both years. Whether or not the CPP profit figure is

Table 14.6   Mr Villa—Income statements and balance sheets, 19X2

		HC £				CPP £
Income statements						
Sales		23,000	×110/110			23,000
less: Cost of goods sold		12,000	×110/105			12,571
Gross profit		11,000				10,429
less: Expenses	6,500		×110/110	6,500		
Depreciation	1,500		×110/100	1,650		
		8,000				8,150
Operating profit		3,000				2,279
Loss on holding net monetary assets			(5,000×5/105)			238
		3,000				2,041
Balance sheets						
Equipment at cost		15,000	×110/100			16,500
less: Accumulated depreciation		3,000	×110/100			3,300
		12,000				13,200
Current assets: Stock	14,400		×110/110	14,400		
	3,000		×110/105	3,143		
	17,400			17,543		
Cash at bank	7,100			7,100		
		24,500				24,643
		36,500				37,843
Ownership interest: Opening balance		30,000				30,000
Capital maintenance reserve						
—beginning of year				1,500		
—adjustment for year				1,627		
		–				3,127
		30,000				33,127
Retained profit						
—beginning of year	3,500			2,675		
—net profit for year	3,000			2,041		
		6,500				4,716
		36,500				37,843

reduced depends as a general rule upon the relative size of the adjustments in the income statement, i.e. the adjustments made in respect of cost of goods sold, depreciation, and the loss, or gain, on holding net monetary assets or liabilities.

Capital intensive companies which own large amounts of plant and equipment would be expected to show a CPP depreciation figure considerably higher than its historical cost counterpart (particularly if items had been purchased, say, fifteen or twenty years previously); companies carrying a high level of stocks and work in progress would report a higher cost of goods sold figure; and companies with large cash balances would disclose sizeable losses from holding net monetary assets. Table 14.7 lists a selection of industry groups in the UK in order of the average difference between historical and CPP income figures. The figures are old. They are taken from the results of a study[1] published in 1974, the only year all UK quoted companies were required to prepare CPP accounts (as a supplementary statement to the historical cost accounts)[2]. We have no reason to believe that the *rankings* would be significantly different at the present time, although of course the *absolute* percentage figures may well be so.

Table 14.7   Average percentage change in CPP income
compared with historical cost income for selected UK
industries, 1973–74

	%
Motors and distributors	−65
Electricals	−60
Textiles	−40
Engineering (general)	−35
Engineering (heavy)	−20
Tobacco	−5
Stores	0
Breweries	+30
Entertainment and catering	+50
Property	+430

The figures in Table 14.7 illustrate a clear distinction in effect between manufacturing companies, whose reported earnings are generally reduced under CPP accounting, and service companies whose earnings are often increased. Among the manufacturing industries, companies in the motor, engineering and textile groups (for example, Dunlop, Babcock and Wilcox, and Courtaulds) suffer particularly badly as the result of high depreciation

---

[1]Parker, P. and Gibbs, M., 'Inflation accounting and its effects', *Accountancy*, September 1974.

[2]Accounting Standards Committee, *Accounting for Changes in the Purchasing Power of Money*, Provisional Statement of Standard Accounting Practice No. 7., Institute of Chartered Accountants in England and Wales, 1974.

charges and the tendency in these industries for companies to carry high levels of stocks and work in progress. Tobacco companies such as British American Tobacco (BAT) suffer less from the effect of increased depreciation charges, but their CPP earnings are affected by their high stock levels.

Among the service industries, property companies (e.g. Land Securities, and Metropolitan Estates) reported the highest increases in CPP income over historical cost income. Property companies do not depreciate their properties. Such properties are not treated as fixed assets, but rather as assets to be traded and therefore as current assets. The most significant adjustment in the CPP income statement of property companies is the gain from monetary liabilities, as property companies are traditionally very highly geared. Breweries (e.g. Bass Charrington, and Whitbread) and hotel chains (e.g. Trust House Forte) are also highly geared, and the depreciation charges on their buildings are low relative to income. Several industries are little affected by any change from historical cost to CPP accounting. Although stores (e.g. Marks and Spencer, Debenhams, and W.II. Smith) are adversely affected by their high levels of stocks, they benefit from having sizeable net monetary liabilities. These arise because, although purchases are made on credit, most sales are cash transactions and hence these companies have relatively few debtors.

Care must be taken in interpreting these results, especially when the difference between the CPP and HC reported income figures is affected most by the gain or loss on holding monetary items. An investor should not be misled into a panic sale of shares in a 'cash-rich' company simply because reported CPP income is lower than reported HC income. The cash, which under CPP accounting would produce a loss on holding monetary assets, might have been accumulated to make a potentially profitable investment in the future, or it may make the company an attractive proposition for a takeover bid by another company. Either way the investor, and the share price, should be little affected by the CPP figures. Conversely one might be wary of a company whose CPP earnings are higher than its HC earnings because of a large gain from holding monetary liabilities—the level of borrowing might presage severe financial difficulties. This serves to remind us of a point we have made previously—that the measurement of liquidity is a separate matter from the measurement of profitability. It is important to analyse both of these areas when assessing a company's position and prospects, and particularly so during a period of rapidly rising prices. We return to this particular theme in Chapter 16.

14.4   An Evaluation of Current Purchasing Power Accounting

In Chapter 12 we explained that the determination of income depends both upon how an entity values its assets and how it maintains its capital. Under the historical cost method of accounting, assets are valued at their original cost, capital is maintained in money terms, and income is generated as a result of actual transactions. We have, in earlier chapters, discussed the possible merits of historical cost accounting. For example, as historical costs are based upon the exchange value of past transactions, the accounting figures are considered to be both objective and easily verifiable. In addition, by providing a reliable record of past transactions, the accounting numbers enable the owners to exercise some stewardship control over the managers. Finally, historical cost accounting has the advantage of being (comparatively) cheap to implement.

Recently, however, some doubts have been expressed about these alleged benefits. For example, objectivity is reduced significantly when organisations are free to select from any one of the many available depreciation and stock valuation methods (see Chapters 9 and 10); and perhaps stewardship can be viewed in a wider sense to involve more than simply 'looking after' the owners' assets—it might also be defined to include the operations of those assets, i.e. users may want information which will enable them to evaluate an entity's past performance and to assess its likely future performance; and, as we saw in Chapter 12, the existence of changing price levels can distort the message conveyed by historical cost data.

From Tables 14.4 and 14.6 we see that under CPP accounting assets are 'valued' in pounds of current purchasing power, capital is maintained in terms of general purchasing power, and income is affected not only by transactions but also by the amount of monetary assets and liabilities held by the entity during the year. Nevertheless, CPP accounting does not represent a fundamental shift away from historical cost accounting; indeed CPP financial statements are prepared by applying only one general price index to the existing set of historical cost accounts. In consequence, many of the advantages and disadvantages of historical cost accounting are applicable also to CPP accounting.

For example, the application of one general index does little to change the extent to which historical cost figures are seen to be both relatively objective and easily verifiable; and the cost of preparing CPP accounts imposes no great burden. In addition, it might be argued that the stewardship function can be fulfilled more completely by CPP accounting, i.e. by separating operating profit from any gain or loss on holding monetary items, the CPP method goes some way to highlight two separate aspects of managerial performance, those of operating efficiency and financial management.

However, the close association of CPP and historical cost accounting produces disadvantages also. This is particularly the case when interpreting the amounts placed upon the organisation's assets. CPP amounts are no more than restated historical costs. The values of assets in a CPP balance sheet and the depreciation and cost of goods sold figures in a CPP income statement do *not* reflect current replacement costs or realisable values except by chance, i.e. unless such costs and values have increased at exactly the same rate as the general price index since the assets were purchased. As we explained in Chapter 12, a general index represents a weighted average of the prices of numerous specific items. It is possible, therefore, for the prices of assets owned by one organisation to rise significantly during the year, the prices of assets owned by another organisation to fall during the year, and the general index to remain unchanged.

As the CPP valuation does not reflect the current value of an asset, it is difficult to attach much significance to an asset's CPP valuation. A student at Manchester University once defined it as 'the amount of money you would need now to buy the same basket of consumer goods you could have bought, but didn't, when you bought the asset instead'. A less cynical definition is 'the current purchasing power of the money originally invested in the asset'.

It is perhaps the indiscriminate application of one general index to all non-monetary assets which limits most severely the usefulness of CPP accounting. Below we use two hypothetical examples to illustrate how the use of a general index can generate potentially misleading information.

In 1982 Nissan, the Japanese car manufacturing company, announced a tentative plan to build a factory in the UK. Two towns shortlisted for the possible site were Shotton, in Clwyd, and Washington, in Tyne and Wear. Suppose that a national supermarket chain decided to build a new store in the 'successful' town and in a move to beat an anticipated increase in the price of land purchased, in 1982, for £200,000 each, suitable sites in both Shotton and Washington. In March 1984 Nissan announced that the new plant would be built in Washington. Suppose that following the Nissan announcement, the supermarket site in Washington was valued at £350,000, and the site in Shotton at £225,000. In its historical cost accounts, prepared at 31 March 1984, the supermarket chain would report both sites at a historical cost of £200,000, and in its CPP accounts, both sites would be restated to £215,700 (£200,000×345.5/320.4, 345.5 and 320.4 being the RPI values at the relevant dates in 1984 and 1982, respectively). Both the CPP method and the historical cost method fail to distinguish between assets, the prices of which are changing at different rates. However, the fact that some revaluation adjustment is made to the historical cost figures might mislead some users into believing that the CPP figures do represent current replacement costs, or realisable values. If so, the method may be criticised under the criterion of understandability.

A similar problem arises when identical assets are purchased at different points in time. Suppose our hypothetical supermarket chain had decided many years previously to situate its head office in the City of London. In 1970 it purchased one of two identical office blocks for £2 million. In 1980, the number of head office staff having increased dramatically, it purchased the second, identical office block for £10 million. At the end of 1983, the market value (current cost) of each office block was £14 million. In its historical cost accounts, the company would report the properties at £2 million and £10 million respectively, and in the CPP accounts the values would be £9.2 million (£2 million×335.1/73.1) and £12.7 million, (£10 million×335.1/263.7) respectively. Neither the historical cost nor the CPP figures approximate to the current market values of the office blocks.

Thus, CPP accounting can be seen to be inflexible in its valuation of assets. If two assets are purchased at the same time for the same price, they will continue to be reported as having identical historical, or CPP, costs *even if their current costs diverge*. Conversely, if identical assets are purchased for different prices at different times it is most unlikely that they will be given the same CPP valuation even though their market values are identical. Not only does this suggest inconsistency but it reduces the comparability between the accounts of different entities owning identical assets. These criticisms highlight a fundamental problem inherent to both the historical cost and CPP methods of accounting. They take no account either of movements in the *relative prices* of different assets or of changing technology, and as a result they view a business more as a financial entity than an operating entity. In the next chapter we shall examine the extent to which this problem is overcome by the replacement cost method of accounting.

In this section we have focused exclusively upon the advantages and disadvantages of applying a general price index to restate the historical costs of an entity's assets. We have not evaluated the use of a general price index to maintain the general purchasing power of the owner's capital (ownership interest). There is a specific reason for this. This method of capital maintenance is not restricted to CPP accounting (see Table 12.7, page 268) and we shall consider it in the context of other capital maintenance concepts in the following chapter.

Discussion Topics

1   Explain the inherent differences between transactions-based and forecast-based approaches to income measurement.

2   'CPP accounting adds nothing to historical cost accounting which is useful to users.' Discuss this comment.

3   Explain the concept of the gain or loss on holding net monetary assets. Why is this gain or loss shown in the income statement?

4   Explain the constituent elements of the index used to restate HC accounts into CPP accounts. What information is necessary to enable a complete restatement to be made for the first time?

5   Explain the elements which normally make up the adjustment to ownership interest in CPP accounting. Why do such adjustments exactly equal the amount produced by multiplying the opening ownership interest by the change in the RPI?

6   Which industries are likely to suffer most in terms of the impact on net income under CPP accounting?

7   What are the advantages of applying CPP accounting to a set of published accounts.

Further Reading

Baxter, W.T. *Inflation Accounting*, Philip Allan, 1984, Chapter 7.

Scapens, R.W., *'Accounting in an Inflationary Environment'*, 2nd Ed, Macmillan, 1981, Chapters 3 and 4.

Whittington, G., *Inflation Accounting: An Introduction to the Debate*, Cambridge University Press, 1983, Chapter 4.

Exercises
(See also the exercises at the end of Chapter 15.)

14.1   On 1 January 19X8 Titus started a business selling home-brewing kits. On that date he paid into the bank £100,000 of which £70,000 was used to buy premises on a new industrial estate.

On 30 June 19X8 he bought 20,000 units of stock for £80,000 on credit. On 31 December, when the replacement cost of stock was £5 per unit, he sold 10,000 units for cash at £7.50 per unit and paid the amount of £80,000 due to his suppliers.

At the end of the year an identical buiding, recently completed on the estate, was purchased by another firm for £80,000, although a valuer valued Titus' building at only £72,000 on 31 December.

Titus depreciates fixed assets on a straight line basis over 10 years, assuming zero residual vaue.

The Retail Price Index moved as follows:

1 January 19X8	100
30 June 19X8	110
31 December 19X8	120

- (a)   Prepare for Titus a balance sheet at 31 December 19X8, and an income statement for the year ended 31 December 19X8, in terms of:
    (i)   historical cost accounting;
    (ii)   current purchasing power accounting.
  (b)   Comment on the usefulness of the accounts you have prepared in (a) (i) and (ii) above.

14.2   Elvira Ltd was incorporated on 1 January 19X7. On that date it issued for cash
100,000 £1 ordinary shares at a price of £1.50 each. On the same date the
company purchased for cash fixed assets costing £100,000 and stock costing
£20,000.

   During 19X7 Elvira Ltd's sales amounted to £90,000, of which £50,000
had been received by 31 December. Purchases of stock during the year were
£80,000 (excluding the purchase made on 1 January). All purchases were on
credit, and £12,000 was owing to creditors on 31 December. Other expenses
for the year (excluding depreciation) were £18,000 all paid in cash. Sales,
purchases (excluding the purchase made on 1 January) and other expenses
occurred evenly throughout the year.

   The fixed assets bought on 1 January had an expected life of five years,
and no expected scrap or resale value at the end of that time. The company
wishes to provide for depreciation using the straight line method. No other
fixed assets were bought, and none were sold, during the year.

   Stock on hand at 31 December 19X7 had cost £30,000, and had been
purchased evenly during the last six months of the year.

   The following indices are available:

Date	Current cost of fixed assets	Current cost of stock	General price level
1 January 19X7	390	150	170
31 December 19X7	430	180	194

* (a)   Prepare the profit and loss account of Elvira Ltd for the year ended
        31 December 19X7, and its balance sheet at that date, using 'pounds
        of current purchasing power' as the unit of measurement.
  (b)   Explain briefly the advantages and disadvantages of this method of
        reporting business performance, and consider which companies in
        which situations would be most affected by its implementation.

   (*Hint*: For *calculation* purposes, where transactions occurred evenly
throughout the period, assume that they occurred at one time midway through
the period.)

Chapter 15

Replacement Cost Accounting

In this chapter we examine one system of accounting which incorporates the impact of changes in the specific prices of assets owned by an organisation. The system is known as replacement cost accounting and, as its title suggests, it produces income statements and balance sheets calculated on the basis of the (hypothetical) cost to the organisation of replacing its assets. In other words the system presumes the organisation will continue into the future (i.e. it will be a going concern) by replacing its existing assets as and when necessary. Replacement cost accounting is a widely advocated variant of current cost or current value accounting. Like historical cost accounting it incorporates the buying prices of assets, but it differs from historical cost accounting in one important respect; historical cost accounting deals with *past* purchase prices, whereas replacement cost accounting deals with *current* purchase prices. Like historical cost accounting, replacement cost accounting matches costs with revenues: however the integral difference is that replacement cost accounting matches the *current* replacement cost of resources used, rather than the *past* costs of such resources. Thus a replacement cost income statement will show figures for depreciation and cost of goods sold which differ from those in an historical cost sense if the asset prices to which these expenses relate have increased (or decreased) during the period. Before we begin our exposition of replacement cost accounting, a few words of background are necessary to explain its contemporary relevance.

15.1 Historical Costs and the Changing Environment

Figure 15.1 shows the after-tax net income of UK companies for the 10 year period 1970 to 1979. It is based on historical cost calculations and shows an encouraging picture of steadily increasing net income throughout the decade—and yet many UK companies experienced severe difficulties during the 1970s. Some were forced into liquidation when they failed to generate sufficient *cash* resources to pay for more highly priced labour, materials and capital equipment; investment in fixed assets by manufacturing industry in 1979 was lower in real (i.e. inflation-adjusted) terms than it had been in 1970; and unemployment continued to rise into the 1980s. So what happened to the encouraging income trend illustrated in Figure 15.1?

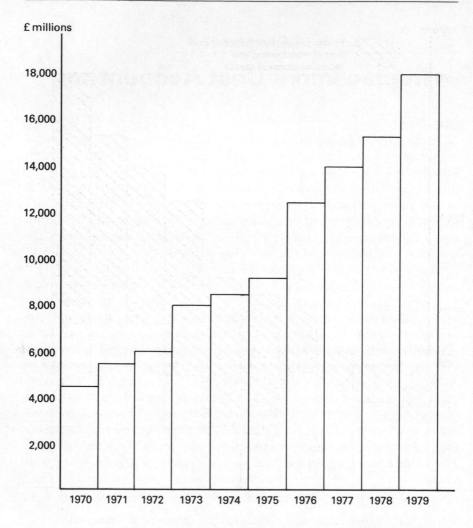

£ millions

Figure 15.1   UK industrial and commercial companies' income before interest but after tax, 1970–79.

The answer is that much of the historical cost income was required to maintain and *replace* existing fixed assets and stocks. Figure 15.2 reveals the extent to which the historical cost income of UK industrial and commercial companies was pre-empted by this requirement. The shaded area represents the expenditure required to *maintain* and *replace* the *current* investment in buildings, plant and stocks, i.e. the expenditure on 'real', or 'growth', investment has not been included. The graph which emerges (i.e. below the shaded area) highlights the difficulties faced by UK companies in 1974 and 1975 in particular, and is consistent with the liquidity crises experienced by many companies during those two years. Figure 15.2 also indicates the

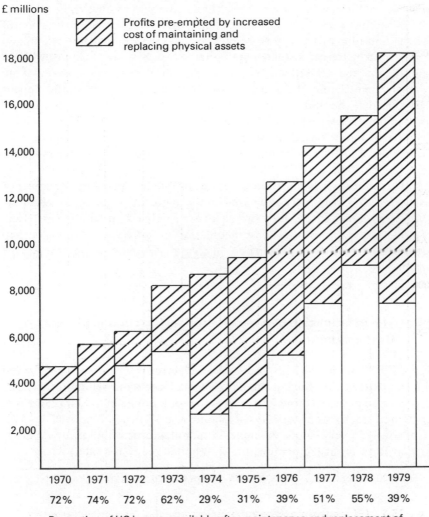

£ millions

Profits pre-empted by increased cost of maintaining and replacing physical assets

Proportion of HC income available after maintenance and replacement of physical assets (%)

Figure 15.2   UK industrial and commercial companies income before interest but after tax, 1970–79.

percentage of the reported historical cost income which was available after the maintenance and replacement of existing physical assets. Less than 30% was available for other purposes in 1974, and the figure did not rise above 55% for the remainder of the decade.

The government and the accounting profession became increasingly concerned that users of accounting reports might be misled into making incorrect and costly decisions. For instance, investors may make poor decisions about buying or selling shares on the basis of reported historical cost income; creditors may not recognise that a company is physically contract-ing, as the historical cost statements could give an incorrect impression of growth and reinvestment; and employees' negotiators may be encouraged by reported historical cost income to pursue excessive wage claims, without realising that the full settlement of such claims could affect the survival of the company, and hence the job security of its workforce. It would appear desirable that the underlying economic situation is clearly disclosed to all users of financial statements. One way of achieving this objective is to report an income figure based upon the procedures illustrated in Figure 15.2 instead of, or in addition to, the historical cost income as reflected in Figure 15.1.

The above issues illustrate potential problems caused by the effect of rising prices on historical cost income at the aggregate level in the UK in the 1970s. Let us now turn to the example of Mr Shielfield, to examine the effect of rising prices on historical cost income for an *individual* business, and to identify the relationship between historical cost and replacement cost income.

15.2   The Relationship between Historical Cost and Replacement Cost Income

Suppose Mr Shielfield buys and sells an electronic space-war game called 'Ledger Attack'. By buying the games for £5 each and selling for £12, he expects to show a profit of £7 on each game sold. For an individual game (i.e. an item of stock) his historical cost income is as shown in Figure 15.3. (This is, of course, a very simple example. A manufacturer would incur expenses to transform input factors into finished goods ready for sale.)

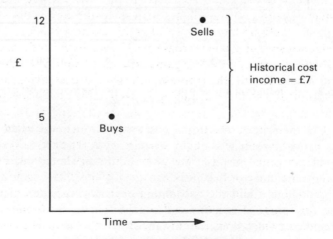

Figure 15.3   Historical cost income.

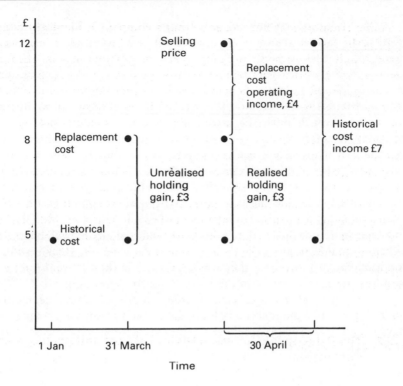

Figure 15.4.

Suppose Mr Shielfield purchases his first electronic game on 1 January, for £5. On 31 March his supplier announces a price increase of £3, to £8. Under historical cost accounting this price increase would not be recorded by Mr Shielfield. Replacement cost accounting, however, requires that the replacement costs of assets are matched against current revenues, and thus Mr Shielfield would update the cost of all his existing stock to £8 (Figure 15.4). This corresponding unit increase of £3 is usually termed a *holding gain* or a *revaluation surplus*. Holding gains arise as a result of holding, rather than using, assets. Strictly, they represent the gain, or cost saving, accruing to an organisation as a result of acquiring an asset at the time it was purchased rather than at the later time it is used or sold. As the game is still held by Mr Shielfield on 31 March the holding gain is, as yet, *unrealised*. We will presume throughout the rest of this example that Mr Shielfield's capital is maintained in *money* terms (i.e. the amount of his balance sheet figure for capital is not adjusted to reflect price changes). *Under this method all holding gains are treated as additions to income, rather than as additions to capital. This is an important assumption and should be continually borne in mind when interpreting the figures.* Later in the chapter we show the effect on the treatment of holding gains of different capital maintenance concepts.

On 30 April Mr Shielfield sells the game for £12. The historical cost profit is £7, but this can now be divided into two components—a replacement cost operating profit of £4, and a *realised* holding gain of £3. The dichotomy between operating profit and holding gains is an important characteristic of replacement cost income; the recognition of two distinct components of income should give users additional information. The historical cost approach blurs the distinction between holding and operating activities; results of the two types of activity are not reported separately and increases in asset values are recognised only when the asset is sold or otherwise disposed of. For example, if Mr Shielfield makes up his accounts to 30 April, the historical cost income of £7 will equal the replacement cost income of £7 (both income figures comprising replacement cost operating income of £4, and a realised holding gain of £3). If, however, Mr Shielfield's financial year ends on 31 March, his historical cost income will be reported as zero in that year, and £7 in the following year when the stock is sold. The replacement cost income will be reported as £3 in the first year (an unrealised holding gain), and £4 in the second year (operating profit).

Thus, although historical cost income comprises both replacement cost operating income and realised holding gains, the holding gains may already have been recognised (as unrealised gains) in the replacement cost accounts of a previous period.

15.3   Main Differences between Replacement Cost and Historical Cost Accouting

Both historical cost and replacement cost methods of accounting are transactions-based approaches to reporting business performance. However, we have identified some important differences of principle between the two methods, and in this section we make use of a simple example to illustrate and explain these differences. Let us look more closely at the totality of Mr Shielfield's operations.

Suppose Mr Shielfield commences business on 1 January 19X0. On that date he pays £100 from his own resources into the business bank account and uses the money to buy 20 units of stock at a cost of £5 each. On 31 December 19X0 he sells 10 units of stock for £12 per unit and buys a further 10 units at a cost of £8 each. On 31 December 19X1 he sells 10 units of stock for £15 per unit and buys a further 14 units at a cost of £10 each. All purchases and sales are for cash. For simplicity, we assume that Mr Shielfield undertakes no transactions other than those described above during the two year period.

Mr Shielfield's historical cost accounts for the two years, assuming use of the FIFO stock flow assumption (see Chapter 10), are shown in Table 15.1. In Table 15.2 we show the accounting equation entries required to

Table 15.1   Mr Shielfield—Historical cost income statements and balance sheets

		19X0 £		19X1 £
Income statements				
Sales	(10×£12)	120	(10×£15)	150
less: Historical cost of stock sold	(10×£5)	50	(10×£5)	50
Historical cost income		70		100
Balance sheets				
Ownership interest:				
Opening balance		100		170
add: Income for the year		70		100
		170		270
Stock	(10×£5 +10×£8)	130	(10×£8 +14×£10)	220
Bank balance	(100−100 +120−80)	40	(40+150 −140)	50
		170		270

record Mr Shielfield's transactions using the replacement cost method. Mr Shielfield's replacement cost accounts for the two years are shown in Table 15.3. Assuming that capital is maintained in *money* terms, the replacement cost accounts differ from the historical cost accounts in two main respects:

1. *Net income*: Under the historical cost approach, net income is defined as revenues less the historical costs of the resources used in earning them. Under the replacement cost approach, income is split into two components—operating income and holding gains. *Operating income* is defined as revenues (as under historical cost) less the replacement costs of the resources used. *Holding gains* are increases in the monetary values of assets held during the period covered by the income statement. Thus Mr Shielfield's *operating income* for 19X0 is £40 (10 units sold at £12 per unit less the current replacement cost of the units at the date of sale, i.e. less 10 units at £8). Similarly, his operating income for 19X1 is £50 (10 units sold at £15 per unit less the current replacement cost of the units sold, 10 units at £10). Mr Shielfield's *holding gains* for 19X0 are £60 (an increase from £5 to £8 during the year in the replacement cost of each of the 20 units held during that period). His holding gains for 19X1 are £40 (an increase from £8 to £10 in the replacement cost of each of the 20 units held during the year).

The holding gains of a period may be either *realised* (if the asset has been sold or used during the period) or *unrealised* (if the asset is held at the end of the period). So, for example, Mr Shielfield's holding gains of £60 for 19X0 comprise £30 realised gains (£3 per unit on the 10 units sold) plus £30 unrealised gains (£3 per unit on the 10 units held at the end of the year which

Table 15.2   Mr Shielfield—Accounting equation entries: replacement cost

	Stock +	Cash at bank	= Ownership interest	+ Operating income	+ Holding gains
	£	£	£	£	£
19X0					
1 January:					
Owner pays in capital		100	100		
Purchases stock (20 units)	100	(100)			
31 December					
Increase in replacement cost of stock (£3)	60				60
Sells stock (10 units)		120		120	
	(80)			(80)	
Purchases stock (10 units)	80	(80)			
Transfer income			100	40	60
Balances	160	40	200	(40)	(60)
19X1					
31 December:					
Increase in replacement cost of stock (£2)	40				40
Sells stock (10 units)		150		150	
	(100)			(100)	
Purchases stock (14 units)	140	(140)			
Transfer income			90	50	40
Balances	240	50	290	(50)	(40)

Table 15.3   Mr Shielfield—Replacement cost income statements and balance sheets

	19X0	£	£	19X1	£	£
Income statements						
Sales	(10×£12)		120	(10×£15)		150
less: Replacement cost of stock sold	(10×£8)		80	(10×£10)		100
Replacement cost operating income			40			50
Holding gains:						
Realised	(10×£3)	30		(10×£2)	20	
Unrealised	(10×£3)	30	60	(10×£2)	20	40
Total replacement cost income			100			90
Balance sheets						
Ownership interest:						
Opening balance			100			200
add: Income for the year			100			90
			200			290
Stock	(20×£8)		160	(24×£10)		240
Bank balance			40			50
			200			290

were bought at the start of the year). Similarly, the holding gains of £40 for 19X1 comprise realised gains of £20 (£2 per unit on the 10 units sold) and unrealised gains of £20 (£2 per unit on the 10 units held at the end of the year which were in stock at the beginning of the year). The categorisation of holding gains as either realised or unrealised is helpful in reconciling historical cost and replacement cost income figures, as we explain shortly.

2.   *Asset Value*: Under the historical cost approach, we have seen that assets are generally valued for balance sheet purposes at their original costs less accumulated depreciation. Under the replacement cost approach assets are included in the balance sheet at their current values (i.e. net replacement cost) at the balance sheet date. Thus Mr Shielfield's stock at the end of 19X0 is included in his balance sheet at £160 (20 units at a replacement cost value at the end of 19X0 of £8 per unit). Similarly, stock at the end of 19X1 is valued for balance sheet purposes at £240 (24 units at £10 per unit, the replacement cost at the balance sheet date). Broadly speaking, replacement cost means the cost of replacing an asset of similar age and condition or, more specifically, the cost of replacing the *services* given by a similar asset. For fixed assets, this value may sometimes be difficult to determine directly, particularly where no efficient second-hand market for the asset exists. For example, it is relatively easy to determine the net replacement cost of a six year old Ford Escort car, but not of a six year old grinding machine. In such

cases, net replacement cost is often approximated by including the replacement cost of an equivalent *new* asset (i.e. taking account of technological change) and deducting from it an appropriate amount for accumulated depreciation (based, of course, on the replacement cost rather than the historical cost of the asset).

Mr Shielfield's accounts, prepared on the replacement cost basis described above, are shown in Table 15.3. We now use the figures for year 2 from Tables 15.1 and 15.3 to summarise broadly the relationships between replacement cost and historical cost measures of income and position.

- *Replacement cost income* and historical cost income for a period differ in their treatment of holding gains. Total replacement cost income comprises replacement cost operating income plus all holding gains which *arise* during the period. Historical cost income comprises replacement cost operating income plus all holding gains which are *realised* during the period. Hence, for the second year of Mr Shielfield's business, the replacement cost income (operating income plus holding gains, £90) equals historical cost income (£100) plus unrealised holding gains *arising during the period* (£20) minus holding gains realised during the period but which *arose during previous periods* (£30, being the gain made during 19X0 on the 10 units purchased at the start of that year which were sold in 19X1. This gain is included in the historical cost income for 19X1 but has already been included in the replacement cost income for 19X0 as an unrealised gain).

- *The replacement cost* of assets at the end of a period is comprised of the historical cost value plus any holding gains relevant to the assets. The replacement cost value of Mr Shielfield's stock at the end of the second year (£240), equals the historical cost value (£220) plus the sum of all holding gains that have arisen during the current and previous periods and that have not been realised by the end of the period (i.e. £20 is the unrealised gain on the 10 units of stock purchased at the end of 19X0 which are still held at the end of 19X1).

The effect of the above relationships is that, in order to convert historical cost records and accounts to a replacement cost basis, three main adjustments are required:

(a) *Asset values* are increased (or decreased) each period to reflect changes in their replacement costs. Only assets whose values are not fixed in money terms (i.e. non-monetary assets) are affected, e.g. fixed assets and stock. The monetary values of other (i.e. monetary) assets, e.g. cash and debtors, whose values are fixed in money terms, require no adjustment.

(b) *Unrealised holding gains* on non-monetary assets are calculated for each period as they arise, and are included in total replacement cost income for the period in which they arise.

(c)   *Operating costs* for each period are changed, where necessary, to convert them from historical to replacement costs. Strictly speaking, the current costs of *all* resources should be matched against revenues at the date of sale. In general, adjustments are required only to depreciation charges on fixed assets and to the cost of using stock, both of which are based on the balance sheet values of assets which are changed under the replacement cost approach. The costs of other resources, for example, wages, lighting, heating, rent, vehicle maintenance and fuel, and so on, tend to be paid at approximately the same time as the resources are used and, in consequence, their actual (original) cost is equal to their replacement cost at the date of use.

At the simplest level, the procedure for converting historical cost accounts to replacement cost accounts is straightforward. The values of non-monetary assets are regularly (at least at the end of each accounting period) updated to their replacement costs. The double entry is completed by increasing net income by the same amount—the holding gains on the assets. When assets are used or sold, the cost of using or selling them is based on their (updated) replacement costs. The procedure is illustrated in the next section.

We began this chapter by noting that interest in replacement cost accounting in the UK was stimulated by the belief that historical cost accounting 'overstated' the reported income figure during a period of rising prices. And yet, despite rising prices, the replacement cost income of Mr Shielfield in 19X0 is greater than the corresponding historical cost income. The explanation of this apparent contradiction is straightforward. The move from a historical cost *valuation of assets* to a replacement cost valuation results in an increase in reported net income for Mr Shielfield because unrealised holding gains are included in the total replacement cost income figure. However, how much of that income is set aside to maintain the value of capital depends upon the *capital maintenance concept* adopted. Figure 15.2 (page 307) illustrated the current cost income figure for UK companies after capital had been maintained in terms of operating capacity, i.e. *no holding gains* were included in the income figure. In the replacement cost financial statements of Mr Shielfield money capital only is maintained and *all holding gains* are included in the income figure. As we noted in Chapter 12, the reported income figure depends upon both the asset valuation method and the capital maintenance concept adopted. In Section 15.5 we shall examine further the effect on replacement cost income of adopting different methods of capital maintenance.

15.4   Illustration of Replacement Cost Accounting

In this section we illustrate the major principles involved in preparing a set of accounts based on replacement costs. We do not, however, distinguish between realised and unrealised holding gains. The main purpose of this distinction, introduced in the previous section, is to reconcile historical cost and replacement cost measures of income. The distinction is not of fundamental importance to an understanding of the principles of replacement cost adjustments. Also, for simplicity, we assume that all transactions occur on the first or last day of an accounting period. The procedures involved for more frequent transactions are the same in principle but considerably more complex in practice, and are outside the scope of this text.[1] Our aim is to explain the basic characteristics of replacement cost accounting methods in sufficient detail to highlight the respect in which they differ from historical cost methods and to permit an evaluation of their potential usefulness.

We shall use the business transactions of Mr Villa, introduced in the previous chapter, to illustrate the application of replacement cost principles. The business transactions, discussed in Table 14.1 are reproduced in Table 15.4 and the historical cost accounts from Table 14.3 are reproduced in Table 15.5. Table 15.6 shows Mr Villa's accounting equation entries for 19X1 using replacement cost accounting. The entries differ from those in

Table 15.4   Mr Villa—Business transactions

Mr Villa commences business as a retailer on 1 January 19X1. He undertakes the following transactions during the subsequent two years. All transactions are for cash.

1 January 19X1
1. Pays £30,000 into the business bank account.
2. Buys equipment for £15,000. The equipment has an expected life of 10 years, at the end of which it will have no scrap or resale value. Mr Villa wishes to apply the straight line method of depreciation to the equipment.
3. Buys 2,000 units of stock at £5 per unit.

31 December 19X1
4. Sells 2,000 units of stock for £10 per unit.
5. Pays expenses of £5,000.
6. Buys 2,500 units of stock for £15,000 (i.e. at £6 per unit, representing a 20% price increase during the year).
    (Note: The price of *new* equipment like Mr Villa's is now £16,500 representing a 10% price increase during the year.)

31 December 19X2
7. Sells 2,000 units of stock for £11.50 per unit.
8. Pays expenses of £6,500.
9. Replaces stock for £14,400 (i.e. 2,000 units at £7.20 per unit, representing a 20% price increase during the year).
    (Note: The price of *new* equipment like Mr Villa's is now £18,150 representing a 10% price increase during the year.)

---

[1]Readers interested in investigating more complex current cost methods will find a comprehensive coverage in E.O. Edwards and P.W. Bell, *The Theory and Measurement of Business Income,* University of California Press, 1961; and in T.A. Lee, *Income and Value Measurement: Theory and Practice,* Nelson, 1974.

Table 15.5   Mr Villa—Historical cost income statements and balance sheets

	19X1		19X2	
	£	£	£	£
Income statements				
Sales		20,000		23,000
less: Cost of goods sold		10,000		12,000
Gross profit		10,000		11,000
less: Expenses	5,000		6,500	
Depreciation	1,500		1,500	
		6,500		8,000
Net income		3,500		3,000
Balance sheets				
Ownership interest:				
Opening balance		30,000		33,500
add: Net profit for the year		3,500		3,000
		33,500		36,500
Equipment at cost		15,000		15,000
less: Accumulated depreciation		1,500		3,000
		13,500		12,000
Current assets: Stock	15,000		17,400	
Cash at bank	5,000		7,100	
		20,000		24,500
		33,500		36,500

Table 14.2 (page 291, based on the historical cost method) in a number of important respects. The first is that income is split into two parts: operating income and holding gains. Entries recording the receipt of capital and the acquisition of assets (transactions (1), (2) and (3)) are the same as under the historical cost method. At the time an asset is acquired, its replacement cost is equal by definition to its actual (historical) cost. Changes to entries in the accounting equation occur when asset values are updated to replacement costs for the purpose of calculating operating costs and closing balance sheet values. Thus the value of equipment is increased by 10% (i.e. by £1,500) at the end of the year, and the value of stock by 20% (i.e. by £2,000). The accounting entry in each case is to increase asset value and increase holding gains. At the end of each period holding gains, together with operating income, are transferred to ownership interest.

When assets are used or sold, their replacement cost at this date is transferred from the asset column to operating income. Thus the cost of goods sold (i.e. the replacement cost of the stock sold on 31 December) is £12,000 (2,000 units sold at a replacement cost, at the date of sale, of £6 per unit). Similarly, the depreciation charge of £1,650 is 1/10 of the equipment's replacement cost at the date of use (£16,500). Note that the same basis of

Table 15.6 Mr Villa—Accounting equation entries 19X1: replacement cost

	Equip-ment £	+	Stock £	+	Cash at bank £	=	Ownership interest £	+	Operating income £	+	Holding gains £	
1 January:												
Transaction (1)	15,000				30,000		30,000					
Transaction (2)			10,000		(15,000)							
Transaction (3)					(10,000)							
31 December:												
Holding gain—equipment	1,500										1,500	
Holding gain—stock			2,000								2,000	
Transaction (4)			(12,000)		20,000				20,000			Sales
									(12,000)			Cost of goods sold
Transaction (5)					(5,000)				(5,000)			Expenses
Transaction (6)			15,000		(15,000)							
Depreciation (16,500÷10)	(1,650)								(1,650)			Depreciation
									1,350		3,500	Income/Holding gains
Transfer operating income and holding gains to ownership interest							4,850		(1,350)		(3,500)	
Balances	16,500 (1,650)	+	15,000	+	5,000	=	34,850	+	0	+	0	

depreciation (straight line, ten year life, no ultimate resale or scrap value) is used here as for the historical cost method. Other expenses of £5,000 are charged against income at the same amount as under historical cost—they are paid for at approximately the same time as they are used and in consequence their actual (original) cost is a close approximation to their replacement cost at the time of use.

The effect of the above entries is to show an operating income for the year based on the matching of revenues with replacement costs (at the date of use) of resources used in earning them; holding gains equal increases in values of assets held during the year; and the balance sheet values of assets equal their replacement costs at the balance sheet date.

The entries for 19X2, shown in Table 15.7, broadly follow the same lines as those in Table 15.6. The only major difference relates to the treatment of the equipment, and arises because the organisation is no longer in its first year of trading. Before examining the appropriate entries for equipment we shall introduce the principles involved by way of a simple illustration.

Consider the case of a businessman who purchases a machine for £600 at the beginning of 19X1. He expects it to last for three years and to have no scrap or resale value at the end of that time. He adopts the straight line method of depreciation and each year his historical cost depreciation charge is £200. At the end of the three years the whole of the historical cost of the machine has been charged to the income statement and the book value of the asset has been reduced to zero. The situation is illustrated in the first two columns of Table 15.8.

Assume now that the (replacement) cost of a new machine increases by 10% per annum, so that at the end of each of the 3 years the replacement cost of a new machine is £660, £726 and £798 respectively (table 15.8, column (c)). The annual depreciation charge is calculated as one-third of the replacement cost at the end of each year, i.e. £220 ($£660 \times 1/3$), £242 ($£726 \times 1/3$), and £266 ($£798 \times 1/3$), as shown in column (d) of Table 15.8. However, the principle of depreciation is to allocate the cost of an asset over its useful life, and the sum of these annual charges, £728, does not amount to the *replacement* cost of a new machine at the end of year 3, which is £798. The machine, although worthless, would be carried in the replacement cost balance sheet as follows:

	£
Machine—gross replacement cost	798
—accumulated depreciation	728
—net replacement cost	70

The reason for this 'shortfall' of accumulated depreciation charge is as follows. Although the depreciation in 19X1 (£220) is one-third of the gross replacement cost at the end of 19X1 (£660) it is not one-third of the gross

Table 15.7   Mr Villa—Accounting equation entries 19X2: replacement cost

	Equip-ment £	+	Stock £	+	Cash at bank £	=	Ownership interest £	+	Operating income £	+	Holding gains £	
1 January:												
Balances	16,500		15,000		5,000		34,850		0		0	
	(1,650)											
31 December:												
Holding gain—equipment	1,650										1,650	
Holding gain—stock			3,000								3,000	
Transaction (7)			(14,400)		23,000				23,000			Sales
									(14,400)			Cost of goods sold
Transaction (8)					(6,500)				(6,500)			Expenses
Depreciation (18,150÷10)	(1,815)								(1,815)			Depreciation
*'Backlog' depreciation	(165)										(165)	
Transaction (9)			14,400		(14,400)							
									285		4,485	Income/Holding gains
Transfer operating income and holding gains to ownership interest							4,770		(285)		(4,485)	
	18,150	+	18,000	+	7,100	=	39,620	+	0 +		0	
	(3,630)											

*Accumulated depreciation required at end of year 2 (2/10×£18,150)   £3,630

Accumulated depreciation provided (opening balance £1,650 plus current year's charge £1,815)   £3,465

Additional (backlog) depreciation required   £ 165

Table 15.8   **Backlog depreciation**

| | Historical cost | | Replacement cost | | |
	Gross cost in balance sheet (a) £	Depreciation charge in income statement (b) £	Gross cost in balance sheet (c) £	Depreciation charge in income statement (d) £	Backlog depreciation (e) £
1/ 1/19X1	600		600		
31/12/19X1	600	200	660	220	
31/12/19X2	600	200	726	242	22
31/12/19X3	600	200	798	266	48
		600		728	70

replacement cost at the end of 19X3 (£798). Hence, each year the previous years' depreciation charges must be 'topped up' to ensure that the net replacement cost of a fixed asset comprises the gross replacement cost of a new asset less the current cost of the accumulated depreciation. This depreciation 'top up' is called *backlog depreciation*. In column (e) of Table 15.8 the backlog depreciation for 19X2 (£22) tops up the first year's depreciation from £220 to £242. In 19X3 the backlog depreciation of £48 tops up the depreciation charges of the two previous years from £242 each to £266 each.

Returning to the example of Mr Villa and to Table 15.7, the price of new equipment at the end of 19X2 is £18,150 which represents an increase (holding gain) of £1,650 over the price of new equipment at the beginning of the year. Depreciation for the year (at 10% p.a.) is £1,815 and this amount is charged in the income statement for 19X2. If no further entry were made, the value of the equipment at the end of the year would be a 'gross' (pre-depreciation) value of £18,150, less accumulated depreciation of £3,465 (comprising £1,650 set aside in 19X1 and £1,815 set aside in 19X2). But the equipment is now two years old (out of a total life of ten years), and, given that it is expected to have no eventual resale or scrap value and that straight line depreciation is to be used, the accumulated depreciation should equal 2/10 of £18,150, i.e. £3,630. The shortfall between the actual provision of £3,465 and this figure of £3,630 is £165—the backlog depreciation for 19X2—and represents the updating required to the accumulated depreciation provisions of previous years. In our example, previous years' depreciation provisions amount to £1,650 (i.e. one year's provision at the current price prevailing at the end of 19X1). This figure must be updated to the price prevailing at the end of 19X2, i.e. it must be increased by 10% (£165) to reflect price increases during 19X2. In general, the backlog depreciation for a fixed asset for any year equals the accumulated depreciation provision at the start of the year multiplied by the percentage increase in the price of the asset during the year. Further adjustments may be necessary when assets are bought or sold during a year, to ensure that accumulated depreciation at the end of the year fully reflects the year-end values of assets.

In Table 15.7 we have deducted backlog depreciation from the asset equipment (i.e. added it to the accumulated depreciation on equipment) and subtracted it from holding gains. It is a moot point whether the amount should be subtracted from holding gains or from operating income. The treatment we have adopted results in operating income being charged only with the replacement cost of using the asset for the year under consideration. It also results in a 'net' holding gain on fixed assets of £1,485 (£1,650–£165) which equals 10% (the rate of increase in the asset's value during the year) of the asset's written down value at the start of the year (£16,500–£1,650). On the other hand, if Mr Villa distributed his entire operating income each year, insufficient funds would be retained in the business to replace the equipment at the end of its life. We consider this question further in Section 15.5

    Table 15.9 shows Mr Villa's replacement cost income statements and balance sheets for 19X1 and 19X2, based on the figures in Tables 15.6 and 15.7. Many of the figures in Table 15.9 differ from their historical cost counterparts in Table 15.5. Replacement cost operating income in each year is less than historical cost income because although revenues are unchanged, costs are increased to current levels. On the other hand, when the unrealised gains on assets are included, total replacement cost income exceeds historical cost income, which recognises only the gains realised on stock sold and on that part of the equipment that has been used (as we illustrated earlier). The replacement cost balance sheet values of equipment (and stock in 19X2) exceed the historical cost figures. The same situation would likely arise also in respect of other non-monetary assets during a period of rising prices.

Table 15.9   Mr Villa—Replacement cost income statements and balance sheets

	19X1		19X2	
	£	£	£	£
Income statements				
Sales		20,000		23,000
less: Cost of goods sold		12,000		14,400
Gross profit		8,000		8,600
less: Expenses	5,000		6,500	
Depreciation	1,650	6,650	1,815 ✻	8,315
Operating income		1,350		285
Holding gains		3,500		4,485
Total replacement cost income		4,850		4,770
Balance sheets				
Ownership interest:				
Opening balance		30,000		34,850
add: Total income for the year		4,850		4,770
		34,850		39,620
Equipment at gross replacement cost		16,500		18,150
less: Accumulated depreciation		1,650		3,630 ✻
		14,850		14,520
Current assets: Stock	15,000		18,000	
Cash at bank	5,000	20,000	7,100	25,100
		34,850		39,620

15.5   Current Costs and Alternative Capital Maintenance Concepts

Our primary purpose thus far in this chapter has been to explain the fundamental differences between historical cost and replacement cost income statements and balance sheets. We have not yet considered the relative merits of other alternative measures of current cost such as realisable value, and opportunity value, or the usefulness of current cost methods as opposed to historical cost methods. Both of these issues are discussed in Chapter 17. The answers to both questions depend on a consideration of the purposes and uses of accounting reports, and on the extent to which alternative reporting methods satisfy such purposes. There are no easy answers! To argue (as is sometimes done) that replacement cost method is more 'realistic' or 'truthful' than the historical cost method not only begs the question of what is meant by 'realism' and 'truth', but also seems to us to be of little help until it is agreed that the qualities of realism and truth are the *only* qualities of importance in evaluating accounting methods. The information that is most realistic or truthful may not for example be the most useful input to users' decision models.

Neither have we thus far considered the effect of adopting different capital maintenance concepts in conjunction with the replacement cost method of asset valuation. Both the examples of Mr Shielfield and Mr Villa value assets by reference to replacement costs, and maintain capital *in money terms*. The main difference between financial statements prepared under different capital maintenance concepts lies in the way in which holding gains on non-monetary assets are reported in the income statement. If operating capacity is maintained, holding gains are reported as part of capital maintenance. If owners' purchasing power is maintained, part of the holding gains are reported in the income statement and the remainder as part of capital maintenance.

Table 15.10 shows the effect of the three different concepts of capital maintenance on the financial statements of Mr Villa for 19X1. Only extracts from the financial statements are presented because the balance sheet values for assets and liabilities, and the income statement entries for current revenues and replacement costs, *are identical under all three methods*. If the business maintains its capital in terms of operating capacity no holding gains are included in the income statement. By implication such gains are not available for distribution and total income is equal to operating income. In such cases, replacement cost income may be considerably lower than historical cost income if asset prices are rising. As assets sold or used during the year are charged to the income statement at their replacement cost, the operating income figure represents the surplus after charging sufficient to ensure that the company can maintain its fixed assets and stocks at their present level. The replacement cost/operating capacity method of accounting emphasises the entity's ability to continue its operations at the same level of activity in the future. As the Chairman of Pilkington plc commented in this particular context, "At least when we break even we know we can continue forever".[2]

---

[2]*Investors Chronicle*, 20 January 1984.

Table 15.10   Mr Villa—Alternative concepts of capital maintenance

	Money		Owners' purchasing power		Operating capacity	
	£	£	£	£	£	£
Income statement						
Operating income		1,350		1,350		1,350
Holding gains	3,500		3,500		3,500	
less: Capital maintenance adjustment	–	3,500	1,500	2,000	3,500	–
Total replacement cost income		4,850		3,350		1,350
Balance sheet						
Ownership interest:						
Opening balance		30,000		30,000		30,000
Capital maintenance adjustment		–		1,500		3,500
		30,000		31,500		33,500
Total income for the year		4,850		3,350		1,350
		34,850		34,850		34,850

This method can be categorised as adopting an *entity* view of accounting in that it maintains the 'well-offness' of the entity as a whole rather than the well-offness of any individual participant group. To that extent it can be argued that the adoption of the current cost/operating capacity method of accounting represents a shift away from the traditional emphasis on shareholders as the focus of financial statements. By emphasising the entity's viability as a going concern it provides information of wider interest to those interested in its future.

A proprietary view of an organisation is, as we noted earlier, one which sees the organisation as an extension of the owners' personal property, i.e. the organisation is a legal structure by which means the owners' assets are managed. According to this view, financial statements should consist primarily of reports to the owners. The current cost/money capital, and current cost/owners' purchasing power methods of accounting are consistent with this approach. As Table 15.10 shows, all or part of the holding gains which have arisen during the year are added to replacement cost operating income to arrive at total replacement cost income. If the *total* replacement cost income of Mr Villa's business was distributed to him, i.e. if the distribution was greater than the replacement cost operating income, Mr Villa might be realising the benefits of the holding gains whilst at the same time running down the level of his future operations.

Of course, the decision to make a distribution to owners depends upon other factors in addition to the current year's income figure. (We noted in Chapter 12 that it cannot automatically be assumed that if an organisation wished to distribute its profits, sufficient cash would be available for this purpose.) Nevertheless, it is clear from Table 15.10 that if Mr Villa was hoping to pay himself a handsome amount at the end of the year, he would draw more encouragement from the income figures generated by the two proprietary methods of accounting than from the income figure produced by the replacement cost/operating capacity method.

It is worth noting that the capital maintenance adjustment required to maintain the owners' purchasing power is calculated by applying the increase in the Retail Price Index to the ownership interest balance at the beginning of the year ($£30,000 \times 5\% = £1,500$ in the case of Mr Villa). The rationale for this adjustment was explained in Chapters 12 and 14. If the increase in the RPI is greater than the increase in the prices of the entity's own assets, as reflected in the figure for holding gains, the capital maintenance adjustment required to maintain the owners' purchasing power will be greater than the holding gains included in the income statement. In this instance, total replacement cost income under the replacement cost/owners' purchasing power method would be lower than replacement cost operating profit.

Discussion Topics

1   Explain how accounting methods of measuring income and value may be categorised according to the asset valuation method and the capital maintenance concept they adopt.

2   Distinguish between 'replacement cost operating income' and 'holding gains', and discuss the possible importance of the distinction.

3   Explain the difference between 'realised' and 'unrealised' holding gains.

4   Describe the main respect in which replacement cost measures of income and value differ from their historical cost counterparts.

5   Outline the main adjustments which are necessary to convert historical cost to replacement cost accounts.

6   Explain the meaning, treatment, and importance of 'backlog depreciation'.

7   Why is it important to distinguish between 'monetary assets' and 'non-monetary assets' when preparing a set of replacement cost accounts?

Further Reading

Baxter, W.T., *Inflation Accounting*, Philip Allan, 1984, Chapters 8–10.

Edwards, E.O. and Bell, P.W., *The Theory and Measurement of Business Income*, University of California Press, 1961.

Scapens, R.W., *Accounting in an Inflationary Environment*, 2nd Ed., Macmillan, 1981, Chapters 5 and 6.

Whittington, G., *Inflation Accounting: An Introduction to the Debate*, Cambridge University Press, 1983, Chapter 5.

Exercises

15.1 Manrico Ltd is a small limited company which rents its property to tenants. Its balance sheet at 1 January 19X7 is as follows:

	£	£
Fixed assets		
Freehold property (original cost *and*		
current value at 1 Jan. 19X7)		6,000
Current assets		
Rent due from tenants	500	
Cash	1,000	1,500
		7,500
less: Current liabilities		
Expenses owed by Manrico Ltd		300
		7,200
Represented by:		
Share capital		
5,000 Ordinary shares of £1 each		5,000
Retained profits		2,200
		7,200

Manrico Ltd's transactions for the year to 31 December 19X7 are as follows:

1. Borrows £15,000 from Fiordiligi Finance Ltd.
2. Buys additional property for cash of £20,000.
3. Receives rent from tenants of £8,500, representing the amount due at 1 January 19X7, and all rent due in respect of 19X7.
4. Pays expenses of £4,300 being expenses owing at 1 January 19X7, and all expenses due in respect of 19X7.
5. Buys 2,000 £1 shares in Pamina Ltd for £2,000.

You are told:

(i)   The total market value of the freehold property at 31 December 19X7 is £50,000.

(ii) The market value of a £1 share in Pamina Ltd at 31 December 19X7 is £1.50.

- (a) Prepare for Manrico Ltd a balance sheet at 31 December 19X7 and an income statement for the year ended 31 December 19X7, using historical cost accounting.
- (b) Prepare for Manrico Ltd a balance sheet at 31 December 19X7 and an income statement for the year ended 31 December 19X7, using

replacement cost accounting, maintaining capital at its money level.
(c)   Comment on your results.

(*Note*: Ignore depreciation and changes in the *general* level of prices).

15.2 Mr Publius commenced business on 1 July 19X7. On that date he paid £20,000
into the business bank account from his personal savings. On the same date he
purchased a machine for £13,000 and 10,000 units of stock at 50p per unit. He
estimated that the machine would last for 8 years, at the end of which time it
would have a scrap value of £1,000. Mr Publius wishes to use the straight line
method of providing depreciation on the machine.

On 30 June 19X8 Mr Publius sold 8,000 units of stock for £11,000 and
paid operating expenses amounting to £4,500. He also purchased a further
9,000 units of stock at 55p per unit. At 30 June 19X8 the cost of machines like
the one owned by Mr Publius was 15% higher than at 1 July 19X7.

- (a)   Prepare Mr Publius' income statement for the year ended 30 June
        19X8 and balance sheet as at that date using *each* of the following
        methods:
        (i)   historical cost accounting;
        (ii) replacement cost accounting, maintaining capital at its money
              level.
- (b)   Discuss the relative usefulness of the figures you have calculated.

15.3 Lohengrin Ltd was incorporated on 1 April 19X6. The company's accounts for
the year ended 31 March 19X7, prepared on a conventional historical cost
basis, are shown opposite.

The directors of Lohengrin Ltd wish to redraft the accounts so that assets
are valued at their replacement costs at the end of the year and trading and
operating costs are included at estimated replacement costs at the date of sale.

Sales and operating expenses occurred evenly throughout the year. Of the
£490,000 spent on purchases, £110,000 was used to buy stock on 1 April 19X6
and the remainder was spent evenly throughout the year. The stock held on 31
March 19X7 was purchased evenly between 1 October 19X6 and 31 March
19X7. All fixed assets were purchased on 1 April 19X6.

The following indices are available:

	1 April 19X6	*31 March 19X7*
Replacement cost of stock	138	162
Replacement cost of fixed assets	180	200
Retail price index	170	188

- (a)   Prepare a revised profit and loss account and balance sheet for
        Lohengrin Ltd for the year ended 31 March 19X7, in accordance
        with the wishes of the directors. Provide for capital maintenance in
        terms of maintaining the operating capacity of the business.
- (b)   Show how the figures you have prepared in (a) above would alter if
        no explicit capital maintenance adjustment was made, i.e. if share-
        holders' equity was maintained at its money level at 1 April 19X6.
- (c)   Comment on the likely usefulness to shareholders of the figures you
        have calculated in (a) and (b) above, and of the historical cost
        accounts provided in the question.

(*Hint*: For *calculation* purposes, where transactions occurred evenly
throughout a period, assume that they occurred at one time midway through
the period.)

Profit and loss account for the year ended 31 March 19X7

	£	£
Sales		680,000
Cost of goods sold:		
Purchases	490,000	
Stock at 31 March 19X7	140,000	
		350,000
Gross profit		330,000
Operating expenses	160,000	
Depreciation	120,000	
		280,000
Net profit, added to reserves		50,000

Balance sheet at 31 March 19X7

	£	£		£	£
Ownership interest			*Fixed assets*		
Issued ordinary			Cost	600,000	
shares of £1		500,000	Depreciation	120,000	
Reserves		50,000			
					480,000
		550,000			
Current liabilities			*Current assets*		
Trade creditors	80,000		Stock	140,000	
Bank overdraft	180,000		Debtors	190,000	
		260,000			330,000
		810,000			810,000

15.4 Mr Cavaradossi commences business as a manufacturer of scarpias on 1 June 19X7. On that date, he pays £6,000 into a business bank account from his personal bank account, and buys 200 units of raw material at £20 per unit.

During the year ended 31 May 19X8, 150 units of raw material are converted to 150 scarpias. The remaining 50 units of raw material are still in stock at 31 May 19X8.

On 31 May 19X8, Mr Cavaradossi pays from the business bank account production workers' wages of £7,000 and other expenses amounting to £4,000. On the same date he sells 150 scarpias at £100 each, and pays the proceeds into the business bank account. He also replaces the 150 units of raw material used, at the current market price of £30 per unit.

During the year ended 31 May 19X8, the general price index increased from 200 to 220.

- (a) Prepare Mr Cavaradossi's income statment for the year ended 31 May 19X8 and balance sheet as at that date using each of the following methods:
    - (i)   historical cost accounting;
    - (ii) replacement cost accounting, maintaining capital in terms of operating capacity;

(iii)   replacement cost accounting, maintaining capital in terms of general purchasing power.

(b)   Comment on the relative usefulness of the figures you have calculated.

15.5   Ms Tosca starts up her business on 1 January 19X7, with £300 cash and £2,000 stock. The stock comprises two identical items which were acquired immediately prior to the start of the period (i.e. the current value at the start of the period was £1,000 for each item).

During the year to 31 December 19X7, work is performed on one stock item only, the wages for which are paid on 31 December and amount to £500.

On 31 December, the worked stock item is sold for £2,200, and replaced by an unworked item costing £1,500.

The increase in the general price index for the year is 20%.

●   (a)   Prepare Ms Tosca's balance sheet at 31 December 19X7 and her income statement for the year ended on that date, using each of the following methods:
   (i)   historical cost accounting;
   (ii)   replacement cost accounting—maintaining capital by a general price index;
   (iii)   replacement cost accounting—maintaining the operating capacity of the business;
   (iv)   current purchasing power accounting.

(b)   Comment on the relative merits of the alternative capital maintenance concepts used in (a) above.

15.6   On 1 January 19X0 Mr Tristan started a business selling video cassettes. On that date he put £5,000 of his own money into a separate business bank account, and later wrote out a cheque for £1,200 to purchase a new TV and video player for showing video cassettes to customers in his store.

On 30 June 19X0 he bought 1,000 video cassettes for £8,000 cash. On 31 December 19X0 he sold 850 cassettes for £20 each and bought a further 500 cassettes at £11 each. Both these transactions were for cash.

At the end of the year he incurred but did not pay £840 of operating expenses. He also learned that the cost of a new TV and video player, identical to those he bought on 1 January 19X0, was now £1,500.

Mr Tristan has decided to depreciate his video equipment on a straight line basis over three years.

During 19X0 the increase in the general price level was as follows:

From 1 January – 30 June	5.55%
1 July – 31 December	6.32%
1 January – 31 December	12.22%

●   (a)   Prepare Mr Tristan's profit and loss account and balance sheet for 19X0 under the following accounting methods:
   (i)   historical cost;
   (ii)   current purchasing power;
   (iii)   replacement cost with the '*money*' concept of capital maintenance.

(b)   Show the effect on the profit and loss account and balance sheet if the *operating capacity* concept of capital maintenance was used in (iii) above.

(c)   Describe the adjustments you would need to make to (iii) above to reflect the *shareholder purchasing power* concept of capital maintenance.

15.7 Tamino Ltd buys and sells papagenos. The company prepares its accounts annually to 31 December. During the year ended 31 December 19X9, it undertook the following transactions in papagenos:

		Units	Price per unit £
1 January	Stock on hand	0	–
2 January	Purchases	4,000	6.00
30 June	Purchases	6,000	8.00
31 December	Sales	8,000	10.00

The purchase price of papagenos at 31 December was £9.00 per unit.

- (a)   Calculate the gross profit made on the sale of papagenos during the year ended 31 December 19X9 *and* the balance sheet value of the stock of papagenos held at 31 December under each of the following methods:
    - (i)   historical cost accounting, using the first in, first out (FIFO) stock flow assumption;
    - (ii)   historical cost accounting, using the last in, first out (LIFO) stock flow assumption;
    - (iii) historical cost accounting, using the weighted average stock flow assumption;
    - (iv)   replacement cost accounting.
- (b)   Discuss the relative merits of the above four methods for calculating cost of goods sold and the balance sheet value of stock.

15.8 The balance sheet of Wotan Ltd at 1 January 19X4, prepared using the replacement cost method of accounting is as follows:

	£	£
Fixed assets		
Land		10,000
Building, at replacement cost	37,500	
less: Accumulated depreciation	(7,500)	30,000
Equipment, at replacement cost	48,000	
less: Accumulated depreciation	(16,000)	32,000
		16,800
Stock		
Net monetary assets		18,750
		107,550
Represented by:		
Issued capital		60,000
Retained profit		47,550
		107,550

During the year to 31 December 19X4, Wotan Ltd earned sales revenue of £53,200, made purchases of stock of £36,000 and incurred general expenses of

£8,900. All sales, purchases and general expenses took place evenly throughout the year.

Closing stock, which cost £17,800, was purchased evenly during the last six months of the year.

Depreciation, using the straight line method, is charged on the average replacement cost during the year. Both the building and the equipment were purchased on 1 January 19X0, when their estimated useful lives were 20 years and 12 years respectively. No fixed assets have been bought or sold since that date.

The following price indices have been made available:

	General		Specific		
		Land	Building	Equipment	Stock
1/1/X4	200	100	150	110	125
31/12/X4	240	105	150	120	145

- (a) Prepare the profit and loss account and balance sheet for Wotan Ltd for the year ended 31 December, 19X4. Use replacement cost accounting and maintain capital in terms of operating capacity. Include a statement which analyses the total holding gains for the year.
  (b) Discuss the major practical problems companies might have in implementing a replacement cost accounting system for their financial statements.
  (c) Would you expect to see share prices change as a result of the publication of replacement cost financial statements? Give your reasons.

Part 5

Interpretation and Evaluation

Chapter 16

Interpretation of Accounts: Ratio Analysis

In previous chapters (for example, Chapters 3 and 12) we have suggested that users of financial statements require future-orientated information to make rational economic decisions. This future-orientated information includes management's estimates of the amount of and risk attached to the entity's future cash flows. We concluded, however, that direct forecasts and forecast-based approaches to the measurement of income and value are unlikely to be included in published financial statements in the foreseeable future, and have thus focused our attention on the income statements and balance sheets produced by transactions-based approaches (i.e. approaches based on the use of historical cost, current purchasing power, and replacement cost). This leads us to repeat the question asked at the end of Chapter 3 (page 45):

> How should users of financial statements analyse and interpret the (historical) data provided in order to obtain the (predictive) information required?

In this chapter we shall attempt to answer this question. In particular we shall consider how we might interpret the data provided in the financial statements in order to estimate an entity's future cash flows and their associated risk.

16.1 The Role of Ratio Analysis

A popular means of interpreting published financial data involves the calculation of a variety of key ratios. The term *ratio analysis* describes such an exercise. Ratio analysis is based on the notion that the analysis of absolute figures may not be the best means available of assessing an organisation's performance and prospects. For example, an annual profit of £20,000 may represent a good level of performance for a local grocer with one shop but a poor achievement for a large company owning a chain of grocery stores. One possible reason for this is that the two businesses may use very different amounts of capital. Thus the local grocer may be using capital of £50,000,

335

whereas the large company may have capital employed of £50 million. A more meaningful way of measuring profitability would be to relate the profit figure to the capital employed as a ratio or a percentage. Hence the local grocer's return is 40% (£20,000 divided by £50,000, expressed as a percentage) and the large company's is 0.04% (£20,000 divided by £50,000,000×100). These ratios better indicate the success of the two businesses in their use of capital.

The above example demonstrates one way in which ratio analysis might be used to measure profitability. Profitability is, however, not the only aspect of performance which can be measured by the use of ratios. Ratio analysis may also be used to measure liquidity and solvency. One of the most important purposes of ratio analysis is to help users to appraise an organisation's past performance and, from that appraisal, to make judgments about its likely future performance. For example, suppose that a firm has regularly increased its capital employed and has managed to sustain a ratio of profit to capital employed of between 20% and 25% p.a. Those interested in predicting the firm's future performance might use this information together with estimates of the firm's future capital employed, as part of a process to predict its future surpluses. Of course, the prediction process is likely to include other variables relating, for example, to environmental conditions, including the rate of inflation, and to other ratios that measure organisational performance. Nevertheless, each key ratio should throw some light on at least one aspect of the firm's activities and, as such, should be of some value.

For example, in order to facilitate the prediction of an organisation's future performance and its associated risk, we might wish to calculate and evaluate ratios under three general headings—liquidity, longer-term solvency, and profitability.

- *Liquidity* is concerned with the organisation's current financial position, and in particular with its capacity to pay its debts as they arise in the short term. If an organisation has a liquidity problem, there is an increased risk of its failing to generate *any* future cash flows.
- *Longer-term solvency* is concerned with the organisation's ability to meet its longer-term financial commitments. It is often related to the composition of its capital structure. For example, a company financed predominantly by loan capital must meet its (high) interest payments as they fall due. The potential consequences of failing to meet these payments increases the risk attached to estimates of the company's future performance.
- *Profitability* is concerned with how effectively an organisation has used its available resources. As we suggested above, an examination of a company's past profitability ratios might be useful in predicting its likely future performance.

We shall discuss the usefulness of particular ratios under these three headings in later sections of this chapter.

16.2   Limitations of Ratio Analysis

Before we begin our examination of particular ratios, we offer some words of warning. Although ratio analysis may be a useful way of interpreting certain types of financial information, its powers should not be overestimated. Its usefulness is restricted in at least two important respects. First, if ratios are calculated from the figures in conventional (i.e. historical cost) accounts, they may not reflect the current (replacement) values of assets or the current costs of operations. This will be a problem if users wish to predict an organisation's future performance *and* if they find current values and current costs more helpful for this purpose than historical figures. We argue in the following chapter that *both* of these conditions are likely to exist.

Secondly, we must be careful in interpreting particular ratios in isolation. For example, is a ratio of profit to capital employed of 15% p.a. good or bad? The answer depends on the individual circumstances. In an environment where inflation is running at 5% p.a., a 15% return is probably satisfactory, whereas it is almost certainly unsatisfactory if the annual rate of inflation is 100%. Similarly, an annual return of 15% may be acceptable for an organisation which operates in a low risk line of business but unacceptable for one operating in a highly uncertain and risky environment. In other words, different values of the same ratio (for example, the profitability ratio) may be *expected* for different types of organisation, different points or periods in time and different environmental conditions. This complicates the setting of 'target' ratios for an organisation. A typical response to this problem is to *compare* the ratios of the organisation with the ratios of organisations in a similar line of business, operating in a similar environment during the same period of time[1], and with the ratios of the same organisation for previous (and possibly—via budgets—future) periods. Unfortunately, neither of these solutions is completely satisfactory. First, comparisons with other firms may be invalid if the other firms use different accounting conventions (for example, concerning fixed asset and stock valuation). In consequence similar underlying performances may reveal quite dissimilar ratios and vice versa. Secondly, comparisons of an organisation's current performance with its previous performance may be misleading if the environment in which the organisation operates changes (for example, if the rate of inflation changes or if its line of business becomes more or less competitive), or if the organisation changes its mix of products.

These limitations do not mean that ratio analysis should be discarded as a means of interpretation. Such a course of action would be appropriate only if ratio analysis provided decision makers with information (*additional* to that which they already have) which has a value less than the costs of

---

[1]See, for example, *Industrial Performance Analysis,* ICC Information Group Ltd, London, 1983. The financial statements of 12,000 companies are analysed and aggregated into twenty-five major industrial groupings. Eighteen key ratios covering liquidity, solvency and profitability are produced for each grouping.

undertaking the analysis. Rather the limitations mean that ratios should be interpreted with care, and that other factors should be considered in evaluating an organisation's performance.

16.3   Illustration of the Calculation and Usefulness of Ratios

We now illustrate the calculation of a number of financial ratios, and discuss their particular limitations and usefulness. We do not attempt to consider every ratio that might be calculated from a set of financial statements. Almost any pair of figures from an income statement and balance sheet could be combined to provide a ratio and clearly some combinations are likely to be more helpful than others. We attempt to identify the more important ratios that should form a part of any evaluation of organisational performance. Other ratios may be appropriate for other situations and analyses.

Two general points relating to the calculation of ratios deserve mention. First, some ratios compare a figure from the income statement (which covers a *period* of time) with a figure from the closing balance sheet (which relates to a *point* in time). An example is the ratio of profit to capital employed. This procedure is acceptable provided that no substantial changes have occurred to the relevant balance sheet figures during the period covered by the income statement. Otherwise, it may be necessary to use an average of opening and closing balance sheet figures to provide a proper and consistent basis for ratio calculation. Consider the case of an organisation that gradually increases its capital employed from £200,000 to £400,000 during an accounting period. During the same period, its profit is £40,000. Profit as a percentage of capital at the end of the period is 10% (£40,000 divided by £400,000×100). But the capital employed was less than £400,000 for most of the period, and was as low as £200,000 at the start of the period. In such situations, ratios might be better calculated by taking the average balance sheet value of capital employed, rather than the end-period figure. Thus capital employed may be taken as £300,000 [(£200,000+£400,000)÷2], giving a profit percentage of $13\frac{1}{3}$% (£40,000÷£300,000×100).

The second point relates to the way in which ratios are expressed. Some ratios are expressed in their 'raw' form (i.e. as ratios), some as percentages and some as periods of time. This variety of expression is employed to help users to better understand the resultant figures; all results could be expressed as ratios but some would be less meaningful in this form. The various forms of presentation, and their usefulness, will be apparent in the example to which we now turn.

The summarised historical cost income statements and balance sheets of Maine Ltd for years 1 and 2 are shown in Table 16.1. The company's performance for the two years may be analysed under the three general headings of liquidity, longer-term solvency and profitability.

Table 16.1   Maine Ltd—Income statements and balance sheets

	Year 1 £	Year 2 £
Income statements		
Sales	900,000	1,200,000
Cost of goods sold (all variable)	720,000	840,000
Gross profit	180,000	360,000
Overhead expenses, excluding interest	133,800	252,500
Net profit before interest	46,200	107,500
Debenture interest payable	0	25,000
Net profit, added to reserves	46,200	82,500
Balance sheets on 31 December		
Land and buldings at cost	150,000	325,000
Plant and machinery at written-down value	60,000	197,500
Stocks (at original cost)	53,000	53,000
Debtors	100,000	200,000
Cash	27,000	27,000
	390,000	802,500
Creditors	(60,000)	(140,000)
Total assets less current liabilities (Net assets)	330,000	662,500
Issued ordinary share capital	250,000	250,000
Reserves	80,000	162,500
Owners' capital employed	330,000	412,500
10% debentures (issued 1 January, Year 2)	0	250,000
Total long-term capital employed	330,000	662,500

Liquidity

Liquidity ratios provide some indication of an organisation's current financial position. Financial statement users will likely be interested in liquidity ratios because a weak liquidity position entails an increased challenge to the achievement of long-term objectives (including the generation of future cash flows). This might lead the user to reassess his estimate of the company's future performance, and/or to discount the future cash flows at a higher discount rate. Taken in conjunction with flow of funds statements (which we discuss in Chapter 18), liquidity ratios provide information about the organisation's ability to generate *cash* and may suggest, by highlighting inefficiencies, ways in which the cash position could be improved. Liquidity ratios are normally presented either as ratios or as time periods and in this section we consider five main liquidity ratios.

Working capital ratio. The working capital ratio, or 'current ratio', is calculated as follows:

$$\text{Working capital ratio} = \frac{\text{Current assets}}{\text{Current liabilities}}$$

This ratio indicates the firm's ability to meet its short-term cash obligations (current liabilities) out of its current assets without having to raise finance by borrowing, issuing more shares, or selling fixed assets, all of which might adversely affect the firm's ability to generate future net cash flows for the existing participants. The figures for Maine Ltd are:

	Year 1	Year 2
Working capital ratio	$\dfrac{(53,000+100,000+27,000)}{60,000}$	$\dfrac{(53,000+200,000+27,000)}{140,000}$
	$=3:1$	$=2:1$

If this ratio provides some indication of an entity's current financial position, one might expect that the higher the ratio the better it is. However, a very high ratio can cause almost as much concern as a very low ratio. A very low ratio might indicate that the company will be unable to meet its short-term obligations as they fall due. A very high ratio might cause the user to query why so much capital has been invested in current assets.

For example, a high ratio arising because the organisation holds an abnormally high level of stock at the year end might imply that the firm is experiencing difficulties in selling its products; an abnormally high level of debtors might imply that the firm is experiencing difficulties in collecting cash from its credit customers or that it has extended the credit period to maintain sales in the face of falling demand; a high cash balance might imply the lack of any current worthwhile projects in which to invest.

To determine whether Maine's working capital ratio is within acceptable bounds we could calculate the working capital ratios of other companies in the same industry. There is no general optimal value for the working capital ratio. Indeed there is no general optimal value for most liquidity ratios. The best ratio for a particular organisation depends on various factors, including the nature of its business and the environment in which it operates. A ratio value that is ideal for one firm may indicate disaster for another.

For example, businesses which carry very little stock, e.g. airlines, or do not normally extend credit to customers, e.g. food retailers, will have a low working capital ratio. Some relevant working capital ratios for 1983 are British Airways 0.68; Sainsbury's 0.55; Tesco Stores 0.78. Businesses which carry high levels of stock and which allow debtors to pay over a longer period, e.g. those in the motor industry, will have a higher working capital ratio (for example, that of Ford Motor Company is 1.82; of Lucas Industries 1.75). Whether the working capital ratio for Maine Ltd is satisfactory depends upon the norm for other firms in the same industry. If we discover that similar firms continue to operate successfully with working capital ratios within the range of 1.5:1 to 2.5:1 then the decline in Maine's ratio from 3:1 to 2:1 suggests a movement towards the norm. The crucial question, however, is whether the decline from 3:1 to 2:1 is a permanent change or the first stage in a longer-term trend. In the former case, the change may indicate efficient working capital management; the company is tying up less capital in net current assets. In the latter case, a continuation of the trend may result in impending liquidity problems for the company.

The working capital ratio suffers two particular limitations. First, the stock component of current assets is included in our example at its historical cost. However, a principal aim of the ratio is to indicate whether the firm can meet its short-term liabilities out of current assets. The cash and debtors figures (subject to an estimate of those debtors who may default) represent a realistic estimate of the cash available to the company in the near future. The historical cost (and even the replacement cost) of stock is not such a realistic estimate. The *current selling price* of the stock, less any costs still to be incurred prior to sale, would be a better measure of its potential contribution to the firm's liquidity.

Second, the ratio depends on the definitions adopted for the classification of fixed and current assets. As we noted in Chapter 6, different asset classifications may be used which may in turn lead to different working capital definitions. In this respect, the speed at which raw materials are converted into finished goods and sold to customers is important. For example, should raw materials and work in progress be included in the working capital ratio as current assets, if they are not to be converted into finished goods and sold for many months?

Liquid ratio. One simple, if crude, way of avoiding such problems is to exclude stock from the working capital ratio. The liquid ratio, or, as it is sometimes described, the 'quick' or 'acid test' ratio, is calculated from the following expression:

$$\text{Liquid ratio} = \frac{\text{Liquid assets (i.e. current assets excluding stock)}}{\text{Current liabilities}}$$

This ratio represents a more stringent test of an organisation's ability to pay its debts as they fall due. This is particularly true in a time of crisis. Stock is excluded for the reasons given above. The resultant figures for Maine Ltd are:

	Year 1	*Year 2*
Liquid ratio	$\dfrac{(100,000+27,000)}{60,000} = 2.1:1$	$\dfrac{(200,000+27,000)}{140,000} = 1.6:1$

Once again, there is no general optimal value for the liquid ratio. To the extent that it measures an organisation's ability to pay its debts in a crisis one might expect that it should not normally fall below 1:1. However, even this rule of thumb is inappropriate in some cases. Most companies do not experience continuous crises and users might consider managers to be excessively conservative if they always carry extra liquid assets as insurance against the occurrence of an unlikely event. As with the working capital ratio, there exists for each industry a range within which the liquid ratio is deemed satisfactory.

In certain industries the manner in which trade is conducted dictates that the 'normal' liquid ratio is less than 1:1. A large supermarket chain which buys all its stock on credit and makes all sales for cash would carry few debtors. It is unlikely that such a business would need a cash balance equal to its liabilities (implying a liquid ratio of 1:1 as debtors are negligible). This situation is confirmed by a glance at the liquidity position of two national supermarket chains, Tesco Stores and Sainsbury's, as reflected in their balance sheets on 26 February 1983 and 26 March 1983 respectively (Table 16.2).

Table 16.2   Tesco Stores and Sainsbury's—Balance sheets on 26 February 1983 and 26 March 1983, respectively

	Tesco's £m	Sainsbury's £m
Current assets:		
Stock	175.0	141.5
Debtors	9.3	17.3
Cash	57.2	39.0
	241.5	197.8
Current liabilities	308.9	360.0
Working capital ratio	0.78	0.55
Liquid ratio	0.22	0.16

In most circumstances these companies can rely on regular cash receipts from customers to pay creditors as they fall due. As far as Maine Ltd is concerned, its immediate liquidity position seems secure, although it is necessary to determine whether the fall in the liquid ratio between years 1 and 2 is permanent or indicative of a longer-term trend.

The liquid ratio does not provide a complete picture of an organisation's ability to survive a liquidity crisis. A strong liquid ratio might suggest that the organisation is having difficulty in collecting its debts, whereas a low figure for current liabilities might suggest that creditors are insisting upon speedy payment. In this instance, the ratio may overstate the company's ability to survive a liquidity crisis.[2] On the other hand, the ratio ignores other means

---

[2]Earlier in this section we suggested that ratios might be interpreted in conjunction with flow of funds statements to provide information about the company's ability to generate cash. We shall examine flow of funds statements in Chapter 18.

available to the organisation for raising cash to settle its short-term liabilities. For a highly respected company, a ratio of less than 1:1 might be acceptable because the company's bankers are willing to provide bridging finance in the event of a temporary liquidity crisis.

Debtor payment period. An increase in either the liquid or the working capital ratio may be the result of an increase in the debtors figure—perhaps because more goods have been sold on credit, or debtors have been allowed more time to pay, or a combination of the two. The debtor payment period measures the average length of time taken by debtors to pay amounts due to the organisation. It is an important aspect of the assessment of management's ability to control working capital and is calculated as follows:

$$\text{Debtor payment period} = \frac{\text{Debtors}}{\text{Credit sales}} \times 12$$

Multiplying the ratio of debtors to credit sales by 12 expresses the payment period in months. Weeks or days could equally well be used. Assuming that all sales are on credit, the figures for Maine Ltd. are:

	Year 1	*Year 2*
Debtor payment period	$\frac{100,000}{900,000} \times 12 = 1.3$ months	$\frac{200,000}{1,200,000} \times 12 = 2.0$ months

A long debtor payment period may have disadvantages. For example, the organisation may incur high interest costs on the working capital needed to finance debtors, and also run the risk of incurring bad debts. An increase in the payment period may indicate that the organisation is attracting less creditworthy customers, from whom it is more difficult and costly to extract due payments and/or that there are inefficiencies in credit control management. Thus the increase in the debtor payment period of Maine Ltd might be viewed with some concern. On the other hand, a longer payment period may mean that fewer customers are taking advantage of any discounts offered, with a consequent reduction in that expense.

Creditor payment period. The creditor payment period may also be expressed in months, weeks or days. Expressed in months, it is calculated as follows:

$$\text{Creditor payment period} = \frac{\text{Creditors}}{\text{Credit purchases}} \times 12$$

The creditor payment period represents the average length of time taken by an organisation in paying amounts due to its creditors, and is another indicator of the success of management's working capital policies. Assuming that all purchases are on credit, and that stock levels remain constant (so that purchases equal cost of goods sold), the figure for Maine Ltd are:[3]

	Year 1	Year 2

Creditor payment period $\dfrac{60,000}{720,000} \times 12 = 1.0$ month $\quad \dfrac{140,000}{840,000} \times 12 = 2.0$ months

Maine Ltd has increased the average time taken to pay creditors, perhaps because of cash flow difficulties. An undesirable consequence of this increase may be the loss of discounts for early payment. On the other hand, the company has persuaded its suppliers to advance more credit, thus reducing the need to raise finance from other sources. An important question is whether the increased credit is available permanently. If not, Maine Ltd will have to make arrangements to replace it with other sources.

Stock holding period. The stock holding period (or 'stock turnover period') may also be expressed in any time dimension. Expressed in months, it is calculated as follows:

$$\text{Stock holding period} = \frac{\text{Stock}}{\text{Cost of goods sold}} \times 12$$

This ratio measures the average length of time during which an organisation holds its stock. For manufacturing firms separate calculations are strictly necessary for raw materials, work in progress and finished goods. The figures for Maine Ltd are:

	Year 1	Year 2

Stock holding period $\dfrac{53,000}{720,000} \times 12 = 0.9$ months $\quad \dfrac{53,000}{840,000} \times 12 = 0.8$ months

The stock holding period is an important aspect of the evaluation of an organisation's working capital management. A long holding period, implying high stock levels relative to the amount of goods sold, has some advantages—for example, it reduces the risk of stock levels falling to zero (stockouts) and the resultant inability to satisfy demand, and it provides

---

[3]In Chapter 10 (page 189) we defined cost of goods sold as:

Cost of goods sold = Opening stock + Cost of production − Closing stock

For an organisation which undertakes no production (for example a retail firm) 'cost of production' is equl to purchases of stock. If the organisation's accounts do not indicate the amount of purchases, the figure may be calculated by substituting 'purchases' for 'cost of production' in the above expression and rearranging, i.e.:

Purchases = Cost of goods sold + Closing stock − Opening stock

If 'cost of production' includes costs which are not incurred on credit (for example, productive wages and machine depreciation), it is necessary to estimate what proportion of the total 'cost of production' is in respect of credit purchases.

more scope for bulk buying and large scale production runs which may produce quantity discounts and other economies of scale. Alternatively it might indicate the existence of 'slow-moving' or obsolete stock. On the other hand, a short period, implying low stock levels, also has advantages. In particular it leads to lower storage, interest and other costs of holding stock. As with the other working capital ratios, it is hard to say whether Maine's stock holding period is optimal. A period of less than one month seems at first sight to be rather low, but this would not necessarily be the case for an organisation dealing in perishable goods, for example a fishmonger or a greengrocer. It would be very low, however, for a business engaged in the manufacture of heavy engineering plant or construction (e.g. the stock holding periods in 1983 of Ford Motor Company and George Wimpey were 3 months and 4.5 months respectively).

In this section we have already mentioned two reasons why the various liquidity ratios should be interpreted with care — first, that different industries have different norms, and second, that a high ratio may give a misleading impression of financial strength whilst disguising an inefficient use of funds. A third reason (alluded to earlier in this chapter) concerns the danger in selecting any single figure for an entity's balance sheet, i.e. a single balance sheet figure may be unrepresentative of the year's balance on any particular element of working capital. Managers have been known to manipulate individual working capital figures at the year-end in order to produce apparently healthy ratios. This practice is known as 'window dressing'.

A common form of window dressing involves the raising of a short-term loan towards the end of the financial year[4]. For example, suppose a company which prepares its accounts on 31 December, has the following liquid ratio on 27 December 19X0:

$$\frac{\text{Liquid assets}}{\text{Current liabilities}} = \frac{900,000}{1,200,000} = 0.75:1$$

The ratio for the company at the end of the previous year was 0.85:1 and the norm for the industry is within the range 0.8:1 to 1:1. The management could increase the liquid ratio to a figure comparable with that of last year and to within the industry's acceptable range by borrowing, say, £600,000 as a short-term loan. The effect of this transaction would be to increase *both* liquid assets (cash) *and* current liabilities (short-term loan) by £600,000. The new liquid ratio would be calculated as:

$$\frac{\text{Liquid assets}}{\text{Current liabilities}} = \frac{1,500,000}{1.800,000} = 0.83:1$$

---

[4]For a report of an example of window dressing investigated by the Department of Trade, see 'Manipulation by Ashbourne board', *The Guardian,* 13 October 1978.

Longer-term solvency

Long-run solvency is concerned with the ability of a company to survive over many years. Declining liquidity and profitability ratios can provide an indication of long-run difficulties. In addition, survival may also be affected by the organisation's long-term financial commitments. These commitments are often closely related to the manner in which the organisation finances its operations.

We discussed capital structure in Chapter 11 (pages 206–209) and explained the importance of an organisation's gearing ratio. The gearing ratio is presented usually as a proportion or as a percentage, and may be calculated from the following expression, which relies on balance sheet data:

$$\text{Gearing ratio} = \frac{\text{Long-term fixed interest capital}}{\text{Total long-term capital employed}}$$

An alternative gearing ratio is the ratio of fixed interest capital to equity capital. Both measures indicate the relationship between an organisation's loan and equity capital. The figures for Maine Ltd, using the first ratio described above,[5] are:

	Year 1	*Year 2*
Gearing ratio	$\dfrac{0}{330,000}=0$	$\dfrac{250,000}{662,500}=0.377$ or 37.7%

Maine Ltd has increased its gearing from zero to nearly 38%. This increase should be of interest to any user who wishes to estimate the future cash flows accruing to the shareholders of Maine Ltd, and the risk attached to those cash flows. Its impact can be seen more clearly in the income statement. In year 2 Maine Ltd pays debenture interest of £25,000. This payment must be made whether or not the company generates a profit, and we saw in Chapter 11 (see Table 11.1) that the profit available for the shareholders of a geared company is more sensitive to changes in pre-interest profit than is the profit available to the shareholders of a purely equity financed company, which was Maine Ltd's position in year 1.

The issue of new loan capital often has both benefits and costs for the owners of a company. We shall see in the next section that one effect of issuing debentures is to increase the return to the owners of Maine Ltd (as the new loan capital has a cost below the return which Maine Ltd earns on its

---

[5]The figures for Maine Ltd, using the second ratio described in the text are:

	Year 1	*Year 2*
Gearing ratio	$\dfrac{0}{330,000}=0$	$\dfrac{250,000}{412,500}=0.606$ or 60.6%

It is imperative that the reader of accounts is consistent in his use of *one* of the two ratios described when comparing the gearing ratios of different companies or of the same company over time.

total capital). At the same time, <u>the increased gearing ratio has resulted in an</u> <u>increase in the financial risk of the owners</u>. Both of these effects are reflected in the income statement and this has led to the emergence of an income statement ratio which measures the impact of gearing. <u>The 'times interest</u> covered' ratio calculates the number of times the interest payment is <u>'covered' by the net profit before interest</u>. The figures for Maine Ltd using this ratio are:

$Year\ 1$ $Year\ 2$

Times interest covered
$$\frac{46,200}{0} = \infty \qquad \frac{107,500}{25,000} = 4.3 \text{ times}$$

One advantage of the income statement ratio is that it focuses upon the *impact* of the change in capital structure. It provides information which might be used as direct input into a decision model assessing the longer-term solvency of the business, i.e. in estimating future cash flows and their associated risk. In addition, <u>gearing ratios calculated from balance sheet</u> <u>figures are of limited use if they are based on the book values of loan and</u> <u>equity capital</u>. The use of market values provides a better measure of the long-term capital position of the organisation.

Profitability

In Chapter 5 we described the activities of a business organisation in terms of a *transformation process,* i.e. the process by which the raw factors of production are converted or transformed into the finished goods sold by the organisation. Thus <u>an assessment of an organisation's profitability is an</u> <u>attempt to evaluate how efficiently the management has carried out the</u> <u>transformation process</u>. By evaluating the management's past performance <u>we may discover information which can be used as a basis for predicting</u> <u>future performance</u>. Profitability ratios indicate how efficiently organisations have used their available resources. Such ratios are normally presented as percentages and, in general, the higher the profitability percentage, the better is the aspect of the organisation's performance to which the ratio relates.

Earlier in this chapter we suggested that absolute profit figures may not be the best means available of assessing performance, and that the assessment of profit relative to the capital employed might produce a more useful indication of performance, i.e. one would be less happy with a profit of £20,000 on an investment of £50 million, than with a profit of £19,000 on an investment of £50,000. Consequently, we require some indicator of profitability which measures the profit earned relative to the economic resources available. One such measure, perhaps the most widely quoted of all ratios, is the *return on investment* series of ratios.

Return on investment is not a single ratio. There are many different levels of return—gross profit, net profit, profit available to shareholders, etc.—and many definitions of the investment in (capital employed by) the organisation—shareholders' funds, all long-term capital, long- and short-term capital, etc. These various definitions can produce a series of useful ratios (rates of return) but it is important that the construction of each ratio entails consistency of numerator and denominator, i.e. that the definition of profit is consistent with the definition of capital employed. For example, the appropriate return on shareholders' funds is the profit available to shareholders, and the appropriate return on long-term capital employed is the profit available to all providers of long-term capital, i.e. the profit before interest payable on long-term loans. We begin by examining the return on long-term capital.

Return on long-term capital. This measure may be calculated from the following expression:

$$\text{Return on long-term capital} = \frac{\text{Net profit before interest}}{\text{Total long-term capital employed}} \times 100$$

The ratio is consistent insofar that capital employed is based on total long-term funds used by the entity and profit is measured before deducting *any* returns to the providers of long term capital. The figures for Maine Ltd are:

	Year 1	*Year 2*
Return on long-term capital	$\frac{46,200}{330,000} \times 100 = 14.0\%$	$\frac{107,500}{662,500} \times 100 = 16.2\%$

From Table 16.1 we can see that the amount of long-term capital employed is matched by the amount of total assets less current liabilities (also referred to as 'net assets'). Hence this ratio could also be expressed as:

$$\text{Return on net assets} = \frac{\text{Net profit before interest}}{\text{Net assets}} \times 100$$

The return on long-term capital ratio measures the return achieved on the total long-term capital available to managers, i.e. for every £1 of long-term capital invested in the company, the managers of Maine Ltd generated 14 pence in net profit before interest in year 1 and 16.2 pence in year 2. This ratio is sometimes used as an indicator of the overall effectiveness of a business—the numerator encompasses most items in the income statement (sales less all production, selling and administrative costs) and the denominator encompasses all items in the balance sheet (i.e. total long-term capital, or total assets less current liabilities). However, this very generality limits the usefulness of the ratio as a means of evaluating an organisation's performance. For example, we can see that Maine's return increased in year 2, but we do not know *why* it increased, or *whether* the increased return is a good indicator of the return likely to be achieved in the future. We thus need to disaggregate the ratio into its component parts.

The transformation process described in Chapter 5 provides a clue as to how the ratio may be analysed. Entities transform raw materials into finished goods and sell them to customers. To generate a profit the entity must sell its goods and services at a price sufficient to cover its costs. Hence, the success of an enterprise in generating a profit depends upon its ability to:

(a)   generate sales from the available economic resources; and
(b)   produce income from the sales generated.

The rate of return on long-term capital employed can thus be broken down into two component parts. The first measures how intensively the management has utilised the available resources to generate sales, and is called the 'utilisation' or 'asset turnover' ratio. The second measures the proportion of sales which is converted into net profit, i.e. the net profit as a percentage of sales. This method of separating the rate of return ratio into its component parts was developed by the American company E.I. Dupont de Nemours. The Dupont formula for the return on long-term capital can be expressed as follows:

$$\frac{\text{Return on}}{\text{long-term capital}} = \text{Utilisation ratio} \times \text{Net profit percentage}$$

which can be expressed as:

$$\frac{\text{Net profit before interest}}{\text{Long-term capital}}$$

$$= \frac{\text{Sales}}{\text{Long-term capital}} \times \frac{\text{Net profit before interest}}{\text{Sales}} \times 100$$

We now examine each part in turn.

(a)   *Utilisation, or asset turnover, ratio*: This ratio measures how efficiently the available resources are used to produce sales. The 'available resources' may be described either as the long-term capital made available to the organisation, or as the net assets under the organisation's control. The ratio may be calculated from the following expression:

$$\text{Utilisation ratio} = \frac{\text{Sales}}{\text{Long-term capital or net assets}}$$

The ratio shows how much in sales revenue is generated from each £1 of long-term capital invested in assets. The higher the ratio the more intensive is the use of assets. The figures for Maine Ltd are:

	Year 1	*Year 2*
Utilisation ratio	$\frac{900,000}{330,000} = 2.73$	$\frac{1,200,000}{662,500} = 1.81$

Thus for every £1 of long-term capital invested, Maine generated £2.73 of sales revenue in year 1, and £1.81 of sales revenue in year 2. This ratio provides some information as to how intensively resources have been utilised. For example, if two companies in the same industry own identical assets and set the same selling price for their product, the company utilising the assets more intensively will generate the higher sales revenue.

One limitation of the utilisation ratio is its use of a figure (for long-term capital) from the balance sheet which may be untypical of the capital employed throughout the rest of the year. We noted earlier that one way of reducing this problem is to use an average of the opening and closing balances.

(b)   *Net profit percentage*: This measure may also be termed the 'net profit margin'. The net profit percentage is calculated from the following expression:

$$\frac{\text{Net profit}}{\text{percentage}} = \frac{\text{Net profit before interest}}{\text{Sales revenue}} \times 100$$

The ratio measures the percentage of sales revenue generated for the providers of all long-term capital after excluding the cost of goods sold and other operating costs. The figures for Maine Ltd are:

	Year 1	*Year 2*
Net profit percentage	$\dfrac{46,200}{900,000} \times 100 = 5.1\%$	$\dfrac{107,500}{1,200,000} \times 100 = 9.0\%$

For each £1 of sales revenue generated, Maine earned 5.1 pence of net profit in year 1, and 9 pence of net profit in year 2.

Separation of the ratio into the two elements permits further analysis of the causes of the increase in the percentage of return on long-term capital employed, as follows:

	Utilisation ratio	×	*Net profit percentage*	=	*Return on long-term capital*
Year 1	2.73	×	5.1%	=	14.0%
Year 2	1.81	×	9.0%	=	16.2%

These figures indicate that, in year 2, Maine Ltd generated fewer sales per £1 invested, but that on average each £1 of sales produced a higher net profit. This increase in the net profit margin more than compensated for the fall in the utilisation ratio, with the result that the return on long-term capital increased from 14% to 16.2%.

A Dupont style analysis encourages a further disaggregation of these ratios. For example, a change in the net profit percentage may be due to changes in the variable operating costs per unit, to changes in fixed operating costs, or to changes in the gross profit percentage. We shall examine one of these possible reasons, a change in the gross profit percentage.

(c) *Gross profit percentage*: The gross profit percentage or 'gross profit margin' is calculated from the following expresson:

$$\text{Gross profit percentage} = \frac{\text{Gross profit}}{\text{Sales revenue}} \times 100$$

This ratio measures how much each £1 of sales revenue earns as gross profit. The figures for Maine Ltd are:

	Year 1	*Year 2*
Gross profit percentage	$\frac{180,000}{900,000} \times 100 = 20.0\%$	$\frac{360,000}{1,200,000} \times 100 = 30.0\%$

Thus, for each £1 of sales revenue generated, Maine Ltd earned 20p gross profit in year 1 and 30p gross profit in year 2.

Changes in the gross profit percentage may be due to:

- Changes in the selling prices of products. For example, Maine may have increased its selling prices whilst managing to hold down the cost of goods sold.

- Changes in the cost of goods sold per unit of output. Such changes may result from changes in input prices or changes in the efficiency with which inputs are used. For example, suppose Maine held constant its selling prices over the two year period. The increase in sales revenue from £900,000 to £1,200,000 would represent an increase of one-third in the *physical* volume of sales (300,000/900,000). If the costs of goods sold are all variable, changes in the physical volume of sales would not of themselves affect the gross profit percentage (because both sales revenue and cost of goods sold would rise proportionately) although they would of course affect the *absolute* gross profit figure. A one-third increase in the volume of goods sold should result in an increase in the cost of goods sold figure for Maine Ltd to £960,000 (£720,000 × $1\frac{1}{3}$). As the cost of goods sold figure in year 2 was only £840,000, Maine Ltd might have reduced unit input costs and/or improved the efficiency of production.

- Changes in the mix of products sold. For example products with higher gross profit percentages may be substituted for products with lower margins. Even if sales prices, input prices and the efficiency of production were unchanged throughout the two years, Maine's gross profit could have been increased by switching into products yielding a higher margin, e.g. if the whole of Maine's increase in sales (£300,000) was due to the launch of a new product with a gross profit margin of 60%, the total gross profit would increase by £180,000 to £360,000 and the average gross profit percentage would increase from 20% to 30%.

It is beyond the scope of this book to consider any further disaggregation of the return on long-term capital ratio, but even so we have identified some potentially useful information. The increase in the return on long-term capital was achieved by increasing the net profit margin. This more than compensated for the fall in asset, or capital, utilisation. The increase in the net profit margin was in turn the result of an increase in the gross profit margin. We cannot identify the particular reason(s) for the increase in the gross profit margin from the financial statements themselves, but that information may be available elsewhere in the company's annual report (for example, in the supplementary notes and other statements), or from other sources.

The return on long-term capital employed is an 'entity' ratio. It shows the return to all providers of long-term capital and is therefore unaffected by changes in a company's capital structure, i.e. its mix of equity and debt capital. The derivation of the return on long-term capital is the same whatever the proportion of total capital supplied by loan creditors. However, as we noted in the section dealing with 'solvency' ratios, the introduction of debt finance can have a significant effect upon the returns to shareholders and their associated risk. This suggests a need to consider also a 'proprietary' ratio which focuses upon the owners of the company.

Return on owners' capital employed. This measure is also called the 'equity return', the 'return to ordinary shareholders' or the 'return on ordinary capital employed'. The return may be calculated from the following expression:

$$\text{Return on owners'} \atop \text{capital employed} = \frac{\text{Net profit after interest}}{\text{Owners' capital employed}} \times 100$$

Note that in order to ensure consistency between the numerator and the denominator, the former is measured as the profit available for owners (i.e. after interest payable) and the latter as owners' capital (i.e. excluding other sources of capital such as long-term loans). The figures for Maine Ltd are:

	Year 1	Year 2
Return on owners' capital employed	$\frac{46,200}{330,000} \times 100 = 14.0\%$	$\frac{82,500}{412,500} \times 100 = 20.0\%$

In year 1 the return on owners' capital employed (14.0%) is identical to the return on long-term capital employed because the owners' capital represents the only long-term capital employed. In year 2, the company borrows £250,000 by issuing debentures. The owners' return increases to 20% and the overall return on long-term capital increases to 16.2% (as we calculated earlier).

The increased capital raised during year 2 has apparently been used efficiently. The *marginal* return on the new capital is 18.4% ((107,500−46,200)÷(662,500−330,000)×100). Of the new capital raised (£332,500), £82,500 is from equity in the form of retained profits and

£250,000 from the issue of new 10% debentures. Because the new debentures, which represent most of the new capital raised, require a lower return
(10% p.a.) than is being earned on the new capital (18.4%), the owners'
return increases by more than the total return. Thus the increase in owners'
return is due partly to increased overall profitability and partly to the
introduction of 'cheap' debt financing. On the other hand, the owners'
return is now subject to increased financial risk as a result of the change in
capital structure. We noted earlier that Maine Ltd now has an obligation to
pay debt interest of £25,000, whatever its net income.

16.4   Limitations of Historical Cost Ratios

We have mentioned previously that the numerator and the denominator of a
given ratio should be consistent, i.e. profit available to shareholders should
be related to shareholders' capital employed; profit before interest should
be related to all long-term capital employed, etc. In addition, the numerator
and demoninator should be expressed in measurement scales which are
comparable and which thus produce a meaningful result. For example, the
ratio of liquid assets (in £) to current liabilities (also in £) produces a
meaningful result (i.e. the proportionate excess, or shortfall, of liquid assets
over current liabilities), whereas a ratio of sales (in £) to the average age of
fixed assets (in years) does not.

On the face of it, the ratios we have examined in this chapter appear to
produce meaningful results—the measurement scales appear to be in har-
mony. For each ratio both the numerator and denominator are expressed in
pounds (£). For example, the utilisation ratio, expressed as

$$\frac{\text{Sales in £}}{\text{Long-term capital in £}}$$

produces a ratio for Maine Ltd in year 2 of

$$\frac{£1,200,000}{£662,500} = 1.81$$

Similarly the utilisation ratio for the Ford Motor Co. for the year ended 31
December 1983 calculated from its published historical cost financial statements is

$$\frac{£3,511 \text{ million}}{£1,662 \text{ million}} = 2.11$$

We have interpreted this ratio as the amount of sales revenue generated
for each £1 of long-term capital invested in the company. But consider what
is the aim of producing this (or any other) ratio. We are interpreting
historical data in order to obtain predictive information. We are interested in

the current year's amount of sales revenue generated per £1 of capital invested largely as a basis for predicting future years' sales revenues (and, eventually, cash flows). Would an extra £1 invested in Ford at the beginning of 1984 generate an additional £2.11 of sales revenue? It is unlikely because the numerator and the denominator of the utilisation ratio are not in fact consistent with each other. It is not sufficient that they are both expressed in £s. The sales figure is expressed in £s reflecting current (1983) prices, but the long-term capital figure comprises amounts invested over a period of many years. If we describe the denominator as 'net assets' the problem is clearer. The denominator includes assets at their historical costs, which may reflect some prices which existed prior to 1960 (property) and prior to 1975 (plant and machinery).

The utilisation ratio for Ford, as calculated above, should, strictly, be described as follows:

$$\text{Utilisation ratio} = \frac{\text{Sales (1983 prices)}}{\text{Net assets (1960–1983 prices)}} = 2:11$$

In other words, if Ford could obtain another £1 of capital in 1983 *and invest it in net assets at prices reigning in the period 1960–1983* then the ratio of 2:11 represents a good indicator of future utilisation ratios. However, Ford must purchase assets at their current prices, and hence a better indicator of future asset utilisation would be represented by a ratio calculated as follows:

$$\text{Utilisation ratio} = \frac{\text{Sales (1983 prices)}}{\text{Net assets (1983 prices)}}$$

This ratio requires all assets in the balance sheet to be restated at their current costs. From the published current cost accounts[6] of Ford (which approximate replacement costs in most cases) we can calculate this new utilisation ratio as

$$\frac{\text{£3,511 million}}{\text{£2,165 million}} = 1.62$$

which is significantly lower than the historical cost ratio of 2:11.

A similar problem affects the ratio for the net profit percentage, which was expressed previously as:

$$\text{Net profit percentage} = \frac{\text{Net profit before interest in £s}}{\text{Sales in £s}}$$

The net profit percentage calculated from the historical cost financial statements of Ford is

---

[6]At the current time, all quoted companies are required to publish supplementary Income Statements and Balance Sheets prepared according to the principles of Current Cost Accounting. This requirement is contained in Statement of Standard Accounting Practice No. 16 (SSAP 16), *Current Cost Accounting,* The Institute of Chartered Accountants in England and Wales, March 1980.

$$\frac{£214 \text{ million}}{£3,511 \text{ million}} \times 100 = 6.1\%$$

However, although sales are expressed in current (1983) prices, net profit is not. Many components of net profit are expressed in 1983 prices (sales, wages, rent, rates, heating, etc.) but depreciation, in particular, is based upon prices which existed at the time of purchase of the relevant assets. As we have already noted these assets may have been bought as long ago as 1960. Similar problems can occur if older items of stock are included in cost of goods sold. Both problems can be avoided by the use of current costs in the income statement. The net profit percentage for Ford derived from the published current cost accounts is:

$$\frac{£96 \text{ million}}{£3,511 \text{ million}} = 2.7\%$$

We explained earlier that if the asset utilisation and net profit percentage ratios are multiplied, they produce a return on investment ratio as follows:

$$\frac{\text{Sales}}{\text{Net assets}} \times \frac{\text{Net profit before interest}}{\text{Sales}}$$

$$= \frac{\text{Net profit before interest}}{\text{Net assets}}$$
$$\text{(or long-term capital employed)}$$

Closer examination of the component part of the ratio reveals that the 'sales' figures cancel out and what remains is a ratio which comprises, for Ford, a net income figure calculated using a mixture of historical prices from 1960–1983, and a net asset figure calculated using a (different) mixture of historical prices from 1960–1983. The resulting figure is unlikely to be useful to decision makers. Table 16.3 illustrates the difference between the return on net asset ratios for Ford calculated under the historical cost and current cost asset valuation methods. The breakdown of the ratio into its component parts shows that the difference in the two return figures is caused primarily by the much lower net profit percentage reported under the current cost method.

Table 16.3   Historical cost and current cost return on net assets ratios for Ford Motor Company Limited, 1983

	Asset utilisation	×	Net profit percentage	=	Return on net assets
Historical cost	2.11	×	6.1%	=	12.9%
Current cost	1.62	×	2.7%	=	4.4%

Source: Ford Motor Company Limited, *Annual Report and Accounts,* 1983.

The potential usefulness of a return on investment figure, both as an indicator of overall performance and as a guide to future performance, would appear to demand that the constituent elements of the income statement and the balance sheet be expressed in comparable current prices. Had Maine Ltd used some form of 'current' cost accounting, the return on investment ratio would have provided a much better indication of management's efficiency in using resources. For example, if asset values and operating costs had been based on replacement costs, the ratio would have provided an indicator of management's ability to generate sufficient funds to replace assets as they are used, and hence to ensure the long-run survival of the company.

In times of rising prices we would expect historical cost returns on historical capital employed (net assets) to be higher than replacement cost (operating) returns on replacement cost capital employed, where capital employed is defined in terms of operating capacity (i.e. holding gains are taken into the balance sheet rather than the income statement). However, the difference between the two returns will not be identical for each company. Differences between the historical cost and current cost returns on capital employed for five UK companies are shown in Table 16.4. The returns of these particular five companies were selected because they are indicative of the relationship between the historical cost and current cost returns (compiled under SSAP 16—see footnote 6) earned during 1980 by the leading 140 UK companies researched by Phillips and Drew[7]. The ranking of the five companies on the basis of current cost percentages is significantly different from the ranking based on historical cost percentages.

Table 16.4   Selected returns on capital employed

Company	Historical cost return on historical cost long-term capital employed %	Current cost return on current cost long-term capital employed %
DRG (Dickinson Robinson Group)	13	2
Pilkington	11	5
Taylor Woodrow	10	7
Lucas Industries	9	(2)
Debenhams	8	6

Historical cost and current cost 'returns' are defined as pre-tax profit before net interest payable.

Source: Phillips and Drew, 'Full Disclosure of CC Profits and Assets', *Accounting Research,* 24 August 1981.

[7]Phillips and Drew, 'Full disclosure of CC profits and assets', *Accounting Research*, 24 August 1981.

The altered ranking is due in part to the differential effects which price changes can have on different industries as a result of differences in the nature and size of fixed assets and stocks, and because different industries traditionally have different debtor/creditor relationships. For example, the four companies selected as the leading companies in the packaging and paper sector reported current cost returns on capital employed figures which were on average 67% lower than their historical counterparts. The eleven leading stores, however, reported current cost return on capital employed figures only 40% lower on average than their historical cost figures. Such industry effects help to explain why the current cost return for DRG (packaging and paper) was 85% lower than its corresponding historical cost figure, whereas Debenhams (stores) current cost return was only 25% lower than its historical cost figure (Table 16.4).

The usefulness of other profitability ratios is similarly limited if costs are measured on an historical rather than a current cost basis. For example, an organisation exhibiting a satisfactory gross profit percentage, i.e. a surplus of sales revenue over the historical cost of stock used, may not be generating sufficient funds either to replace the stock at current prices or to meet its operating costs.

Similar criticisms can be levelled at the ratio expressing the return on owners' capital employed. The figure for owners' capital employed is based on the historical value of capital provided, both in the form of capital paid in and in the form of retained profits (reserves). As far as shareholders are concerned, the real cost of their investment in the company (the 'opportunity cost' of their investment) is represented by the amount sacrificed by not selling their shares, i.e. the *market value* of their shares. The same is true for potential buyers of shares who have to pay the *market* value rather than the book value to acquire shareholdings. This problem would still exist if the company used some form of current cost accounting, although the differences between the 'book' figures used in the ratio and the 'relevant' return and income figures described above may be smaller. The return to ordinary shareholders depends on the dividends they receive and expect to receive and on the market value of their shares. Neither of these is included in the calculation of return on owners' capital based on the company's income statement and balance sheet, although, in practice, the ratio of a quoted company's net profit (or earnings) to its market price—known as the price-earnings ratio—is often used as an indicator of success.

In addition, profit after interest may have little relationship to cash paid to or available for the owners of Maine Ltd. As we argued in Chapters 12 and 13, the owners' return depends both on the cash distributed by the business during the period and on the value of the business at the end of the period, which in turn depends on the cash expected to be distributed in future periods.

16.5   Summary of the Analysis

The financial ratios we have calculated for Maine Ltd for years 1 and 2 are summarised in Table 16.5. In spite of the limitations we have discussed, the ratios, together with the financial statements shown in Table 16.1, do provide a picture of the change in Maine's performance and position between the two years, and may be used as *part* of a process to predict its likely future performance. Maine Ltd has increased its capital during year 2 by £332,500, comprising £82,500 retained profits and £250,000 new debentures. The new capital has been used primarily to purchase additional land and buildings and plant and machinery; the increase in debtors is financed almost entirely by an increase in creditors.

Table 16.5   Maine Ltd—Summary of financial ratios

	Year 1	Year 2
Liquidity		
Working capital ratio	3.0:1	2.0:1
Liquid ratio	2.1:1	1.6:1
Debtor payment period	1.3 months	2.0 months
Creditor payment period	1.0 month	2.0 months
Stock holding period	0.9 month	0.8 month
Capital structure		
Gearing ratio	0	37.7%
Times interest covered	∞	4.3
Profitability		
Return on total long-term capital	14.0%	16.2%
Utilisation ratio	2.73	1.81
Net profit percentage	5.1%	9.0%
Gross profit percentage	20.0%	30.0%
Return on owners' capital	14.0%	20.0%

The expansion appears to have been successful. Although fewer sales were generated per pound invested in net assets, sales increased during year 2 by $33\frac{1}{3}$% while cost of goods sold increased by only $16\frac{2}{3}$%. This resulted in an increase in gross profit from 20% to 30%. Overhead expenses increased by nearly 90%, but the company was still able to increase its return on total capital employed from 14% to 16.2%. Because of the increase in gearing (from zero to nearly 38%) return on owners' capital increased from 14% to 20%, benefitting from both the introduction of 'cheaper' debt financing and the increase in total return. The liquidity ratios appear satisfactory for both years. Decreases in the working capital ratios and increases in the debtor and creditor payment periods between years 1 and 2 may be cause for concern if they indicate the start of a longer-term trend. On the other hand, if the changes are permanent they may indicate increased efficiency in the management of working capital. Although the increase in gearing has resulted in an increased equity return, it has also increased the financial risk borne by ordinary shareholders. As we noted earlier, a more reliable indicator of the success of the expansion for equity holders would include consideration of its impact on the market value of their shares.

In this chapter we have discussed the usefulness and limitations of a number of important financial ratios concerned with liquidity, solvency and profitability. Many ratios are limited by the fact that they are based on historical cost accounting measures. We have argued that, despite this limitation, they are of some use in appraising an organisation's past performance, and in making judgments about its likely future performance. We cannot stress too strongly that ratio analysis is not a substitute for forecasts of future sales, costs and cash flows, but rather that it is part of the process for generating and corroborating such forecasts. Hence, a key question concerning the success of the expansion of Maine Ltd, discussed in this chapter, is: 'To what extent will the improved performance resulting from the expansion be sustained in the future?' It is forecasts, not measures of past performance, that are of importance to the decision models of users of financial reports.

Discussion Topics

1 You have been approached by a bank manager who has asked you to advise him as to whether he should make a loan to a client. The client, who is a retailer, has provided copies of his profit and loss accounts and balance sheets for the past three years. Describe how you would assess the client's current liquidity position and his liquidity prospects.

2 Discuss the main roles and limitations of ratio analysis, and explain the extent to which ratio analysis alone can be used to appraise an organisation's performance.

3 For each of the following ratios, explain briefly how the ratio is calculated, describe the aspects of an organisation's activities about which it provides information, and discuss the ratio's particular limitations:
   (a) Working capital ratio
   (b) Liquid ratio
   (c) Creditor payment period
   (d) Stock holding period
   (e) Debtor payment period
   (f) Gearing ratio
   (g) Return on total capital
   (h) Return on owners' capital
   (i) Gross profit percentage
   (j) Net profit percentage

4 Discuss the problem of establishing 'benchmarks', with which a particular firm's ratios may be compared.

Further Reading

Altman, E.I., 'Financial ratios, discriminant analysis and the prediction of corporate bankruptcy', *Journal of Finance,* September 1968.

Dev, S., 'Ratio analysis and the prediction of company behaviour', in Edey, H. and Yamey, B.S., *Debits, Credits, Finance and Profits,* Sweet and Maxwell, 1974.

Elam, R., 'Predictive ability of financial ratios', *Accounting Review,* January 1975.

Horrigan, J.O., 'Some empirical bases of financial ratio analysis', *The Accounting Review,* July 1965.

Lev, B., *Financial Statement Analysis: A New Approach,* Prentice-Hall International, 1974.

Tarmari, M., *Financial Ratios: Analaysis and Prediction,* Paul Elek, 1978.

Exercises

16.1 The following are summaries of the published accounts of Siegmund Ltd for the past two years:

Balance sheets as at:	*31 October 19X6*		*31 October 19X7*	
	£'000	£'000	£'000	£'000
Ordinary share capital		1,200		1,200
Retained profits		270		290
		1,470		1,490
10% loan stock		800		800
		2,270		2,290
Fixed assets:				
Land and buildings, at cost	520		550	
less: Accumulated depreciation	80	440	90	460
Machinery and vehicles, at cost	1,120		1,340	
less: Accumulated depreciation	580	540	750	590
		980		1,050
Current assets:				
Stock, at lower of cost or market value	830		980	
Debtors, less provision for doubtful debts	650		570	
Cash	120		40	
	1,600		1,590	
less: Current liabilities (creditors)	310	1,290	350	1,240
		2,270		2,290

Profit and loss accounts, year ended	31 October 19X6		31 October 19X7	
	£'000	£'000	£'000	£'000
Sales revenue		2,200		3,200
less: Cost of sales		1,610		2,590
Gross profit		590		610
less: General expenses	210		230	
Depreciation	160	370	180	410
Operating profit		220		200
less: Loan interest		80		80
Net profit for the year		140		120
add: Retained profits at beginning of year		300		270
Available for distribution		440		390
less: Dividends paid		170		100
Retained profits at end of year		270		290

No fixed assets were sold during either year. All dividends due had been paid by 31 October 19X7.

● Interpret the above accounts for a shareholder in Siegmund Ltd who is not familiar with accounting practices. Calculate any ratios that you think may be helpful to the shareholder in appraising the company's performance, and comment on the limitations of such ratios for financial analysis.

16.2 Hagen is considering whether or not to invest a substantial portion of his private capital in Siegfried Ltd. He asks for your advice.

Your main source of information about Siegfried Ltd is the balance sheet and profit and loss account for the year to 31 December 19X4:

Balance sheet as at 31 December 19X4			£
Fixed assets			
Land and buildings (at cost)			200,000
Plant and machinery (at cost less depreciation)			800,000
			1,000,000
Trade investments (at cost)			50,000
Current assets			
Stocks		450,000	
Debtors		1,050,000	
Cash		50,000	
		1,550,000	
less: Current liabilities			
Creditors	400,000		
Taxation	150,000	550,000	1,000,000
			2,050,000
Represented by:			
Share capital and reserves			
Ordinary shares of £1 each			1,500,000
Retained profits			550,000
			2,050,000

Profit and loss account for the year to 31 December 19X4		£
Sales		3,000,000
less: Cost of sales		1,990,000
Gross profit		1,010,000
less: Operating expenses	410,000	
Bad debts	150,000	
Depreciation	110,000	670,000
Net profit before taxation		340,000
Taxation based on profit above		150,000
Net profit after taxation		190,000
Dividend at 10% on ordinary shares		150,000
Profit retained		40,000
Retained profits, brought forward		510,000
Retained profits in balance sheet		550,000

You also ascertain that Siegfried Ltd has been in business for five years, and produces plastic toys. The current market value of its ordinary shares is 125p each.

- (a)   Advise Hagen as to his proposed investment on the basis of the available information.
- (b)   Advise Hagen what additional information he should seek about the financial affairs of Siegfried Ltd before making a final decision.

16.3   Sharpless Ltd is an old-established firm which manufactures machine parts for the textile industry. For some time now the company's profits have been declining and this year as you prepare to audit the accounts you determine to examine the situation thoroughly.

You have in your possession the most recent statistics published by the Centre for Inter-Firm Comparison which state that in this particular industry the average company:

1.   sells 90p of sales for every £1 invested in assets;
2.   earns a gross profit of 15% on each sale;
3.   returns a net profit, before interest, of 10% on total assets employed, and provides shareholders with an earnings return of 12% on their capital employed;
4.   has on average a stock turnover period, a debtors' credit period and a creditors' credit period of 9 weeks, 8 weeks and 7 weeks respectively.

On arrival at the company, you are presented with the 'draft accounts' for 19X8 prepared by the unqualified book-keeper who heads the accounts department. These draft accounts are shown opposite.

During your visit, the directors announce their intention of paying a dividend of 4p per share.

Profit and loss account

	£
Depreciation—plant and machinery	15,000
Cost of goods sold	415,000
Debenture interest	12,000
Taxation	6,000
Depreciation—motor vehicles	10,000
General expenses	52,000
	510,000
Sales	530,000
Net profit	20,000

Balances after completing profit and loss account

	£'000
Plant and machinery—cost	300
Motor vehicles—cost	90
Accrued expenses	10
Stock on 31 December 19X8	220
Taxation liability	20
Trade creditors	60
Land and buildings—cost	330
Share capital (£1 shares)	270
Reserves at 1 January 19X8	322
Profit for the year	20
Debtors	105
Cash	117
8% debentures	150
Accumulated depreciation:	
Plant and machinery	240
Motor vehicles	70

- (a) Prepare a profit and loss account for Sharpless Ltd for the year ended 31 December 19X8, and a balance sheet as at that date.
- (b) Draft a report to the chairman of Sharpless Ltd giving reasons for your concern about the company's position, and suggesting possible future action to be taken by the company.

16.4 On the next page are percentages, etc., for samples of companies in the following industries:

Brewing	Building materials' manufacturers
Cotton (spinning and weaving)	Entertainment and sport
Building and construction	Retail distribution

- Try to identify each industry in the table by comparing it with 'all companies' bearing in mind the obvious facts about each, and also the information given. The order of the columns (A, B, C, etc.) is not necessarily that of the above list.

	All companies	Industry					
		A	B	C	D	E	F
Assets as % of net assets (i.e. total assets minus total current liabilites)							
Fixed assets	52	39	61	84	45	58	94
Stocks	39	46	20	14	63	33	11
Debtors	24	15	22	8	52	28	7
Cash and securities	20	21	24	14	22	25	14
Total assets	135	121	127	120	182	144	126
Bank overdraft	4	2	2	1	11	2	6
Dividends, tax due and other provisions	12	10	11	8	15	19	8
Trade and other creditors	19	9	14	11	56	23	11
Total current liabilities	35	21	27	20	82	44	26
Gearing ratio—range in which median company is found		0–10	0–10	11–20	0–10	11–20	11–20

*Percentage of fixed interest and fixed (preference) dividends to total income.

Brewing: Stocks deteriorate fast. Little credit is given or received.

Cotton (spinning and weaving): Raw materials are bought on 10 days' credit, and sales are on 14 days' credit. Spinners can buy at cheaper prices and get a better range of choice just after the harvest. In the above sample most of the companies prepared their accounts soon after the harvest. The problems facing the industry make borrowing difficult.

Building: The workload is variable. Contracts take a long time to finish. Some big jobs are overseas. Much of the work is done by subcontractors. Costing is slow, and 'retention money' is often held by the customer until the work proves satisfactory. Because of the dangers of taking credit too soon for profit on contracts, debts are often valued at cost and included with stock (which may also include some land and plant).

Building materials' manufacturers: Trade creditors are rather low because of vertical integration. Production may be continuous, and investment in plant high per man. Trade is poor in winter, and so (if the firm's year ends then) liquidity must be ample yet debtors may be low compared with 'all companies'.

Entertainment and sport: This includes cinemas, stadiums, etc.

Retailing: Although some firms sell for cash only, others give extended credit (e.g. hire purchase). Wholesalers may provide much of the finance.

16.5 Mr Pinkerton's accounts for 19X6 were as follows:

Profit and loss account, year ended 31 December 19X6

	£	£
Sales		40,000
less: Cost of goods sold		32,000
Gross profit		8,000
less: General expenses	2,000	
Depreciation	3,000	5,000
Net profit		3,000

Balance sheet as at 31 December 19X6

	£		£	£
Capital account	30,000	Fixed assets		
		at cost	45,000	
		less: Depreciation	15,000	30,000
Creditors				
(for goods)	4,000	Current assets:		
		Stock	4,500	
Bank overdraft	5,500	Debtors	5,000	9,500
	39,500			39,500

The following information describes Mr Pinkerton's transactions during the year ended 31 December 19X7:

1. Sales increased by 10%.
2. The gross profit rate was 25% of sales.
3. General expenses (all paid in cash) were £2,500.
4. Depreciation of fixed assets was £3,000.
5. The average period of credit allowed to debtors was 3 months.
6. The average period of credit allowed by creditors was 2 months.
7. The stock turnover was 8 times per year.

The average period of credit allowed to debtors and by creditors, and the stock turnover rate are calculated using the *average* of the balances at 1 January 19X7 and 31 December 19X7, for debtors, creditors and stock respectively. All purchases and sales of goods were on credit.

● Prepare Mr Pinkerton's profit and loss account for the year ended 31 December 19X7, and his balance sheet as at that date.

16.6   The following balances have been extracted from the books of Isolde Ltd as at 30 September 19X1:

	£
Creditors	18,900
Sales	240,000
Land at cost	54,000
Buildings at cost	114,000
Furniture and fittings at cost	66,000
Bank overdraft	18,000
Depreciation—buildings	18,000
—furniture and fittings	30,000
Discounts received	5,292
Unappropriated profit at 1 October 19X0	6,000
Provision for doubtful debts	2,448
Goodwill	49,200
Cash in hand	696
Stock at 1 October 19X0	42,744
Interim dividend on preference shares	1,800
Rates	6,372
Wages and salaries	24,000
Insurance	5,688
Returns inwards	1,116

General expenses	1,308
Debtors	37,920
Purchases	131,568
Debenture interest	1,200
Bad debts	2,028
5% debentures	48,000
6% £1 preference shares	60,000
£1 ordinary shares	60,000
General reserve	30,000
Share premium	3,000

Additional information:

1. Stock on hand at 30 September 19X1 was £46,638.
2. Insurance paid in advance was £300.
3. Wages owing were £840.
4. Depreciation is to be provided at 10% on the cost of buildings and at 20% on the written down value of furniture and fittings.
5. Provision for doubtful debts is to be reduced to 5% of debtors.
6. Debenture interest outstanding is £1,200.
7. The directors propose to pay a 5% ordinary dividend and the final preference dividend and to transfer £24,000 to general reserve.

- (a) Prepare the profit and loss account of Isolde Ltd for the year ended 30 September 19X1 and a balance sheet as at that date.
  (b) Examine the accounts you have prepared in (a) above and then answer the questions below:
    (i) How did the share premium account arise?
    (ii) How could the goodwill account have arisen?
    (iii) What is the rate of return on net capital employed and what is the significance of this figure?
    (iv) Which of the reserves are capital reserves and which are revenue reserves, and what, in principle, is the difference between the two?
    (v) The company is relatively highly geared; what does this mean?

Chapter 17

Evaluation of Alternative Accounting Methods

In Chapter 2 we suggested that most users of financial statements have two main, interdependent information requirements:

(a) forecasts of some aspects of the future performance of the reporting entity, and

(b) regular reports explaining both differences between forecast and actual performance, and changes in forecasts if expectations have changed.

While the need for, and requirements of, forecasts may differ from user to user, we suggested that most users are interested in the cash flows of the entity. However, what appears beneficial to the interests of one, or more, groups of participants may be detrimental to the interests of others. Management, who may have most to lose by the disclosure of forecasted information, comprise a powerful lobby opposing such disclosures. As a result some participants are deprived of a basic input for their decision models, i.e. forecasts of future cash flows.

The information currently disclosed in financial statements is concerned with *past* performance and *current* position. External users must analyse and interpret this historical information in order to estimate an entity's *future* business performance and financial position. This leads us once more to the following fundamental question:

How should users of financial statements analyse and interpret the (historical) data provided in order to obtain the (predictive) information required?

In previous chapters we have discussed some means for choosing between alternative reporting methods (Chapters 4, 12 and 13), described historical cost, current purchasing power and replacement cost approaches to the measurement of income and value (Chapters 5–11, and Chapters 14 and 15), and explained how financial statements might be interpreted to analyse organisational performance (Chapter 16).

In those chapters we discussed and made a preliminary evaluation of the alternative accounting treatments available for particular items. However, a full assessment of the usefulness of particular accounting treatments involves a consideration of broader issues, such as the choice of a basis of valuation. For example, in Chapter 9 we compared and contrasted different historical cost based depreciation methods but pointed out that a more fundamental question concerns whether depreciation should be based on historical cost, current cost, or some other measure. The purpose of this chapter is to take a wider view of some of the issues raised in previous chapters, and to evaluate the alternative accounting methods described previously.

We first review the possible criteria for selecting between alternative accounting methods and describe the general characteristics by which such accounting methods may be classified. We then apply the criteria to a broad evaluation of the alternative accounting methods. Our conclusions are tentative, reflecting the differences of opinion and lack of empirical (i.e. real-world) evidence that presently exist in the area of financial reporting.

17.1 Criteria for Choice of Accounting Method

In Chapter 4 we discussed various criteria for choice of accounting method. We here review and, to a limited extent, expand those arguments. The problem of deciding what financial information ought to be reported is complicated by the existence of different users of accounting reports, and thus of possible conflicts in preferences for information.

Broadly, the problem of choice can be attacked in either of two ways. The first approach might be termed the *user decision orientated* approach. This entails an identification of the main groups of users and an assessment of the ability of alternative accounting methods to satisfy their information requirements. The assessment is often based on an examination of users' decision models. User decision orientated approaches were discussed in Chapter 2. We include in this section a summary of those discussions. The second approach is more limited and concerns the choice of accounting methods for quoted (listed) companies only. It might be termed the *efficient capital market* approach. This approach involves an examination of the efficiency of the capital market (i.e. the Stock Exchange) in incorporating accounting (and other) information in share prices, and is thus concerned mainly with the allocation of investors' resources.

User decision orientated approach
The user decision orientated approach considers the ability of alternative accounting methods to provide information useful to users' decision models. Initially, the information requirements of each user group (e.g. shareholders, employees, creditors, etc.) are considered separately. When (and if) the best reporting method is agreed for each group, the further question arises as to whether the various methods can be combined into one general

purpose report, or whether the best methods for each group differ so much that a special report must be provided for each group. The five steps involved in applying a user decision orientated approach are:

1. Identify groups of users and determine the information requirements of each group.
2. Specify alternative reporting methods.
3. Specify a testing procedure which relates the available courses of action (alternative accounting methods) to the information requirements of each group.
4. Use the testing procedure to select the best reporting method for each group, after taking account of the cost of implementing each reporting method.
5. Assess the extent to which the various preferred reporting methods might be combined in a general purpose report.

The results of the above procedure are unlikely to remain stable through time. For example, users' understanding of accounting information may change and thus their responses to alternative reporting methods may alter. It is therefore important that the procedure should be regularly repeated.

In Chapter 2 we identified the following external user groups for consideration: employees and trades unions; government; creditors and lenders; customers; shareholders and investment analysts. We considered their decisions and suggested the sort of accounting information which might be of help to them. Although we did not attempt to develop detailed decision models for each group, our analysis suggested that for major decisions, information relating to some aspects of an entity's future performance was relevant. This led us to the conclusion that competing accounting methods should be (at least partially) assessed against two interdependent criteria: their *predictive value* (i.e. their usefulness in enabling users to estimate future relevant events) and their *control* properties (i.e. their usefulness in assisting users to monitor an organisation's performance through time).

This analysis was based primarily on our assumptions about the sort of decisions taken by different users. This type of *a priori* analysis, based on assumptions and opinions, suffers the weakness that it is not supported by *empirical* evidence (i.e. it is not supported by observations of real world behaviour). Ultimately, the only way of resolving disputes concerning the usefulness of alternative accounting methods is by gathering empirical evidence about the extent to which, and the ways in which, the alternative methods are used. At least three variants of this approach are available: (1) ask a sample of users what sort of information they require, using questionnaire and interview techniques; (2) conduct controlled experiments, by providing a sample of users with alternative forms of accounting information and asking them to make hypothetical decisions on the basis of that information; (3) observe and analyse the actual decisions taken by users in response to available information.

None of these variants is free from problems. For example, variant 1 involves the selection of a representative (unbiased) sample of users and the design of a questionnaire that does not influence their replies; variant 2 relies on the responses of users to hypothetical decisions in the same way as they would react to real-world problems; variant 3 requires the researcher to distinguish between users' actions which are motivated by the information provided, and those that result from other factors, such as changes in environmental conditions. In addition, all three variants suffer the disadvantage that users' responses may be conditioned by the sort of information they are receiving at present and have been accustomed to receive in the past. A reliable empirical experiment would involve the provision of a variety of information for a long period of time, before we could test users' preferences for particular information. In respect of alternative asset valuation methods this procedure should be facilitated by recent accounting standards in the UK, USA, and elsewhere, which require certain organisations to provide both current cost and historical cost information.

Efficient capital market approach

Efficient capital market tests are a form of the third empirical approach discussed above. Such tests involve an analysis of decisions taken by users in response to available information. In particular they are concerned with the speed with which, and the extent to which, accounting and other information is reflected in current share prices. For example, studies have been undertaken which examine the reaction of share prices to the announcement of accounting numbers (e.g. annual earnings numbers) and to changes in accounting methods (e.g. methods of calculating depreciation and of valuing stock or fixed assets). The capital market is said to be efficient if it responds rapidly and without bias to new information. However, the efficient capital market approach is concerned only with the allocation of investors' resources and is thus of little help in assessing the usefulness of accounting reports to other participants.

In addition to its limited scope, the efficient capital market approach is concerned primarily with the efficiency of the market in processing available information, i.e. it is (self-evidently) not concerned with alternative but as yet unprovided accounting information. Thus capital market efficiency cannot, by itself, be used to assess the *desirability* of alternative accounting methods, although it may be of some use in assessing their *effects*.

One important test of capital market efficiency asks the following question. Can the market (e.g. the London Stock Exchange) distinguish between accounting information that signals a 'real' change in an organisation's position or performance (for example, information about increased turnover that might lead to an increase in distributable cash flows in the future) and information that is 'cosmetic' and has no implications for the 'real' position of an organisation (for example, information about increased earnings resulting purely from a change in depreciation method)? In practice, there may be few changes to accounting methods that are entirely 'cosmetic'. A change in an organisation's depreciation method may seem at first sight to have no 'real' information value in the sense that it signals no 'real' change in the organisation's performance (i.e. it does not change its cash flows). On further investigation, though, it might be found to influence the timing of the organisation's cash receipts (if, for example, the organisation is involved in government contracts under which payments are related to accounting costs such as depreciation) or its taxation liability (for example, in countries such as the USA where the accounting charge for depreciation forms the basis for the tax allowance for depreciation). If the capital market *is* able to distinguish between 'real' and 'cosmetic' changes ('real' changes thus having an effect on share prices, 'cosmetic' changes having no such effect) then at least organisations need not spend time (and incur costs) in choosing between accounting methods, the differences between which are purely 'cosmetic'. In such cases, any one method contains the same amount of information as any other.

Interpersonal utility comparisons

In our discussions of both user decision orientated and efficient capital market approaches we have noted the problem caused by the existence of potential conflicts between and within groups concerning the provision of relevant information. *Intergroup* conflicts arise when the provision of certain information is beneficial to one group and harmful to another (for example, increased information to employees may enable them to negotiate higher wages, one result of which may be an increase in the selling price which is passed on to customers). *Intragroup* conflicts arise when information benefits certain members of a particular user group but is disadvantageous to other members of the same group. (For example, a company operating two separate plants might pay the same wage rate to employees in both locations based upon the joint output of the two plants. Disaggregated information which showed one plant to be more productive might prove to be helpful to one group of employees in subsequent wage negotiations, but detrimental to the interests of the other group.) Intergroup and intragroup conflicts are inevitable in such situations. The resolution of such conflicts requires some form of social value judgment, i.e. a judgment as to whether the benefits to one group or subgroup arising from a change in accounting method outweigh the costs to others in *social* terms. Social value judgments may have to be made ultimately by government, or by another body (such as the accounting profession) with the implicit or explicit approval of government.

Other criteria

Our approach thus far has suggested that *in our opinion* relevance to user decisions (i.e. predictive value and control) should, in most cases, be regarded as the most important criterion for evaluating accounting methods. In Chapter 4 we categorised the main criteria for choice as relating to either the *usefulness* or the *feasibility* of alternative accounting methods. Within the category of usefulness we included *predictive value and control* (discussed above) and also *timeliness, comparability, objectivity* and *understandability*. The criterion of timeliness suggests that the usefulness of accounting information is greater, the shorter the time period between the outcome and the report of an event. Comparability (often termed 'consistency') means that accounting information should be prepared on comparable bases both through time and between organisations. Objectivity is concerned primarily with the extent to which accounting information is free from bias. Understandability means the extent to which those who use accounting information understand the basis upon which it has been prepared.

The set of criteria relating to the feasibility of accounting methods encompasses *verifiability* and *measurability*. Verifiability relates to the extent to and ease with which the information contained in an accounting report can be checked. The criterion of measurability suggests that an accounting system which enables more factors to be measured (with some degree of certainty) is to be preferred.

In Chapter 13 we described the nature of economic (forecast-based) measures of income and value and suggested that they might provide a benchmark against which various (transactions-based) accounting approaches might be evaluated. This role for economic measures is based on the *a priori* argument that they have high predictive value and control properties. Thus an accounting method that is consistently a good estimator of economic measures should be ranked highly.

The criteria developed thus far are concerned primarily with the benefits associated with different accounting methods. We should not forget that the choice of accounting method depends also on its associated costs. The best accounting method is the one with the greatest surplus of benefits over costs. For this purpose, costs include not only the costs of producing and analysing the information, but also the costs suffered by particular participants if information is disclosed which is detrimental to their interests.

The identification of an optimal accounting method would be straightforward if one method were superior to all others in terms of its ability to satisfy *all* criteria, including that of cost. As we shall see in later sections, this is not the case—different criteria are probably best satisfied by different accounting methods. Furthermore, there is no easy way of expressing benefits in a common unit of measurement. In consequence we believe that an unambiguous cost–benefit analysis of alternative methods is not possible at present. We shall attempt to identify strengths and weaknesses of particular accounting methods and use the results to make a preliminary assessment of their relative merits. Our inability to draw firm conclusions about the superiority of some methods over others simply reflects the present state of accounting as a developing discipline.

17.2   Alternative Accounting Methods for External Reporting

Accounting reporting methods may be classified according to two characteristics—their asset valuation method and their capital maintenance
concept (see Chapter 12, pages 262–267). The asset valuation method
determines the value of assets in the balance sheet and the operating costs in
the income statement. The capital maintenance concept determines how
much of income is set aside to maintain the value of the invested capital.

Assets may be valued, and costs determined, using one of the following
five transactions-based methods:

1. Historical cost.
2. Historical cost adjusted by a general price index.
3. Current cost/value: (a)   Replacement cost
                        (b)   Realisable value
                        (c)   'Value to the firm'.

We have examined and discussed in previous chapters the nature of
historical cost, adjusted historical cost and replacement cost asset valuations. The realisable value of an asset is the price at which the asset could be
sold in a normal business transaction. 'Value to the firm' involves the
comparison of various asset valuation methods. It is defined as the *lower* of
replacement cost and value in use, where value in use is the *higher* of
realisable value and the discounted present value of the net future benefits
expected from use of the asset. If this seems difficult to understand at the
moment, we shall explain more fully its calculation, and that of realisable
value, later in this chapter.

Capital may be maintained using:

1. Maintenance of money capital.
2. Maintenance of the general purchasing power of owners' equity.
3. Maintenance of operating capacity (i.e. maintenance of the physical
   capability of the enterprise).

We have not included economic measures of income and value in the
above categorisations because we do not see them as feasible methods of
reporting business performance; their importance is as benchmarks against
which alternative transactions-based methods can be assessed. We have also
excluded other possible methods (for example, cash flow accounting[1]) which
do not fit in easily with the traditional framework for measuring and reporting income and value. Such methods represent a radical departure from
present practice and, in our view, are unlikely in the foreseeable future to
replace reports based on the measurement of income and value. Our purpose in this chapter is to evaluate existing methods and others that we
believe might replace (or supplement) them. In the next two sections we
evaluate the alternative capital maintenance concepts and asset valuation
methods described above.

---

[1]Cash flow accounting will be discussed further in Chapter 18.

17.3   Evaluation of Capital Maintenance Concepts

In Chapter 15 (pages 323–326) we compared and reached some conclusions as to the relative merits of alternative capital maintenance concepts. We now summarise those conclusions. The justification for making capital maintenance adjustments (i.e. those based on maintaining the firm's operating capacity or the general purchasing power of owners' funds) is that they avoid the distribution of the organisation's 'real' capital. This justification places a substantial emphasis on the measurement of income, in terms both of amounts currently available for distribution and of the prediction of future performance.

However, one might argue that it may not be in the interests of those associated with an organisation to maintain its real capital. It might be better in certain cases to increase current distributions (to owners, employees and so on) and reduce the scale of future activities if parts of the organisation's activities are unprofitable or are located in a contracting sector of the economy. For example, an organisation which manufactures calculators may be acting in the best interests of its participants if it decides to reduce its production of battery-powered calculators, particularly if it decides instead to make solar-powered calculators. Distribution decisions should be based on investment and financing opportunities available and expected to become available and on the consumption preferences of the participants, rather than on accounting measurements of past performance.

The criteria discussed earlier in this chapter are similarly not affected significantly by the choice of a capital maintenance concept. The main difference between financial statements prepared using different capital maintenance concepts lies in the way in which holding gains on non-monetary assets (primarily stock and fixed assets) are reported. We discussed this at some length in Chapter 15. If capital is maintained in money terms, holding gains are reported in the income statement. If operating capacity is maintained, holding gains are reported as part of ownership interest in the balance sheet. If owners' purchasing power is maintained, part of the holding gains are reported in the income statement and the remainder as part of ownership interest. Thus although the choice of capital maintenance concept affects directly an organisation's net income (see Table 12.3, page 263), full disclosure of holding gains should ensure that for all but the most naive user each capital maintenance concept conveys the same information.

17.4   Evaluation of Asset Valuation Methods

Historical cost
From the inception of double-entry recording until some ten or twenty years ago, historical cost was almost universally accepted as the most appropriate

means of measuring costs and assets in external accounting reports. Hence one argument often advanced in its favour is that it has stood the test of time, i.e. it has provided numbers which have been *used* (and presumably deemed to be *useful*). It does not, however, follow that numbers prepared on some other basis could not also have been used, or that a method that was useful in the past will continue to be useful in the future. It is also argued that historical cost numbers are objective because they represent the prices at which actual transactions have taken place and, in consequence, there should be little dispute about whether or not the numbers are 'correct'. The validity of this argument is weakened by the need to match costs with revenues. Matching involves subjectivity. For example, the calculation of the amount of annual depreciation of a fixed asset depends directly on subjective estimates of its remaining useful life and residual value. Similar considerations apply to stock and debtors. Another argument in favour of historical cost relates to the cost of its application. It is frequently argued that it is cheaper to implement than alternative methods, primarily because change would involve additional costs. We discuss the relative cost of other methods below.

Various arguments have been advanced against the use of historical cost, particularly during periods of inflation. Such arguments usually relate to its inadequacy as a means of controlling and assessing the efficiency of resource use. We saw in Chapter 16 that a historical cost balance sheet is not a statement of the current values of assets, and that performance measured against the (outdated) historical cost of resources gives little indication of how well managers have performed in the past or of how well they are likely to perform in the future. These limitations severely restrict the comparability of financial statements prepared on a historical cost basis. It is possible for two organisations to own assets with identical current values and yet report different historical costs in the balance sheet and charge different historical costs in the income statements. As the financial statements of the two organisations lack comparability, so do many of the attendant ratios.

Other disadvantages might be cited. For example, historical costs rarely measure the relevant (opportunity) costs of using resources; and as a consequence of adopting the 'fundamental concept' of prudence, there is widespread use of conservatism in the preparation of financial statements, at the possible expense of such other qualities as relevance. Finally, it is difficult to make a case supporting the predictive value of historical cost numbers; or to establish a relationship between historical cost and economic income. Economic values are forward-looking and based upon estimates of future cash flows. Historical costs are backward-looking and based upon past transactions. Only in those cases where there have been few, or no, environmental changes, e.g. changes in price levels, technology and customer preferences over a period of many years, would these two methods be closely related. These conditions rarely, if ever, exist. We saw in the previous chapter how historical cost profitability ratios can give a misleading indication of future performance if both the income and balance sheet figures include costs and assets at prices which are out of date.

Historical cost adjusted by a general price index

This method 'values' assets in pounds of current purchasing power (CPP). The advantages and disadvantages claimed for CPP figures have, as we mentioned in Chapter 14, much in common with those claimed for unadjusted historical costs. By applying a widely used general index (the Retail Price Index) to the historical cost of past transactions, CPP figures are easily verifiable, and the cost of preparing CPP accounts is not excessive. In addition, by separating operating profit from any gains or losses on holding monetary items, the method highlights two separate aspects of managerial performance—operating efficiency and financial management.

However, the close association of CPP and historical cost methods of asset valuation implies that many of the disadvantages of historical cost apply equally to the CPP method. Objectivity is reduced by the need to make judgments in respect of particular attributes of fixed assets, stock and debtors and although operating profit is separated from gains or losses on holding monetary items, that profit may not itself be a good indicator of managerial performance in the past or in the future. In particular, the values of assets and the cost of using them do *not* reflect current replacement costs or realisable values, unless such costs and values have increased at exactly the same rate as the general price index since the assets were purchased. Furthermore, some users may be misled into believing that the adjusted figures do represent current replacement costs or realisable values, and may make incorrect decisions in consequence. If this is so, the CPP method fails to satisfy the criterion of understandability.

It also fails to satisfy the criteria of consistency and comparability. We noted in Chapter 14 that it is possible for two assets with identical current values to be measured differently under CPP accounting. It is also the case that assets with identical costs at the time of purchase will be reported as having identical CPP (and historical) costs thereafter, even though their current values might diverge. Not only do CPP asset values and income figures lack comparability, but as a result so do any ratios based upon those figures.

Finally, the CPP approach to asset valuation is backward-looking. It is based upon the historical cost of past transactions, and the figures derived from this approach are unlikely to have any relationship with forecast-based figures which determine economic income and value.

Current cost or current value

The terms 'current cost' and 'current value' are used to describe those accounting methods which value assets by reference to current prices. There are a number of asset valuation methods which may be included within this definition. For example, an asset's value may be determined by its current replacement cost as we saw in Chapter 15, or by current selling price, or by its value 'in use', i.e. a value based upon its contribution to the organisation's business. We deal in turn with each of the three variants of current cost.

(i)   *Replacement cost*. We have seen that an important characteristic of replacement cost accounting is its recognition of different aspects of managerial activity via the separate treatment of operating income and holding gains. Operating income is calculated by matching revenues with the current replacement costs of operating resources. Holding gains are increases in the replacement costs of assets occuring during the accounting period. The split is significant because, as we suggested in Chapter 15 (pages 324–325), it may help to satisfy the criteria of predictive value and control.

An operating surplus suggests that the organisation has generated sufficient revenue to cover the current replacement costs of the resources. This *may* suggest that it will be able to continue doing so in the future, although a fuller judgment depends on forecasts of how future economic conditions will be likely to affect the organisation. Nevertheless, the information provided is more current than that revealed by historical cost income statements, and it tackles a fundamental problem facing most organisations, i.e. their ability to replace resources as they are used.

Holding gains suggest changes in the cash-generating potential of assets. A positive holding gain (increase in an asset's value) usually results from an increase in the future benefits the asset is expected to provide; this implies that a present holding gain indicates an increase in future operating income.[2] Thus holding gains (or losses) provide some indication of possible changes in the trend of operating income. The dichotomy between operating income and holding gains may also be useful in assessing the efficiency of managers. It may aid decisions (by shareholders) as to whether to retain or replace the management and/or whether to increase its remuneration. It emphasises two different aspects of management activity: the success of managers in purchasing assets in advance of a price rise (measured by holding gains), and the efficiency of managers in operating assets (measured by operating income).

It is also argued that replacement cost asset values provide information useful in predicting future performance. The current replacement cost of an asset reflects, to some extent, the future benefits likely to be derived from its use. This suggests a possible link between replacement cost and economic value. For example, few organisations would replace assets unless the future

---

[2]An increase in an asset's value does not always imply an increase in future operating income. For example, an asset's value may increase if it is used in an industry whose members enjoy some degree of monopoly protection. If the monopoly protection is removed, new firms may enter the industry to take advantage of the 'monopoly' profits, thus bidding up the price of the asset but also reducing the expected profits of each existing member of the industry because total industry profits now have to be shared between more firms.

discounted benefits (economic value) exceed the purchase price (replacement cost). The extent to which likely future benefits are reflected in current replacement cost depends on the nature and efficiency of the market in which the asset is traded.

The final advantage claimed for replacement cost is that, relative to historical cost, it increases the degree of comparability between the reports of different organisations. The values of assets and operating costs are measured in terms of current prices, so that similar organisations reporting on the same date should disclose costs and values computed on comparable bases, even if the age structure of their assets is different. The same cannot be said of historical cost accounts. As we saw in Chapter 16, it is essential that assets and operating costs are measured in terms of current prices in order to produce meaningful ratios which evaluate an organisation's past performance, compare that performance with other similar organisations, and estimate the organisation's likely future performance.

Various criticisms have been levelled against the use of replacement costs in financial statements, for example that replacement cost figures are expensive to calculate. During the 1980s many large organisations in the UK and USA have been required to prepare and publish replacement cost information. Most organisations have chosen to continue to record transactions at historical cost and to make periodic revisions to incorporate changes in replacement cost. These revisions have usually been made once a year, at the year-end, although some companies have made quarterly or, occasionally, monthly revisions. Although this sort of procedure involves additional clerical costs, there is evidence to suggest that the extra cost of annual revisions is slight, particularly in relation to the cost of maintaining the basic historical cost records.[3]

A second argument frequently advanced against replacement cost accounting is that it lacks objectivity; the adjustments required to the basic historical cost records may be based on indices of specific price changes published by the Central Statistical Office, on manufacturers' price lists or on information gleaned from the internal records of the organisation. In other words, there may be several different 'replacement costs' for the same asset, unless it is traded in a very efficient market. For example, the cost of a two year old British Leyland Metro may vary depending upon its condition and upon the source from which it is acquired. However, although there may not be a unique replacement cost for a two year old Metro (or for many other assets), it may still be that net replacement cost is more 'objective' as a valuation basis than written-down historical cost. We noted above that

---

[3]See, for example, R.W. Scapens, A.J. Southworth, G.H. Stacy, *Case Studies in Current Cost Accounting,* Institute of Chartered Accountants in England and Wales, 1983; Anthony Hope, *Accounting for Price-level Changes—A Practical Survey of Six Methods,* Institute of Chartered Accountants in England and Wales Research Committee Occasional Paper No. 4, 1974; R.C. Dockweiler, 'The practicability of developing multiple financial statements: a case study', *The Accounting Review,* October 1969.

subjective estimates of remaining life and residual value are required to calculate historical cost. The calculation also depends on the chosen method of depreciation. It is possible (even probable) that if a number of accountants were asked to estimate the replacement cost and written-down historical cost of a two year old Metro, and were given no further guidance as to which valuation conventions to use, their estimates of replacement cost would be less widely dispersed than those of historical cost. Thus, insofar as a consensus view may be taken as a measure of objectivity, replacement cost figures may well be more objective than historical costs, particularly in relation to assets which have an active second-hand market.

A final problem concerns the definition of replacement costs when technology is changing. An organisation may own an asset (Mark I) which has been superseded by a more efficient one (Mark II). Is the appropriate replacement cost of the Mark I asset the cost of buying another Mark I asset of similar age and condition, or is it the cost of acquiring the same production potential from a Mark II asset? The latter seems more likely, as it appears more likely that the organisation would buy a Mark II asset if it had to replace its asset. However, it may be difficult (and hence costly) to calculate the cost of obtaining, from the Mark II asset, services identical to those available from the Mark I. For example, suppose the Mark I model has a production capacity of 200,000 units p.a., and the Mark II has a production capacity of 300,000 units p.a. Under these conditions the replacement cost of the *services* provided by the Mark I asset would appear to be two-thirds of the appropriate written-down cost of a Mark II asset. However, the Mark II model might process a different mix of raw materials, use more, or less, labour and power, have a different maintenance contract etc.—all of which affect the cost of replacing the services provided by the Mark I model.

(ii) *Realisable value*. The realisable value of an asset is the price at which the asset could be sold in a normal business transaction. This may be very different from the amount that would be raised in a forced liquidation. For example, a second-hand car dealer, forced to dispose of his entire stock of second-hand cars within a few days, may have to accept much lower prices than he could obtain by selling them in the normal course of his business over a period of three or four months.

Perhaps the most popular argument in favour of realisable value as a measure of the current value of an asset is that it is the most appropriate indication of the *sacrifice* involved in using the asset, i.e. by using the asset the organisation is foregoing the opportunity to sell it. It is sometimes argued that avoidance of the cost of replacing an asset is not an alternative available to an organisation once the asset has been purchased. For example, suppose a company purchases a machine for £20,000 in 19X0. In 19X2 the replacement cost of a two year old machine is £17,000 and the realisable value is £11,000. It is argued that the sacrifice involved in using the asset in 19X2 is the £11,000 foregone—the £17,000 does not measure any form of sacrifice made by the company.

This line of argument has led some proponents of the realisable value method to claim that the realisable value of an asset is relevant to *all* decisions concerning its use, i.e. sale of the asset should always be considered as one possible course of action. These lines of argument have their roots in the concept of relevant costs for management decisions concerning the use of assets,[4] but seem basically to be flawed for the purpose of selecting a valuation method for external reports. First, they are not consistent even with the logic of determining relevant costs for decisions. The replacement cost of an asset is very often the relevant (opportunity) cost of using it; if the asset is to be replaced eventually, the relevant cost of its use is the amount the organisation must pay to acquire a replacement. (This point is clarified further in the later discussion of 'value to the firm'.) Second, there seem to be no obvious reasons to assume that a cost which is relevant to managers, who must make decisions about the optimal use of assets, is also relevant to external users, who generally have no control over such decisions.

There is, however, a more persuasive argument for using realisable values in external reports. The basis of this view is that they provide an indication of an organisation's ability to adapt to changing environmental and economic conditions, particularly in the short run. An organisation that is unable to adapt in the short run may not survive to the long run. One aspect of an organisation's adaptability is its ability to raise cash to undertake new investment. To some extent, this depends on its ability to generate funds to repay long-term capital and to pay interest. It also depends on its ability to raise capital quickly to exploit short-term opportunities. The realisable values of the organisation's assets are an important contributory factor to this ability. They indicate the amounts that could be raised quickly to finance new investments, both by selling the assets themselves and by pledging them as security for loans from banks and other lenders. In Chapter 16 (page 341) we suggested that an analysis of an organisation's liquidity position would be more meaningful if non-monetary assets such as stock and work in progress were always valued at their realisable values.

In discussing the merits of replacement costs we argued that they provide a yardstick against which to assess management's ability to generate sufficient funds to replace assets as they are used. Realisable values provide a different yardstick: one that indicates management's ability to generate a better return than could be achieved by selling the organisation's assets and investing the proceeds elsewhere. This yardstick indicates one ambivalent characteristic of realisable value systems—they concentrate heavily on the short-run performance of an organisation and on its potential liquidation rather than on its performance as a going concern. This emphasis may be inappropriate for an organisation operating in a healthy economic environment, although it could provide important information about an organisation struggling to survive in a weak or declining economy.

[4]See, for example, John Arnold and Tony Hope, *Accounting for Management Decisions,* Prentice-Hall International, 1983, Chapter 6.

This concentration upon short-run performance suggests that, *a priori,* realisable values are unlikely to be good indicators of future performance. A going concern, by definition, is expected to continue to operate into the foreseeable future and hence replace its assets as they wear out. Even if the going-concern assumption is relaxed, realisable values will be accurate predictors of future cash flows only if the assets are sold off individually.

The idea that an organisation's assets might be sold and the proceeds invested elsewhere implies a *proprietary* view of the firm, i.e. the realisable value method views the organisation as a collection of assets which can be (broken up and) sold by the managers or the owners at any time. This view conflicts with the more generally accepted *entity* view of the firm, as a collection of individuals or groups (participants) whose collective participation is essential for the continued existence of the organisation. This view was described in Chapter 1.

Additional arguments have been advanced against the use of realisable values. As with replacement costs, they may involve additional preparation costs. A further difficulty lies in the treatment of highly specialised assets, for example oil rigs and specialised manufacturing plant. Such assets may cost many millions of pounds but, because of their highly specialised nature, may have very low realisable values almost immediately after acquisition. Realisable value accounting may therefore result in the whole cost of an asset being written-off early in its life. Whether or not this is a desirable consequence depends on the uses of the information. It is a very conservative treatment, resulting in extremely low income figures during the first year or so of an asset's life, and relatively high income figures (via low or non-existent depreciation charges) thereafter. In some respects, a realisable value income statement would approximate a statement of past cash flows. Again, this suggests that realisable values do not provide a sound basis for forecasting an organisation's likely future performance. Indeed the case for using realisable values is rarely, if ever, argued in terms of their predictive value. This final criticism may be the most pertinent. If, as we have argued, predictive value is a crucial attribute of any reporting method, the fact that little (successful) attempt has been made to show that realisable value numbers possess this attribute suggests that they may not represent a useful basis of asset valuation.

(iii) *Value to the firm*. Value to the firm (or 'deprival value') has its roots in economics, and is related closely to the concept of opportunity cost. It is the current cost asset valuation method recommended by the UK professional accountancy bodies.[5] The means of determining the value to the firm of an asset is depicted in Figure 17.1, and illustrated in Table 17.1.

The term 'deprival value' provides a clue as to the rationale behind this

---

[5]See Statement of Standard Accounting Practice No. 16 *Current Cost Accounting*, The Institute of Chartered Accountants in England and Wales, March 1980, particularly paragraphs 42 and 43.

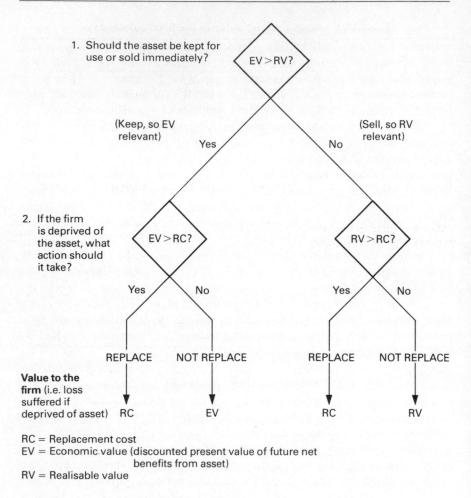

1. Should the asset be kept for use or sold immediately?

EV > RV?

(Keep, so EV relevant)   Yes

No   (Sell, so RV relevant)

2. If the firm is deprived of the asset, what action should it take?

EV > RC?

RV > RC?

Yes   No

Yes   No

REPLACE   NOT REPLACE   REPLACE   NOT REPLACE

Value to the firm (i.e. loss suffered if deprived of asset)   RC   EV   RC   RV

RC = Replacement cost
EV = Economic value (discounted present value of future net benefits from asset)
RV = Realisable value

Figure 17.1   The determination of the 'value to the firm' of an asset it owns.

method of asset valuation. In essence the method asks the following question. 'What would be the cost incurred by the firm if it was deprived of a particular asset?' Would management replace it with another, similar asset (in which case the cost to the firm would be the replacement cost)? Or would management decide the asset was not worth replacing (in which case the cost to the firm would be the revenue foregone from being unable to sell the asset or to use it in the business)? Thus the deprival value, or value to the firm, depends upon the relationship between the replacement cost, realisable value and economic value (discounted present value) of an asset.

We should begin our analysis of the concept of 'value to the firm' by asking two questions. First, should the asset be kept for use or sold immediately? The answer depends on the relationship between economic value and

Table 17.1   Illustration of 'value to the firm' calculations

	Asset A £	Asset B £	Asset C £	Asset D £
Replacement cost	200,000	180,000	18,000	63,000
Realisable value	100,000	15,000	30,000	6,000
Economic value	250,000	60,000	500	1,000
Stage 1 Calculate 'value in use' (equal to the *greater* of realisable value and economic value)	250,000	60,000	30,000	6,000
Stage 2 Calculate 'value to the firm' (i.e. the loss the firm suffers if deprived of the asset, given by the *lower* of replacement cost and value in use)	200,000	60,000	18,000	6,000
Value to the firm	Replacement cost	Economic value	Replacement cost	Realisable value

realisable value. If the economic value of the asset is greater than its realisable value it should be kept. If the realisable value is greater than the economic value it should be sold. One would therefore expect most fixed assets to have an economic value greater than their realisable value (otherwise the assets would already have been sold). Most items of stock will, however, have a realisable value higher than their economic value. The higher of these two values is often called the 'value in use'. Hence the value in use for items of stock is generally their realisable value.

Second, we should ask, 'What action should the firm take if it is deprived of the asset?' The answer depends on the relationship between its replacement cost and its value in use. If replacement cost is less than value in use, it is worthwhile replacing the asset, and the sacrifice suffered by the firm as a result of deprival is the replacement cost of the asset. If replacement cost is greater than value in use, it is not worthwhile replacing the asset, and the loss suffered by the firm is the asset's value in use. The rules for determining value to the firm should become clearer if we apply them to particular types of asset. We thus consider each of four asset types illustrated in Figure 17.1 and Table 17.1. The first branch of Figure 17.1 corresponds to Asset A in Table 17.1. These figures could describe a profitable fixed asset. It has an economic value greater than its realisable value, so the organisation would continue to use the asset, and as the replacement cost is lower than the economic value, the organisation would replace the asset in the event of deprival. Replacement cost (£200,000) is thus the relevant value to the firm.

The second branch of Figure 17.1 corresponds to Asset B in Table 17.1. Asset B best describes an old item of plant with little, or no scrap value. The company still finds it worthwhile to operate the machine (rather than sell it) but could not generate sufficient revenue to warrant replacing it. Consequently, if deprived of the asset the company would not replace it and would incur a cost equal to the net revenue foregone (the economic value of £60,000).

The third branch corresponding to Asset C might represent a profitable line of stock. The company itself cannot use the items but their realisable value is high. Clearly the company would wish to continue selling this product and if deprived of its present stock it would replace it. The value to the firm is the replacement cost of £18,000.

Finally, the fourth branch corresponding to Asset D might describe a line of obsolete stock which could be sold only at a heavily discounted price, or an obsolete fixed asset awaiting disposal. The company would aim to sell the asset rather than keep it, but would not replace the asset if deprived of it. The value to the firm is the realisable value of £6,000.

The examples and analysis above result in the following concise definition of value to the firm: *the lower of replacement cost and value in use, where value in use is the higher of realisable value and economic value.*

The main argument for 'value to the firm' as the appropriate basis of valuation is that the value to a firm of an asset it owns is the difference between the value of the firm with the asset and its value if it was deprived of the asset. The arguments are analogous to those used to determine the relevant cost (opportunity cost) of using particular items of stock or particular machine services. As a measure of the cost of using particular assets, there seems little doubt that value to the firm is useful to *management* in making resource allocation decisions. However, our concern is with the usefulness of asset valuation methods to users *other than* managers and there is no reason to assume that what is useful to managers (who have control over particular resources) is also useful to other users (who generally have not). The usefulness of value to the firm to non-management groups must be argued using other criteria.

Figure 17.1 and Table 17.1 show that for most fixed assets and items of stock, value to the firm is represented by replacement cost. Realisable values and economic values are relevant only where changing technological factors and demand conditions result in the unprofitability of replacement when the asset reaches the end of its useful life. Insofar as replacement cost is the appropriate measure, the arguments we outlined earlier for and against its use also apply here. Arguments for and against the use of economic value were discussed fully in Chapter 13. For both replacement cost and economic value we have presented *a priori* arguments in their favour on grounds of their predictive value. It seems likely that asset values based on value to the firm, which entails the calculation of both replacement cost and economic value, are also likely to provide information that has predictive value. Indeed, provided that the values *and bases of valuation* of individual assets or groups of assets are reported, it may be that value to the firm has more predictive value than replacement cost alone, as it does not involve reporting the replacement cost of assets that will not be replaced.

If individual values and bases of valuation are not disclosed for individual assets or groups of assets, value to the firm may be less useful. Thus users attempting to interpret such figures will be faced with values for a variety of assets, and will not know which are replacement costs, which are economic values, which (possibly) are realisable values and which are a mixture of the three. If, as is likely, prediction models require different treatments for different valuation bases, users will be unable to make full use of the information in the report.

A major disadvantage of value to the firm as a method of asset valuation is that of cost. In particular, the need to calculate the economic values of *all* assets (in order to determine the value in use) imposes a substantial cost on preparers.

17.5   Conclusions

Having discussed possible criteria to evaluate alternative accounting methods and having applied those criteria to the various capital maintenance concepts and asset valuation/cost determination methods, we may now make some tentative observations. Remember that we categorised criteria under the three main headings of *usefulness, feasibility* and *cost*. First we suggest that the choice of a capital maintenance concept is not of great importance. Different concepts involve little more than either the alternative positioning of holding gains, or the inclusion of general price change information that is already available from other sources. These concepts are not concerned with more fundamental problems of disclosure. No one capital maintenance concept seems to provide more information to users than any other.

The same is not true of alternative asset valuation methods. Fundamental differences exist between methods based on historical costs and those based on current costs. Our *a priori* analysis suggested that current-cost-based methods are likely to be more useful to external users than those based on historical costs. In particular, the role of current cost methods as inputs to prediction models (their predictive value and control properties) seems to be more obvious. In addition, the measurement of current costs seems, in most cases, to be no less feasible than the measurement of historical costs when the latter involve subjective allocations (for depreciation, cost of stock used and so on). Though current cost systems are more costly to operate, we would argue that, on balance, the additional cost is more than justified by their extra usefulness.

The choice between alternative current cost systems is more difficult. Our analysis suggested that there is little to choose between them on grounds of either feasibility or cost. However, replacement cost methods seem to be superior in terms of their usefulnes. The *a priori* arguments in favour of the predictive value and control properties are much stronger than those for realisable value systems; primarily because replacement cost measures focus on the long-term prospects of an organisation, whereas realisable value measures place heavy emphasis on the short term. In order to provide maximum information, it may be that *both* replacement cost and realisable value measures should be reported. The use of deprival values as estimates of current costs, involving measures based on a mixture of replacement costs, realisable values and economic values, may increase the usefulness of a system based only on replacement costs or realisable values. On the other hand, the determination of deprival values requires the calculation of three separate values for each asset and thus is likely to be more costly than the consistent use of only one valuation method.

The arguments discussed in this chapter suggest that either replacement costs or deprival values are better bases for accounting systems than are other methods. However, as we have pointed out, these arguments are predominantly *a priori* (they are based on our opinions)—final judgment on the choice of accounting method must await extensive empirical testing of hypotheses concerning the usefulness, feasibility and cost of alternatives. Such testing is possible now that the accountancy professions of a number of Western countries have recommended at least some organisations to report both historical cost and current cost numbers for a significant period of time.

We should point out that there is evidence to suggest that our preference for current-cost-based systems is not universally shared. For example, the vehemence of the recent debate as to the continuation of the applicability of SSAP 16, which requires the disclosure of detailed current cost information by large organisations, suggests that many practising accountants, both in industry and within the profession, disagree strongly with the need for companies to produce current cost information. It may well be that the bases of their arguments are somewhat different from those put forward in this and earlier chapters, i.e. they may not regard predictive value and control information as paramount. Indeed, a frequently advanced argument against current cost accounting, which we find a little difficult to accept, is that the cost of producing such information is prohibitive, and in many cases is greater than the attendant benefits.

In Chapter 2 we argued that most users of financial statements require the following information for at least some of their decisions:

(a)   a statement of forecasts of the organisation's expected future cash flows; and

(b)   a statement of the organisation's actual cash flows together with an explanation of the differences between the forecast and the actual cash flows.

We concluded that it was unlikely that forecasts of future cash flows would be published in the foreseeable future and that a statement of income was preferred to a statement of actual cash flows as a means of reporting past performance. In consequence, much of this book has been concerned with describing, explaining and analysing various methods of income, or accrual, accounting. We have described in detail a number of transactions-based methods of accrual accounting. Each has been evaluated according to a wide range of criteria, although our primary concern has been to identify that method which best satisfies the users' needs for predictive value and control information.

Our choice of reporting methods for evaluation has clearly been restricted. By eliminating forecast-based approaches as being infeasible, we have considered only transactions-based approaches. By accepting the traditional preference for accrual accounting over cash flow accounting we have considered only those methods which can be expressed in the traditional framework of an income statement and balance sheet. Our objective has been to ascertain whether any transactions-based method of accrual accounting could satisfy the more important information requirements of financial statement users. We have discovered that no one method of accounting can provide all the information required by all users. Hence, whichever method is adopted, there will be a need for *additional* information to be provided outside the restrictive framework of the income statement and balance sheet. In Chapter 18 we consider one such additional source of information, the funds flow statement.

Discussion Topics

1   'The "opportunity values" (or "deprival values") of assets are clearly relevant to managers who have to make decisions about the utilisation of the assets. But why should they be of any interest to those, like employees and investors, who generally have no control over the uses to which individual assets are put?' Explain and discuss.

2   Outline the main characteristics of efficient capital markets research, and discuss the usefulness and limitations of such research as a means of choosing between accounting methods.

3   Describe the methods available for determining empirically the information needs of the users of accounts, and discuss the problems associated with each method.

4   Discuss the view that conflicts between and within groups of users of accounting statements cannot be resolved analytically and that, in consequence, it is impossible to define optimal accounting procedures.

5 Describe and evaluate the main arguments advanced for and against the use of each of the following methods of asset valuation in accounting reports:
   (a)   Replacement cost
   (b)   Realisable value
   (c)   Historical cost
   (d)   Value to the firm.

6 "The point at issue, of course, is not *whether* to value by current entry or exit prices, but *when* to shift from entry to exit values." (E.O. Edwards, 1975.) (Note that entry and exit prices mean replacement costs and realisable values respectively.) Explain and discuss this statement, and consider the *relative* merits of replacement cost and realisable values as means of attributing current values to assets and costs in accounts.

7 Explain and illustrate what you understand by 'user decision orientated' approaches to the choice of accounting method.

8 Discuss the view that 'the correct measurement of income is the *only* important feature of external accounting reports'.

9 Discuss whether historical cost accounting measures are more objective than those based on the use of current values.

10 Explain and illustrate how to calculate the 'value to the firm' of an asset it owns.

Further Reading

Arnold, J., 'Capital market efficiency and financial reporting', in Carsberg, B.V. and Dev, S. (eds), *External Financial Reporting,* Prentice-Hall International, 1984.

Baxter, W.T., *Inflation Accounting,* Philip Allan, 1984, Chapter 12.

Beaver, W.H., *Financial Reporting: An Accounting Revolution,* Prentice-Hall International, 1981.

Carsberg, B., Arnold, J. and Hope, A. 'Predictive value: a criterion for choice of accounting method', in Baxter, W.T. and Davidson, S. (eds), *Studies in Accounting,* Institute of Chartered Accountants in England and Wales, 1977.

Chambers, R.J., *Accounting, Evaluation and Economic Behaviour,* Prentice-Hall International, 1966.

Cowan, T.K., 'Accounting in the real world', *Accounting and Business Research,* Autumn 1983.

Drake, D., and Dopuch, N., 'On the case for dichotomizing income', *Journal of Accounting Research,* Autumn 1965.

Edey, H.C., 'CCA and HCA; fact and fantasy', *Accountancy,* August 1982.

Inflation Accounting Committee, *Report of the Inflation Accounting Committee,* Cmnd. 6225, HMSO, 1975.

Lee, T.A., 'Reporting cash flows and net realisable values', *Accounting and Business Research,* Spring 1981.

Parker, R.H. and Harcourt, G.C. (eds), *Readings in the Concept and Measurement of Income,* Cambridge University Press, 1969, Section II.

Penman, S.H., 'What is net asset value?—an extension of a familiar debate', *The Accounting Review,* April 1970.

Revsine, L. *Replacement Cost Accounting,* Prentice-Hall International, 1973.

Sterling, R.R. (ed), *Asset Valuation and Income Determination—A Consideration of Alternatives,* Scholars Book Co., 1971.

Tweedie, D., 'Breaking free of the CCA impasse', *Accountancy,* October 1984.

Westwick, C.A., 'The lessons to be learned from the development of inflation accounting in the UK', *Accounting and Business Research,* Autumn 1980.

Whittington, G., *Inflation Accounting: An Introduction to the Debate,* Cambridge University Press, 1983, Chapter 6.

Woodham, J., 'A proposal for reform', *Accounting and Business Research,* Summer 1984.

Exercises

17.1 You are the auditor of two manufacturing companies, Musetta Ltd and Mimi Ltd, both of which were incorporated on 1 January 19X8. Each company issued 300,000 shares of 25p each on that date. During the year to 31 December 19X8 both companies undertook the *same* basic economic events and in January 19X9 they each present you with their draft accounts for auditing.

The first thing you notice is that the profit and loss accounts and the balance sheets are not at all similar, and a telephone conversation with the accountants at the two companies reveals that the accountant at Musetta was under instruction to produce accounts which would impress the shareholders with the company's first year of trading, whilst the accountant at Mimi was instructed to avoid giving the employees any ammunition for their impending wage claim.

The economic events for 19X8 for both companies were as follows:

1. Both companies bought raw materials on credit during the year as follows:

1 January	50,000 units	at 25p each
1 March	40,000 units	at 40p each
1 April	40,000 units	at 50p each

    Each unit of sales consumed one unit of raw material. At the end of the year, Musetta and Mimi each owed £25,000 for materials.
2. Production began on 1 May, and sales amounted to 100,000 units at £1 each. By 31 December, the companies had each received £75,000.
3. Plant was bought for £60,000 at the start of the year by both companies. From your experience of other companies, you ascertain that the plant will last between 5 and 10 years, and that the scrap value can vary from zero to £6,000.
4. For both companies, productive wages were £13,000; indirect costs (factory power, light, heat, etc.) £7,800, and administrative salaries £17,200.

5. Both companies incurred general overheads of £15,000 during the year, of which £10,000 was spent on the development of a revised product to be marketed in 19X9, and £2,000 was spent on an advertising campaign to be run over the next three years.

- (a) Reproduce the profit and loss accounts for both companies for the year ended 31 December 19X8, and the balance sheets as at that date, bearing in mind that both accountants were aware of the basic accounting conventions.
  (b) Calculate the following ratios: asset utilisation, profitability and return on capital employed. Are the differences material?
  (c) Does it matter that companies have considerable discretion over the methods they can use for preparing accounts? Would it be 'better' if all companies used the same methods?

17.2 Your client, Mr Colline, is considering purchasing the consultancy practice of Mr Benoit. Mr Benoit's latest balance sheet is as follows:

Balance sheet at 31 October 19X7

Capital account		£	Fixed assets		£
Balance at 1 November			Freehold premises,		
19X6		31,000	at cost		25,000
add: Net profit for			Office equiment,		
the year		8,600	at cost	3,200	
		———	less: Depreciation	800	2,400
		39,600			———
less: Drawings		9,500	Motor vehicle,		
		———	at cost	3,800	
		30,100	less: Depreciation	1,900	1,900
					———
					29,300
Current liabilities			Current assets		
Accrued expenses	400		Debtors		3,800
Bank overdraft	2,600	3,000			
	———	———			———
		33,100			33,100
		———			———

Mr Colline estimates that the current values of Mr Benoit's fixed assets are:

	Replacement cost £	Realisable value £
Freehold premises	40,000	38,000
Office equipment	3,800	1,000
Motor vehicle	2,300	1,500

In addition to the fixed assets, Mr Colline would take over the current assets and liabilities. He believes that £500 of the debtors are irrecoverable.

Mr Benoit's net profits for the past five years (calculated on the conventional historical cost basis) have been as follows:

		£
Year ended 31 October	19X3	7,000
	19X4	7,400
	19X5	8,800
	19X6	8,200
	19X7	8,600

Mr Colline has recently inherited £200,000 which is at present earning an annual rate of interest of 10%. If he buys Mr Benoit's business he will pay for it out of this inheritance. Mr Colline is presently employed at an annual salary of £4,000, and would relinquish his employment in order to run the business.

● Draft a report to. Mr Colline advising him, on the basis of the above information, how much he should offer for Mr Benoit's business. Include in your report a note of any additional information that you think would be useful before a final decision is made.

Chapter 18

Flow of Funds Statements

Most business organisations engage in financing, investment and operating activities in order to generate a profit. So far in this book we have described and analysed two major financial statements which provide information on an organisation's business activities. The balance sheet describes the organisation's financial position at a point in time. In the balance sheet, the results of investment activities are represented by assets and the results of financing activities are represented by liabilities and owners' equity. The income statement describes what happened to the organisation during the period between two balance sheets. However, the income statement reflects only *operating* activities. It focuses upon the matching of revenues and costs. It does not reflect the consequences of the *financing* and *investment* decisions taken between two balance sheet dates. A financing decision might involve an issue of shares, or the taking out of a long-term loan. An investment decision might involve the purchase of fixed assets, or the repayment of a long-term loan.

Thus neither the balance sheet nor the income statement can provide the answers to such important questions as:

- In which new financing and investment activities did the organisation engage during the year?
- How much of the new investment was generated by the organisation's operations and how much was provided by increased borrowing or increased share capital?
- Why did the mix of assets change during the year?
- Where did the organisation raise funds in order to redeem its long-standing debt?

Yet the answers to these questions are essential for an assessment of an organisation's future prospects because the financing and investment decisions taken in one year affect an organisation's liquidity, solvency and profitability for many years in the future.

There is therefore a need for a financial statement which explains the changes between two balance sheets; which discloses where management invested existing funds (i.e. employed the organisation's capital) in order to satisfy the interests of participants; and which discloses the sources from which management obtained additional funds to take advantage of new opportunities and satisfy the unfulfilled needs of the participants. Such a statement exists. The result of these 'financial management' decisions are disclosed in a *flow of funds statement* (also called a *source and application of funds statement* or a *source and uses of funds statement*).

The nature of the accounting process dictates that each application of funds must be offset by one or more sources of funds and that a given source of funds must be offset by one or more applications. For example, the purchase of plant and machinery may be financed by funds provided partly by a reduction in the cash balance and partly by an increase in long-term loan capital. Similarly, funds raised by an issue of share capital may be used to purchase stock, pay off trade creditors and increase the bank balance. This description of the dual nature of the sources and uses of funds should be familiar. We adopted a similar approach to introduce double-entry book-keeping and the accounting equation in Chapter 6. In fact there is a very close relationship between the flow of funds statement and the balance sheet, and in its simplest form the flow of funds statement merely describes the changes in an organisation's assets, liabilities and owner's equity be-tween two balance sheet dates. By showing where management committed available funds (uses), acquired additional funds (sources), reduced existing investments (sources), and reduced outstanding claims against the organisa-tion (uses), the funds flow statement should assist an external user in an evaluation of the effect of financial management decisions taken during the year. As we explained in Chapter 16 when examining ratio analysis, the user must then decide whether these movements are 'normal' (in relation to past movements and comparable industry data) or are 'abnormal' and thus require further analysis.

18.1   The Definition of 'Funds'

There are several ways of defining 'funds'. Most people would probably interpret the term 'funds' to mean 'cash', as in "I can't go to the pub tonight because I'm short of funds". Such an interpretation would produce a flow of funds statement which concentrates upon the movement or flow of cash. This is a valid interpretation and we examine cash flow statements in Section 18.4. However, for most organisations cash flows are part of a wider move-ment of funds.

For example, suppose on 30 December a company held a cash balance of £80,000 and had outstanding debtors of £220,000. Together the two accounts constitute 'liquid assets' of £300,000. If £100,000 was received from various debtors on 31 December, the balances on the two accounts at the year-end would show cash of £180,000 and debtors of £120,000. There has been a significant increase in the cash balance, and a significant decrease in the debtors figure, but *no change* in the total of liquid assets. A similar situation could arise in the case of trade creditors. The balance on the trade creditors' account represents an outflow of cash in the near future. Hence, the liquidity position of a company with a cash balance of £150,000 and trade creditors outstanding of £120,000, would not change significantly if the company paid £80,000 to its suppliers. The new account balances would show cash of £70,000 and trade creditors of £40,000 and the net difference would remain at £30,000. This type of transaction, which has a significant effect upon an organisation's cash position, but not upon its liquidity position, has led many writers and analysts to focus upon a wider definition of funds than is provided by cash alone.

One approach has been to look at the changes in an organisation's working capital (current assets less current liabilities) rather than changes in the cash balance. The working capital cycle, or operating cycle, of a business is the length of time required for a company to transform cash into stock, stock into debtors and debtors into cash again. This cycle is a continuous process and at various stages within the cycle the cash balance will fluctuate as a result of day-to-day operating decisions, although the working capital balance will remain unchanged. If we can imagine 'working capital' as comprising one account, it is clear that a receipt of cash of £100,000 from debtors does not alter the working capital balance and would not therefore be treated as a flow of (working capital) funds. Similarly, the payment of cash to trade creditors, and the purchase of stock for cash or on credit do not represent a flow of funds into or out of working capital, but rather a rearrangement of the balances within working capital.

The choice of a cash-based or a working-capital-based funds statement depends upon the potential use of the information. From the broad perspective of appraising *financial management* decisions, as distinct from *operating* decisions, participants may be more interested in identifying whether more or fewer funds have been tied up in working capital as a whole, than whether they have been shifted between the individual components of working capital. If, however, participants are interested specifically in the liquidity position of the organisation they may be very interested to learn that the cash balance has been maintained only by slowing down the payment of cash to creditors, or that the overdraft has risen significantly because of an increased investment in stock. In the following sections we shall consider the preparation and interpretation of both cash-based and working-capital-based funds flow statements.

18.2   Sources and Uses of (Working Capital) Funds

We noted previously the close relationship which exists between the balance sheet and the flow of funds statement. The balance sheet depicts the sources and uses of funds at a point in time, and the flow of funds statement depicts the sources and uses of funds over a period of time, i.e. between two balance sheet dates. Let us explore this relationship further in order to identify the major sources and uses of (working capital) funds.

The basic expanded accounting equation is expressed as:

$$FA + CA = CL + LTL + OI + NI \qquad (18.1)$$

where FA is fixed assets, CA current assets, CL current liabilities, LTL long-term liabilities, OI ownership interest, and NI net income (revenue − expenses). We can rearrange this expression to focus upon the working capital position:

$$CA - CL = LTL + OI + NI - FA \qquad (18.2)$$

Using the symbol Δ to mean 'change in' we can see that any *changes* in working capital must be balanced by one or more changes in the accounts on the right-hand side of the equation:

$$\Delta(CA - CL) = \Delta LTL + \Delta OI + \Delta NI - \Delta FA \qquad (18.3)$$

No matter how complex a company's flow of funds statement might appear, or how many items appear on the statement, expression 18.3 shows that there are only four basic sources, and four basic uses, of funds which can explain a change in working capital. Thus, an *increase* in working capital (strictly an increase in the investment of funds in working capital), must be financed from one or more of the four sources of funds represented on the right-hand side of expression 18.3, i.e. an *increase* in long-term liabilities (e.g. new borrowing), an *increase* in ownership interest (e.g. a new share issue), an *increase* in net income (e.g. income from operations), and/or a *decrease* in fixed assets (e.g. the disposal of plant).

Conversely, a *decrease* in working capital represents fewer funds invested in working capital, and means that funds are available for use elsewhere. Again this will be reflected in the accounts on the right-hand side

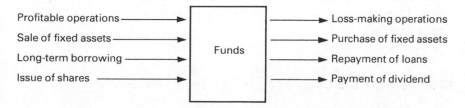

Sources of working capital funds   **Uses of working capital funds**

Profitable operations ⟶ | Funds | ⟶ Loss-making operations
Sale of fixed assets ⟶   ⟶ Purchase of fixed assets
Long-term borrowing ⟶   ⟶ Repayment of loans
Issue of shares ⟶   ⟶ Payment of dividend

Figure 18.1   Common sources and uses of working capital funds.

of expression 18.3, i.e. as a *decrease* in long-term liabilities (e.g. repayment of a loan), a *decrease* in ownership interest (e.g. payment of a dividend), a *decrease* in net income (e.g. a loss), and/or an *increase* in fixed assets (e.g. purchase of machinery). The common sources and uses of working capital funds are summarised in Figure 18.1.

   The above analysis of the sources and applications of funds provides a useful starting point for the preparation of flow of funds statements, to which we now turn.

18.3   Illustration of the Preparation of Flow of Funds Statements

The balance sheets of Wembley Ltd, at 31 December 19X0 and 31 December 19X1, together with its summarised income statement for the year to 31 December 19X1, are shown in Table 18.1. No fixed assets were sold during 19X1 (i.e. the increase in the cost of fixed assets represents the purchase of new assets). The directors of Wembley Ltd have expressed their concern over two matters. First, although they are aware that the company has expanded significantly during 19X1, it is not clear how this ex-

Table 18.1   Wembley Ltd—Balance sheet and income statement

Balance sheet as at 31 December	19X0 £'000	19X0 £'000	19X1 £'000	19X1 £'000
Fixed assets at cost	195		310	
less: Accumulated depreciation	70	125	95	215
Current assets: Stock	40		70	
Debtors	25		30	
Cash	30		20	
	95		120	
less: Current liabilities	60		80	
		35		40
		160		255
Issued share capital		100		120
Reserves (retained profit)		60		135
		160		255

Income statement 19X1	£'000
Net profit before depreciation	100
less: Depreciation for the year	25
Net profit, added to reserves	75

pansion has been financed, and in particular whether the funds raised are available on a long term basis. Secondly, they cannot understand why the company's cash balance has fallen by £10,000 during 19X1 despite the retention of profits of £75,000 for that year. A flow of funds statements should help to explain the situation.

A flow of funds statement describes the changes in assets, liabilities and owners' equity (uses and sources of funds) between two balance sheet dates. A very crude statement could therefore be prepared by simply recording the change in balance sheet figures. Details are given in Table 18.2. Even from this crude statement we can identify which account balances have changed most significantly and therefore which have provided or used more funds.

Table 18.2   Wembley Ltd—Changes in financial position, 19X1

| | Balance at end of: | | Changes in balance |
	19X0 £'000	19X1 £'000	during 19X1 £'000
Fixed assets, at cost	195	310	$+\Delta 115$
Accumulated depreciation	(70)	(95)	$+\Delta (25)$
	125	215	$+\Delta\ 90$
Stock	40	70	$+\Delta\ 30$
Debtors	25	30	$+\Delta\ \ 5$
Cash	30	20	$-\Delta\ 10$
Current liabilities	(60)	(80)	$+\Delta (20)$
	160	255	$+\Delta\ 95$
Issued share capital	100	120	$+\Delta\ 20$
Reserves	60	135	$+\Delta\ 75$
	160	255	$+\Delta\ 95$

(For example, Wembly Ltd has generated funds by earning a profit—from its regular operations—and has invested a considerable sum in fixed assets.) However, a more informative presentation would *explain* the changes which have occurred. In this and the following section we shall prepare statements which explain the changes in Wembley's working capital, and cash, balances.

Expression 18.3, reproduced below, indicates the format for a flow of funds statement which focuses on the change in working capital:

$$\Delta(CA-CL)=\Delta LTL+\Delta OI+\Delta NI-\Delta FA \qquad (18.3)$$

This implies that the flow of funds statement should first indicate the amount of the change in working capital, and secondly *explain* the reason for that change by identifying changes in the sources and uses of funds elsewhere.

The calculation of the change in the working capital of Wembley Ltd is straightforward, and is illustrated below:

	31 December	*19X0* £'000	*19X1* £'000	*Change* £'000
Stock		40	70	+30
Debtors		25	30	+ 5
Cash		30	20	−10
		95	120	+25
Current liabilities		(60)	(80)	(+20)
Working capital		35	40	+ 5

Working capital has increased by £5,000 during 19X1, i.e. an additional £5,000 has been invested in the working capital of the business. The second stage of the statement should explain from where those additional funds were raised.

Let us examine the nature of the transactions which gave rise to Wembley's financial position at the end of 19X1. Table 18.3 presents the accounting records of Wembley Ltd for 19X1. The transactions are self-explanatory. Now, suppose that the 'working capital' accounts (stock, debtors, cash and current liabilities) are aggregated into one working capital account. This is indicated by those accounts falling within the broken lines in Table 18.3. The balance on this aggregate account increases by £5,000 over the year, i.e. closing working capital balance of £40,000 (70,000+30,000+20,000−80,000) less the opening balance of £35,000 (40,000+25,000+30,000−60,000). Our aim is to explain how an additional £5,000 was raised to invest in working capital.

Clearly, transactions that involve *only* working capital accounts cannot explain the increase, as they have no effect on the aggregate working capital figure. For example, transactions (1), (2) and (5) alter the balances on individual working capital accounts but leave the aggregate working capital figure unchanged. Similarly, transactions which do not involve *any* working capital accounts cannot explain the increase because they also have no effect on the aggregate working capital figure. For example, transaction (8), the depreciation of fixed assets, affects only the fixed asset (accumulated depreciation) account and the income statement.

The only type of transaction which can explain a change in working capital is therefore one which involves *both* working capital *and* non-working capital accounts. In Table 18.3 this type of transaction is illustrated by transactions (3), (4), (6) and (7), and these four transactions explain the increase in working capital during 19X1:

Table 18.3   Wembley Ltd—Accounting equation entries, year to 31 December 19X1

	Fixed assets £'000	+	Stock £'000	+	Debtors £'000	+	Cash £'000	=	Current liabilities £'000	+	Share capital £'000	+	Income £'000
Balances brought forward	125		40		25		30		60		100		60
Transactions:													
1. Purchase of stock on credit			330						330				
2. Cash payment to suppliers							(310)		(310)				
3.} Sale of stock on credit			(300)										(300)
4.					400								400
5. Cash receipts from customers					(395)		395						
6. Issue of shares							20				20		
7. Purchase of fixed assets	115						(115)						
8. Depreciation	(25)												(25)
Balances at end of 19X1	215		70		30		20		80		120		135

Working capital accounts (spanning Stock, Debtors, Cash, Current liabilities)

£'000

Sources of funds:
(3) and (4) Generated from operations   100
(6) Issue of shares   20

                                               120

Uses of funds:
(7) Purchase of fixed assets   115

Surplus=increase in working capital   5

It is clear from this analysis that the depreciation charge is excluded from the flow of funds statement. As we explained in Chapter 9, depreciation is merely a book-keeping entry which allocates the cost of an asset over its useful life—it has no effect upon working capital; it does not represent a movement of funds. The movement of funds in relation to fixed assets is represented by the amount spent on purchasing (and received on selling) fixed assets during the year. Therefore, the amount of funds generated from operations is calculated by deducting from sales revenue only those costs which affect working capital, e.g. cost of goods sold (which affects stock), wages (cash), interest (cash or current liabilities), etc. This calculation is straightforward in the case of Wembley Ltd, because it incurred only one 'working capital' cost during the year. The funds generated from operations amount to £100,000, i.e. sales £400,000 less cost of goods sold £300,000.

However, most organisations incur many more costs which affect working capital, and the amount of funds generated from operations can be calculated more simply by taking the net profit figure and *adding back* those (relatively few) expenses which do *not* affect working capital, i.e. do not involve a movement of funds. For Wembley Ltd, therefore, the funds generated from operations can be calculated as follows:

                                               £'000
Net profit per income statement   75
Add back items not involving a movement of funds:
   depreciation   25

Funds generated from operations   100

This form of presentation has occasionally misled users into believing that depreciation is a source of funds, because it is added to net profit. We have already addressed this issue, somewhat briefly, in Chapter 9 (page 149). We hope that the explanation above has avoided this confusion. The depreciation charge is a book entry which does not involve any movement of funds. Charging more or less depreciation has no effect whatsoever on the funds generated from operations. For example, if the depreciation charge in 19X1 for Wembley Ltd was £40,000, the net profit would fall to £60,000 (i.e. £100,000 – £40,000) and in the flow of funds statement, *the funds generated from operations would remain unchanged at* £100,000. Because the depreciation charge has been *deducted* to calculate net profit it must be *added back* to calculate the working capital funds generated from operations.

The final presentation of Wembley Ltd's flow of funds statement for 19X1, prepared on a working capital basis, is illustrated in Table 18.4. Many companies prepare their funds flow statements on a working capital basis. The funds flow statement (here called a Source and Application of Funds Statement) of Boddington's Breweries plc for the year to 31 December 1983, reproduced in Table 18.5, provides a good example of this treatment.

Table 18.4   Wembley Ltd—Flow of funds statement to explain change in working capital, 19X1

	£'000
Source of funds	
Net profit for the year	75
add back: Items not involving the movement of funds:	
depreciation	25
Funds generated from operations	100
New shares issued	20
	120
Use of funds	
Purchase of fixed assets	115
Increase in working capital	5
Analysis of change in working capital	
Increase in stocks	30
Increase in debtors	5
Decrease in cash	(10)
	25
Increase in current liabilities	20
Increase in working capital	5

The flow of funds statements described so far in this chapter have analysed the change in a company's working capital (rather than its cash balance) over an accounting period. Such statements direct the attention of the reader towards an assessment of the broader financial management decisions taken by the organisation. For example, it is clear from Table 18.1 that Wembley Ltd has expanded significantly in 19X1—net assets increased from £160,000 to £255,000 over the year. The flow of funds statement in Table 18.4 explains where the expansion occurred and how it was financed.

**Table 18.5   Boddingtons' Breweries plc and subsidiary company—
Group source and application of funds, year ended 31 December 1983**

	1983		*1982*	
	£'000	£'000	£'000	£'000
Source of funds				
Profit on ordinary activities before taxation		9,095		8,609
Adjustment for items not involving the movement of funds: depreciation		850		786
Funds generated from operations		9,945		9,395
Other sources				
Proceeds from sale of investments	–		1,528	
Proceeds from sale of properties	130		165	
Proceeds from sale of plant and equipment	51		80	
Shares and loan stock issued in consideration of acquisition of subsidiary	–		23,652	
Loan stock of subsidiary	–		120	
		181		25,545
		10,126		34,940
Application of funds				
Purchase of tangible assets	6,287		15,069	
Purchase of investments	–		1,552	
Taxation paid	3,894		1,656	
Dividends paid	1,847		1,624	
Trade loans less repayments	252		1,134	
Debentures redeemed	1		24	
Premium on acquisition of subsidiary	–		8,721	
Expenses of share and loan stock issue	–		671	
		12,281		30,451
(Decrease)/increase in working capital		(2,155)		4,489
Applied to/(derived from)				
Stocks	370		1,054	
Debtors	672		2,053	
Leasing	1,355		–	
Creditors	(325)		(1,691)	
		2,072		1,416
Net liquid funds				
Certificates of tax deposit	–		719	
Bank loan	(700)		–	
Cash at bank and in hand	(3,527)		2,354	
		(4,227)		3,073
		(2,155)		4,489

Most of the increase in Wembley's net assets is the result of a major investment in fixed assets, financed primarily out of funds generated from operations. The increase in working capital is very small. The directors of Wembley might wish to consider the wisdom of financing most of the company's capital expenditure with funds generated from operations (and of financing all of the capital expenditure with funds provided by share-holders). They might consider also why the increase in working capital is so small. We can see from Table 18.4 that stock and debtors required an additional investment of £35,000 in year 2, but that £30,000 of this amount was financed by reducing the cash balance (£10,000) and increasing the amount of current liabilities outstanding (£20,000), i.e. the individual com-ponents of working capital have been managed so that few additional working capital funds are required.

It would still not be clear to the directors whether the increases in the stock, debtors and creditors figures reflect an increase in the volume of goods sold, or whether they signal difficulties in moving stock (e g old product lines), collecting debts (e.g. low credit rating of customers) and paying creditors (e.g. a shortage of cash). Such information might be obtained from the use of selective ratios such as the stockholding period, debtors' collection period and creditors' payment period discussed in Chapter 16.

This use of a flow of funds statement to analyse the (detailed) liquidity position of an organisation has led an increasing number of companies to publish a cash-based, rather than a working capital-based, flow of funds statement. We examine cash-based flow of funds statements in the following section.

18.4   Sources and Uses of (Cash) Funds

The conversion of a working capital-based flow of funds statement (Table 18.4) into a cash-based statement is simple. Rearranging the basic account-ing equation (expression 18.1) we can express cash in terms of all other accounts, i.e. if:

$$\text{Cash} + (\text{Other CA} - \text{CL}) = \text{LTL} + \text{OI} + \text{NI} - \text{FA} \tag{18.4}$$

then:

$$\text{Cash} = (\text{CL} - \text{Other CA}) + \text{LTL} + \text{OI} + \text{NI} - \text{FA} \tag{18.5}$$

and movements in the non-cash components of working capital (CL – Other CA) now represent a source or a use of cash. For example, an increase in the stock and debtors figures implies that additional cash has been tied up in these assets and therefore represents a use of cash. An increase in current liabilities implies a delay in the payment of cash to short-term creditors and represents a source of cash to the company.

With regard to the presentation of a cash-based flow of funds statement, expression 18.5 indicates that the first stage will present the change in the cash balance only and that the non-cash components of working capital will be transferred into the main body of the statement. An increase in non-cash working capital will represent a use of funds, and a decrease will represent a source of funds. Table 18.6 presents a cash-based flow of funds statement for Wembley Ltd for 19X1. The change in the cash balance over the year is presented at the bottom of the statement. The additional cash invested in stock and debtors over the year is £35,000, of which £20,000 has been financed by increasing current liabilities. The balance of £15,000 represents a net increase in non-cash working capital and hence a use of cash funds. All other entries in the cash-based statements are identical to those in the working capital-based statement presented in Table 18.4.

Table 18.6   Wembley Ltd—Flow of funds statement to explain change in cash balance, 19X1

		£'000
Source of funds		
Net profit for the year		75
Adjustment for items not involving the movement of funds:		
depreciation		25
Funds generated from operations		100
Net shares issued		20
		120
Use of funds		
Purchase of fixed assets		115
Change in working capital:		
Increase in stock	30	
Increase in debtors	5	
Increase in current liabilities	(20)	
		15
		130
Decrease in cash		(10)
Analysis of change in cash balance(s)		
Decrease in cash balance		(10)

An example of a cash-based flow of funds statement is illustrated in Table 18.7. The John Lewis Partnership plc owns almost one hundred department stores and supermarkets. From the bottom of the statement we can see that in the year to 28 January 1984 the company increased its cash balances by £5,504,000 and reduced its bank overdraft by £4,002,000—a

Table 18.7   John Lewis Partnership plc—Statement of source and use of funds for the year ended 28 January 1984

	Years ended January				
	1980 £'000	*1981* £'000	*1982* £'000	*1983* £'000	*1984* **£'000**
Source of funds					
Arising from trading:					
Profit before Partnership bonus and taxation	35,507	33,975	35,757	38,832	**58,827**
Adjustment for items not involving a movement of funds:					
Depreciation	6,669	8,436	10,600	12,405	**12,851**
Profit on sale of fixed assets	(280)	(1,937)	(3,610)	(638)	**(1,051)**
	41,896	40,474	42,747	50,599	**70,627**
Funds from other sources:					
Proceeds from sale of fixed assets	1,764	4,186	8,600	2,268	**3,688**
Bank loans	2,992	3,000	1,000	3,000	**–**
Total inflow	46,652	47,660	52,347	55,867	**74,315**
Use of funds					
Additions to land and buildings	17,116	19,135	18,470	13,016	**17,708**
Additions to fixtures and fittings	11,963	10,974	12,982	13,624	**18,108**
Acquisition of subsidiary*	–	–	–	953	**6,540**
Repayment of bank loans and debentures	745	308	502	261	**10,883**
Corporation tax paid	2,533	368	2,377	(707)	**4,737**
Dividends paid	405	393	362	367	**367**
Partnership bonus	13,880	14,679	12,641	15,715	**17,023**
	46,642	45,857	47,334	43,229	**75,366**
Increase/(decrease) in working capital					
Stocks	10,235	4,229	9,617	2,395	**7,108**
Debtors	11,185	5,186	3,248	7,903	**8,703**
Creditors	(11,701)	(5,705)	3,584	(6,051)	**(26,368)**
Total outflow	56,361	49,567	63,783	47,476	**64,809**
Net inflow/(outflow)	(9,709)	(1,907)	(11,436)	8,391	**9,506**
Increase/(decrease) in cash	(9,709)	(1,907)	(1,598)	139	**5,504**
(Increase)/decrease in bank overdraft	–	–	(9,838)	8,252	**4,002**

*Net assets of the subsidiary acquired during the year:

	£'000
Land and buildings	4,500
Stocks	1,598
Debtors	1,712
Creditors	(1,295)
Cash	25
	6,540

net cash inflow over the year of £9,506,000. This increase in the net cash balance of £9.5 million is explained as follows. The company raised funds of £74.3 million during the year, of which £70.6 million was generated from operations. Funds totalling £75.4 million were applied in the purchase of fixed assets, the repayment of loans and the payment of tax, dividends and bonuses. This would have resulted in a net cash outflow of £1 million, but the company reduced its investment in working capital by £10.5 million, releasing cash for use elsewhere and contributing to the net cash inflow of £9.5 million.

Although it is standard accounting practice for a flow of funds statement to be included in the financial statements of most large organisations in the UK,[1] there is no standard form of presentation. We have already seen that some companies prepare working capital-based statements (Table 18.5) and others prepare cash-based statements (Table 18.7). There is also a variety of formats within these two broad approaches. For example, Marks and Spencer plc (Table 18.8) presents its flow of funds statement in the form of a ledger account with opening and closing balances which can be reconciled to the balance sheet.

In addition, the definition of 'funds' adopted by Marks and Spencer is somewhere between 'cash funds' and 'working capital funds'. Most large organisations do not hold all their surplus cash in bank accounts. It is sound financial management to invest excess cash in government stocks or perhaps in the shares of publicly quoted companies. These investments are usually called *short-term investments* and are categorised as current assets in the balance sheet. Because they represent a (short-term) alternative to holding cash, many companies which publish a cash-based flow of funds statement analyse the movements in 'cash and short-term investments'.

It should not matter whether an organisation publishes a flow of funds statement prepared on a working capital or a cash basis. The reader wishing to compare the statements of one or more organisations can easily produce one from the other by relocating the non-cash components of working capital. In Table 18.9 we present a summarised flow of funds statement for Boddingtons', John Lewis Partnership and Marks and Spencer in a common cash-based format. This form of statement recognises the role played by working capital in the operating cycle of a business by presenting the change in working capital immediately following the figure for funds generated from operations. In this format the statement should not only enable the reader to identify clearly the investing and financing activities of each company's management over the past year, but also facilitate the reconciliation of the net income with the movement in the cash balance.

For example, both Boddingtons' and Marks and Spencer increased their investment in working capital over the year. This means that less cash

---

[1]Statement of Standard Accounting Practice Number 10, *Statement of Source and Application of Funds,* The Institute of Chartered Accountants in England and Wales, June 1978.

Table 18.8   Marks and Spencer plc and subsidiaries—Consolidated source and application of funds for the year ended 31 March 1984

	1984 £m	1983 £m
Cash and short-term funds at 1 April 1983	**172.1**	151.5
Source of funds		
Arising from trading		
Profit on ordinary activities before taxation	**279.3**	239.3
Depreciation	**39.9**	30.3
Sales of fixed assets	**4.5**	2.1
	323.7	271.7
From other sources		
Shares issued under employees' share schemes	**4.8**	5.0
	500.6	428.2
Application of funds		
Payment of dividends	**69.8**	61.7
Payment of taxation	**71.3**	99.6
Purchase of assets leased to third parties	**76.8**	35.3
Purchase of other fixed assets	**120.4**	110.5
Miscellaneous	**(1.4)**	(1.1)
	336.9	306.0
Increase (decrease) in working capital		
Stock	**30.8**	19.6
Debtors	**(9.5)**	5.9
Creditors over one year	**(1.2)**	(4.5)
Creditors under one year (excluding taxation and dividends):		
Bills of exchange	**9.5**	22.0
Bank loans and overdrafts	**13.6**	(59.7)
Other	**(15.0)**	(33.2)
	28.2	(49.9)
	365.1	256.1
Cash and short-term funds at 31 March 1984	**135.5**	172.1

Cash and short-term funds comprise cash at bank and in hand and current asset investments.

was available for use elsewhere, i.e. the increase in working capital is *deducted* from the funds generated from operations in order to arrive at the figure representing cash generated from operations. Conversely, the management of John Lewis Partnership released cash for use elsewhere by decreasing the amount invested in working capital. Partly as a result of this

**Table 18.9   Common format flow of funds statement
to explain changes in cash balances of three UK companies**

	Boddingtons' £'000	John Lewis Partnership £'000	Marks and Spencer £'000
Sources of funds			
Profit on ordinary activities	9,095	58,827	279,300
Adjustment for items not involving the movement of funds:			
Depreciation	850	12,851	39,900
Other	–	(1,051)	4,500
Funds generated from operations	9,945	70,627	323,700
(Increase)/decrease in working capital	(2,072)	10,557	(28,200)
Cash generated from operations	7,873	81,184	295,500
Other sources:			
Sale of fixed assets	181	3,688	–
Issue of shares	–	–	4,800
Total inflow	8,054	84,872	300,300
Application of funds			
Tax paid	3,894	4,737	71,300
Dividends paid	1,847	367	69,800
Bonus paid	–	17,023	–
Purchase of fixed assets	6,287	42,356	197,200
Repayment of loans, etc.	253	10,883	–
Others	–	–	(1,400)
Total outflow	12,281	75,366	336,900
Net inflow/(outflow)	(4,227)	9,506	(36,600)
Analysis of changes in cash balances			
Increase/(decrease) in cash and short-term funds	(3,527)	5,504	(36,600)
(Increase)/decrease in bank loans and overdrafts	(700)	4,002	–
	(4,227)	9,506	(36,600)

management of working capital, John Lewis Partnership was able to finance its tax and dividend payments and its capital expenditure from cash generated from operations. (It was also able to repay some of its outstanding debt.) The cash generated from the operations of Boddingtons' and Marks and Spencer was more than sufficient to cover the tax and dividend payments but was insufficient to also finance all the capital expenditure. Consequently the cash balances of both companies fell during the year.

18.5   Cash Flows and Net Income

Although it does not matter whether the flow of funds statement is prepared on a working capital or a cash basis, it is important that the statement provides the external user with sufficient disaggregated information to identify and evaluate the results of management's investment and financing decisions. The importance of this disaggregation must be assessed in the context of the evaluation of cash-based and income-based measures of business performance introduced in the earlier chapters. In Chapter 4 we noted that most external users of financial statements would benefit from the publication of a statement of an organisation's actual cash flows, because cash is essential for the survival of an organisation; it is well understood by all external users; it is an objective method of reporting business performance; and it provides useful control information against which to compare previous estimates of performance.

Nonetheless, historical cash flows are thought to be potentially misleading for two reasons. First, the pattern of an organisation's cash surpluses or deficits through time may be erratic—for example, because fixed assets are bought more intensively in some years than in others, even though they may be used on a regular and steady basis. Such erratic cash flow patterns may be misleading to users who wish to make predictions of the organisation's *long-term performance,* particularly if the predictions are based on changes in the organisation's cash resources over only a small number of years. It is sometimes argued that 'smoothed' income figures may give a better indication of an organisation's ability *in the long term* to generate surpluses to pay dividends, settle debts, pay wages, pay taxes and so on. Secondly, cash flows are sometimes criticised for reporting on the *financial activity* of the receipt and payment of cash rather than the *economic activity* of buying and selling goods and services. Together these two criticisms may imply that cash flow statements do not provide a reliable measure of past economic performance, nor a sound basis for predicting future cash flows.

However, flow of funds statements similar to those illustrated in Table 18.9 would appear to go some way to answer these criticisms. First, the various sources and uses of cash are disclosed separately. The cash flows generated from the operations of the company are not distorted by large, irregular capital expenditures. Secondly, operating figures based on accrual accounting (i.e. profit from operations, and funds generated from operations) and operating figures based on cash flows (i.e. cash flows generated from operations) are both disclosed in the statement. This enables users to assess the results of both 'economic' and 'financial' activities during the year.

It may still be the case that a time series of income figures gives a better indication of the organisation's ability in the long term to generate surpluses. However, we observed in Chapter 16 that some organisations may never attain the 'long term' because of liquidity problems in the short or medium term. It might be argued that 'erratic' cash flows provide the users of financial statements with valuable information about the *riskiness* of the organisation's activities. In the *short to medium* term an organisation may report positive income figures and yet have no cash to pay its liabilities as they fall due. There are many reasons why an organisation's cash flows may' be significantly lower than its income figures (e.g. the incurrence of capital expenditure which is continually in excess of the annual depreciation charge; a steady build-up of stock which is not reflected in the cost of goods sold; the recognition of revenues prior to the receipt of cash) all of which should be made clear to external users.

The analysis in this section, in this chapter, and in many previous chapters, suggests that no one method of accounting can evaluate satisfactorily all aspects of an organisation's performance and prospects. At the very least, one must examine an organisation's profitability, liquidity and solvency and this can be achieved only by a careful analysis of the figures provided in the balance sheet, the income statement *and* the flow of funds statement. It is not, and never has been, a question of choosing between accrual accounting and cash flow accounting—both are necessary for an external user to evaluate an organisation's past performance and to estimate its future performance.

Discussion Topics

1 Explain why an examination of an organisation's cash resources may be a crucial part of an evaluation of its performance and prospects.

2 'Cash flow is the life-blood of any organisation. Thus cash flow statements, and not income statements, should be included in financial reports.' Discuss.

3 Outline the main sources and applications of an organisation's funds.

4 Distinguish between operating, financing and investment decisions. Why is it important to understand their nature?

5 Discuss the difference between working capital-based and cash-based definitions of funds. Why is it important to understand the difference? How might such different definitions affect users' decisions?

6 Why is depreciation not a source of funds? Can you think of any other income statement expenses which would be treated in the same way as depreciation when preparing a flow of funds statement?

Further Reading

Egginton, D.A., 'In defence of profit measurement: some limitations of cash flow and value added as performance measures for external reporting', *Accounting and Business Research*, Spring 1984.

Lawson, G.H., 'Cash-flow accounting', *The Accountant,* 28 October and 4 November 1971.

Lee, T.A., 'A case for cash flow reporting', *Journal of Business Finance,* Summer 1972.

Lee, T.A., 'The cash flow accounting alternative for corporate financial reporting', in van Dam, C. (ed.), *Trends in Managerial and Financial Accounting,* Martinus Nijhoff, 1978.

Lee, T.A., 'Cash flow accounting and reporting', in Lee, T.A., (ed.), *Developments in Financial Reporting,* Philip Allan, 1981.

Lee, T.A., 'Cash flow accounting and the allocation problem', *Journal of Business Finance and Accounting,* Autumn 1982.

Lee, T.A., 'Laker Airways—the cash flow truth', *Accountancy,* June 1982.

Mason, J., 'Funds statements—time to end the confusion', *Accountancy,* December 1983.

Exercises

18.1 Biterolf Ltd is a retailing company with numerous stores throughout the UK. It is proposing to open a new store on 1 January 19X6. Initially, the store will be opened for a trial period of six months. Biterolf Ltd will provide any funds required by the new store during the trial period. Biterolf's finance director provides you with the following estimates relating to the new store:

1. Freehold property will be purchased on 1 January 19X6, for £100,000 due when the property is purchased.
2. Fittings and equipment costing £30,000 will be purchased and paid for on 1 January 19X6. They will have an estimated life of 10 years.
3. Sales:

January 19X6	£10,000
February 19X6	£15,000
March 19X6 and subsequent months	£20,000 per month

4. Purchases:

January 19X6	£120,000
February 19X6 and subsequent months	£15,000 per month

5. One half of all sales will be for cash. The remainder will be on credit, and payment for these sales is expected two months after the sale is made.
6. All purchases will be on credit. One month's credit will be taken.
7. Other expenses are expected to amount to £2,500 per month, payable as they are incurred.

- (a) Prepare a cash budget for the new store covering the trial period from 1 January to 30 June 19X6, showing the funds that will be required from Biterolf Ltd month by month.
- (b) On the basis of the estimated figures, advise the directors of Biterolf Ltd whether the new store is likely to be profitable.

18.2 The following are the balance sheets of Kurwenal Manufacturing Ltd as at 31 December 19X6 and 19X7:

	19X6		19X7	
	£	£	£	£
Fixed assets, at cost	28,200		36,900	
less: Accumulated depreciation	9,300		14,400	
		18,900		22,500
Current assets:				
Stock	15,300		17,700	
Debtors	7,500		7,800	
Cash	1,500		300	
	24,300		25,800	
less: Current liabilities	5,700		3,900	
		18,600		21,900
		37,500		44,400
Issued share capital		24,000		24,000
Retained profits		13,500		20,400
		37,500		44,400

Your client, Mr Kurwenal, owns most of the shares in the company. He writes to you as follows: "I always thought I was in business to make profits. Now I am not so sure. In 19X7 I made a profit of £6,900 and did not draw any dividend from the company. Despite this, the company had even less cash at the end of the year than at the beginning. Perhaps I should try to make a loss in 19X8!"

- (a) Draft a reply to Mr Kurwenal, explaining to him in non-technical terms the relationship between profits and changes in cash balances. Include in your reply a statement of source and application of funds for the company for 19X7. (No fixed assets were sold or scrapped during 19X7.)
- (b) Discuss briefly the importance of both profits and changes in cash balances to a business enterprise.

18.3   The balance sheets of Flosshilde Ltd for the past two years are shown overleaf. No property or fittings were sold during the year ended 30 September 19X6. However, some plant was sold on 1 October 19X6 for £8,000. This plant had cost £34,000 and had been written down to £16,000 by the date of sale. The loss on sale of £8,000 had been deducted from profit for the year ended 30 September 19X6. No dividends were paid or proposed for the year to 30 September 19X6.

- (a) Prepare a flow of funds statement for Flosshilde Ltd for the year ended 30 September 19X6.
- (b) Describe briefly the usefulness of such a statement in assessing the performance of Flosshilde Ltd.

Balance sheets at 30 September	19X5		19X6	
	£'000	£'000	£'000	£'000
Fixed assets				
Freehold property at cost		232		232
Plant and machinery at cost	354		420	
less: Depreciation	128		152	
		226		268
Fittings at cost	104		120	
less: Depreciation	34		40	
		70		80
		528		580
Current assets				
Stock	52		108	
Debtors	30		24	
Cash	108		80	
	190		212	
Current liabilities	38		26	
		152		186
		680		766
Capital				
Issued share capital		400		400
Profit and loss account		280		286
14% debentures (irredeemable)		–		80
		680		766

18.4 Marcello Manufacturing Co. Ltd makes a single product for which the demand has now stabilised at a sales level of approximately £500,000 p.a. The business was started on 1 November 19X5 and accounts have been prepared for the first two years by the company's unqualified book-keeper.

Balance Sheets

	31 October 19X6	31 October 19X7
	£	£
Cash	64,500	43,000
Debtors	42,000	69,000
Stock	28,500	37,500
Plant	78,000	132,500
	213,000	282,000
Capital (90,000 shares of £1 each)	90,000	90,000
Retained profits	27,000	34,050
Creditors	66,000	37,500
Reserves:		
Tax	18,000	40,500
General	–	45,000
Depreciation	7,800	19,050
Contingency	4,200	6,900
Dividend	–	9,000
	213,000	282,000

Profit and loss accounts

Year ended	31 October 19X6	31 October 19X7
	£	£
Materials used	108,000	126,000
Factory wages	153,000	157,500
Factory rent and other expenses	69,000	73,500
Depreciation reserve	7,800	11,250
Office expenses	34,500	39,000
Contingency reserve	4,200	2,700
General reserve	–	45,000
Tax reserve	18,000	40,500
Dividend reserve	–	9,000
Net profit for the year	27,000	7,050
Total sales	421,500	511,500

No plant was sold during the year ended 31 October 19X7. No dividend was paid for 19X6. The managing director proposes that a dividend of 10p per share should be paid in respect of the year ended 31 October 19X7 and has instructed that a reserve be established for this in the above accounts. The other directors are concerned about the proposed payment; they argue that the accounts reveal falling profits and a declining cash balance and that in the circumstances no dividend should be paid.

● Prepare a brief report to the directors advising them on the position. If you think it helpful, include in the report a revised presentation of the profit and loss accounts and balance sheets for the two years and a flow of funds statement for the year ended 31 October 19X7.

(*Note*: On inquiry you discover that the 'contingency reserve' is for doubtful debts, and is fully justified by the delays in payment of the debtors in question.)

18.5 Professor Parpignol (ex professor of accounting) had been out of a job for 12 months but he still liked to visit the university campus now and again to relive past triumphs. As he sank his eighth pint of beer in a corner of a local public house, he was approached by a former colleague from the Medical School, Dr Goro. As always happened on these occasions, Dr Goro wanted to discuss his latest financial problem whereas Professor Parpignol wanted advice on his latest squash injury.

At the cost of two extra pints Dr Goro got his way. His problem concerned a company in which he had invested in the hope of receiving regular dividends and a capital growth. He produced the latest set of accounts which he had received that morning. The Chairman's Report stated that the company had recently invested in new capital equipment which would increase profits in the future, but that the consequent cash shortage meant that no dividend could be paid this year. A Statement of Source and Application of Funds was included to explain the position.

Dr Goro was confused. In the Statement depreciation was added back to net profit as a 'source'. "If depreciation is a source of cash then the more capital equipment the company has, the greater is the depreciation figure and so the greater the source of cash. So where *is* the cash? And if there isn't enough cash at present why not depreciate some more?"

Professor Parpignol sent his friend away to replenish the glasses and turned to the Notes to the Accounts. Under the note on fixed assets he saw the following:

	19X1	19X2
	£	£
Plant and equipment	576,000	735,000
less: Accumulated depreciation	315,000	265,000
	261,000	470,000

Glancing through the rest of the accounts he noted that new capital equipment bought during the year had cost £512,000, that old plant had been sold at a loss of £107,000, and that the year's depreciation charge had been £143,000.

When Dr Goro returned, Professor Parpignol passed him a beermat on which he had made a few jottings. These consisted of a reconstruction of the plant and equipment information to show how the figures had been arrived at, and an indication of which figures would appear in the Source and Application of Funds Statement.

Dr Goro was astounded. It all began to make sense now. He turned to thank the Professor—but too late. He was already sliding beneath the table.

- (a) What were the jottings that had so astounded Dr Goro? Reconstruct the year's changes on fixed assets and the Source and Application of Funds entries which Professor Parpignol had produced.
- (b) Is Dr Goro right in his belief that depreciation is a source of cash?
- (c) In a wider context discuss the wisdom of a company policy that leads it to undertake expansionary investments to the exclusion of the current dividend.

18.6 Rodolfo forms a company to start a new business on 1 January 19X4. He plans to provide the necessary capital in the form of a subscription for £1 ordinary shares. The following estimates are made about the first six months' business:

	£
Equipment bought for cash, January	3,000
Stock of goods bought on credit, January	5,500
Sales per month, January to March	2,800
Sales per month, April to June	7,600
Rent per annum, payable quarterly in advance	800
General expenses, per month, cash outlay	350

The estimated gross profit percentage is 25% on sales value
Stock is to be maintained always at £5,500
Creditors will allow one month's credit. Customers are to be allowed two months' credit
An interim dividend of £1,000 is, if profit allows, to be paid at the end of June.

Assume all payments will be made at the end of the month in which they fall due. Depreciation on equipment for the half-year is to be £150.

- (a) Calculate the capital Rodolfo should raise if the maximum financial need in the first six months is to be met, but no more.
- (b) Draft the final accounts for the half-year (profit and loss account and balance sheet), on the assumption that Rodolfo pays in the necessary capital, as calculated in (a), on 1 January.

18.7 Klingsor Clothing Ltd was recently formed by Mr Parsifal to manufacture a new type of waterproof clothing. In its first month of operations, the firm was involved in the following transactions:

May 1   (i)   Parsifal invested £10,000 cash into the business.
          (ii)   Waterproof material was bought on credit for £1,700. This
                 amount was paid to the supplier on 15 June.
          (iii) Two part-time employees were hired to assemble the water-
                 proof clothing. They were each to be paid £200 per month on
                 the last day of the month.
May 2   Cutting and sewing machinery was purchased. Parsifal paid £7,200 in
          cash for this equipment.
May 5   Parsifal signed an agreement with a local outdoor pursuits retailer to
          supply waterproof garments in May and June (half the order being
          delivered in each month). The total order price was £3,600, £1,000 of
          which was paid to Klingsor Clothing at the time the order was agreed.
          The remainder would be paid at the end of June.
May 30   The employees were paid. Parsifal counted his stock and found that
          £700 of material had not been used. One-half of the waterproof
          clothing order was delivered as per the agreement.

Parsifal tells you that the equipment has a three year life with zero scrap value,
that no additional waterproof material was purchased in May and that he had
no finished items of waterproof clothing nor any work in progress at the end of
May.

- (a)   Prepare a statement of the operating cash flows occurring in the
        month of May.
- (b)   Prepare a conventional profit and loss account (income statement)
        for the month of May.
- (c)   Compare the two statements and explain which one appears to give
        the better measure of performance.
- (d)   Consider why company financial accounts are published every year.
        Would longer (e.g. every two years) or shorter (e.g. every 6 months)
        time periods be better for external users of the company's accounting
        information?

Chapter 19

Summary and Review

This book has been concerned with the provision of information by organisations to their participants. Its approach reflects our view that the purpose of accounting is to provide information useful for decision-making. This particular emphasis was reflected in Part 1, where we considered the information requirements of the users of financial accounts. In Parts 2, 3, and 4 we described and explained the concepts and principles which presently underlie the preparation of financial accounts and discussed several reporting methods which have been suggested as modifications or alternatives to existing practice. In Part 5 we discussed the interpretation and evaluation of alternative financial accounting methods in the context of the basic framework developed in Part 1.

In this final chapter, we review the objectives of the book and the main principles suggested for the evaluation of financial accounting procedures. We then outline the limitations to the scope of the book, given that it is impossible to cover all aspects of financial accounting in a single text! Finally, we consider the current state of financial accounting and suggest some directions in which it might develop in the future.

19.1   Review of Objectives

We summarised our objectives in the Introduction as follows:

1.   To provide a framework for the evaluation of alternative methods of financial accounting, based on the assumption that the primary purpose of financial accounting is to provide information which is useful for decisions.
2.   To explain the fundamental concepts and principles underlying historical cost accounting, so that the reader of financial reports may understand more clearly the basis upon which such reports are prepared and appreciate both their strengths and their limitations.
3.   To describe and evaluate alternative approaches to the measurement of an organisation's performance and position.

4. To instil in the reader a critical and analytical attitude to financial accounting, which will enable him to understand and evaluate future changes to financial accounting practices.

Each of these objectives can be attained only by the application of certain principles to the evaluation of alternative financial accounting methods. We now turn to a summary of those principles.

19.2 The Main Principles

Although there is no universally accepted definition of the objective and subject matter of accounting or of its role, our view is well reflected in two definitions which we introduced in Chapter 2 (page 20):

> (Accounting is) the process of identifying, measuring and communicating economic information to permit informed judgments and decisions by the users of the information.[1]

> . . . the fundamental objective of corporate reports is to communicate economic measurements of and information about the resources and performance of the reporting entity useful to those having reasonable rights to such information.[2]

Both definitions suggest that, in order to assess the value of accounting information, it is necessary to consider who are the *users* of the information and what are the *decisions* they might take. As decisions are concerned with choices between alternative future courses of action, information useful for decisions generally relates to the future. This is true for virtually all users and decisions although, of course, the precise information required may vary from user to user and from decision to decision. However, the information currently provided in financial accounts is almost always concerned with past performance and present position. Users must analyse and interpret this historical information in order to make their predictions. This difference in time between the period to which the information relates and that for which it is useful led us to ask the following fundamental question in Chapter 3 (page 45):

> How should users of financial statements analyse and interpret the (historical) data provided in order to obtain the (predictive) information required?

The answer to this question provides the key to the evaluation of alternative accounting methods. Perhaps the most important criterion for choosing an

---

[1] American Accounting Association, *A Statement of Basic Accounting Theory*, AAA, 1966, page 1.

[2] Accounting Standards Committee, *The Corporate Report*, ASC, 1975, page 28.

accounting method is the extent to which it provides relevant information, i.e. information which helps users in their predictions. Of course, other criteria must also be considered, for example the feasibility and cost of alternative methods. We discussed some of these criteria in Chapter 4. Nevertheless, any evaluation of a financial accounting system which ignores its potential relevance to users' decisions is likely to be vacuous.

19.3 Limitations to the Scope of the Book

It is not possible in a single (introductory) text to consider all the concepts and practices necessary to understand the role and scope of financial accounting. Our main aim throughout has been to provide a conceptual foundation and framework rather than to offer a detailed explanation of current practices. This aim accords with our objective of instilling in the reader a critical and analytical attitude to financial accounting, which will enable him to understand and evaluate future changes to financial accounting practices. Hence one limitation to the scope of the book is that we have not covered in detail the very large number of requirements imposed on the preparers of accounts in the UK by accounting standards and company law. We have mentioned these only where necessary, and then only to amplify arguments. In our view such an emphasis would use valuable space and would detract from our main objectives by overwhelming the reader with extensive practical details before he had grasped the essential conceptual issues.

Limitations of space have also prevented us from exploring, in as much detail as we would have wished, the financial accounting problems which face both public sector and not-for-profit organisations. Not all participants in these types of organisation will have the same aims and thus require the same information as those in the organisations on which we have concentrated. In consequence, it is possible that financial accounting systems relevant to private sector, profit-orientated organisations will not be so for other types of organisation. We should stress, however, that the main principles introduced in Part 1 and many of the concepts and procedures described in Parts 2, 3, and 4 are applicable to all reporting organisations.

19.4 The Current State of Financial Accounting

Historical cost accounting has been the basis of accounting practice since the time of its development in the fourteenth and fifteenth centuries. However, during the second half of the twentieth century it has been the subject of increasing criticism, resulting primarily from changes in the environment in which organisations exist. The fact that historical cost accounting has been broadly successful in satisfying demands during the past five centuries says much for its durability and usefulness; it does not mean, however, that it will necessarily continue to meet those demands in a future environment which is likely to be volatile and unpredictable.

In this section we consider four particular respects in which environmental changes have induced or are likely to induce pressures for change in extant financial accounting methods.

Inflation

As we explained in Chapter 12 and subsequently, the existence of inflation complicates considerably the problem of interpreting the meaning of historical cost accounts; historical cost numbers are a disparate batch of figures, based on units of measurement (£'s arising at different times in the past) which are not comparable. The *problem* is widely recognised by the accountancy profession throughout the Western world—unfortunately there is little agreement concerning the appropriate *solution*. Accounting for changing prices is an area which is likely to occupy accountancy practitioners and academics for some years to come.

Complexity

Most organisations now operate in environments which are far more complicated than those faced by their predecessors. Advances in transportation and communications during the twentieth century have resulted in the creation and expansion of vast multinational companies such as General Motors, Unilever, ICI, and Ford, as well as in the growth of much smaller organisations which, while still operating within one country, have a much wider geographical and product coverage than previously. A single income statement and balance sheet may be of use to the participants in a centrally located organisation with only a small number of activities, but of how much use are they to the participants of ICI, say, which has divisions active in agriculture, fibres, general chemicals, industrial explosives, oil, organic chemicals, paint and decorative products, petrochemicals and plastics, and which manufactures in over fifteen countries around the world? The need for much more disaggregated information than is currently available is apparent, and it seems likely that this is an area for future developments in financial accounting.

Information technology

The advances in information technology which have taken place during the past twenty years and which are likely to move even faster in the future may well prove to be the most significant environmental change to influence the content and form of financial accounts. It is now possible to manipulate and access data at a speed which was unimaginable only ten or twenty years ago.

Changes in information technology have already had a major impact on the internal accounting procedures of organisations. They have, as yet, had less influence on the ways in which an organisation's performance and position are reported to its external participants. That situation is almost sure to change as national and international communications networks provide the facilities for households, businesses and other organisations to be linked together and to transmit information between themselves at high speed and low cost. For example, it is easy to imagine that by the end of this century a company's accounts will no longer be printed and distributed by post to its shareholders but rather each shareholder will enjoy direct access to the company in respect of the particular information which he requires (subject, of course, to considerations of such matters as confidentiality). It is impossible to predict all the changes which will occur to financial accounting as a result of new information technology; however, it is probable that they will be extensive and important.

Users

Financial reports have traditionally been addressed to an organisation's owners (shareholders) and creditors (including the providers of long-term loan capital). As we noted in Part 1, many other groups and individuals participate in an organisation and are affected by its actions. The rights of these other participants to receive information are increasingly being recognised. The present importance of the net income or net profit figure (available for owners) reflects the traditional orientation of financial accounts towards the providers of capital. As the claims of other participants, for example employees, customers, and government (representing society at large) are admitted it is likely that alternative forms of report will be developed to satisfy their information requirements.

The above brief review of the current and likely future state of financial accounting suggests that many changes will be necessary before the end of the twentieth century. We hope that an understanding of the framework, principles and concepts which we have developed in this book will be of some help in an evaluation of those changes.

Discussion Topics

1 'Users of financial accounts need information about the future. The accounts provide information about the past.' Explain and discuss this apparent dilemma.

2 Outline the major changes likely to be seen in financial accounting practices in the next twenty years.

3 Speculate on ways in which advances in information technology might affect the reporting practices of organisations in the future.

4   Discuss the extent to which the information requirements of all groups of users of an organisation's accounts are satisfied at present.

5   In what respects might participants in public sector and not-for-profit organisations require different information from that which is useful to participants in private sector, profit-orientated organisations?

Exercise

19.1   Mr Tannhauser started business on 1 January 19X3. The following is an extract from a letter he wrote to you on 1 January 19X4:

"My transactions for 19X3 were as follows. On 1 January, I opened a business bank account and paid £30,000 into it from my savings bank account. I purchased some office equipment for £1,500. (As you know, I use one room of my private house as an office.) I expect that this equipment will last at least 10 years, although it will be worth very little at the end of that time. Indeed, I would probably not get more than £150 if I were to sell it now, even though the cost of replacing it with similar second-hand equipment would be at least £1,800. I also bought a van on 1 January which cost me £4,500. I expect to sell this at the end of 19X4. When I bought it I thought I would get at least £3,000 for it in December 19X4 but with the current fuel situation that looks like an overestimate. Only yesterday my local garage offered me £2,700 for it, although I saw a similar model advertised for sale today at £3,600.

As to trading activities, I bought 2,000 donners in January for £6,000. I sold 1,500 of these immediately at £6 each and still have the rest. The current selling price of donners is £3.30 but I am keeping those that I have not sold as I am expecting a rise in the price shortly. It could even reach £6 again by the end of 19X4. Maybe I should buy some more! In April I bought 10,000 used loges for £15,000. This turned out to be a bad buy. I did manage to sell 4,000 in September for £4,500 but the best offer I have had for the rest is £3,000 and I do not feel inclined to take such a heavy loss yet. In July I managed to pick up 500 fasolts cheap (only £15 each) and sold them immediately to Mr Fafner for £18,000. He paid me £12,000 in September and still owes me the balance. I am a little worried because I have not seen him at the golf club since September and there is a persistent rumour that he is on the verge of bankruptcy. At least all my other transactions were for cash. My last transaction was in October when I bought 10,000 frohs for £22,500 which I paid in cash. I sold 4,000 of these in November for £12,000 and another 4,000 in December at £3.75 each. The current selling price is £3.90.

Overhead expenses were fairly low. I spent about £60 a month on petrol and maintenance for the van and about the same amount again on other expenses. I transferred £600 each month from the business account to my private account. (My monthly salary before I went 'self-employed' was £600 and I did not see why I should work for myself for less!)

What bothers me is whether I made the right move in setting up on my own. I have given up a safe job and 10% p.a. interest on the money I withdrew from my savings bank account (£30,000 in the business bank account may seem a bit high to you but I think this sort of sum is necessary to clinch unexpected deals). I thought that you, as an accountant, might be able to let me know how much I made during 19X3."

● Draft a reply to Mr Tannhauser answering, as far as you think possible, the questions in the final paragraph of the above extract. Include in your reply a discussion of the income measurement problems raised by the various transactions undertaken by Mr Tannhauser during 19X3.

Index